W9-CQJ-947

WITHDRAWN

OPERA

GARLAND REFERENCE LIBRARY
OF THE HUMANITIES
(VOL. 468)

OPERA:
A Research and Information Guide

Guy A. Marco

GARLAND PUBLISHING, INC. · NEW YORK & LONDON
1984

Library of Congress Cataloging in Publication Data

Marco, Guy A.
Opera : a research and information guide.

(Garland reference library of the humanities ; v. 468)
Includes indexes.
1. Opera—Bibliography.   2. Operas—History and
criticism—Bibliography.   I. Title.   II. Series.
ML128.04M28   1984   016.7821   83-49312
ISBN 0-8240-8999-5

Cover design by Laurence Walczak

Printed on acid-free, 250-year-life paper
Manufactured in the United States of America

For Norma and Siegmund

J'ai trouvé mon Eurydice,
Rien n'égale mon bonheur.

ACKNOWLEDGMENTS

Most of the research for this book was carried out at Stanford University, the University of California (Berkeley), the University of Chicago, and the Library of Congress. My gratitude is offered to the librarians of those institutions who provided access and assistance. Dena Epstein, University of Chicago, deserves special mention. I also wish to thank a number of persons who helped with the identification, location, or description of materials: Olga Buth, Molly Engelbrecht, Thomas Heck, Karen Marco, Katherine Rivera, and Andrea Schacter.

CONTENTS

FOREWORD

What a superb undertaking! When one considers the almost endless ramifications of the art of opera, it is clear that a critical bibliography of opera must be a frightening prospect to anyone bold enough to venture upon it. Yet there is a crying need for just such a work. Despite the growing body of serious musicological work on opera, there is probably no other field of music so rife with amateurish popularizers and pseudo scholarship. And there is none so full of booby traps for the humble music lover in search of hard facts. When such a "standard" work as Kobbé can pass through edition after edition with egregious errors uncorrected and with at least one of its descriptive analyses translated word for word (including subjective judgments) from a well-known dictionary of opera, it is clear that the layman needs guidance. And all of us, including professionals, are necessarily laymen in some aspect of operatic history or performance.

Guy Marco, like all good scholars, invites additions, corrections, and comment from his readers. They will be forthcoming, for perfection is even more of a dream in this field than many others. Donald Grout's bibliography for his *Short History of Opera* includes some 3,900 items. Dr. Marco has listed and annotated just over 700, although many additional items are cited in passing. That is already a brave number in a brave undertaking. May it continue to expand and refine and put us all into Dr. Marco's debt.

Edward O.D. Downes

INTRODUCTION

"Save the time of the reader" is the most important of Shiyali Ranganathan's Five Laws of Library Science. A bibliographer is a librarian without walls, guided by the same precepts and values. I think of readers coming to a bibliography as they would to a reference desk in a library, looking for starting points, for the shortest distances to desired facts or materials. And just as the reference librarian endeavors to assist inquirers whatever their purpose or background, and to save their time, so does a bibliography offer expeditious guidance to all who consult it.

The guidance provided by this book, as the title suggests, is both for scholars involved in research and for anyone—specialist or layman—who simply wants a fact or two about opera. (The scholars will not need such help until they wander out of the comfortable confines of their specializations.) I hope that the materials I have cited here will lead each user to the full benefit of cumulative musicological study, whether in the shape of a full historical account, a theoretical speculation, or a plain collection of facts. Indeed, certain inquiries may well be satisfied at once by the bibliography itself, apart from the contents of materials cited. While this is neither a dictionary of opera nor a history of that intriguing art, it does convey some facts directly: the correct names of operas and relevant dates, for example; and basic information on opera companies, theaters, and certain individuals. But *au fond* it is a bibliography: an inventory of useful materials in which answers to questions will be found, and in which the results of research are delineated.

It seems that no earlier annotated bibliography of opera exists, aside from the treatments of opera within works of wider scope. Certainly the immensity of the literature has been a deterrent to anyone with bibliographic intentions; the number of writings on Wagner alone had already exceeded 10,000 a hundred years ago.

We now confront millions of potential inclusions. Numbers apart, the books and articles on operatic topics carry various levels of physical or intellectual inaccessibility. As objects, they are hard to find. Great libraries have collected them rather haphazardly; indexes have identified relatively few of them. Once locatcd, they challenge the reader with their language barriers. These obstacles impeded my work, as they would anyone's. I cannot claim to have examined even a large segment of the literature. What I think I have done is to discover the core of that literature; those writings that present what Patrick Wilson calls the "verified public knowledge" of the field, and those writings that point bibliographically to other writings of possible utility. These at least have been my objectives, my selection criteria.

Beyond the identification of the core literature, I have sought to describe it with precision. The reader is entitled to expect a full and accurate display of the publication data on each work, with all names and words rendered correctly in their respective languages. And the reader may reasonably expect—in a book that claims to be a time-saver—a concise summary of the content and reference features of each work cited. I have made a particular point of noting the presence of indexes, chronologies, and bibliographies in the works cited; and I have in many cases described those features in some way that might help the reader judge their value for some specific purpose. (For instance, I refer to an index as "expansive" if its entries are subdivided for enhanced access; and I try to call attention to bibliographies that have incomplete data in their citations.)

I have taken the term "opera" in its usual sense, as a dramatic action in which the dialogue is primarily sung rather than spoken. Operetta and its parallel genres like *Singspiel* are considered selectively; the American musical is omitted. Only the European tradition is covered, together with its North and South American manifestations. All the writings included are in European languages.

My method has been *de visu* examination insofar as possible. Alternatively I have relied on descriptions by others; now and again I have listed a work unseen, on the basis of apparent importance—in such cases I have warned the reader with appropriate disclaimers. Generally I have accepted the authority of the

Library of Congress for transliterations, forms of names, and bibliographic data. The compilation of entries took place in 1983, and the cutoff date for inclusions was December 1.

One subdivision of the topic is entirely excluded: individual biography. A new publication covers this ground so thoroughly that it would be a loss rather than a saver of time to essay even partial duplication. *Opera and Concert Singers: An Annotated International Bibliography of Books and Pamphlets* by Andrew Farkas (New York: Garland, 1984), will guide the reader to all known biographical works about singers and other persons in the operatic world of past and present.

I respectfully invite users of this volume to advise me of omissions, errors, or other infelicities they may notice. If there is a revised edition, it will benefit from comments received.

Guy A. Marco
Washington, D.C.
1983

Opera

USERS' NOTE

Many entries throughout this book carry references to the author's *Information on Music* (Libraries Unlimited, 1975-84, 3 volumes). These citations appear in the form *IOM-0002*, where the numeral refers to the item's entry number in that work.

I. ENCYCLOPEDIAS AND DICTIONARIES

Opera in General Works

*Operatic terminology, topics, and personalities are covered,
to some extent, in all the music encyclopedias and dictionaries;
indeed, many facts about opera are found in such nonmusical
compilations as the* New Encyclopaedia Britannica *or* Webster's
Third New International Dictionary of the English Language.
*Although it might seem reasonable to begin a fact search--or
the exploration of a particular subject--in the most specialized
reference books available, that decision properly depends upon
the kind of information wanted.   It happens that certain of the
general works are much more up to date than any specifically
musical (or operatic) counterpart.   Another advantage in the
use of general rather than musical encyclopedias is that they
have superior indexing.   All the major English-language general
encyclopedias, except the new* Britannica, *have excellent name/
topic indexes, while none of the important musical encyclopedias
have any indexing at all.*
    *It is not possible to comment here on the musical content
of nonmusical works.   A convenient guide to these materials
is IOM, especially volume 1, chapters 1 and 2.   Some comprehensive musical reference works which have great utility for information on opera are the following:*

1. Apel, Willi. *Harvard Dictionary of Music.* 2d ed. Cam-
    bridge, Mass.: Belknap Press of Harvard University
    Press, 1969. xv, 935 pp. IOM-0002 ML 100 A64
    The standard source of definitions and concise topical
    articles for English readers; no biographical entries,
    however. "Opera" is a useful historical orientation,
    written by Donald Jay Grout. There are also brief entries
    for many individual operas, with stylistic observations
    (not the plots), and articles on related subjects, such as
    Overture, Recitative, Zarzuela, and Aria. No index; weak
    bibliographies.

2. *Die Musik in Geschichte und Gegenwart; allgemeine Enzyklo-
      pädie der Musik....* Hrsg. von Friedrich Blume. Kassel:
      Bärenreiter, 1949- (in progress). IOM-0058 ML 100 M92
      Fourteen volumes, plus a supplement of two volumes, issued
   through 1983; index to be published. The finest of the
   multivolume music reference works, written by leading
   international scholars. Base set contains some 9,000
   articles, all in German, with about 7,100 illustrations.
   Comprehensive work-lists for most composers, and extensive
   bibliographies (which unfortunately offer incomplete data
   and are presented in a forbidding format). Entries for
   individual cities cover operatic history and life and
   usually include pictures of opera houses. The most useful
   articles are cited in IOM, especially volume 3; those
   citations are not repeated in the present work.

3. *The New Grove Dictionary of Music and Musicians.*   Ed. Stan-
      ley Sadie. London: Macmillan; dist. in U.S. by Grove's
      Dictionaries of Music, Washington, D.C., 1980.   20 vols.
      ISBN 0-333-23111-2 IOM-1333 ML 100 N48
      With 18 million words, 22,500 articles, and 2,500 inter-
   national contributors, *New Grove* is clearly the monument
   among English-language music reference works. Sad to say,
   it is uneven and undependable as an information source.
   Many valuable long articles, including "Opera" in volume
   13 (pp. 544-647), and good short accounts of individual
   cities with facts on opera and illustrations of opera
   houses. The most significant entries are cited in IOM,
   volume 3, with critical comments. Users of *New Grove*
   should be ready for problems. First of all, it has no
   index--and the cross-reference apparatus is unsteady.
   Further, the article bibliographies are poorly organized,
   incomplete, and erratic in what they include, and devoid
   of essential facts for individual entries (no pagination
   for journal articles, no publishers for monographs).
   Editorial policy on inclusion of topics--in particular
   articles on individual musicians--is a mystery that has
   puzzled most reviewers of *New Grove*; and the wide scatter-
   ing of factual errors has rendered consultation of the
   work an anxious experience. Coverage of North American
   and Latin American music is especially deficient (an
   American counterpart work is now in preparation); a
   chronicle of omissions and mistakes, by Robert Murrell
   Stevenson, appeared in the *Inter-American Music Review*,
   3-2 (Spring-Summer 1981): 159-207.

4. Pratt, Waldo Selden. *The New Encyclopedia of Music and
    Musicians*. New and rev. ed. New York: Macmillan, 1929.
    969p. IOM-0084 ML 100 P87
    Useful, despite its age, for coverage of singers who
    are not found in more recent works and interesting for
    personal evaluations of them by the editor (e.g., of the
    contralto Pisaroni: "Though her voice was noble and her
    acting impressive, her homeliness of face checked her
    success"). Another good feature is the musical gazetteer
    (pp. 901-960), which identifies musical organizations,
    individuals, concert halls, and opera houses of each city
    (not premieres, however). All facts given by Pratt are
    best verified in later sources.

*Many other general musical reference titles are to be found in
library collections. Some of them, such as those of Riemann
(IOM-0063), Thompson (IOM-0065), Michel (IOM-0072), Gatti
(IOM-0081), and Pena (IOM-0083), may be of value for information on their countries of origin, as well as on universal
topics; but in most cases what they have to offer will duplicate
coverage of items 1-4, above, and items to be cited later in
this volume.*

Specialized Works on Opera

*We now consider the most useful encyclopedic approaches to
opera: books that present data on various facets of the art.*

5. Rosenthal, Harold D., and John Hamilton Warrack. *The
    Concise Oxford Dictionary of the Opera*. 2d ed. London:
    Oxford University Press, 1979. 561p. IOM-1366a
    ML 102 O6 R67
    Topical and biographical articles; operatic history of
    major cities, with important premieres; opera composition
    in individual countries. Entries for each major opera,
    for operatic characters and arias. Articles on literary
    figures (e.g., Byron, Cervantes) citing operas based on
    their writings. Bibliographic references are incomplete
    and seem to have been chosen at random. No index; no
    illustrations. The most valuable single reference work
    available.

6. Kloiber, Rudolf. *Handbuch der Oper*. 9. Aufl. Kassel:
    Bärenreiter, 1978. 2 vols. 875p. ISBN 3-761-904229,

3-761-804237   MT 95 K66

Gives detailed consideration to 180 operas in the current performance or recorded repertoire (the selection
reveals a German slant). Facts included for each work:
synopsis, instrumentation, duration (not in every case,
and occasionally dubious), premiere date, publication,
historical background, voice types used. There is also
a list of composers and their works, with brief comments
on style, cities of premieres, and other notes on performance history. An interesting, if perhaps overelaborate,
table lists operatic roles by voice type--including such
impressionistic categories as soubrette, dramatic coloratura,
lyric mezzo-soprano and dramatic alto. There is a list of
arias by voice type, too. Indexed by composer and title.

7.   Moore, Frank L. *Crowell's Handbook of World Opera*. New
        York: Crowell, 1961. 683p. (Reprint--Westport, Conn.:
        Greenwood, 1974.) ISBN 0-8371-6822-8 IOM-1368
        ML 102 06 M6
        A fine variety of information, in dictionary format:
        entries for operas (plot synopses, principal musical
        themes), characters, and topics; opera chronology and
        discography. Useful indexes of roles by voice type or
        by type of ensemble; no general index.

8.   *Enciclopedia dello spettacolo*. Roma: Casa Ed. Le Maschere,
        1954-62. 9 vols. Supplements, 1963, 1966. IOM-1367
        PN 1625 E7
        An Italian-language work covering the stage arts.
        Operatic entries include singers, composers, cities and
        countries, and topics. Good illustrations and bibliog-
        raphies. Base set and supplements indexed in a separate
        volume that appeared in 1968.

9.   Ewen, David. *The New Encyclopedia of the Opera*. 3d ed.
        New York: Hill and Wang, 1971. vii, 759p.
        ISBN 0-8090-7262-9 IOM-1369 ML 103 06 E9
        Announced as Ewen's 75th book, this is a well-revised
        version of the original *Encyclopedia of the Opera* (1955).
        It presents a vast array of information: operatic terms,
        stories, characters, singers, houses, festivals, literary
        sources, and topical articles. Inaccuracies of historical
        fact appear too frequently to allow a confident approach,
        and the author's historical perspective is--according to
        one reviewer--"simplistic." No index.

10. Orrey, Leslie. *The Encyclopedia of Opera*. London: Pit-
    man, 1976. 376p. ISBN 0-684-13630-9 ML 102 06 E56
    A useful compilation of about 3,000 entries, written
    by 13 scholars (among them Julian Budden, Geoffrey Norris,
    John Tyrrell, and the "advisory editor" Gilbert Chase).
    Articles on individuals, on opera houses, festivals,
    terms, film opera, radio/television opera, and other
    topics. About 700 operas are given separate articles,
    with plot synopses and background information. The
    introduction presents an interesting overview of operatic
    reference books in historical perspective; it announces
    the present work to be the first encyclopedia to be
    illustrated. There are 371 pictures, many in color.
    Names of operas in less-common languages are alphabetized
    only by their English translations. Lack of index is
    troubling, especially since cross-reference practice is
    inconsistent (e.g., nothing in the entry for Budapest
    indicates that a photo of the Operaház appears later in
    the volume, at the entry for Hungary). But in general
    this is an accurate and attractive volume.

11. *Herders Musiklexikon: Oper, Operette, Musical*. Bearb.
    von Gerhard Hellwig. 4 Aufl. Freiburg im Breisgau;
    Basel; Wien: Herder, 1976. 370p. ISBN 3-451-16357-8.
    ML 102 06 H5
    Based on the 1962 *Das grosse Buch der Musik*. Essen-
    tially a collection of plots, but including for each of
    about 500 works considerable background data and names
    of arias or songs (these are in German translation,
    leading to quaint titles like "Good night mein Jemand"
    from *Music Man*). A first-line index gives approximately
    800 songs and arias in original tongues. Also biographical
    and term entries; index of composers and titles.

12. Krause, Ernst. *Oper A-Z; ein Opernführer*. 3. Aufl.
    Leipzig: VEB Deutscher Verlag für Musik, 1978. 704p.
    MT 95 K91
    Basically a book of plot synopses, but containing much
    other information about each work: instrumentation,
    duration of each act, background on the composition
    process, performance history, etc. Many of the operas
    are outside the usual repertoire; e.g., by such composers
    as Jan Cikker, Paul Dessau, Gottfried von Einem, Fritz
    Geissler, Jakov Gotovac, Siegfried Matthus, Gerhard
    Rosenfeld, and Udo Zimmermann. Title and composer index.

13. *Simon and Schuster Book of the Opera: A Complete Reference
     Guide.* New York: Simon and Schuster, 1977.   512p.
     ISBN 0-671-24886   ML 102 06 063   Identical work issued
     as: *Phaidon Book of the Opera.* Oxford: Phaidon, 1979.
     512p.   ISBN 0-7148-1885-2   ML 102 06 0612
     Translated from the Italian *L'opera: repertorio della
     lirica* (Milano: Mondadori, 1977) by Catherine Atthill
     et al.   Synopses and program notes for about 800 operas
     of historic as well as contemporary importance.   Premiere
     data, critical reception, good photographs.   Chronological
     arrangement; thus requiring constant reference to the
     indexes (either title or composer).

14. Brockway, Wallace, and Herbert Weinstock.   *The World of
     Opera; The Story of Its Origins and the Lore of Its
     Performance.* New York: Pantheon, 1962.   731p.
     ML 1700 B86 07
     An excellent handbook of data on 253 operas, generally
     representing the current standard repertoire.   Gives pre-
     miere date and theater, with cast, and a summary per-
     formance history, emphasizing the U.S. and offering
     negative as well as affirmative appraisals.   Information
     is accurate; historical highlights are aptly selected.
     Who remembers the performance of Tristan in which three
     different tenors had a turn at the title role?

II. HISTORICAL STUDIES

General Histories of Music

Except for the New Oxford History of Music, *the principal general histories provide uneven treatment of operatic development. One reason is that Italian and French grand opera was not widely viewed as a topic of musicological concern until after the publication of many major histories. Jay Nicolaisen has pointed out (in* Italian Opera in Transition *(629), p. 271) the imbalance in Paul Henry Lang's* Music in Western Civilization *(New York: Norton, 1941), in which Puccini has one paragraph, Gounod "shares two sentences with two other composers," nothing is said about Boito, Catalani, or Ponchielli; while Richard Strauss has three pages. But even later works present uneven coverage: Richard Crocker's* History of Musical Style *(New York: McGraw-Hill, 1966) has almost identical neglect of the composers just mentioned. Even opera authority Donald J. Grout, in his* History of Western Music *(3d ed., with Claude V. Palisca; New York: Norton, 1980), allows Puccini only eight lines, mentions Boito only as Verdi's librettist, and says nothing about Catalani or Ponchielli. Gounod has part of a paragraph. Of course all these histories do cover certain opera composers and styles; Grout, for instance, gives five pages to Verdi and a page or so each to Rossini, Bellini, and Donizetti. But Rameau and his operas have more attention than any of the Italian masters.*

15. *The New Oxford History of Music.* Ed. Jack A. Westrup et al. London: Oxford University Press, 1954- (in progress). IOM-0101 ML 160 N44

   Opera is covered in all volumes beginning with IV. These have appeared:

   IV. *The Age of Humanism, 1540-1630* (1968). Includes "Music and Drama," by Edward J. Dent, revised by F.W. Sternfeld; and "Early Italian Opera," by Simon Towneley.

V. *Opera and Church Music, 1630-1750* (1975). Includes "Italian Opera from the Later Monteverdi to Scarlatti," by Hellmuth Christian Wolff; "Italian Opera 1700-1750," by Hellmuth Christian Wolff; "The Origins of French Opera," by Margaret M. McGowan; "French Opera from Lully to Rameau," by Paul-Marie Masson; "Opera in England and Germany," by J.A. Westrup.

VII. *The Age of Enlightenment, 1745-1790* (1973). Includes "Promotion and Patronage," "Italian Opera," "German Opera," and "The Operas of Mozart," by Anna Amalie Abert; "The Operas of Haydn," by H.C. Robbins Landon; "Opera in France," by Martin Cooper; "English Opera," by Roger Fiske; "The Rise of Russian Opera," by Gerald Seaman; and "Opera in Spain," by Gerald Abraham.

VIII. *The Age of Beethoven, 1790-1830* (1982). Includes three major essays by Winton Dean: "French Opera," "Italian Opera," and "German Opera," together with a quick look at Polish and Russian works: "Opera in Other Countries," by Gerald Abraham.

X. *The Modern Age, 1890-1960* (1974). Includes "Stage Works, 1890-1918," by Martin Cooper; and "Music in the Soviet Union," by Gerald Abraham, which covers opera to 1960.

Typically a volume of NOHM will offer clear and dependable introductions to its topics, by recognized authorities. Essays are footnoted and provided with numerous musical examples. Each volume has a name index, with titles of compositions listed under composers. Bibliographies are poor: awkwardly arranged, thick with trivia, and lacking basic facts, such as publishers of monographs and pagination of journal articles.

Two other multivolume histories carry some information on opera that is worth mentioning: the Prentice-Hall History of Music *(IOM-0103) and* A History of Western Music *(IOM-0511, 1334, 1335). For factual summaries not readily available elsewhere, one number in each of these sets may be cited:*

16. Béhague, Gerard. *Music in Latin America; an Introduction.* Englewood Cliffs, N.J.: Prentice-Hall, 1979.

xiv, 369p. (Prentice-Hall History of Music Series.)
ISBN 0-136-08919-4 ML 199 B44
Contains discussion, on a general plane, of opera in
Argentina, Brazil, Colombia, Cuba, Mexico, and Peru.
Bibliographic notes, but no bibliography. Name, title,
and topical index.

17. Sternfeld, Frederick William. *Music in the Modern Age.*
New York: Praeger, 1973. 515p. (A History of Western
Music, 5.) ML 197 S7655 M9
The chapters of most interest are "Latin America," by
Robert Murrell Stevenson; "Poland," by Czeslaw Halski;
and "Czechoslovakia," by Brian Large. All give quick
reviews of major names and works, with bibliographies
and discographies. There is an index in the volume, of
names, places, and subjects. (Only two volumes of this
promising series have appeared; the other one deals with
the preopera period.)

Specialized Works on Opera

18. Knapp, J. Merrill. *The Magic of Opera.* New York: Harper
and Row, 1972. x, 371p. ML 1700 K67
History of opera is but one of the topics treated in
this excellent presentation. The book is in fact a general
text on the nature of opera, its terminology, conventions,
and production. It is sensible and scholarly throughout.
Expansive name and topic index.

19. Barblan, Guglielmo, and Alberto Basso. *Storia dell'*
opera. Torino: UTET, 1977. 3 vols. in 6 parts. xx,
546; xii, 630; xii, 536; xii, 474; xii, 522; ix, 651p.
ML 1700 S884
Specialists from several countries contributed chapters
to this imposing work. The first two parts (volume 1)
are devoted to Italy; the next two parts (volume 2) are
about Europe and America; the final parts (volume 3)
consider aspects of the vocal art, give biographical
data on hundreds of singers (many of them quite obscure),
and discuss libretti. There is a name index to all
volumes, and a useful title index in original languages--
a valuable identification tool. One might characterize
the essays here as general outline presentations, in
encyclopedia style. There are few footnotes and few

musical examples; analysis is not emphasized. We will
turn to Barblan primarily for overviews of operatic
development in countries outside the mainstream, and for
facts about lesser-known works. The chapter bibliographies may also be helpful as guides to further research: they are modern and thoughtfully selected, although lacking publisher names for monographs and journal-
article pagination. Countries that are given complete
chapters include the Scandinavian nations, Holland and
Belgium, Portugal, Switzerland, Czechoslovakia, the
USSR, Poland, Spain, Hungary, Yugoslavia, Romania,
Bulgaria, Greece, Canada, and the U.S. Latin American
trends are well summarized in an essay by José López-
Calo.

20. Grout, Donald Jay. *A Short History of Opera*. 2d ed.
        New York: Columbia University Press, 1965. xviii,
        852p. IOM-1370 ML 1700 G83
        The standard history in English; indeed the only modern
     examination of operatic development from the earliest
     efforts to our own time (to 1960). This is a musicological
     presentation by a leading scholar, marked by insights
     into style and movements. A good expansive index of
     names, titles, and topics renders the contents easily
     accessible; here is a fine starting point for investiga-
     tion into subjects like Leitmotif, Patronage, and Singing.
     Much acclaim has been accorded to the bibliography, and
     it is formidable (about 2,700 entries). Yet it is awkward-
     ly arranged (by chapter) and possesses no discernible
     criteria for inclusion. Many items are too trivial to
     be of any interest—two- or three-page "impressions" of
     this or that opera, by forgotten authors—and others
     seem to belong in some other list (e.g., Pastor's *History
     of the Popes*). However, article pagination is given,
     and publishers of books are cited.

21. Donington, Robert. *The Rise of Opera*. Boston and Lon-
        don: Faber & Faber, 1981. 399p. ISBN 0-571-11674-4
        ML 1700 D683 R5
        Covers through 17th century only. The author is an
     important authority, known for his espousal of the so-
     called Jungian approach to interpretation of operatic
     stories. (See entry 524.) This is his major historical
     effort in the genre, well documented and carefully pre-
     sented. A particularly useful presentation is given on
     calendars and dating problems. The bibliography of about

450 entries is well chosen and gives full data. A fine
expansive index of names, titles, and subjects completes
the work, which promises to be the new standard English
history if it moves ahead into later centuries. A shorter
volume by the same author, *The Opera* (New York: Harcourt
Brace Jovanovich, 1978; x, 238p.), cannot be recommended.
It attempts more than its few pages can bear: to be a
general history of opera for scholars and amateurs, and
to be a sounding board for Donington's special theories
drawn from Jung. An imbalance results from the apparent
preference accorded to operas amenable to an archetypical
analysis. Much of the book is expended on plot synopses
in that framework.

This is the most useful narrative history of light opera:

22. Wolff, Hellmuth Christian. *Geschichte der komischen Oper:
     von den Anfängen bis zur Gegenwart.* Wilhelmshaven:
     Heinrichshofen, 1981. 264p. ISBN 3-7959-0304-1
     IOM-1378a ML 1850 W64
     A scholarly account of the genre from the early Renais-
     sance; emphasis on Europe, with some attention to American
     works. Illustrations, extended musical examples, un-
     annotated bibliography of about 150 items. Name and
     topic index.

Collections of Documents

*Collections of documents and contemporary writings about opera
present useful perspectives on the historical pageant. The
most familiar gathering in this category is not entirely concerned with opera but does include important material about it:*

23. Strunk, Oliver. *Source Readings in Music History from
     Classical Antiquity Through the Romantic Era.* New
     York: Norton, 1950. 919p. IOM-0104 ML 160 S89
     A well-chosen, carefully annotated group of 87 writings
     by musicians and critics, with new English translations
     where necessary. Long treatises are represented by brief
     extracts. Among the authors who wrote on opera: Pietro
     de' Bardi, Ottavio Rinuccini, Giulio Caccini, Jacopo Peri,
     François Raguenet, Benedetto Marcello, Jean-Jacques
     Rousseau, Francesco Algarotti, C.W. von Gluck, Carl Maria
     von Weber, Hector Berlioz, and Richard Wagner. Index of
     names.

Three other compilations are devoted entirely to material on opera:

24. Becker, Heinz. *Quellentexte zur Konzeption der europäischen Oper im 17. Jahrhundert.* Kassel: Bärenreiter, 1981. 200p. ML 1703 Q3
    Gives 62 documents in their original languages, without translations; extensive commentaries in German. Topics are Florentine, Venetian, French, and German opera of the 17th century, as discussed by such writers as Jacopo Peri, Giovanni Doni, Marc' Antonio Cesti, Pietro Ziani, Antonio Sartorio, and Jean-Baptiste Lully. Name and title index.

25. Krause-Graumnitz, Heinz. *Vom Wesen der Oper. Opern-komponisten über die Oper.* Berlin: Henschelverlag, 1969. 538p. ML 90 K73
    Letters, prefaces, and other statements by about 100 composers of opera, from Peri to Shostakovich. Sources identified; commentaries; everything is in German. Name and title index.

26. Weisstein, Ulrich. *The Essence of Opera.* New York: Free Press of Glencoe; London: Collier-Macmillan, 1964. 372p. ML 1700 W35
    An anthology of 68 selections on the topic of operatic poetics, the unity of words and music. All are in English, with sources and commentaries. Authors include composers from the Florentines to Stravinsky, and literary figures like Voltaire, Goethe, Schopenhauer, Shaw, Cocteau, Brecht, and Auden. Name and title index.

Chronologies

Chronology is another valuable approach to historical under-standing. No specific chronology of opera has been seen, but operatic highlights appear in many general chronologies. Of these the most useful have been described in IOM, 0105-0112, 1410, 1501. Surely the most interesting of them is:

27. Slonimsky, Nicolas. *Music Since 1900.* 4th ed. New York: Scribner, 1971. 1,595p. IOM-0112 ML 197 S634
    Major events in music from 1900 through July 20, 1969, including opera premieres, dates of composition, odd

occurrences (a stink bomb thrown in the Budapest opera
during the premiere of Křenek's *Jonny Spielt Auf*) and
Slonimsky's ever-peppery, perceptive observations on it
all. Name index, with compositions listed under their
composers.

One of the pillars of opera reference is in chronological
format:

28. Loewenberg, Alfred. *Annals of Opera, 1597-1940.* 2d ed.,
     rev. and corr. Frank Walker. Genève: Societas Biblio-
     graphica, 1955. 2 vols. xxv p., 1,756 columns.
     IOM-1378 ML 102 06 L6.
     A reprint edition (Totowa, N.J.: Rowman and Littlefield,
     1978) was described as "3rd edition, revised and correc-
     ted." This is a reliable, scholarly list of about 3,600
     operas that have been performed, arranged by date of
     premiere. For each work the first and important per-
     formances outside the home country are given, with exact
     dates, language of each libretto and names of translators,
     and miscellaneous observations. Opera titles appear in
     their original languages, with English translations for
     less-common tongues. Indexes by title, composer and
     librettist; also a general index with entries for in-
     dividual countries and for topics. A continuation of
     this work, by Harold Rosenthal, was announced for 1983
     publication: *Annals of Opera, 1940-1981* (London: Calder).

Iconographies

Opera lends itself admirably to pictorial treatment, or iconog-
raphy. Many such treatments are cited in the present volume
under specific approaches that they represent (particular com-
posers, designers, opera houses, etc.). There is one general
iconography of interest:

29. Wolff, Hellmuth Christian. *Oper, Szene und Darstellung*
     von 1600 bis 1900. Leipzig: VEB Deutscher Verlag für
     Musik, 1968. 212p. (Musikgeschichte in Bildern, 4/1.)
     IOM-1371 (series at 0119) ML 89 M9 v.4,1
     Part of a major series of iconographical works. Con-
     sists of more than 200 documented illustrations of pro-
     ductions, costumes, and all kinds of performers. Many
     sketches for stage design, including some published for

the first time.   Unannotated bibliography of about 150
entries; name and topic index.

*Operatic content is found in more general music iconographies
as well; for comments on the major examples see IOM-0113-0136,
and the discussion following 0136.*

III. EDITIONS AND EXCERPTS

In chapter XIV, on individual operas, a number of modern editions are identified. Such information is not offered in detail in this volume because there are two convenient sources for it. The New Oxford History of Music *gives, in each volume, citations to editions of the works of all composers, with indication of operas included.* A History of Western Music, *by Grout, lists collected editions by composer in the bibliography. Several anthologies of music provide a variety of examples from the history of opera. These are especially useful:*

30. *Anthology of Music*. Ed. Karl Gustav Fellerer. Cologne: Arno Volk Verlag, 1955-76. 48 vols. M2 M9872
    Four of the volumes are devoted to opera. Volume 5, ed. Anna Amalie Abert, presents ten extended examples; the composers are Caccini, Monteverdi, Hasse, Lully, Schürmann, Gluck, Dittersdorf, Mozart, Spontini, and Spohr. Volumes 38, 39, and 40, ed. Hellmuth Christian Wolff, deal with different periods. In volume 38 (17th century) there are 25 excerpts, by Archilei, Caccini, Gagliano, Monteverdi, Landi, Staden, Cavalli, Cesti, Sartorio, Ziani, Pallavicino, Legrenzi, Theile, Foertsch, Kusser, Lully, Krieger, Steffani, Scarlatti, and Pollaroli. Vol. 39 (18th century) has 26 excerpts, by Campra, Keiser, Telemann, Handel, Bononcini, Vivaldi, Schürmann, Pepusch, Hasse, Rameau, Leo, Graun, Gluck, La Borde, Hiller, Piccinni, Jommelli, Monsigny, Mozart, Schweitzer, Benda, and Umlauf. Volume 40 (19th century) has 21 examples, by Spontini, Auber, Meyerbeer, Mehül, Gounod, Rossini, Bellini, Verdi, Puccini, Spohr, Hoffmann, Weber, Lortzing, Wagner, Moniuszko, Smetana, Borodin, and Rimskiǐ-Korsakov. The most popular arias are generally avoided, in favor of lesser-known but characteristic pieces. English libretto segments are given, along with commentaries and sources.

31. Brody, Elaine. *Music in Opera: A Historical Anthology*.
     Englewood Cliffs, N.J.: Prentice-Hall, 1970.   604p.
     M2 B857 M9
     About 100 long excerpts, covering all periods. Aria
     texts in original language and English translations,
     stage directions, and commentaries. The composers are
     Peri, Monteverdi, Lully, Purcell, Scarlatti, Keiser,
     Handel, Rameau, Gluck, Pepusch, Pergolesi, Rousseau,
     Hiller, Mozart, Beethoven, Auber, Meyerbeer, Gounod,
     Rossini, Bellini, Donizetti, Weber, Wagner, Verdi,
     Musorgskiĭ, Smetana, Bizet, Massenet, Charpentier,
     Puccini, Debussy, Strauss, Schoenberg, Berg, Gershwin,
     Britten, Stravinskiĭ, Poulenc, and Ginastera. Popular
     arias are mingled with lesser-known numbers. Name,
     title, and topic index.

32. *Historical Anthology of Music*. Ed. Archibald T. Davison
     and Willi Apel. Rev. ed. Cambridge, Mass.: Harvard
     University Press, 1949-50. 2 vols. M2 D25 H6
     In the second volume there are operatic excerpts by
     Peri, Caccini, Monteverdi, Rossi, Cavalli, Landi, Cesti,
     Steffani, Lully, Bononcini, Pepusch, Pergolesi, Jommelli,
     Piccinni, Hasse, Gluck, Hiller, Dittersdorf, Arne,
     Rousseau, Grétry, and Hopkinson. Translations into
     English for the texts; commentaries and notes on sources.

*Garland Publishing has issued some valuable series of scores,
making available works not generally available before:*

32a. *The Ballad Opera; A Collection of 171 Original Texts of
     Musical Plays Printed in Photo-Facsimile*. Sel. and
     arr. Walter H. Rubsamen. New York: Garland, 1974.
     28 vols. ML 48 B18
     These works comprise the entire extant repertoire of
     English, Scottish, Irish, and American ballad opera--the
     18th-century form that led to the comic opera. Among the
     better-known compositions are *The Beggar's Opera*, *Polly*,
     The Devil to Pay, and *The Disappointment*. Scores and
     libretti are printed as they were first published, with-
     out notes, comments, or indexing.

32b. *Italian Opera, 1640-1770*. First series. Ed. with intro-
     ductions by Howard Mayer Brown. New York: Garland, 1977-7?
     60 vols.

Includes the scores and libretti of 50 operas, by such composers as Cavalli, Luigi Rossi, Cesti, Sartorio, Legrenzi, Stradella, Pallavicino, Fux, Scarlatti, Gasparini, Bononcini, Vinci, Galuppi, Perez, Jommelli, and Piccinni.

A second series, 1981-84, comprises volumes 61-97 and includes 31 additional operas and their libretti. This second series is edited with introductions by Howard Mayer Brown and Eric Weimer.

32c. *Early Romantic Opera.* Ed. with introductions by Philip Gossett and Charles Rosen. New York: Garland, 1978-84. 44 vols.

These are full orchestral scores, photocopied from manuscript or rare early printed versions. Major works by Bellini, Rossini, Meyerbeer, Donizetti, Auber, Cherubini, Halévy, Le Sueur, Méhul, and Spontini are included.

IV. TITLE LISTS

Operas

Many writers have been inspired to make lists of operas, in alphabetical order by title or in some cases by composer. Since no two of those inventories list exactly the same titles, and since each compilation offers diverse bits of information about the works enumerated, it is necessary to consider quite a few of them.

33. Clément, Félix, and Pierre Larousse. *Dictionnaire des opéras....* Rev. ed. Arthur Pougin. Paris: Larousse, 1905. 1,203p. (Reprint--New York: Da Capo, 1969; 2 vols.) IOM-1374 ML 102 06 C42
Title of the first edition (1869) was *Dictionnaire lyrique.* A list of about 20,000 operas and comic operas that were actually performed, with dates of premieres, language, number of acts, and names of composers and librettists. Some non-French titles are given only in French translation. Composer index.

34. Riemann, Hugo. *Opern-Handbuch.* 2 Aufl. Leipzig: H. Seemann Nachfolger [189?]. 862p. IOM-1375 ML 102 06 R5
There is no date in this revised edition; the first edition appeared in 1887, and a supplement in 1893 (included in the revision). Operas, operettas, ballets, and other stage works are listed by title. Information given is variable; plot synopses, premiere data, and historical notes may appear. Not all the works were performed. No index.

35. Dassori, Carlo. *Opere e operisti (dizionario lirico 1541-1902)....* Genova: Istituto Sordomuti, 1903. 977p. (Reprint--Bologna: Forni, 1979.) IOM-1377 ML 102 06 D2

A list of 15,406 operas, with premiere dates, and birth/death dates for the composers.

36. Towers, John. *Dictionary Catalog of Operas and Operettas Which Have Been Performed on the Public Stage.* Morgantown, W. Va.: Acme, 1910. 2 vols. (Reprint--New York: Da Capo, 1967.) IOM-1373 ML 102 06 T8
   A list of 28,015 operas, thick with inaccuracies and confusingly alphabetized. Gives the name, nationality, and dates of the composers and alternative or translated titles of each work. Composer index.

37. Stieger, Franz. *Opernlexikon/Opera Catalogue/Lexique des opéras/Dizionario operistico.* Tutzing: Schneider, 1975-1983. Teil 1: *Titelkatalog.* 3 vols. Teil 2: *Komponisten.* 2 vols. Teil 3: *Librettisten.* 3 vols. Teil 4: *Nachträge.* 2 vols. ISBN 3-7952-0165-9 IOM-1372 ML 102 06 S8
   A delayed publication of Stieger's compilation, presented by him to the Austrian National Library in 1934. About 50,000 operas, operettas, Singspiele, and plays with music; and about 6,600 oratorios. Information given for each work: composer, librettist, and premiere facts. Corrections to Clément (33), Riemann (34), and Dassori (35) are offered; but Stieger's list also has many errors. The volumes on librettists give more than 15,000 persons, with the composers and debut data for their scripts. In the *Nachträge* we have some interesting arrangements of historical material: a chronology of operatic performances to 1700; names of Singspiele performed 1701-1900, and of all German stage works, 1901-35; Italian operas, 1701-1800; list of premieres in Italy, 1701-1900; Italian operas premiered outside Italy; and Italian libretti set by non-Italian composers. There is a list of composers by city of birth, by year of birth, and by year of death, with a summary list of those who lived longest and who died youngest. The oldest was neither Auber nor Verdi, but Giacomo Tritto, 1733-1824, who wrote 51 operas before dying at 91.

38. Manferrari, Umberto. *Dizionario universale delle opere melodrammatiche.* Firenze: Sansoni, 1954-55. 3 vols. IOM-1376 ML 102 06 M3
   A list of about 30,000 operatic works, in composer order; gives name of librettist and premiere data.

*And, for a few thousand operas that are in nobody else's
list:*

39. Dramatic Compositions Copyrighted in the United States,
     1870-1916. Washington, D.C.: Government Printing
     Office, 1918. 2 vols. 3,547p. (Reprint--New York:
     Johnson Reprint, 1968.) Z 5781 U5
     The forbidding *Catalog of Copyright Entries* (IOM-0826)
     includes vast quantities of published and unpublished
     music--up to 80,000 items per year. Its content is un-
     digestible, however, since the entries are grouped
     variously from time to time, but never conveniently.
     No cumulative indexing either. So the availability of
     this list, containing more than 60,000 titles, opens the
     door part of the way. About 10 percent of the titles
     seem to be musical: operas, operettas, musicals. The
     publications may be scores, libretti, or both. Raw data
     only, with no extra information. Many of the works
     originated in countries other than the U.S.

*Several major libraries have issued lists of opera scores or
libretti in their collections:*

40. United States. Library of Congress. Music Division.
     Catalogue of Opera Librettos Printed Before 1800,
     prepared by O.G.T. Sonneck. Washington, D.C.: Govern-
     ment Printing Office, 1914. 2 vols. (Reprints--New
     York: Burt Franklin, 1967; New York: Johnson Reprint,
     1970.) IOM-1549 ML 136 U55 C45

41. *Catalog of the Opera Collections in the Music Libraries:
     University of California, Berkeley; University of
     California, Los Angeles.* Boston: G.K. Hall, 1983.
     697p. ISBN 0-8161-0392-5 ML 136 B47 U58
     A pair of lists, by composer, of opera scores in the
     two libraries. About 4,000 entries from UCLA, and
     10,000 from Berkeley. Format is photoreproduction of
     catalog cards, with full bibliographic data. No index.

42. Eckhoff, Annemarie. *Oper, Operette, Singspiel. Ein
     Katalog der Hamburger Musikbücherei.* Hamburg: Hamburger
     Öffentliche Bücherhallen, 1965. 206p. ML 136 H33 O4

About 2,000 entries, in composer order with title index. Gives place and year of premiere, librettist, and
publisher.

43. British Broadcasting Corporation. *Choral and Opera
     Catalogue.* London: British Broadcasting Corporation,
     1967. 2 vols. IOM-0377 ML 128 V7 B76
     Composer and titles lists, with the genres intermixed.
Gives publisher and duration; covers about 60,000 titles.

*Numerous library inventories include operatic works along with
other kinds of music. The major examples are described in
IOM, 0227-0240, 0370-0389. Special notice is due to the outstanding cooperative list for North American libraries:*

44. *National Union Catalog: Pre-1956 imprints.* London: Man-
     sell, 1968- (in progress). IOM-0240 Z 1215 U47
     This massive set is but one component of the *NUC*, the
     world's largest publication. It presents about 10 million
     entries: works that were published before 1956 (together
     with some later items; see note in IOM) and that are
     held by any of 750 cooperating research libraries in the
     United States, Canada, and Mexico. The base set consists
     of 685 volumes; a supplementary set has been issued since
     1980, continuing the numbering (latest one seen is 64).
     Musical works are listed under names of composers, with
     full bibliographic data (format is photoreproduction of
     catalog cards). There are entries for all editions,
     transcriptions, arrangements for other instruments,
     libretti in various languages, etc. Looking in the main
     set for a pair of popular operas, we find 182 entries
     for versions of *Faust* and 289 for *Don Giovanni*.

*Another union list is of great value for its lists of recent
materials:*

45. United States. Library of Congress. *Library of Congress
     Catalog--Music, Books on Music, and Sound Recordings*,
     1953- . Washington, D.C.: Library of Congress, 1953- .
     (Semiannual; annual and quinquennial cumulations.)
     ISBN 0092-2838 IOM-0387 Z 881 U52 M8
     From 1953 to 1972 the title was *Music and Phonorecords*.
The title adopted in 1973 marked the inclusion of entries

from a number of cooperating libraries in addition to
Library of Congress. Contents: materials processed in
one of the cooperating libraries during the time period
of each volume; most publication dates are recent, but
older materials are included if they have just been ac-
quired and cataloged. Genres included are music scores,
books about music, and sound recordings whether of music
or speech. Unfortunately all these categories are
interfiled by author/composer, but a subject index makes
it possible to extract what is wanted. About 20-25 opera
scores and around 200 opera recordings are listed each
year.

Opera is a particular strength in the next collection:

46. New York (City). Public Library. The Research Libraries.
       *Second Edition of the Dictionary Catalog of the Music
       Collection.* Boston: G.K. Hall, 1982. 45 vols.
       ISBN 0-8161-0374-7 ML 136 N5 N573
       The first edition of this catalog appeared in 1964-65
     in 33 volumes and was supplemented in 1966 and 1973
     (IOM-0233). Photoreproductions of about 677,000 cards
     constitute the new edition, including entries for music
     scores and writings about music. Only about 35,000 items
     are new in the second edition, so it is possible to get
     along with the first edition if necessary (most libraries
     have decided to do that). Further supplements are
     available annually from the publisher, as the *Biblio-
     graphic Guide to Music*, 1975- . This *Guide* incorporates
     additions to the New York Public Library and items from
     Library of Congress; scores and books on music are in-
     cluded.

The other great collection with a modern printed catalog:

47. British Library. *The Catalogue of Printed Music in the
       British Library to 1980.* New York and Munich: K.G.
       Saur; dist. by Gale, Detroit, 1980- (in progress).
       ISBN 0-85157-903-5
       This new set replaces various earlier catalogues
     (IOM-0230, 0378, 0423, 0424, 0425); it will include
     about 1 million entries for music scores, in 62 volumes.
     A high degree of overlap is found between this *CPM* and
     NUC-Pre-1956, for earlier materials; but *CPM* will be a

better choice for British compositions. The single composer alphabet will make it somewhat quicker to use than *Music, Books on Music, and Sound Recordings* in a search for recent works. However, there is no subject access to *CPM*.

The next two entries represent different kinds of lists:

48. Gruber, Clemens M. *Opern-Uraufführungen. Ein internationales Verzeichnis von der Renaissance bis zur Gegenwart*. Wien: Gesellschaft für Musiktheater, 1978. ISBN 3-85202-049-2 ML 128 04 G88
    A multivolume work, of which just one volume has been seen: III--*Komponisten aus Deutschland, Österreich und der Schweiz, 1900-1977*. The intention is to list, eventually, all opera premieres with information about them. This third volume is a composer list, with operas and their premiere cities and dates given under the composers' names. About 1,700 composers are included. A title index and a city index offer useful access points. Information is in English, German, French, Italian, Russian, and Spanish.

49. Martin, George Whitney. *The Opera Companion to Twentieth-Century Opera*. New York: Dodd, Mead, 1979. 653p. ISBN 0-396-07594-0 MT 95 M253
    Plot synopses of 78 operas are the focus of this book, but there is also a useful statistics section. The operas chosen are intended to represent the current standard repertoire of works composed in this century: those which are "most performed, which have been recorded, and which seem to be gaining rather than losing popularity" (Preface). Synopses are detailed and accompanied by premiere information and other background commentary. The statistics are extensive lists of the works given in leading opera houses, from the years in which the theaters opened, with tabulations. These are the locations examined: Metropolitan Opera, Covent Garden, Hamburg, Prague, La Scala and Piccola Scala, Parma, Barcelona, Rio de Janeiro, Paris Opéra, Copenhagen, Berlin, Dresden, Brno, Leningrad, Moscow, Budapest, Buenos Aires, Australian Opera, Santa Fe, Glyndebourne, Verona, and Salzburg. The book also has a good bibliography, with complete data, of about 120 items; and there is an expansive index of titles, names, and topics.

Arias and Numbers

*Except for pieces in the most familiar operas, it is quite
difficult to discover the names of arias and other musical
numbers within a given work, or to identify an aria for which
the opera is not known. Perhaps the most useful source of
such information is a commercial service intended for record
shops:*

50. *Phonolog.* Los Angeles: Trade Services Publications,
       1948- . IOM-0483
       A looseleaf service, with replacement pages delivered
     several times each week. Covers all sorts of serious
     and popular music that is currently available on discs.
     Composite recordings are analyzed; i.e., individual
     songs and arias are individually listed--in original
     languages and in English if that appears helpful. So
     if an opera recording is "in print," it should be possible
     to find its musical numbers in *Phonolog.* Research
     libraries often subscribe to it.

51. Barlow, Harold, and Sam Morgenstern. *A Dictionary of
       Opera and Song Themes, Including Cantatas, Oratorios,
       Lieder, and Art Songs.* New York: Crown, 1966. vi,
       547p. IOM-0445 ML 128 V7 B3
       This is a reprint of *A Dictionary of Vocal Themes*
     (Crown, 1950), unchanged except for the title. About
     8,000 short musical themes are given, including thousands
     of opera arias. Good index of titles.

52. Hodgson, Julian. *Music Titles in Translation: A Checklist
       of Musical Compositions.* London: Bingley; Hamden, Conn.:
       Linnet, 1976. 370p. ISBN 0-85157-198-0 (Bingley),
       0-208-01520-1 (Linnet) ML 111 H7
       About 14,000 entries, giving titles of all kinds of
     works in their original languages and in "the most common
     alternative language." Opera arias account for a small
     percentage of the inclusions; it seems that the standard
     repertoire is their source. No index of composers or of
     operas.

*Arias and numbers are sometimes identified in books of opera
plots (items 134 to 145) and in certain opera encyclopedias
(see items 5-11 above).*

V. OPERA HOUSES

Gathered in this chapter are works that describe the opera houses of many countries. Books and articles that are entirely concerned with the theaters of a single country are listed under that country in chapter XV. A useful guide to writings about one aspect of theaters and halls, including but not limited to opera houses:

53. Stoddard, Richard. *Theatre and Cinema Architecture; A Guide to Information Sources.* Detroit: Gale, 1978. 368p. ISBN 0-8103-1426-6 Z 5784 S8 S82
Consists of 1,586 annotated entries--books, pamphlets, and articles--on exterior and interior design, including acoustical questions. Arrangement by country. Reference value of the work is reduced by the absence of diacritical marks in foreign words and names. Index of architects and designers; index of theaters by country.

54. Hughes, Patrick Cairns (Spike). *Great Opera Houses; A Traveller's Guide to Their History and Traditions.* London: Weidenfeld and Nicolson, 1956; New York: McBride, 1959. 362p. IOM-1382 ML 1720 H8
Discusses the major houses in Munich, Vienna, Venice, Milan, Parma, Florence, Rome, Naples, Palermo, Catania, Genoa, Turin, Paris and London; 13 illustrations. The approach is historical but popular (no footnotes). It is a pleasant introduction to many of opera's greatest homes. Bibliography and index.

55. Krause, Ernst. *Die grossen Opernbühnen Europas.* Kassel: Bärenreiter, 1966. 251p. IOM-1383 ML 1720 K73
A photo album of halls in Berlin, Vienna, Milan, Rome, Venice, Paris, London, Glyndebourne, Moscow, Leningrad, Prague, Budapest, Sofia, Warsaw, Stockholm, Zurich, Barcelona, Munich, Dresden, Stuttgart, Hamburg, Frankfurt, Cologne, Düsseldorf, Leipzig, Bayreuth, Salzburg,

and Halle. Most of the views are exteriors, but some
are scenes from productions. Index of persons and opera
titles.

55a. Burian, Karel Vladimir. *Světová operní divadla*. Praha:
     Supraphon, 1973. 222p. and 59 plates. ML 1700 B935
     Although the Czech language may present a barrier, this
     is a useful gathering of facts and pictures on the
     world's opera houses. Dimensions, history, and personali-
     ties of 149 theaters are given, in city arrangement.
     Index of names and theaters.

56. Sachs, Edwin O., and Ernest A. Woodrow. *Modern Opera
     Houses and Theatres*. London: Batsford, 1896-98. 3 vols.
     (Reprint--New York: Benjamin Blom, 1968.) IOM-1384
     NA 6821 S22
     The first two volumes review the architectural history
     and dimensions of leading recent constructions in Europe;
     the final volume is a treatise on theater planning and
     construction, with attention to stage machinery. Cities
     covered are Vienna, Budapest, Prague, Dresden, Halle,
     Berlin, Bayreuth, Worms, London, Wolverhampton, Manchester,
     Bristol, Amsterdam, Brussels, Oslo, Stockholm, Odessa,
     Tiflis, Leningrad, Paris, Monte Carlo, Palermo, Milan,
     Torino, Bilbao, Salzburg, Laibach, Frankfurt, Rostock,
     Essen, Bromberg, Stratford-on-Avon, Leeds, Cambridge,
     Athens, Rotterdam, Bucharest, Geneva, and Zurich. Photo-
     graphs, plans; index.

57. Filippi, Joseph de. *Parallèle des principaux théâtres
     modernes de l'Europe et des machines théâtrales
     françaises, allemandes, et anglaises*. Paris: A. Lévy
     fils, 1860. 163p. plus drawings. (Reprint--New York:
     Benjamin Blom, 1968.) IOM-1385 NA 6821 F5
     A historical survey of theater architecture and planning,
     followed by a technical description of halls in France,
     England, Italy, Germany, Russia, Spain, Belgium, and
     Denmark. Most of the theaters are 19th century, but a
     few are older. 133 plates, including plans.

58. Baur-Heinhold, Margarete. *Baroque Theatre*. Trans. Mary
     Whittall. London: Thames and Hudson; New York: McGraw-
     Hill, 1968. 292p. PN 2174 B32
     Originally: *Theater des Barock* (München: Callwey,
     1966). A cultural approach to theaters in Italy, Germany,

France, Spain, Russia, Switzerland, and Austria; considers patrons, composers, artists, and production matters, as well as the houses themselves, 16 color plates,
191 photos, and 146 figures. Bibliography of about 150
items, incomplete data. Index of names, titles, and
topics.

59. Izenour, George C. *Theater Design*. New York: McGraw-
Hill, 1977. 631p. ISBN 0-07-032086-1 NA 6821 I94
A history of theaters from ancient times, with technical
descriptions and plans and sections that are usefully
drawn to the same scale. Also essays on diverse aspects
of design; acoustics, cost-analysis, etc. About 900 illustrations; index to theaters by type and by location.

60. Aloi, Roberto. *Architetture per lo spettacolo*. Milano:
Ulrico Hoepli, 1958. lxv, 504p.
A useful handbook of about 100 theaters of the world,
most of them dating from the 1950s. Vastly detailed with
technical data ("reinforced concrete roofing 2.36 inches
thick ... cork panels 1.18 inches thick ...") and
profusely illustrated: 21 color plates, 345 black-and-
white photos, and 454 designs. The descriptive matter
is in Italian, French, English, and German. Index of
architects and theaters.

*Several architectural journals offer frequent articles about
design of theaters for music, with photos and plans. Among
these are* Architectural Design, Architects' Journal, *Architectural Review,* Theatre Design and Technology, *and* Architectural Forum. *Many citations to these and other journals are
found in Stoddard (53).*

VI. INTERNATIONAL DIRECTORIES

These are guides to the operatic world: people, companies, theaters, activities. The sources mentioned are current, or at least recent, but there will be some comments on retrospective directories at the end of this section.

61. *Who's Who in Opera; An International Biographical Directory of Singers, Conductors, Directors, Designers, and Administrators*. Ed. Maria F. Rich. New York: Arno, 1976. 684p. IOM-1500 ML 102 06 W5
    Attempts to give some biographical facts about all persons who sang at least five major roles with one of 140 major opera companies or in important festivals since 1971; the result is a collection of 2,350 personal profiles (as the title indicates, various categories of nonsingers are included as well). There is also information on 101 opera companies of the world.

62. *International Music Guide*, 1977- . London: Tantivy; Cranbury, N.J.: Barnes, 1976- . (Annual.) ISBN 0-498-02107-6 IOM-1437 ML 5 I582
    A country-by-country survey of musical life, including opera companies, premieres, festivals, and developments. Names of institutions appear in original languages, with English translations. A similar work in German: Irmgard Bontinck and J. Breuer, *Institutionen des Musiklebens in Europa....* (Wien: Doblinger, 1979; 108p).

63. *International Who's Who in Music and Musicians' Directory*. 9th ed. Ed. Adrian Gaster. Cambridge, Eng.: International Who's Who in Music; Detroit: Gale, 1980. ISBN 0-900332-51-4 (Cambridge), 0-8103-0427-9 (Detroit). IOM-1496 ML 106 G7 W4
    The history of this directory goes back to a 1935 first edition; it has had various titles and publishers. This

edition offers a good universal directory of musical institutions, including opera companies, and of opera
singers. Names of organizations are sometimes in their
own languages, sometimes in English. Many omissions and
an extraordinary number of misprints detract from the
usefulness of the volume. No index.

Three directories are technically international, but the only
countries covered are the United States and Canada:

64. *The Musician's Guide: The Directory of the World of Music.*
        6th ed. Chicago: Marquis Academic Media, 1980. 943p.
        ISBN 0-8379-5601-3 IOM-0146 ML 13 M505
        Publisher has varied since the first edition of 1954.
     Lists of agencies, organizations, libraries, periodicals
     (foreign included in this list), music critics, schools,
     competitions, etc. About 600 U.S. and Canadian opera
     companies are identified--amateur and college groups
     among them--with addresses and names of administrators.
     The "general index" to the volume is really an expanded
     table of contents.

65. *Musical America: Directory Issue*, 1968/69- . Great
        Barrington, Mass.: Billboard, 1968- . (Annual.)
        IOM-0144 ML 12 M88
        Continues an earlier directory issue of *High Fidelity/*
     Musical America. Content similar to that of previous
     item, but has a name index.

66. *Musical Courier Annual Directory of the Concert World*.
        Evanston, Ill.: Summy-Birchard, 1963- . (Annual.)
        Comparable coverage to the two preceding items.

A valuable guide to musical life of several European nations
has appeared in four volumes. Although intended primarily
as aides for travelers who are interested in musical activi-
ties and landmarks, they are useful as reference books as
well. Accurate data are given about organizations, institu-
tions, festivals, libraries, concert halls, opera companies,
and opera houses (seating capacities, hours, and other box-
office information), etc. All volumes are indexed.

67. Brody, Elaine, and Claire Brook. *The Musical Guide to*

Austria and Germany. New York: Dodd, Mead, 1975. xvi, 257p. ISBN 0-396-07217-8 IOM-1438 ML 21 B77

68. ————. *The Music Guide to Belgium, Luxembourg, Holland and Switzerland.* New York: Dodd, Mead, 1977. xvi, 156p. ISBN 0-396-07437-5 IOM-1439 ML 21 B773

69. ————. *The Music Guide to Great Britain.* New York: Dodd, Mead, 1975. 221p. ISBN 0-396-06955-X (Reprint--London: Hale, 1976.) IOM-1440 ML 21 B78

70. ————. *The Music Guide to Italy.* New York: Dodd, Mead, 1978. xvii, 233p. ISBN 0-396-07436-7 IOM-1441 ML 21 B783

Of many directories that treat music festivals this appears to be the most up to date and comprehensive:

71. Smith, Douglas, and Nancy Barton. *International Guide to Music Festivals.* New York: Quick Fox (30 W. 60 St., New York, N.Y. 10023), 1980. 245p. ISBN 0-8256-3165-3 IOM-1447 ML 35 S7
Much detail, even to cost of tickets, on about 600 worldwide festivals of opera, concert music, folk music, and jazz. Index.

Older directories will not be described here, but their value should be mentioned. On one level, they provide for the researcher a slice of the past. On another, they often give facts that are still valid, in more detail than modern publications offer; for example, we find floor plans of opera houses in Scandinavian cities in Eugène d'Harcourt's La musique actuelle dans les états scandinaves, *of 1910 (IOM-1861). Pierre Key's Music Yearbook (IOM-0153) provided directory information on opera companies of the world, lists of singers and premieres, etc., during its period of issue, 1924-38. Other retrospective directories are noted in IOM: 0138-0140, 1442-1443, and 2499. The next item is too old to be current but not old enough yet to be historic:*

72. Ross, Anne. *The Opera Directory.* London: Calder; New York: Sterling, 1961. 566p.

About 7,000 singers listed by voice type; also conductors, producers, designers, etc. Theaters and opera companies of each country are identified correctly in their own languages (except for U.S.S.R., where everything comes out in English). Good list of operas by composer, with dates, number of acts and scenes, premiere facts, cast needed. Casting index: a list of roles and all singers in the *Directory* who sing each role. No index.

VII. OPERA YEARBOOKS

A thin line separates the works in this category from the annual directories described earlier. What we are treating here are annual reviews of operatic performance, rather than revised descriptions of institutions and their personnel; but overlap is frequent between the two groups, and both categories should be consulted to discover a full range of facts.

73. *Oper; Jahrbuch der Zeitschrift "Opernwelt,"* 1966- .
Velber bei Hanover: Opernwelt, 1966- . ML 5 0615
Title and publisher vary. A world review of operatic activity, with details of casts, photographs, critical comments. Also useful feature articles, e.g. in 1981: Denis Vaughan, "Stimm- und Klangqualität im Musiktheater und zu Hause," which considers vocal acoustic characteristics of opera houses in Germany, Austria and Switzerland. The same issue has also an interesting summary of 30 years of the Bayreuth Festival.

74. *Oper Heute: Ein Almanach der Musikbühne.* 1- . 1978- .
Berlin: Henschelverlag, 1978- . ML 1700.1 061
Continues two earlier titles: *Jahrbuch der Komischen Oper Berlin* (1-12, 1960/61-1971/72; IOM-2081) and *Musikbühne: Probleme und Informationen* (1-4, 1974-1977; IOM-1379a). Horst Seeger has been editor through all the title changes. An outstanding reference source, not only for worldwide activity of each year, but for summary articles on individual opera houses and lists of premieres by country. Appropriate citations are made later in this volume.

Convenient digests of each year's operatic highlights are found in the annuals issued by three encyclopedias: Americana,

Britannica, *and* Collier's *(see IOM-0150-0151). The* World
Almanac *(IOM-0155) has useful current data on opera companies
and performances in the U.S. and Canada. An* Opera Annual,
*ed. Harold Rosenthal, appeared in London, 1954/55-1961/62;
it had strong coverage of the seasons in Britain.*

VIII. OPERA PERIODICALS

*Only a few periodicals are concerned exclusively with opera.
These are the principals:*

75. *Central Opera Service Bulletin.* 1- . 1959- . New
    York: Central Opera Service, 1959- . (Quarterly.)
    ML 1 C397
    Informative reports on current productions, especially
    for U.S. and Canada, with full lists of repertoires for
    most companies. Also news items, appointments and resig-
    nations, book reviews, courses, and seminars.

76. *Opera.* 1- . 1950- . London: Seymour, 1950- .
    (Monthly.) ML 5 067
    General articles, reviews of books and records, coming
    events, and comments on performances in U.S. and in some
    foreign cities.

77. *Opernwelt.* 1- . 1960- . Velber bei Hanover: Opernwelt,
    1960- . (Monthly.) ML 5 0672
    See also its yearbook, 58. Publisher and location
    vary. Discussions of performances, worldwide; interviews,
    articles, record reviews.

78. *Opera Journal.* 1- . 1968- . University, Miss.:
    National Opera Association, 1968- . (Quarterly.)
    ML 1 0486
    The Association was organized in 1955; editorial home
    of the *Journal* has varied. Issues include footnoted
    articles, reviews of performances, and reviews of books.

79. *Opera News.* 1- . 1936/37- . New York: Metropolitan
    Opera Guild, 1936- . (Monthly; biweekly during radio-
    broadcast season.) ML 1 0482

Frequency varies. General articles, city reports
(mostly U.S.), coming events in U.S., record reviews.
Detailed program notes for the operas broadcast on
Saturday-afternoon radio.

80. *Opera Quarterly.* 1- . 1983- . Chapel Hill: University
    of North Carolina Press, 1983- . (Quarterly.)
    ISSN 0736-0053
    Volume 1 is the only issue seen. It contains footnoted
    articles by writers who are not established specialists,
    on topics of general appeal ("Opera on Television,"
    "Eros on the Operatic Stage," etc.). One article is
    cited under Haydn (296). Reviews of discs and books.

81. *Opéra; la revue française de l'art lyrique.* 1- . 1910/
    11- . Paris: Opéra, 1910- . (Weekly.) IOM-2031
    ML 5 G82
    The complex history of this journal, the first name of
    which was *Le guide du concert,* is summarized in IOM.
    In its present manifestation it offers detailed calendars
    of operatic events in French cities and a number of
    foreign cities, with reviews and feature articles.

*A useful international journal--not exclusively on opera, but
with strong coverage--is Oper und Konzert, 1963- (IOM-1453),
a monthly. Periodicals of interest for individual countries
are listed in chapter XV.*
*Many opera companies issue periodicals for their sub-
scribers, and every performing group publishes some kind of
program; these local productions are of research interest
for the particular area but are not seriously collected by
any library encountered during the compilation of this volume.
It would seem that the best means of access to that category
of publication would be via direct correspondence with the
individual opera companies.*

IX. LIBRARY RESOURCES FOR OPERATIC RESEARCH

*In the works that follow one may find out which libraries
have particular strengths in certain topics of research interest.*

82. Benton, Rita, ed. *Directory of Music Research Libraries.*
    Kassel: Bärenreiter, 1967– (in progress). IOM-0137
    ML 12 B45
    Four volumes have appeared (publisher varies):
    1) *Canada and the United States*; 2) *Thirteen European
    Countries*; 3) *Spain, France, Italy, Portugal*; 4) *Aus-
    tralia, Israel, Japan, New Zealand.* In preparation:
    5) *Eight European Countries* (Bulgaria, Czechoslovakia,
    Greece, Hungary, Poland, Romania, USSR, Yugoslavia);
    6) *South America, Central America, Mexico and the Carib-
    bean.* An outstanding cooperative work produced by the
    International Association of Music Libraries, initiated
    by the late Dr. Benton. Now issued as part of the *RISM*
    series, *Répertoire international des sources musicales*
    (IOM-0419). General facts about each major library
    (hours, regulations for use, collection size, some
    special strengths) and reference to articles and other
    publications that give more details. Not really arranged
    for the purpose of finding collections on given subjects,
    but can serve that cause with patience on the user's
    part.

83. *American Library Directory.* 36th ed. New York: Bowker,
    1983. 2,057 p. ISBN 0-8352-1694-2
    A descriptive list of all libraries (except elementary/
    secondary school and very small public libraries) in
    the U.S. and Canada, by state or province and by city.
    Gives names of staff--including the music librarian, if
    any--finances, holdings, and special subject collections.
    Details are not generally given on the collections; but
    some libraries have provided rather long lists of in-

dicators (e.g., Chicago Public Library has a set of
Chicago opera programs beginning 1910). Revised an-
nually.

The next item has a subject approach:

84. Ash, Lee. *Subject Collections.* 5th ed. New York:
    Bowker, 1978. 1,184p. ISBN 0-8352-0924-5 Z 731 A78
    Subject and personal-name collections of research
    libraries, public libraries, and museum libraries in
    the U.S. and Canada. Gives useful summaries of collec-
    tion contents in about 40 libraries with opera special-
    ization.

85. Seaton, Douglass. "Important Library Holdings at Forty-
    one North American Universities." *Current Musicology,*
    17 (April 1974): 7-68. ML 1 C98
    This is a general survey of music research holdings,
    in which certain opera collections are identified.
    Some of the special operatic strengths noted are Boston
    University (Risë Stevens Collection); Columbia University
    (Berlioz); Cornell University (18th-19th-century scores);
    Harvard University (Rossini); Indiana University (black
    music; Latin American music); Stanford (recorded sound,
    early singers); University of California, Berkeley (18th-
    century French libretti; 19th-century Italian and
    French scores); University of California, Los Angeles
    (18th-century libretti, including a 117-volume set of
    Venetian works); University of Texas (libretti); Uni-
    versity of Washington (17th-19th century scores);
    University of Western Ontario (editions and manuscripts,
    1751-1800).

86. Bradley, Carol June. *Music Collections in American
    Libraries; A Chronology.* Detroit: Information Co-
    ordinators, 1981. 249p. ISBN 0-89990-002-X
    ML 111 B79
    An inventory of 374 institutions in the U.S., citing
    significant dates, special collections, published cata-
    logs, and writings by and about the library. Index
    identifies major subject collections.

87. Krummel, Donald W., et al. *Resources of American Music
    History: A Directory of Source Materials from Colonial*

Times to World War Two. Urbana: University of Illinois
Press, 1981. vi, 463p. ISBN 0-252-00828-6 IOM-1332w
ML 120 Ur R47
A review of library collections by state, with atten-
tion to materials for historical research. Index of
names, topics, and types of materials.

88. *Music Resources in Canadian Collections.* Ottawa: National
     Library of Canada, 1980. 1 vol. (various paging).
     ISBN 0-660-50451-0 IOM-1332n Z 735 A1088
     Services, facilities, and subject collections of 142
     libraries are described. Name index only.

89. *East Central and Southeast Europe: A Handbook of Library
     and Archival Resources in North America.* Paul Horecky,
     chief ed.; David H. Kraus, assoc ed. Santa Barbara,
     Calif.: Clio, 1976. 467p. ISBN 0-87436-214-8
     IOM-1489 Z 2483 E2
     Collections in about 40 U.S. and Canadian libraries
     are described with respect to coverage of Albania,
     Bulgaria, Czechoslovakia, German Democratic Republic,
     Greece, Hungary, Poland, Romania, and Yugoslavia. Music
     holdings are carefully described. Topic and area index.

90. Benton, Rita. "Libraries--Europe." *New Grove* (3), 10,
     725-797.
     Comments on about 1,500 music collections, arranged
     by country and city. Literature about each institution
     is cited. No index.

91. Lewanski, Richard C. *Subject Collections in European
     Libraries.* 2d ed. New York: Bowker, 1978. 495p.
     ISBN 0-85935-011-8 IOM-1487 Z 789 L4
     Includes information on about 300 music libraries,
     with summary of holdings. No topic index.

92. Albrecht, Otto. "Collections, Private." *New Grove* (3),
     4, 536-558.
     A useful survey of collectors and their collections,
     including facts on changes of ownership, losses, and
     dispersals. Covers 25 countries. Bibliography refers
     to other writings about private collections.

93. Penney, Barbara. *Music in British Libraries: A Directory of Resources.* 3d ed. London: Library Association, 1981. 452p. ISBN 0-85365-981-8 IOM-3546 ML 21 L66
Describes holdings and facilities of 712 libraries. Index of composers cited and of other special collections by subject.

94. *Zenei könyvtárak kalauza. Guide to Music Libraries. Putevoditel' muzykalnyï biblioteke.* Comp. Judit Skaliczki. Budapest: Országos Széchényi Könyvtár, 1981. 64p. IOM-2332b
Written in Hungarian, English, and Russian. Describes 30 music collections. Indexed.

A further level of detail about holdings of libraries is available in the actual catalogs, such as the works already cited (32, 33, etc.). Such catalogs, mostly partial in content, exist in profusion and cannot be identified here. Lists of library catalogs appear in the Harvard Dictionary *(1), in* Music Reference and Research Materials, *by Vincent Duckles (3d ed.; New York: Free Press, 1974), and in IOM.*

X. BIOGRAPHIES

Indexes and Bibliographies

95. *Biography and Genealogy Master Index*. 2d ed. Detroit: Gale, 1980. 8 vols. ISBN 0-8103-1094-5 IOM-0516 Z 5305 U5 B56

    A name index to 350 biographical reference works; more than 3 million citations. *Bio-base* (1981), a microfiche elaboration, offers 4 million citations. A useful spinoff concentrates on musicians and other performers: *Performing Arts Biography Master Index* (1981; 701p. ISBN 0-8103-1097-X PN 1584 A12 P35). It covers 45 sourcebooks not in *BGMI*, including entries from *New Grove*. About 270,000 biographical sketches can be located with this index. While this is a splendid finding tool, it must be said that not all possible references for an individual are indexed, and that the number of citations often varies--for one person--between *BGMI* and *PABMI*.

96. *Biography Index: A Cumulative Index to Biographical Material in Books and Magazines*. New York: H.W. Wilson, 1946- . (Quarterly; annual and triennial cumulations.) IOM-0169 Z 5301 B5

    Indexes biographical writing in some 1,700 periodicals (current issues) and recent books in English; also *New York Times* obituaries. Singers and other musicians, living or dead, are included if they are subjects of articles or books examined. An occupational index offers access by various musical specializations; "Singers" is one such category, and there were about 75 names in a recent quarterly issue.

97. National Association of Teachers of Singing. "Bibliography of Concert and Opera Singers. I: General Books on Singers." By Robert Cowden. *NATS Bulletin*, 26-2 (December 1969): 14-18, 52. IOM-1519 ML 27 U5 N2652

Annotated bibliography of 65 titles, plus ten not annotated, written in various languages from the 17th century to 1968. Further articles by the same author:
"II: Related Books Containing Important Material," *NATS
Bulletin*, 27-2 (December 1970: 24-29, 58 (172 items,
mostly memoirs and interviews); "III: Books on Opera
Houses and Festivals." *NATS Bulletin*, 28-1 (October
1971): 14-15, 19-20 (42 items, all of which include
lists of singers who performed). In all these useful
lists accuracy is good for bibliographic data, and annotations are sharp. Unfortunately, many of the books
cited are unavailable even in large research libraries.

There are two important guides to biographies of special groups:

98. Hixon, Donald L., and Don Hennessee. *Women in Music:
     A Bibliography*. Metuchen, N.J.: Scarecrow, 1975.
     xii, 347p. ISBN 0-8103-0869-2 IOM-0518 ML 105 H6
     An index to information about musicians in 48 standard
     sources, including *Baker's* (87); more than 5,000 names
     included. A useful index makes it possible to locate
     all the sopranos, contraltos, etc.

99. DeLerma, Dominique-René. *Bibliography of Black Music*.
     Westport, Conn.: Greenwood, 1981- . 3 vols. ISBN
     0-313-21340-2, 0-313-23144-3, 0-313-12510-4 IOM-1332e
     ML 128 B45 D34
     The three parts are: 1) *Reference Materials*; 2) *Afro-
     American Idioms*; 3) *Geographical Studies*. A vast
     assembly of citations, more than 88,000 entries, to
     writings about black musicians and their art. Not
     indexed. Planned to be in ten volumes.

This is about Americans only:

100. Jackson, Richard. *United States Music; Sources of
      Bibliography and Collective Biography*. New York:
      Institute for Studies in American Music, Department
      of Music, Brooklyn College of the City University of
      New York, 1973. 80p. IOM-0786c ML 120 U5 J2
      A useful guide to the contents of 90 reference books.
      Of special interest is the listing of persons covered
      in various collective biographies, including *Dictionary*

of American Biography, and *Current Biography* (104).
Quite a few opera singers are found in the name index.

*One writer has provided two useful guides to biographical
materials that are difficult to identify with usual access
aides:*

101.   Douglas, John R. "Publications Devoted to Individual
        Musicians: A Checklist." *Bulletin of Bibliography
        & Magazine Notes*, 33-3 (April-June 1976): 135-39.
        IOM-0517
        Journals, newsletters, etc., centered on certain com-
        posers or performers.

102.   ———. "Musician and Composer Societies: A World
        Directory." *Notes*, 34-1 (September 1977): 39-51.
        Of the 153 societies listed only three are for
        singers: Bjoerling, McCormack, and Steber; but there
        are also many for opera composers.

Collective Biographies

*Each of these volumes presents information about many musicians.
The more general works are listed first, followed by specialized
collections of operatic biography. Individual biographies are
not covered in this volume. An extensive, annotated assemblage
of titles in that category is available in the book already
mentioned in the Introduction: Andrew Farkas,* Opera and Concert
Singers: A Bibliography.

103.   Baker, Theodore. *Baker's Biographical Dictionary of
        Musicians*. 6th ed., rev. Nicolas Slonimsky. New
        York: Schirmer, 1978. 1,955p. ISBN 0-02-870240-9
        IOM-0175 ML 105 B16
        In Slonimsky's hands *Baker's* (first edition, 1900)
        has become the most useful and reliable handbook of
        biography and also the most entertaining of music
        reference tools. The first place to look for accurate
        information on singers of past or present. At the end
        of many articles there are citations to full-length
        biographies.

104. *Current Biography.* New York: H.W. Wilson, 1940–
    (Monthly; annual cumulations.) ISSN 0011-3344
    IOM-0184 CT 100 C8
    An outstanding journal that provides extensive bio-
    graphical coverage of 300-400 persons each year. In-
    formation is personal: there are often descriptions
    (hair and eye color, etc.) and quotations from the
    biographee. Updates and obituaries appear in later
    issues. 30-year index, 1940-70; 10-year index, 1971-
    80; and further cumulative indexing in each issue and
    each annual. An occupation index makes it easy to find
    the musicians, who are numerous. Opera singers are
    well represented; Elly Ameling even made the cover in
    October 1982. (Her hair is "molasses-colored.")

105. Mapp, Edward. *Directory of Blacks in the Performing
    Arts.* Metuchen, N.J.: Scarecrow, 1978. 444p.
    ISBN 0-8108-1126-X PN 1590 B53 M3
    Opera singers are among the 850 blacks whose biog-
    raphies are given in this useful volume. A classified
    index identifies them.

106. *Creative Canada: A Biographical Dictionary of Twentieth-
    Century Creative and Performing Artists.* Toronto:
    University of Toronto Press, 1971. 2 vols. ISBN
    0-8020-3262-1 IOM-0578 NX 513 A1 C7
    Singers are among those included. Index in volume 2.

107. *Encyclopedia of Music in Canada.* Ed. Helmut Kallmann
    et al. Toronto: University of Toronto Press, 1981.
    1,108p.
    In English only; a French edition has been announced.
    More than 3,000 articles, many of them biographical,
    with portraits. Index.

*Many other compilations have important coverage of operatic
biography. New Grove (3) and Pratt (4) have been cited
above. Some others that will be useful, especially for
pre-20th-century artists, include James Duff Brown,* Biographical Dictionary of Musicians, *1886 (IOM-0178); Alexandre
Choron and F.J.M. Fayolle,* Dictionnaire historique des
musiciens, artistes et amateurs, morts ou vivants, *1810-11
(IOM-0181); François Joseph Fétis,* Biographie universelle des
musiciens et bibliographie générale de la musique, *2me éd.,*

1860-66 (IOM-0191); Ernst Ludwig Gerber, Neues historisch-
biographisches Lexikon der Tonkünstler ..., *1812-14 (IOM-0193);*
Sohlmans musiklexikon, *2. ed., 1975-79 (IOM-203**);* Bio-
bibliographical Index of Musicians in the United States of
America Since Colonial Times, *2d ed., 1956 (IOM-0786); and
Otto Mayer-Serra,* Música y músicos de latinoamérica, *1947
(IOM-0839). This is the principal publication devoted in
full to singers:*

108. Kutsch, K.J., and Leo Riemens. *Unvergängliche Stimmen:
      Sängerlexikon.* 2. Aufl. Bern and München: Francke,
      1982. 782p. ISBN 3-7720-1555-7 IOM-1499 ML 400 K98
      While this is the second edition by the present title
      (first was 1975), the work was previously published as
      Kleiner Sängerlexikon (1962, 1966). An English transla-
      tion of the 1966 edition appeared as *A Concise Bio-
      graphical Dictionary of Singers* (Philadelphia: Chilton,
      1969). More than 3,000 artists receive brief, factual
      treatment. Some discographical information included,
      but it is vague and unreliable. Universal coverage,
      but weak for Eastern European singers. No index.

*The other books of singer-biography are listed here in alpha-
betical order by author.*

109. Breslin, Herbert H. *The Tenors.* New York: Macmillan,
      1974. xv, 203p. ISBN 0-02-515000-6 ML 400 B84
      Five leading artists--Corelli, Domingo, Tucker,
      Pavarotti, and Vickers--are discussed by five writers.
      Views of the tenors are given in their own words, on
      conductors, composers, and other things they like and
      do not like.

110. Brook, Donald. *Singers of Today.* 2d ed. London:
      Rockliff, 1958. 200p. ML 400 B871
      Four- or five-page accounts of singers holding the
      stage after 1930: 20 men and 20 women.

111. Celletti, Rodolfo. *Le grandi voci.* Roma: Istituto per
      la Collaborazione Culturale, 1964. xiv, 1p., 1,044
      columns, 1p. IOM-0472 ML 400 C44
      Biographies of 250 singers, with comprehensive dis-
      cographies and 48 portraits.

112. Davidson, Gladys. *A Treasury of Opera Biographies*.
     New York: Citadel, 1955. 352p. ML 400 D32
     Also issued as *Opera Biographies* (London: W. Laurie,
     1955). Popular sketches of about 120 persons, past and
     present, with comments on their voices. No lists of
     repertoire or other factual matter. Bibliography of
     about 50 items. Some portraits. The index of opera
     titles has no discernible value.

113. Ferris, George Titus. *Great Singers*. Rev. ed. New
     York: 1895. 2 vols. (Reprint--Freeport, N.Y.: Books
     for Libraries, 1972.) ISBN 0-8369-7259-7 ML 400 F39
     First published 1879-81. Popular accounts of the
     careers of Bordoni, Gabrieli, Arnould, Billington,
     Catalani, Pasta, Sontag, Malibran, Schröder-Devrient,
     Grisi, Viardot, Persiani, Alboni, Lind, Cruvelli,
     Titiens, and (in the revised edition only) Christine
     Nilsson, Materna, and Patti. No original material, no
     footnotes; but many facts are mixed in with the anec-
     dotes. Not indexed.

114. Heriot, Angus. *The Castrati in Opera*. London: Secker &
     Warburg, 1956. 243p. (Reprints--London: Calder,
     1960; New York: Da Capo, 1975.) ISBN 0-306-80003-9
     (Da Capo) ML 400 H47
     A basic study of the castrati, who comprised--as late
     as the end of the 18th century--70 percent of all male
     opera singers. Filippo Balatri (1676-1756) gets special
     attention. About 50 others have bio-sketches. Foot-
     notes; 101-item bibliography; name and title index. A
     valuable older treatise is Franz Haböck, *Die Kastraten
     und ihre Gesangskunst* (Stuttgart: Deutsche Verlags-
     Anstalt, 1927; xvii, 510p.); includes fine description
     of voice production and accounts of individual singers
     by country. Name index.

115. Honolka, Kurt. *Die grossen Primadonnen, von der Bordoni
     bis zur Callas*. Stuttgart: Cotta, 1960. 286p.
     ML 400 H66
     General narratives on Adriana and Leonora Baroni,
     Giorgina, Maupin, Hasse-Bordoni, Mara, Catalani, Pasta,
     Schröder-Devrient, Sontag, Malibran, Viardot, Lind,
     Patti, Lilli Lehmann, Flagstad, Tebaldi, and Callas.
     Some footnotes and pictures; no index or bibliography.
     A Czech edition, *Slavné primadony* (Praha: Supraphon,

1969), adds information on singers of that nation,
notably Emmy Destinn and Marta Krasova.

116. Klein, Hermann. *Great Women-Singers of My Time*. Lon-
      don: Routledge, 1931. vi, 244p. (Reprint--Freeport,
      N.Y.: Books for Libraries, 1968.) ML 400 K63
      Popular, personal accounts, with some footnotes, of
      Patti, Lucca, Christine Nilsson, di Murska, Trebelli,
      Alboni, Nordica, Sembrich, Melba, Calvé, Albani, Patey,
      Scalchi, Ravogli, Schumann-Heink, Sterling, Materna,
      Brandt, Sucher, Vogl, Reicher-Kindermann, Malten,
      Lehmann, Klofsky, and Ternina. Name index.

117. Krause, Ernst, and Marion Schöne. *Opern Sänger.
      Sechzig Porträts aus der Welt des Musiktheaters*.
      Berlin: Henschelverlag, 1979. 183p. ML 400 K91
      This book, not examined, appears to be an expansion
      of the 1963 work *Opern Sänger. 44 Portrats ...*, by
      the same publisher. The early version consisted of
      biographies, principal roles and photos of contemporary
      East German artists, both male and female.

118. Kühner, Hans. *Grosse Sängerinnen der Klassik und
      Romantik*. Stuttgart: Victoria Verlag Martha Koerner,
      1954. 326p. ML 400 K824
      Apparently supersedes *Genien des Gäsanges aus dem
      Zeitalter der Klassik und Romantik*, by the same author
      (Basel: Trias, 1951). Gives long accounts of Mara,
      Sontag, Malibran, Schröder-Devrient, and Lind. Bib-
      liography of 101 entries; index.

119. Lahee, Henry C. *Famous Singers of Today and Yesterday*.
      Boston: L.C. Page, 1898. ix, 337p. ML 400 L183
      Brief, popular sketches of about 250 persons. Useful
      chronological table that arranges them in order of
      birthdates. Index of names.

120. ――――. *The Grand Opera Singers of Today*. Rev. ed.
      Boston: Page, 1922. x, 543p.
      First published 1912. A running critical commentary,
      with some facts interspersed, about hundreds of singers
      who took the stage in New York, Chicago, or Philadelphia
      during the period after 1903. Name and title index.

121. Mackenzie, Barbara, and Findlay Mackenzie. *Singers of Australia from Melba to Sutherland.* Melbourne: Lansdowne, 1967. xvii, 309p. ML 400 M27
Long, footnoted chapters on Melba and Sutherland; good coverage of Alda, Dawson, J. Brownlee, Marjorie Lawrence; shorter treatment of 60 others. Useful introductory essay on opera in Australia. Bibliography of about 200 books and articles; name index.

122. Müller-Marein, Josef, and Hannes Reinhardt. *Das musikalische Selbstportrait, von Komponisten, Dirigenten, Instrumentalisten, Sängerinnen und Sänger unserer Zeit.* Hamburg: Nannen, 1963. 508p. ML 385 M91
Autobiographical; 50 artists discussing themselves and their work. Includes singers: Berger, Streich, Seefried, M. Lorenz, Leider, Lemnitz, Mödl, Melchior, Varnay, Rosvaenge, Winters, Hotter, Kunz, Ludwig, and Windgassen; and director Rolf Liebermann. Discography for each (identifying the labels only); name index.

123. Pahlen, Kurt. *Great Singers from the Seventeenth Century to the Present Day.* Trans. Oliver Coburn. London: W.H. Allen; New York: Stein and Day, 1973. 266p. ISBN 0-491-01361-2 (London), 0-8128-1698-6 (New York) ML 400 P2413
Originally *Grosse Sänger unserer Zeit* (Gütersloh: Bertelsmann, 1971); also in Spanish as *Grandes cantantes de nuestro tiempo* (Buenos Aires: Emecé Editores, 1973). A popular style of comments on many singers of each era; no footnotes or bibliography. Name index.

124. Pleasants, Henry. *The Great Singers; From the Dawn of Opera to Our Own Time.* New York: Simon and Schuster, 1966. 382p. ML 400 P65
A popular narrative, without footnotes; covers castrati, Golden Age tenors, the early prima donnas, and carries into recent times with Tauber, Tibbett, Anderson, and Flagstad. About 70 artists discussed, with some attempt at historical perspective. Hardly a work of scholarship, but "the basic history in English to date" (Cowden, 81). Weak bibliography of about 100 titles; index of names and titles.

125. Rasponi, Lanfranco. *The Last Prima Donnas*. New York:
      Knopf, 1982. 633p. ISBN 0-394-52153-6 ML 400 R37
      One of the better books about great women singers,
      emphasizing their art over their personalities. Much
      of the material appeared first in *Opera News*. Includes:
      Stignani, Nicolai, Turner, Grob-Prandl, Flagstad, Lubin,
      Konetzni, Grümmer, dalla Rizza, Ursuleac, Duval, Galli-
      Curci, dal Monte, Pagliughi, Carosio, Mazzoleni, Pacetti,
      Cigna, Milanov, Ranczak, Caniglia, Tebaldi, Tellini,
      Saraceni, Laurenti, Kirsten, Pederzini, Höngen, Novotna,
      della Casa, Oltrabella, Carbone, Corradetti, Simionato,
      di Giulio, Watson, Swarthout, Moore, Pons, Bori, Bellin-
      cioni, Stabile, Scuderi, Lotte Lehmann, Jurinac, Seefried,
      Sayao, Favero, Streich, Tess, Mödl, Rethy, Roman, Carteri,
      Cerquetti, and Callas. Useful expansive index of 70
      pages.

126. Rogers, Francis. *Some Famous Singers of the 19th Cen-
      tury*. New York: H.W. Gray, 1914. 128p. (Reprint--
      New York: Arno, 1977.) ML 400 R725
      Some occasional facts are found in this mélange of
      anecdotes and invented conversations. Covers the Garcia
      family, Catalani, Pasta, LaBlache, Rubini, Mourrit,
      Duprez, Sontag, Lind, Grisi, de Condia, and Tamburini.
      No index.

127. Rosenthal, Harold D. *Great Singers of Today*. London:
      Calder & Boyars, 1966. 212p. ML 400 R79
      Facts, dates, and critical opinions about 100 singers,
      male and female; popular style but not chatty. Many
      photos; no bibliography or index.

128. Sargeant, Winthrop. *Divas*. New York: Coward, McCann &
      Geoghegan, 1973. 192p. ML 400 S245 D6
      A disappointing collection of former *New Yorker*
      "Profiles" by the venerable music critic of that maga-
      zine. Mostly anecdotes. Covers Farrell, Horne, Birgit
      Nilsson, Price, Sills, and Sutherland. No index.

129. Schwaiger, Egloff. *Warum der Applaus. Berühmte Inter-
      preten über ihre Musik*. München: Ehrenwirth, 1968.
      348p. ML 394 S39
      Bio-sketches and material from radio interviews, on
      various musicians, including these singers: Berry,

della Casa, Dermota, Fischer-Dieskau, Gedda, Hotter,
Jochum, Ludwig, Prey, Rothenberger, Rysanek, Streich,
Jess Thomas, Varnay, Watson, Windgassen, and Wunderlich.
No index.

130. Steane, J.B. *The Grand Tradition. Seventy Years of
      Singing on Record*. London: Duckworth, 1974. xii,
      628p. ML 400 S821
      An interesting narrative history of operatic and
concert singing as displayed on recordings, with much
discerning critical opinion. Useful chapters on singers
of each country and on the interpreters of Mozart,
Wagner, etc. This is not--despite the implication of
the title--a discography; however, there is an appendix
comparison of recorded performances of 12 arias. Index
of composers with their works; index of names.

131. Thompson, Oscar. *The American Singer. A Hundred Years
      of Success in Opera*. New York: Dial, 1937. 426p.
      (Reprint--New York: Johnson Reprint, 1969.)
      A popular review of careers of Kellogg, Cary, Charles
Adams, Hauk, Juch, Valleria, Albani, Edyth Walker, Telva,
Hackett, Chamlee, etc. Some quotations but no footnotes. Appendix cites early appearances of various
singers in the opera companies of New York, Philadelphia,
and Chicago. No bibliography. Good expansive name
index.

XI. OPERA PLOTS

In an opera, as in a novel, the most accessible element is the
story--an outline of the actions taken by the characters.
Because the plot is approachable it has become the focus of
a large proportion of writing about opera; the story may simply
be paraphrased (as in the anthologies of the present section),
or it may be analyzed closely in an effort to locate the
artistic heart of the work (examples will be presented later).
The paraphrased plot or synopsis of the action is certainly
basic to understanding what is happening, but it does seem
hazardous to assign aesthetic significance to the operatic
story. Music, not libretto, is the meaning-giver. We find
the same general story used again and again by opera composers
(e.g., the Concise Oxford Dictionary of Opera lists about 60
versions of Orpheus; the wide variation in resultant value
must follow from the quality of the score. The novel offers
an apt analogy; it is what the author does with the story-line
that carries the artistic consequence. In both novel and
opera the plot may be trivial or foolish (Vanity Fair, Magic
Flute) while the artistic development of it is supreme. Nor
does a finely wrought, sophisticated story lead necessarily
to a successful musical drama--examples of this kind of
failure are numerous among the attempts of contemporary opera
composers. Nevertheless, plots are important, and they are a
frequent subject of inquiry. The books that follow will provide enough information for most purposes.

132. Drone, Jeanette Marie. *Index to Opera, Operetta and
      Musical Comedy Synopses in Collections and Periodicals.*
      Metuchen, N.J.: Scarecrow, 1978. 177p. ISBN
      0-8108-1100-6 IOM-1381 ML 128 O4 D76
      An important index to 74 opera-plot anthologies and
      the plots found in *Journal of the American Musicological
      Society* (1948-76), *Musical Times* (1971-74), *The New
      Yorker* (1976), and *Opera News* (1949-76). Synopses
      included in dictionaries of opera are not indexed. It
      contains references to 1,605 titles of 627 composers.

Arrangement is by title with a composer index. The
anthologies analyzed are in English and all published
after 1926 in order to coordinate with the next entry.

133. Rieck, Waldemar. *Opera Plots*. New York: New York Pub-
       lic Library, 1927. 102p. ML 128 L4 R4
       An index to about 200 books of synopses, in English,
French, German, and Danish. Arranged under composers'
names. References to 2,775 operas by 998 composers.

Many books cited earlier are useful sources of plots: Kloiber
(6), Moore (7), Ewen (9), Orrey (10), Herders (11), Krause
(12), Simon and Schuster (13), Riemann (34), and Martin (49).
The following selection of plot-collections will add con-
siderably to the range of available synopses.

134. Czech, Stan. *Das Operettenbuch: Ein Führer durch die*
       Operetten und Singspiele der deutschen Bühnen. 4. Aufl.
       Stuttgart: Muth, 1960. 424p. MT 95 C93
       Detailed synopses of about 125 light operas that have
held the German stage. In addition to standard composers like Kálman and Lehár we find the work of many
lesser-known persons; e.g., these (not in Drone): Beneš,
Bromme, Burkhard, Dellinger, Dostal, Goetze, Jarno,
Meisel, Nick, Raymond, Scheu, Schröder, and Vetterling.
But only one American composition is included: *Küss*
mich Kätchen. Yes, all titles and arias are in German
only. A useful feature is the citation of films made
of each operetta, with dates and casts. There are also
brief performance histories and comments. No indexes.

135. Fellner, Rudolph. *Opera Themes and Plots.* New York:
       Simon and Schuster, 1958. xii, 354p. MT 95 F319
       A useful guide to plots of the standard operas, be-
cause the stories are keyed to many brief musical examples (e.g., 34 examples from *Ballo in Maschera*).
Covers 32 operas. Index of texts quoted is in effect
a list of the arias and vocal numbers in all these
works.

136. Kobbé, Gustave. *The New Kobbé's Complete Opera Book.*
       Ed. and rev. Earl of Harewood. 9th ed. New York:

Putnam, 1976. xvii, 1,694p. ISBN 399-11633-8
IOM-1380 MT 95 K52
Gives plot summaries for about 220 operas in the
current standard repertoire of Britain and America.
Includes some historical notes. Name and title index,
and index to a few topics. The title of this well-
known book has varied considerably over its publishing
history, which began in 1919.

137. Lubbock, Mark Hugh. *The Complete Book of Light Opera.*
        With an American section by David Ewen. London:
        Putnam; New York: Appleton-Century-Crofts, 1962.
        xviii, 953p. MT 95 L85
        About 300 plots, covering the European repertoire
     (Audran, Hervé, Oscar Straus, etc.) and American musicals.
     Information given includes premiere date and main cast.
     Name, title and subject index, partly expansive. Another
     book by Ewen includes fewer plots but adds more back-
     ground facts: *The Book of European Light Opera* (New
     York: Holt, Rinehart & Winston, 1962). It has a useful
     chronology and an aria index.

138. Martens, Frederick Herman. *A Thousand and One Nights
        of Opera.* New York and London: Appleton, 1926.
        ix, 487p. (Reprint--New York: Da Capo, 1978.)
        Seems to be the largest collection of plots (1,550),
     but ballets are included as well as operas. Title and
     composer indexes.

139. Melitz, Leo. *Opera Goers Complete Guide.* New York:
        Garden City, 1921. xvii, 508p.
        Plots, names of musical numbers (in English only),
     and casting for 268 works. Useful for many nonstandard
     inclusions, by such composers as Adam, Auber (eight
     operas), Blech, Blockx, Boieldieu, Boughton, Breil,
     Breton, Brüll, Cadman, Erlanger, Février, Goldmark
     (five operas), Massenet (ten operas), and Pfitzner
     (three operas).

140. Newman, Ernest. *Stories of Great Operas.* New York:
        Vintage, 1958. 2 vols.
        Incorporates his *Stories of Famous Operas*, *More
     Studies of Famous Operas*, and *Seventeen Famous Operas.*

(For another of his books, *The Wagner Operas*, see item
509.) These are literate, detailed summaries of the
standard repertoire material, with musical examples
and background information.

141. Payne, Alexis. *Grand opéras du répertoire.* Paris:
      Fayard, 1979. 574p. ISBN 2-213-00675-X
      ML 102 06 P346
      About 120 operas, including the standards of Anglo-
      American seasons and works by French composers. De-
      tailed plots are given, with lists of arias and numbers,
      background data for each opera, and discographies.
      Useful index of characters; also one by title and a
      chronological array. Valuable list of theaters by
      country, with most names in original languages.

142. Renner, Hans. *Oper, Operette, Musical. Ein Führer
      durch das Musik-theater unserer Zeit.* München:
      Südwest Verlag, 1969. 626p. MT 95 R41 06
      Something that appears to be a reprint was advertised
      in a 1980 issue of the *Journal of the American Musico-
      logical Society*: *Renners Führer durch Oper, Operette,
      Musical* (Clifton, N.J.: European American Music Distribu-
      tors); it has not been seen. About 1,000 plots are
      given in the 1969 version, standard repertoire and many
      obscure modern works. Some background facts are given
      with the synopses. Arias are identified in German only,
      and the titles also--in main text and index. There is
      a composer index as well.

143. Schumann, Otto. *Handbuch der Opern.* 10. Aufl. Wilhems-
      haven: Heinrichshofen's Verlag, 1972. 964p. ISBN
      3-7959-0002-6 MT 95 S392
      In addition to standard composers, presents a fine
      cross-section of lesser-known Germans (e.g., Julius
      Weismann, Walter Braunfels, Ottmar Gerster, Erich
      Sehlbach, Mark Lothar) whose works are not indexed by
      Drone. Biographies of the composers; 32 plates; index
      of titles and of characters (with their German names
      only: who remembers Mackie Messer?).

*A comparable collection, also useful for Germans, is Kurt
Honolka's* Grosse Reader's Digest Opernführer *(Stuttgart: Verlag
Das Beste, 1966; 728p.), about 200 plots.*

144. Sénéchaud, Marcel. *Le répertoire lyrique d'hier et
     d'aujourd'hui.* Paris: Billaudot, 1971. 301p.
     Gives plots of 343 works, including the familiar
     pieces, but with good representation of operas popular
     in Paris or by French composers. For instance, we find
     Platée (Rameau), *Le Poirier de misère* (Delannoy), and
     Quand la cloche sonnera (Bachelet), none of which appears
     in Drone's index to plots.

145. *The Victor Book of Operas.* 13th ed., rev. Henry W.
     Simon. New York: Simon and Schuster, 1968. 475p.
     MT 150 V4
     First published in 1912, this familiar work has been
     frequently revised. It covers 120 operas of the standard
     repertoire, with leisurely synopses, photos of famous
     singers in the various roles, and discographies.

XII. OPERA PRODUCTION

*Drawn together under the general heading of "production" are
all aspects of management, direction, design, and staging.
There is a valuable bibliography with which to begin:*

146. Cowden, Robert H. "Acting and Directing in the Lyric
     Theater: An Annotated Checklist." *Notes*, 30-3 (March
     1974): 449-59. ML 27 U5 M695
     Consists of 111 entries, books and articles, in
     English, French, and German. The literature on these
     topics is thin, as Cowden observes, and many of the
     titles included here are of little more than passing
     interest. The following are some of the more substantial
     writings.

Manuals and Guides

147. Central Opera Service, New York. *Opera Manual; A Hand-
     book of Practical Operatic Information.* New York,
     1956. 36p. MT 955 C4
     Discusses about 500 "chamber operas" in terms of pro-
     duction requirements: voices needed and their types,
     sets, acts, duration, publisher. Covers a few standard
     works (*Barber of Seville, Sir John in Love, Tender Land,*
     etc.), but most of the operas are little known.

148. Eaton, Quaintance. *Opera Production, A Handbook.*
     Minneapolis: University of Minnesota Press, 1961-74.
     2 vols. ISBN 0-8166-0689-7 MT 955 E25
     Production information on some 700 operas (in detail)
     and brief notes on another 250 in a supplement. Gives
     plot, duration, casting, publisher or other source of
     score, and much auxiliary guidance. The most important
     of the manuals.

149. Goldovsky, Boris. *Bringing Opera to Life; Operatic
      Acting and Stage Direction*. New York: Appleton-
      Century-Crofts, 1968. x, 424p. ISBN 0-13-083105-0
      ML 1700 G738 B7
      Detailed directions for staging various standard
operas, with diagrams covering all contingencies. Special
attention to presentation of two arias: Cherubino's "Non
so più cosa son" and Leporello's "Il catalogo è questo."
Index of operas.

150. *National Opera Association Catalog ... of Contemporary
      American Operas*. Ed. Arthur Schoep. New York:
      National Opera Association, 1976. ML 128 C4 N27
      Similar to Eaton in format, but restricted to modern
American works and including many not described in Eaton
or the other handbooks of this section.

*This is the only book discovered that takes a broad look at
modern productions:*

151. Nagler, Alois Maria. *Misdirection: Opera Production in
      the 20th Century*. Trans. Johanna C. Sahlin. Hamden,
      Conn.: Archon, 1981. 134p. ISBN 0-208-01899-9
      ML 1700 N33
      Translated from *Malaise in der Oper* (Rheinfelden:
Schäube, 1980). A sour view of Felsenstein, Rennert,
Wieland Wagner, and all the moderns, but interlaced with
facts and good perceptions. Useful also for summary
stage histories of the operas examined: *Don Giovanni*,
Così fan tutte, *Marriage of Figaro*, *Fidelio*, *Flying
Dutchman*, *Aida*, *Tales of Hoffmann*, *Freischütz*, *Carmen*,
and *Rosenkavalier*. Notes; name index.

Individual Producers and Artists

Rudolf Bing

152. Bing, Rudolf. *5000 Nights at the Opera*. New York:
      Doubleday, 1972. ML 429 B613 A3
      A plain autobiography, without notes or reference
features; gives little in the way of facts about his
management of the Metropolitan Opera (1951-72). No
index. The next entry is more useful:

153. ————. *A Knight at the Opera*. New York: Putnam, 1981.
287p. ISBN 0-399-12653-8 ML 429 B52 A33
He really was a knight, having been thus honored in
1971. This review of his career at the Met is chatty
and smug but does offer some interesting letters to and
from Maria Callas and documents revealing Bing's style
in handling stage managers, TV people, unions, and of
course singers. Includes a list of his Metropolitan
repertoire and all the artists who performed, and a list
of his new productions. Index of names and titles.

John Christie

154. Blunt, Wilfrid. *John Christie of Glyndebourne*. New
York: Theatre Arts, 1968. xiii, 303p. ML 429 C53 B6
Concerns the founder of the Glyndebourne Opera (1934)
and his solution of numerous problems involved in making
it one of the leading companies. Discussion of Bing,
the first manager; Carl Ebert, artistic director; Fritz
Busch, conductor; and mezzo-soprano Kathleen Ferrier.
Indexed.

Walter Felsenstein

155. Felsenstein, Walter. *Schriften zum Musiktheater*. Berlin: Henschelverlag Kunst u. Gesellschaft, 1976.
575p. ML 1700.1 F44
The author is best known for his work as Intendant
(Manager) of the Komische Oper, East Berlin. He gives
general ideas on staging and particular approaches to
specific works: *Bartered Bride*, *Carmen*, *Freischütz*,
Falstaff, *Marriage of Figaro*, *Magic Flute*, *Otello*,
Traviata, *Rigoletto*, and some others. List of sources;
chronology of works staged by him, 1926-75; name index.

156. *The Music Theater of Walter Felsenstein: Collected Articles, Speeches, and Interviews*.... Ed. and annotated
Peter Paul Fuchs. New York: Norton, 1975. xx, 188p.
ISBN 0-393-03186-6 ML 429 F43 M9
Included here because it is the only book on Felsenstein in English, but it is of marginal value. Interviews give some insights into various operas and problems. No index.

Fortune Gallo

157. Gallo, Fortune. *Lucky Rooster*. New York: Exposition,
     1967. 304p. ML 429 G153 A3
     Gallo founded the San Carlo Touring Company in 1909.
     His autobiography is not very informative about that
     important organization; it is a tiresome gathering of
     anecdotes and imagined conversations. No notes, index,
     or other reference features.

Giulio Gatti-Casazza

158. Gatti-Casazza, Giulio. *Memories of the Opera*. New
     York: Scribner, 1941. xii, 326p. (Reprint--New York:
     Vienna House, 1973.) ISBN 0-9443-0022-5 ML 429 G17 A3
     The significant contribution of Gatti-Casazza to the
     establishment of the Met as a world-esteemed company
     remains to be adequately documented. His own account of
     that career (1908-35) is vague and chatty, with invented
     conversations and few facts. No notes; no bibliography.
     Index of names, titles, and topics.

Rudolf Hartmann

159. Hartmann, Rudolf. *Oper. Regie und Bühnebild Heute*.
     Stuttgart: Fohlhammer, 1977. 267p. ML 1700 061.
     In English: *Opera* (New York: Morrow, 1972); in
     French: *Les grands opéras. Décor et mise en scène*
     (Paris: Vilo, 1977).
     Hartmann achieved world recognition for his produc-
     tions at Munich (1938-67), and later in other European
     houses. A general essay on stage design, followed by
     illustrated accounts of his settings for *Don Giovanni*,
     Magic Flute, *Fidelio*, *Barber of Seville*, *Don Pasquale*,
     Don Carlos, *Meistersinger*, *Götterdämmerung*, *Tales of
     Hoffmann*, *Pelléas et Mélisande*, and *Frau ohne Schatten*--
     all these productions dating 1962-76. Fine pictures;
     and comments by other stage artists and producers.
     Appendix gives data on the theaters he has worked in,
     from a production viewpoint. Bibliography of about 50
     titles. No index.

160. ————. *Richard Strauss: The Staging of His Operas and
     Ballets*. Trans. Graham Davies. New York: Oxford Univer-
     sity Press, 1981. 280p. ISBN 0-19-520251-1 MT 955
     H3332
     The original was in German: *Richard Strauss: Die Bühnen-
     werke von der Uraufführung bis Heute* (München: R. Piper,
     1980). Interesting details on staging, with notes and
     good pictures. Bibliography of about 50 items; name and
     place index.

Rolf Liebermann

161. Liebermann, Rolf. *En passant par Paris; opéras.* Paris:
     Gallimard, 1980. 457p. ML 1727 L716
     A splendid picture book of productions, covering 55
     operas given at the Paris Opéra. Liebermann was manager
     there from 1973 to 1980, after achieving fame as Inten-
     dant at Hamburg, 1959-73. For each work treated here
     there are details of casting and staff, with perceptive
     commentaries. Some of the less-common operas included
     are *Ariane et Barbe-Bleue, Erwartung, Intégrale* (Satie),
     Marchand de Venise (Hahn), *Moses and Aron, Platée*
     (Rameau), *Tom Jones* (Philidor), and *Véronique* (Messager).
     Liebermann is an advocate of contemporary composers.

Benjamin Lumley

162. Lumley, Benjamin. *Reminiscences of the Opera.* London:
     Hurst and Blackett, 1864. xx, 448p. (Reprint--New
     York: Da Capo, 1976.) ISBN 0-306-70842-6
     ML 429 L95 A3
     As manager of Her Majesty's Theater, 1841-52 and
     1856-59, Lumley was at the center of operatic life in
     London. This is a personal, emotional account of his
     activities (problems, mostly), involving the great
     composers (Donizetti, etc.) and singers. Invented con-
     versations; no notes or index.

James Henry Mapleson

163. Mapleson, James Henry. *The Mapleson Memoirs, 1848-
     1888.* New York: Belford, Clarke, 1888. xi, 392p.
     (Reprint--New York: Appleton-Century-Crofts, 1966.
     346p.)
     Mapleson was active as an impresario in London, 1861-
     89 (Drury Lane, Her Majesty's, Covent Garden), and then
     in America until 1897. This is a chatty, sometimes
     entertaining chronicle of his London adventures; often
     more imaginary than factual. The reprint edition is
     abridged and annotated by Harold Rosenthal, and is
     much preferable to the original; it also includes ap-
     pendixes of interviews, peer observations, and a list
     of persons mentioned with some brief identifications.
     A list of Mapleson's English premieres is of use. Name
     and title index.

Max Maretzek

164. Maretzek, Max. *Revelations of an Opera Manager in 19th-
      Century America.* New York: Dover, 1968. xxxi, 442p.
      ML 429 M32 A3
      This edition incorporates *Crotchets and Quavers* (1855)
      and *Sharps and Flats* (1890) and offers a new introduc-
      tion by Charles Haywood, plus an index. Maretzek was
      another of those colorful impresarios of the Golden
      Age, in continued confrontation with his "rapacious"
      singers, creditors, and tricky competitors. His account
      deals with a long period (1848-90) in New York, where he
      managed the Academy of Music and other companies. Much
      is chatter, and invented conversation, but useful in-
      formation on personalities and conditions of the time
      is pervasive.

Günther Rennert

165. Rennert, Günther. *Opernarbeit: Inszenierungen 1963-
      1973.* Kassel [etc.]: Bärenreiter; München: Deutscher
      Taschenbuch-Verlag, 1974. 263p. ISBN 3-7618-0432-6
      ML 3858 R45
      A picture book of his stage designs, mostly from
      Munich, where he was Intendant from 1967 to 1976.
      Covers standard operas, plus some moderns like Janáček
      and Penderecki--the latter represented by a wild and
      naked scene from *Devils of Loudon.* No notes, no index.

Konstantin Sergeevich Stanislavskiĭ

166. Rumi͡ant͡sev, Pavel Ivanovich. *Stanislavski on Opera.*
      Trans. and ed. Elizabeth Reynolds Hapgood. New York:
      Theatre Arts, 1975. x, 374p. ISBN 0-87830-132-1
      ML 429 S8 R813
      Stanislavskii directed the (new) opera studio of the
      Bol'shoĭ Theater from 1918; in 1924 this became the
      Stanislavskiĭ Opera Studio, and in 1928 the Stanislavskiĭ
      Opera Theatre. His influence on operatic acting was
      considerable, but this book--primarily made up of in-
      vented conversations in which the director gives advice
      on specific roles to various singers--does not do justice
      to his contribution. Rumi͡ant͡sev was a singer and
      director in most of Stanislavskiĭ's productions. No
      bibliography, no index.

Wieland Wagner

167. Skelton, Geoffrey. *Wieland Wagner: The Positive Skep-
      tic.* New York: St. Martin; London: Gollancz, 1971.
      222p. ISBN 0-575-00709-5 (London) ML 429 W135 S6
      An adulatory, undocumented story of Richard Wagner's
      grandson, who was co-director at Bayreuth (with Wolfgang
      Wagner, his brother) from the end of World War II until
      his death in 1966. His staging departed from emphasis
      on scenery and moved toward abstractions. Many good
      photos; list of his productions, 1936-66; bibliography
      of about 20 entries; useful expansive index of names
      and titles.

David Webster

168. Haltrecht, Montague. *The Quiet Showman: Sir David
      Webster and the Royal Opera House.* London: Collins,
      1975. 319p. ISBN 0-00211-1632 ML 429 W378 H19
      A vague account of Webster's career as manager of the
      Royal Opera (Covent Garden), 1945-70. No notes; a weak
      bibliography of about 25 items; index of names and
      titles.

XIII. THEORY, CRITICISM, ANALYSIS

General Views

169. Conrad, Peter. *Romantic Opera and Literary Form.*
      Berkeley and Los Angeles: University of California
      Press, 1977. vii, 185p. ISBN 0-5200-3258-6
      ML 2110 C754
      An examination of Verdi, Wagner, Strauss, and some
      contemporaries in terms of their handling of story and
      literary sources of their stories. The underlying
      assumption--that literary matters are the basic forces
      in opera--and the lack of a coherent terminology put
      this study into the category of question-raiser rather
      than answer-provider. Bibliography of about 50 entries;
      name index, with works cited under composer names.

170. Hanning, Barbara. "The Influence of Humanist Thought
      and Italian Renaissance Poetry on the Formation of
      Opera." Ph.D. dissertation, Yale University, 1969.
      374p.
      Not examined. The author's abstract in *RILM Abstracts*,
      3/1-2 (January-August 1969): 63, says that she has dis-
      cussed the "poetics of the first operas." There is a
      consideration of theories of the affections vis-à-vis
      the Camerata; the Orfeo legend and early libretti; verse
      styles; and the role of the librettists in "determining
      the form and style of the incipient genre."

171. Kerman, Joseph. *Opera as Drama.* New York: Knopf, 1956.
      269p. (Reprint--New York: Vintage, 1959.) ML 3858 K4
      Promotes the primacy of plot and character as operatic
      values. Gives program-note commentaries on several
      standard operas, concentrating on the story-lines. The
      author's literary premises lead him to denounce the
      operas of Puccini and Strauss as "false through and
      through." *Salome* and *Rosenkavalier* are "insincere in

every gesture." No notes, no bibliography. Index of names, titles, and topics.

172. Leibowitz, René. *Les fantômes de l'opéra. Essais sur le théâtre lyrique.* Paris: Gallimard, 1972. 393p. ML 1700 L43

     Says that the point of opera is the creation of character and situation through purely musical means. Analyzes *Fidelio, Euryanthe, Don Carlos, Pique Dame, Tosca, Pelléas,* and works of Monteverdi in order to demonstrate the thesis. Interesting structural study. Notes; no bibliography; no index.

173. Schmidgall, Gary. *Literature as Opera.* New York: Oxford University Press, 1977. xi, 431p. ISBN 0-1950-2213-0 ML 3858 S348

     Examines the process of transforming a work of literature into an opera, following the idea that literary quality of the original ought to be retained. He expresses pessimism about today's operatic composer, who seeks among inferior stage works for material. His analyses, being nonmusical, necessarily miss the points of the works he selects for close study: *Orlando, Alcina, Marriage of Figaro* (where he strains to find a comic theme in the libretto), *Maria Stuarda, Lucia, Benvenuto Cellini, Macbeth, Eugène Onegin, Salome, Wozzeck,* and *Death in Venice.* Backnotes; no bibliography; good expansive index of names, titles, and topics.

Criticism

A major overview of German music criticism:

174. Kirchmeyer, Helmut. *Situationsgeschichte der Musikkritik und des musicalischen Pressewesens in Deutschland.* Regensburg: Bosse, 196X-72. 4 vols. ISBN 3-7649-2019-x ML 3915 K57

     Considers methods and principles of musical criticism, and studies applications in 18th- and 19th-century Germany. The fourth volume deals with Wagner criticism; the sixth is a bio-bibliography of critics. Contains long extracts from contemporary newspaper and journal critiques. Index of names and source journals.

175. Arundell, Dennis. *The Critic at the Opera*. London:
          Ernest Benn, 1957. 424p. ML 1731 A74
          A collection of comments by critics from the 16th to
      the 20th century; running observations and notes by the
      editor. Bibliography of about 120 entries, in chrono-
      logical order, with incomplete data. Expansive index
      of names, titles, topics. Lists of theaters, works,
      singers, composers, and conductors.

*The remaining citations in this section are about individual
critics.*

176. Aldrich, Richard. *Musical Discourse from the New York
          Times*. New York: Oxford University Press, 1928.
          305p. ML 60 A5
          The author was music editor of the *New York Times*,
      1902-23. He offers sophisticated comments on musical
      events, including opera; with interesting pieces on
      Jenny Lind and Adelina Patti.

177. Hanslick, Eduard. *Music Criticisms, 1846-99*. Trans.
          and ed. Henry Pleasants. Baltimore: Penguin, 1950.
          313p. ML 60 H2492
          One of the most famous writers of musical criticism,
      Hanslick wrote for the Vienna *Presse* and *Neue freie
      Presse*. His novel concept that the value of music comes
      from its pure, nonreferential character (independent of
      program, or dramatic text) is significant in the history
      of aesthetics. His views were applied harshly, however,
      and Wagner (a "referentialist") was among those to bear
      his scorn. Wagner turned him into Beckmesser. Most of
      the essays in this collection are about Wagner themes;
      but there are also opinions of Patti, Lilli Lehmann,
      Otello, and *Hansel and Gretel*. Name index. This is
      the only English translation of Hanslick criticism, but
      the serious student will need to look at the German
      originals. A convenient reprint of the "Collected
      Musical Criticism of Eduard Hanslick" was published
      in nine volumes by Gregg (Farnborough, England) in
      1971--ISBN 0-576-28228-6.

178. Henderson, William James. *The Art of Singing*. New
          York: Dial, 1937. xviii, 509p. (Reprint--Freeport,
          N.Y.: Books for Libraries, 1968.) MT 820 H496 A8

Includes *The Art of the Singer* (1906) and articles
from the *New York Sun*. Henderson (1855-1937) was critic
for the *Sun* and for the *New York Times*; his reviews of
opera are of special value. Among the singers discussed:
Calvé, Tetrazzini, Viardot, Galli-Curci, Patti, Farrar,
Maurer, Jeritza, Lilli Lehmann, Hauk, Pons, Melba,
Sembrich, Flagstad, and Schumann-Heinck. Index of names
and titles.

179. Hogarth, George. *Memoirs of the Opera in Italy, France,
      Germany and England*. 2d ed. London: Richard Bentley,
      1851. 2 vols. (Reprint--New York: Da Capo, 1972.)
      ISBN 0-306-70256-8 ML 1700 H72
      The first edition (1838) had the title *Memoirs of the
      Musical Drama*. Hogarth lived from 1783 to 1870; he was
      critic for the London *Morning Chronicle* and for the
      Daily News. This collection includes important commen-
      taries on Gluck and Piccinni, Mozart, *The Beggar's Opera*,
      and Jommelli and critiques on many singers, among them
      Farinelli, Caffarelli, Gizziello, Carestini, Guarducci,
      Durastanti, Guadagni, Mingotti, Mara, Millico, Cecilia
      Davies, Rauzzini, Agujari, Banti, Todi, Paccierotti,
      Rubinelli, Marchesi, Billington, Grassini, Braham,
      Catalani, Bertinotti, Tramezzani, Naldi, Vestris, Fodor,
      Camporese, Ambrogetti, Pasta, Velluti, Sontag, and
      Malibran. Engraved portraits; no index.

180. Klein, Hermann. *Thirty Years of Musical Life in London,
      1870-1900*. New York: Century, 1903. xvii, 483p.
      ML 285.8 L8 K6
      Klein, who lived 1856-1934, wrote for the London
      Sunday Times. This collection has notes, portraits,
      and an excellent expansive index of names. There are
      essays of special interest on the de Reszkes, Patti,
      Sembrich, Lucca, Bispham, Melba (her debut), Schumann-
      Heink, Alvary, and Nordica.

181. Lonchampt, Jacques. *L'opéra d'aujourd'hui, journal de
      musique*. Paris: Éditions du Seuil, 1970. 301p.
      ML 60 L847
      Articles from *Le monde*, 1960-70, covering performances
      in Paris and elsewhere in Europe. Some of the less-
      common operas reviewed include *Passion grècque* (Martinů),
      Antigone, and *Aventures du roi pausole* (Honegger),
      Miguel Manara (Tomasi), *Les canuts* and *Les hussards*

(Kosma), *Andrea del Sarto* (Lesur), *L'opéra de poussière*
(Landowski), *La rêve de Liu Tung* (Isang Yun), and others
by Semenoff, Macha, Klebe, Duhamel, Prey, Pousseur,
Manzoni, Goehr, and Bennett. Composer and title index.

182. Marcello, Benedetto. *Il teatro alla moda*. Venezia:
       Borghi di Belisania per A. Licante, ca. 1720.
       A satirical and entertaining essay that sharply criti-
       cizes operatic practice of the time. Frequently trans-
       lated (see list in Grout, *Short History of Opera* (16),
       p. 663). The most useful English rendition is: "Il teatro
       alla moda," trans. Reinhard G. Pauly, *Musical Quarterly*,
       34 (1948): 371-403; 35 (1949): 85-105. The translator
       has provided valuable footnotes and helpful explanations.
       The same author has also written an important study of
       the essay: "Benedetto Marcello's Satire on Early 18th
       Century Opera," *Musical Quarterly*, 34 (1948): 222-233,
       which gives interesting material on stage devices and
       on other operatic satires of the period.

183. Porter, Andrew. *Music of Three More Seasons, 1974-1977*.
       New York: Farrar Straus Giroux, 1978. 667p.
       ML 60 P895 M88
       Interesting reviews by an English critic who wrote for
       the *New Yorker* magazine for several seasons of opera;
       these are all extracts from the magazine. (An earlier
       collection, *A Musical Season, 1972-1973*, is also worth
       looking at.) Expansive index of names and places.

184. Wellesz, Egon. *Essays on Opera*. Trans. Patricia Kean.
       London: Dennis Dobson, 1950. 158p. ML 1700.1 W42
       Reflections on the early days of opera in Vienna,
       Italians at the Austrian court, operatic form, and a
       valuable discussion of Cesti's *Pomo d'oro* (pp. 54-81).
       No index.

XIV. STUDIES OF INDIVIDUAL OPERAS

The works cited in this chapter are concerned with specific operas, or with several operas by one composer. By grouping them under composer' names, we can compare various approaches to each composer's output. In many instances the operas are discussed within a biographical context, so a number of biographies will be found; however, biographies that do not include substantial attention to operatic writing are in general omitted.

Two expressions are used frequently in the annotations to give the reader a tangible impression of the sort of approach taken by the authors. By far the most common approach in the literature on individual operas is the "program note." This term refers to the kind of general description that is usually found in the concert or opera program booklet: a plot synopsis, with background facts on the circumstances of the composer at work, some comments on the libretti vis-à-vis the original literary work, and perhaps some information about the premiere. A program note is accessible to nonspecialist readers; it is not footnoted and does not present original material.

In contrast to the program note there is "analysis." Analysis attempts to describe a work intensively with regard to its form, structure, harmonic and melodic elements, style, and technique. The analyst aims at specialized readers, and endeavors to provide an original viewpoint that to some extent "explains" a work. Documentation of previous analyses (footnotes, bibliography) is a typical feature. Analysis may have diverse starting points, or theoretical premises; indeed, specialists in analysis may be gathered under various headings or "schools," just as literary critics may be identified with distinctive labels.

Length of presentation does not distinguish a program note from an analysis, nor does the author's announced intention. Finally, it should be stressed that neither mode is superior sui generis; each may serve its purpose well or poorly, and both purposes are worthy. In scholarly writing, however, there is a clear trend away from program notes toward some kind of analysis; so a large proportion of the recent writing cited below will represent analytic approaches.

*Certain selection criteria have been applied in choosing
the books, articles, and other materials listed in this chapter. From the immense literature on major composers only a
handful of titles could be included. These are, for the most
part, recent scholarly works, or "classic" studies, or works
with strong bibliographic orientation (those that guide the
reader to other writings). For lesser-known composers it has
been necessary to select from what is available. In all cases
preference has been given to writing in English, French, German,
Italian, and Spanish; but material in other languages is included as required by the circumstances.*

185.   One useful series is cited frequently: *Avant-scène
        opéra* (Paris, 1976-). It consists of handbooks on
        individual operas, each containing the libretto in the
        original language and in French, together with program
        notes and articles by various specialists, and many
        photographs.

186.   There are other handbook series worthy of attention.
        The "Rororo Opernbücher" began in 1981 under the
        editorship of Attila Csampai and Dietmar Holland.
        Publisher is Ricordi in Munich, with Rowohlt Taschen-
        buch Verlag in Reinbek bei Hamburg. Announcement of
        the series states that these operas will be included:
        Meistersinger, *Don Giovanni*, *Otello*, *Boris Godunov*,
        Bohème, *Fidelio*, *Freischütz*, and *Magic Flute*. Two have
        been seen: *Die Zauberflöte--Texte, Materialen, Kommentare*
        (1982) and *La Bohème* (1981). They offer scholarly
        essays on genesis and productions, chronologies, letters,
        analyses, bibliographies, discographies, and the libretto
        in German (also in Italian for *Bohème*). No indexes.

187.   The "Cambridge Opera Handbooks" began to appear in
        1981, issued by Cambridge University Press. Each volume
        consists of essays by various authors; typically, they
        deal with the libretto, the premiere and later produc-
        tion history, and miscellaneous studies. The six volumes
        that have come out are all cited below, at their respective
        operas: *Kat'a Kabanová*, *Orfeo* (Gluck), *Don Giovanni*,
        The Rake's Progress, *Peter Grimes*, and *Parsifal*. A
        Falstaff handbook was announced but not seen; one on
        Norma is in preparation.

188.   Eight volumes have been seen in another distinguished
         series: "English National Opera Guides." Operas covered
         are *Cenerentola*, *Aida*, *Magic Flute*, *Fidelio*, *Traviata*,
         Tristan, *Otello*, and *Rosenkavalier*. They are published
         by John Calder (London) and Riverrun Press (New York).
         Contents of the volumes include photos, essays by
         specialists, libretto in original language and English,
         musical themes, bibliography, and discography. Publica-
         tion began in 1980.

         Another new series, "Metropolitan Opera Classics" (New
         York: Little, 1983-), has had good reviews. None of
         the three volumes issued has been examined.

While some cross-referencing is offered in the annotations,
it is assumed that the reader will bear in mind the possible
utility of general works discussed earlier (histories, ency-
clopedias, biographies, etc.) and will also make use of the
index.
     Names of operas appear in their original languages and in
English translations as appropriate; the translations are the
most common forms, as shown in standard sources. Composers'
names and dates usually follow the authority of the Library
of Congress.

                     Antonio Maria Abbatini
                      (ca. 1609-ca. 1677)

189. Murata, Margaret. *Operas for the Papal Court, 1631-*
      1668. Ann Arbor, Mich.: UMI Research, 1981. x, 474p.
      ISBN 8357-1122-6 ML 1733.8 R6 M97
      Based on the author's dissertation (University of
      Chicago, 1975). The attention is focused on Giulio
      Rospigliosi (Pope Clement IX), whose worldly pastime
      was authorship of libretti for operas. Two of his
      texts were set by Abbatini: *Dal male il bene* (1653;
      with Marazzoli) and *La comica del cielo* (1668); both
      are analyzed carefully here from historical and stylis-
      tic viewpoints. Appendix of sources: manuscripts,
      library locations, editions, anthologies. Good expansive
      index of names, titles, and topics; also a first-line
      index to arias. Bibliography of about 250 entries,
      with full data.

Daniel François Esprit Auber
(1782-1871)

190. Pendle, Karin. *Eugène Scribe and French Opera of the
      Nineteenth Century.* Ann Arbor, Mich.: UMI Research,
      1977. vi, 624p. ISBN 8357-1004-1-S83 ML 1727 P398
      This work, like the preceding entry, is about a famous
      librettist. Scribe (1791-1861) wrote the texts for
      many composers: Boieldieu, Meyerbeer, Halévy, and Auber.
      This book, based on the author's dissertation (Univer-
      sity of Illinois, 1970), has much detail on Auber's
      work, with special attention to *La muette de Portici*
      (1828). It has extensive backnotes and a bibliography
      of about 300 entries with full data. Expansive index
      of names, titles, and topics. An article drawn from
      this material, with the same title as this book, ap-
      peared in *Musical Quarterly*, 57-4 (October 1971): 535-
      561.

Béla Bartók
(1881-1945)

Duke Bluebeard's Castle, *also known as* Bluebeard's Castle *or*
The Castle of Duke Bluebeard *(A kékszakállú herceg vára), pro-
duced in 1918, was Bartók's only opera; it has not spawned a
large literature. Some comments are found in Halsey Stevens,*
The Life and Music of Béla Bartók *(London: Oxford University
Press, 1964). The following may be useful:*

191. Rhodes, Sally Ann. "A Music-Dramatic Analysis of the
      Opera Bluebeard's Castle by Béla Bartók." M.A.
      thesis. Eastman School of Music, University of
      Rochester, 1974. 2 vols.
      Not examined. In *RILM Abstracts*, 8-2/3 (May-December
      1974): 212, the author abstract reveals an emphasis on
      form and tonal structure.

Ludwig van Beethoven
(1770-1827)

Fidelio *(1805) was Beethoven's only completed opera; it has
not received the massive critical examination of his instrumental works. Willy Hess is one scholar who has given it
much study:*

192. Hess, Willy. "Fünfzig Jahre im Banne von Leonore-
      Fidelio." *Beethoven-Jahrbuch*, 9 (1973-77): 167-184.
      A summary of research on the opera, with special con-
      cern for the versions of 1805 and 1806 and differences
      between manuscript and printed editions. List of all
      writings by Hess on the opera.

This is a detailed examination of the libretto versions:

193. Ruhnke, Martin. "Die Librettisten des Fidelio." *Opern-
      studien. Anna Amalie Abert zum 65. Geburtstag*, ed.
      Klaus Hortschansky, pp. 121-140 (Tutzing: Schneider,
      1975). ISBN 3795-20155-1 ML 55 A15
      Compares the 1805 and 1806 versions with a later
      libretto of 1814 and an earlier one of 1798.

*Avant-scène opéra, 10 (May-June 1977), offers various perspec-
tives on Fidelio. There is also an "English National Opera
Guide" (188).*

Vincenzo Bellini
(1801-1835)

*Recent biographies have concentrated on events of the com-
poser's life rather than on his music. This book has some
discussion of the operas:*

194. Brunel, Pierre. *Vincenzo Bellini*. Paris: Fayard, 1981.
      431p. ISBN 2-213-00263-5 ML 410 B44 B89
      A footnoted biography; attention to the operas is
      limited and concentrates on text (quotations are in
      French translation); no musical examples. Useful work-
      list, alphabetical and classified. Bibliography of
      about 200 entries; discography; index of names, titles,
      and topics.

The most thorough study of the operas in book form:

195. Lippmann, Friedrich. *Vincenzo Bellini und die italien-
      ische Opera seria seiner Zeit. Studien über Libretto,*

Arienform und Melodik. Köln and Wien: Böhlau, 1969.
xii, 402p. (Analecta musicologica, 6.)
A scholarly analysis, with focus on libretto, structure of the aria, and general melodic style. Comparisons
with work of Rossini, Donizetti, and other contemporaries.
Discussion of sources, autographs, early editions, etc.
Bibliography of about 150 entries, some annotated. No
index.

Another important treatise remains unpublished:

196. Greenspan, Charlotte. "The Operas of Vincenzo Bellini."
      Ph.D. dissertation. University of California, Berkeley,
      1977. 383p.
      Considers the context in which the ten operas were
      written: his singers, audience, theaters, etc.; libretti,
      orchestration. Not examined; information from author's
      summary in *RILM Abstracts*, 9-3 (September-December 1977):
      300.

I Capuleti e i Montecchi

*Critics who take a literary view of opera have denigrated
this work because of its unfaithfulness to Shakespeare. A
recent study clears the air:*

197. Collins, Michael. "The Literary Background of Bellini's
      I Capuleti ed i Montecchi." *Journal of the American
      Musicological Society*, 35-3 (Fall 1982): 532-538.
      ML 27 U5 A83363
      (Capuleti is sometimes seen with two t's; and the
      conjunction may be either "e" or "ed.") Conjectures,
      convincingly, that the librettist Romani was not adapting
      Shakespeare at all but drawing on quite different ver-
      sions of the romance. Useful bibliographic notes.

I puritani di Scozia

198. Petrobelli, Pierluigi. "Bellini e Paisiello. Altri
      documenti sulla nascita dei Puritani." *Il melodramma
      italiano dell'ottocento: studi e ricerche per Massimo
      Mila*, pp. 351-364. Torino: G. Einaudi, 1977.
      ML 1733.4 M5

Offers the idea that Bellini kept Paisiello's works
before him as a frame of reference as he planned
Puritani. Discusses the early sketches.

La sonnambula

199. Degrada, Francesco. "Prolegomeni a una lettura della
Sonnambula." *Il melodramma italiano dell'ottocento:
studi e ricerche per Massimo Mila*, pp. 319-350.
Torino: G. Einaudi, 1977. ML 1733.4 M5
Recounts the genesis of the libretto and gives program notes on the music. Useful citations of earlier
writings about the opera; 13 musical examples.

Alban Berg
(1885-1935)

*No other composer has been responsible for such an important
scholarly literature in the period immediately following his
death. In view of the stunning complexity of the two operas,
Wozzeck (1925) and Lulu (1937), it is all the more remarkable
that an array of perceptive analysis took shape so quickly.
The highly selective group of citations that follow are intended to represent the highlights of that array, and to
offer--through their notes and bibliographies--guidance to
the remaining writings. A good historical summary of Berg
literature is found in Mark DeVoto's review of Jarman's book,
in* Journal of the American Musicological Society, *33-3
(Summer 1980): 407-412.*

200. Reich, Willi. *Alban Berg, Leben und Werk*. Zürich:
Atlantis-Verlag, 1963. 239p. ML 410 B47 R342. In
English: *The Life and Works of Alban Berg*. Trans.
Cornelius Cardew. New York: Harcourt, Brace & World,
1965.
Reich, a pupil of Berg, has been regarded as his
"official" biographer; this book includes edited versions of writings by Berg about *Wozzeck*. With 41 backnotes, 38 musical examples. Rather rudimentary attempts
at structural analysis, seemingly oblivious of the
studies by other scholars. Name and title index.

201. Redlich, Hans F. *Alban Berg: Versuch einer Würdigung*.
Wien: Universal, 1957. 393p. In English (abridged):

Alban Berg: The Man and His Music (London: Calder, 1957).

Redlich uncovered much new source material and offered a revision of Berg's *Wozzeck* lecture that differed from that of Reich. His analyses moved toward the sophistication of the next wave of scholars; had he not died before his revised edition could be completed, he might have been important in that wave.

202.   Perle, George. *The Operas of Alban Berg. I: Wozzeck.*
       Berkeley and Los Angeles: University of California
       Press, 1980. xvii, 231p. ISBN 0-5200-344-06
       ML 410 B47 P45
       Now considered to be the leading authority on Berg's music, Perle has been writing intriguing articles on *Wozzeck* and *Lulu* for 25 years. He offers extremely detailed analyses of pitch and structural organization in these twelve-tone works, and also an acerbic review of what other scholars have written. Perle steps away from the large-scale total-unity approach of many contemporary opera specialists; he identifies the components of Berg's atonal universe, and relates music to text at specific moments, but does find it worthwhile to seek unification of those components into a "single comprehensive system."

203.   Jarman, Douglas. *The Music of Alban Berg.* Berkeley
       and Los Angeles: University of California Press, 1979.
       xii, 266p. ISBN 0-5200-348-56 ML 410 B47 J37
       After some brief attention to biography and documents, this outstanding study moves on to the music and covers it thoroughly: pitch organization, rhythm, and macro-structure as well as smaller structures (in this respect taking a broader view than Perle). Jarman acknowledges all earlier studies and adds to them. There are 210 musical examples; a work-list (including manuscripts and sketches, with locations); a fine bibliography of about 150 items, fully described; and an expansive index of names, titles, and topics.

204.   Carner, Mosco. *Alban Berg: The Man and the Work.* 2d ed.
       London: Duckworth, 1983. xx, 314p. ISBN 0-7156-0769-3
       ML 410 B47 C28
       The first edition came out in 1975; it was translated into French in 1979. This now stands as the principal

biography. It includes some musical analysis (most importantly of *Lulu*), with notes and musical examples. Perle's work appears to have been ignored. A basic work-list; short bibliography (about 70 items), with incomplete data; expansive index of names and titles.

It must be said that the other recent biography, by Karen Monson, is unsatisfactory, even as a popular treatment. Paolo Petazzi's 1977 book consists of little more than program notes and does not even have an index.

Wozzeck

A recent study of the libretto is of interest:

205. Radice, Mark A. "The Anatomy of a Libretto: The Music Inherent in Buchner's Woyzeck." *Music Review*, 41-3 (August 1980): 223-233.
    Considers the folksongs in the Buchner text, versions seen by Berg, overall structure of the opera. Useful references to previous scholarship.

A good general approach to the opera, with complete libretto, is provided by Avant-scène opéra, *36 (1981). See also Perle (202). A steady source of new data and speculation is the* Newsletter *of the International Alban Berg Society (Durham, N.C.: The Society, 1968-   ).*

Hector Berlioz
(1803-1869)

The basic guide to Berlioz scholarship is:

206. Holoman, D. Kern. "The Present State of Berlioz Research." *Acta musicologica*, 47-1 (1975), 31-67.
    ML 5 I6
    A lucid, learned summary of biographical and analytical studies. It has not been thought necessary to repeat here the titles cited by Holoman, except for a few modern landmarks. Some works that appeared after 1975 are also identified below.

207.   Hopkinson, Cecil. *A Bibliography of the Musical and
        Literary Works of Hector Berlioz*. 2d ed. Tunbridge
        Wells, Eng.: R. Macnutt, 1980. xix, 230p. ISBN
        0-907180-00-0 ML 134 B5 H79
            This is a facsimile reprint of the 1951 edition, with
        additions and corrections. Arranged by title, it gives
        all known editions in all countries, with detailed
        descriptions and locations. Does not discuss performances.
        22 plates; general index.

208.   Berlioz, Hector. *The Memoirs of Hector Berlioz....*
        Trans. and ed. David Cairns. Corrected ed. New
        York: Norton, 1975. 636p. ISBN 0-393-00698-0
        ML 410 B5 A42
            Aside from certain emendations, this is the same text
        as the first edition (London: Gollancz, 1969). It is
        an excellent rendering of Berlioz's delightful and
        illuminating recollections, with full scholarly ap-
        paratus. The period covered is 21 March 1848 to 1 Jan-
        uary 1865, during which he wrote *Les troyens* and
        Béatrice et Bénedict and experienced at least one
        trauma (a chapter begins: "Calamity--I become a critic").
        Cairns holds that, despite the humor and romantic
        panache of the memoirs, they are basically accurate.
        "Errors and disputed points" are discussed, as are the
        sources. An appendix presents descriptions of Berlioz
        by his contemporaries; a glossary identifies persons
        mentioned and gives bio-sketches of them, and also
        identifies places and institutions. An expansive index
        of names and titles.

209.   Berlioz, Hector. *New Letters of Berlioz, 1830-1868*.
        With introduction, notes, and English translation by
        Jacques Barzun. New York: Columbia University Press,
        1954. xxxi, 322p. (Reprint, as "2d ed."--Westport,
        Conn.: Greenwood, 1974.) ISBN 0-8371-3251-7
        ML 410 B5 A33
            A bilingual, annotated edition, with bibliography.
        No index.

210.   Barzun, Jacques. *Berlioz and the Romantic Century*. 3d
        ed. New York: Columbia University Press, 1969. 2 vols.
        ML 410 B5 B2
            The first edition was 1950; a second edition of 1956
        had a variant title: *Berlioz and His Century* (reprinted--

Chicago: University of Chicago Press, 1982). The standard biography, but as Holoman points out it does not fully replace the pioneering studies by Adolphe Boschot.

Several important dissertations have appeared:

211. Gräbner, Eric Hans. "Berlioz and the French Operatic Tradition." Ph.D. dissertation. York University (England), 1967. 250p.

Not examined; author summary in *RILM Abstracts*, 4-2 (May-August 1970): 147, indicates an emphasis on sociocultural contexts for the major operas. Gräbner is an editor for the New Berlioz Edition and has written significant Berlioz analysis.

212. Langford, Jeffrey Alan. "The Operas of Hector Berlioz: Their Relationship to the French Operatic Tradition of the Early Nineteenth Century." Ph.D. dissertation. University of Pennsylvania, 1978. 459p.

Not examined. From *RILM Abstracts*, 12-2 (May-August 1978): 188, we learn that there is major attention to the macrostructure of *Les troyens*. All the works are examined in the light of French operatic traditions.

213. Stuart, James F. "The Dramatic World of Hector Berlioz." D.M.A. dissertation. University of Rochester, 1969.

Not examined. Described by Holoman as treating the operas in relation to French traditions and offering a list of "all Parisian productions that may have influenced Berlioz in his study of operatic design."

Several writings by Brian Primmer and by Edward T. Cone are described by Holoman.

Les troyens

214. Section 2c of *Hector Berlioz: New Edition of the Complete Works* (Kassel: Bärenreiter, 1970) gives the score and an elaborate historical and critical commentary, with sources, sketches, editions, and variant readings. Written in English, French, and German, under the editorship of Hugh MacDonald, who presented this material

originally as his Ph.D. dissertation: "A Critical Edition
of Berlioz's Les Troyens" (Cambridge University, 1968;
4 vols.).

Another dissertation is described by the author in RILM Abstracts, *9-1/2 (January-August 1975): 77.*

215. Goldberg, Louise. "Les Troyens of Hector Berlioz: A
      Century of Productions and Critical Reviews." Ph.D.
      dissertation. University of Rochester, 1974. 2 vols.
      A history of staged and concert productions of the
      various versions, with data on casts, dates, and cuts;
      and an annotated bibliography of the reviews of each
      performance.

On The Damnation of Faust *there is an issue of* Avant-scène
opéra *(no. 22). Finally, the reader is referred to the*
Berlioz Society Bulletin *(London, 1952- ; quarterly), which
has carried many features on the operas, notably in the series
beginning Winter 1982 under the editorship of David Cairns.*

Georges Bizet
(1838-1875)

216. Dean, Winton. *Georges Bizet, His Life and Work.* 3d ed.
      London: Dent, 1975. x, 306p. ML 410 B62 D28
      (Reprint in paperback, 1977.)
      The first edition was 1948, second edition 1965. A
      popular biography, with program notes on the operas.
      Work-list, glossary of persons cited in the text, bib-
      liography of about 100 items (incomplete data). Name
      and title index.

Carmen

A good introduction is provided by Avant-scène opéra, *26 (1980).*
*Two accounts of recent productions make an interesting com-
parison:*

217. Koerth, Manfred. *Felsenstein inszeniert Carmen; Doku-
      mentation.* Berlin: Akademie der Künste der Deutschen
      Demokratischen Republik, 1973. 127p. ML 410 B62 K6

218. Phillips, Harvey E. *The Carmen Chronicle: The Making of
      an Opera.* New York: Stein & Day, 1973. 288p. ISBN
      0-8128-1609-9 ML 410 B62 P65
      Describes the planning of Gentele's 1972 production
      at the Met; unfortunately in a very chatty style, with
      invented conversations. The Koerth presentation of
      Felsenstein is more sober and informative.

219. Wright, Lesley A. "A New Source for Carmen." *19th Cen-
      tury Music,* 2-1 (July 1978): 61-69. ML 1 N714
      Examines the so-called censor's libretto; discusses
      variant readings and sources. A new "revision chronology"
      is proposed, in contrast to that in Fritz Oeser's edition.
      Good references to earlier work.

Marc Blitzstein
(1905-1964)

220. Dietz, Robert James. "The Operatic Style of Marc Blitz-
      stein in the American 'Agit-prop' Era." Ph.D. disser-
      tation. University of Iowa, 1970. 475p.
      Appears to be the only full-length study of this com-
      poser's music. Not examined; author's summary in *RILM
      Abstracts,* 4-2 (May-August 1970): 153, indicates that
      the approach is essentially sociophilosophical. A bib-
      liography and a work-list are included.

François Adrien Boieldieu
(1775-1834)

221. Favre, Georges. *Boieldieu: sa vie, son oeuvre.* Paris:
      1944-45. 2 vols. ML 410 B69 F35
      A scholarly biography, well footnoted; letters and
      documents included. Synopses and program notes on the
      operas, with handwritten musical examples that are dif-
      ficult to decipher. Work-list (titles only, without
      details), bibliography, and name index.

Arrigo Boito
(1842-1918)

222. Nardi, Piero. *Vita di Arrigo Boito.* Verona: Mondadori,
      1942. 753p. ML 410 B72 N2
      A revised edition, not seen, came out in 1944. This
      is the standard biography, and, since most of the con-

siderable literature on Boito preceded it, it stands as a summary of scholarship. A scholarly work, with ample footnotes and an expansive index. Operas receive program-note treatment.

See also the section on Boito in Jay Nicolaisen, Italian Opera in Transition, 1871-1893 *(629).*

Giovanni Bononcini
(1670-1747)

223. Wolff, Hellmuth Christian. "Bononcini--oder die Relativität historischer Urteile." *Revue belge de musicologie*, 11 (1957): 3-16. ML 5 R292
    A well-documented study of Bononcini's style and the context of his times. Useful comments on the writings of other scholars and quotations from them. Observes that there is no thorough analysis of the operas. Wolff's opera chapter in *New Oxford History of Music*, 5, has useful information on Bononcini.

224. Lindgren, Lowell. "The Three Great Noises 'Fatal to the Interests of Bononcini.'" *Musical Quarterly*, 61-4 (October 1975): 560-583.
    General biographical background, and details on Bononcini's misguided activities in London after 1720. Lindgren's dissertation, not examined, is the most substantial treatise: "A Bibliographic Scrutiny of Dramatic Works Set by Giovanni and His Brother Antonio Maria Bononcini" (Ph.D. dissertation. Harvard University, 1972; xii, 1,094p.). It includes a work-list and thematic catalog.

George Frederick Bristow
(1825-1898)

225. Gombert, Karl Erwin. "'Leonora' by William Henry Fry and 'Rip van Winkle' by George Frederick Bristow; Examples of Mid-Nineteenth Century American Opera." D.A. dissertation. Ball State University, 1977. 264p.
    Appears to be the first full-length perusal of these works; not examined.

Benjamin Britten
(1913-1976)

226. White, Eric Walter. *Benjamin Britten: His Life and Operas*. 2d ed. London: Faber and Faber, 1983. ISBN 0-571-18066-3 ML 410 B853 W4
      The publishers have chosen a confusing way of identifying various versions of this work. The first edition was 1948, a second edition appeared in 1954, and a clearly labeled third edition in 1970. So the new "2d" is a further revision of the "3d." It is mainly a collection of program notes; in the author's words: "These little essays ... lay no claim to offer musical analyses in depth." Useful chronology of published works and a list of premieres. Good illustrations, weak bibliography of about 25 items; index of names, titles, and topics.

227. Evans, Peter. *The Music of Benjamin Britten*. Minneapolis: University of Minnesota Press, 1979. 564p. ISBN 0-8166-0836-9 ML 410 B853 E9
      There is some structural analysis here--e.g., in the treatment of *Billy Budd*--but essentially Evans has written sophisticated program notes. More than 300 musical examples; work-list; bibliography of about 75 entries (incomplete data); name index.

228. Howard, Patricia. *The Operas of Benjamin Britten: An Introduction*. London: Barrie & Rockliff; New York: Praeger, 1969. 236p. ISBN 214-66055-9 (New York). MT 100 B778 H7
      Synopsis and program notes for each opera, with 102 musical examples. There is no reason to consult this book if Evans is available. No bibliography; no index.

229. Herbert, David. *The Operas of Benjamin Britten: The Complete Librettos*. New York: Columbia University Press, 1979. xxxi, 382p. ISBN 0-2310-48688 ML 49 B74 H5
      A useful handbook of the opera texts, with 140 plates that illustrate costumes and sets of the premieres. Includes some essays by librettists and designers. Bibliography of 13 items; expansive index of names, titles, and topics.

A Midsummer Night's Dream

230. Bach, Jan Norris. "An Analysis of Britten's A Midsummer
      Night's Dream." D.M.A. dissertation. University of
      Illinois, 1971. 424p.
          Not examined. According to the author, in *RILM Ab-
      stracts*, 5-2 (May-August 1971): 178, this is an "attempt
      to determine the degree of architectonic thought in
      Britten's compositional procedures." There is also
      discussion of sources and the libretto. Bibliography,
      work-list, discography, and index.

Peter Grimes

231. Brett, Philip, ed. *Benjamin Britten: "Peter Grimes."*
      New York: Cambridge University Press, 1983. 225p.
          A "Cambridge Opera Handbook." According to the pub-
      lisher's announcement, consists of a collection of
      essays and materials on the opera. Not seen.

Peter Grimes and *Turn of the Screw*

232. Deavel, R. Gary. "A Study of Two Operas by Benjamin
      Britten: Peter Grimes and Turn of the Screw." Ph.D.
      dissertation. Eastman School of Music, University
      of Rochester, 1970. 344p.
          Not examined. The author says, in *RILM Abstracts*,
      4-2 (May-August 1970): 153, that "the analysis includes
      a discussion of form, tonal organization, and those
      aspects of musical grammar that establish each work's
      individual identity." Libretti are compared with the
      literary works from which they are drawn. Bibliography;
      no index.

Giulio Caccini
(1546-1618)

Some fine material on Caccini (and also Peri and Monteverdi)
is presented in this article:

233. Pirrotta, Nino. "Early Opera and Aria." *New Looks at*
      Italian Opera (620), pp. 39-107. ML 1733.1 A92
          Considers the nature of the aria and problems of
      definition and form in opera of the period.

Alfredo Catalani
(1854-1893)

Interest in Catalani has waned among scholars. The only recent writing of consequence is Nicolaisen's study in his Italian Opera in Transition, 1871-1893 *(629). This is the standard biography:*

234. Gatti, Carlo. *Alfredo Catalani, la vita e le opere.*
    Milano: Garzanti, 1953. 250p. ML 410 C37 G3
    A life story, with program notes on the operas.

Pier Francesco Cavalli
(1602-1676)

235. Glover, Jane. *Cavalli.* New York: St. Martin; London:
    Batsford, 1978. 191p. ISBN 0-71341-0078 (London)
    ML 410 C37 G56
    A fine synthesis of what is known about the composer,
    whose operas were performed more than those of anyone
    else during his era. Biographical data are included,
    but operas are the main focus. Backnotes, musical ex-
    amples, references to earlier scholarship; the bibliog-
    raphy has about 300 entries (incomplete information).
    List of all the operas, with dates, premiere, manuscript
    locations, and comments. Excellent expansive index of
    names, titles, and topics.

Two older works remain highly useful for their detailed approaches:

236. Wellesz, Egon. "Cavalli und der Stil der venezianischen
    Oper von 1640-1660." *Studien zur Musikwissenschaft,*
    1 (1913): 1-103.
    Extended excerpts in score, with perceptive struc-
    tural analyses; consideration of choral writing, instru-
    mentation, and aria style. Notes; no index.

237. Prunières, Henry. *Cavalli et l'opéra vénetien au XVIIe*
    siècle. Paris: Rieder, 1931. 120p. ML 410 C3913 P7
    Scholarly discussion of the period and of Cavalli's
    works; a few footnotes, extended musical examples. 40
    pictures of scenes from productions. Bibliography of
    about 30 entries. No index.

*Two dissertations should be mentioned.   Information is from
author summaries in* RILM Abstracts.

238.   Clinkscale, Martha Novak.   "Pier Francesco Cavalli's
          Xerse."   Ph.D. dissertation.   University of Minnesota,
          1970.   2 vols.   893p.
          Biography; relations with librettists and fellow com-
          posers; and analysis of the opera *Xerse* (1654 or 1655).
          In volume 2 there is a modern edition of the complete
          opera.   Bibliography; thematic catalog.   No index.
          RILM Abstracts, 4-1 (January–April 1970): 25.

239.   Rosand, Ellen.   "Aria in the Early Operas of Francesco
          Cavalli."   Ph.D. dissertation.   New York University,
          1971.   x, 390p.
          Considers the operas of 1639–45, observing "changes
          in dramatic structure and expressive language leading to
          mature Baroque opera."   Arias are categorized as serious,
          comic, or laments.   *RILM Abstracts*, 502 (May–August
          1971): 162.

Antonio [Pietro] Cesti
(1623–1669)

The major recent writings are dissertations:

240.   Schmidt, Carl B.   "The Operas of Antonio Cesti."   Ph.D.
          dissertation.   Harvard University, 1973.   2 vols.
          1,721p.
          The author states (*RILM Abstracts*, 9-1/2 [January–
          August 1975]: 53) that he has included a documented
          biography and a "bibliographical scrutiny of all Cesti's
          operas."   Descriptions and locations of 130 libretti
          and about 30 full scores and aria collections.   Style
          analysis of several works, notably *La Dori*, for which
          a complete transcription is provided.   Bibliography,
          work-list; no index.

241.   Holmes, William Carl.   "Orontea: A Study of Change and
          Development in the Libretto and Music of Mid-Seventeenth
          Century Italian Opera."   Ph.D. dissertation.   Columbia
          University, 1968.   iv, 282p.
          Not examined.

See also his:

242. Holmes, William Carl. "Giacinto Andrea Cicognini's and
         Antonio Cesti's Orontea, 1649." *New Looks at Italian
         Opera* (620), pp. 172-219.

Schmidt also has a useful journal article:

243. Schmidt, Carl B. "Antonio Cesti's *Il pomo d'oro*: A
         Reexamination of a Famous Hapsburg Court Spectacle."
         Journal of the American Musicological Society, 29-3
         (Fall 1976): 381-412. ML 27 U5 A83363
         Establishes that the premiere took place in July
      1668 rather than 1667, as given in standard sources.
      Discusses new material that had been presumed lost.
      Another good commentary on this opera, by Egon Wellesz,
      has already been cited (184).

                  Petr Il'ich Chaĭkovskiĭ (Tchaikovsky)
                            (1840-1893)

*The operas have been largely neglected by scholars. Program
notes are given in Gerald Abraham's* Slavonic and Romantic
Music *(662a) and in the newest full-length work:*

244. Brown, David. *Tchaikovsky: A Biographical and Critical
         Study.* London: Gollancz; New York: Norton, 1978- .
         ISBN 0-393-07535-2 (New York) ML 410 C4 B87
         Projected as 4 volumes, of which two have appeared:
      1) *The Early Years, 1840-1874* (1978); 2) *The Crisis
      Years, 1874-1878* (1982). Covers *Eugene Onegin*, *Mazeppa*,
      Queen of Spades, and *The Sorceress*. Synopses and back-
      ground information; 95 musical examples in volume 1,
      another 152 examples in volume 2. The biography is
      well documented with primary sources. Name and title
      index.

                       Luigi Cherubini
                         (1760-1842)

245. Willis, Stephen. "Luigi Cherubini: A Study of His Life
         and Dramatic Music, 1795-1815." Ph.D. dissertation.
         Columbia University, 1975. 429p.
         Not examined.

*An article by Alexander Ringer, "Cherubini's Médée and the
Spirit of French Revolutionary Opera,"* Essays in Musicology
in Honor of Dragan Plamenac *(Pittsburgh: University of Pittsburgh Press, 1969), 281-299, gives social context and program
notes.*

Domenico Cimarosa
(1749-1801)

246. Johnson, Jennifer Elizabeth. "Domenico Cimarosa (1749-
     1801)." Ph.D dissertation. University of Wales,
     1976. 3 vols. 1,124p.
     Not examined. In *RILM Abstracts*, 10-3 (September-
     December 1976): 339, the author says that a chronology
     is established for all compositions, with a thematic
     catalog. Manuscript sources and printed editions,
     libretti, and performances are noted for all the operas,
     and "certain features of his operatic style are described."
     Bibliography; no index.

Il matrimonio segreto

247. Dietz, Hanns-Bertold. "Die Varianten in Domenico
     Cimarosas Autograph zu Il matrimonio segreto und ihr
     Ursprung." *Musikforschung*, 31-3 (1978): 273-284.
     ML 5 M9437
     Discusses variants between the composer's autograph
     and the version used for the premiere (1792); compares
     other copies and editions.

Claude Debussy
(1862-1918)

248. Abravanel, Claude. *Claude Debussy: A Bibliography*.
     Detroit: Information Coordinators, 1974. 214p.
     ML 113 D483 #29
     A thorough inventory of 1,854 books, articles, and
     dissertations written about Debussy; full bibliographic
     data, but no annotations. On *Pelléas et Mélisande*, his
     only opera, we find a listing of premiere reviews from
     France, Germany, Austria, Czechoslovakia, and the U.S.,
     and then 142 writings about the work. Index of names.

*Avant-scène opéra, 9 (March-April 1977), gives useful essays;
performance history, including all casts of Paris productions*

and productions at *La Scala, Covent Garden, Rome, the Metro-politan, and Florence; and a short bibliography (about 20 items, with incomplete data). No index.*

Paul Dessau
(1894-1979)

249. Nadar, Thomas Raymond. "The Music of Kurt Weill, Hanns Eisler and Paul Dessau in the Dramatic Works of Bertolt Brecht." Ph.D. dissertation. University of Michigan, 1974. 346p.
Includes discussion of Dessau's opera *Die Verurteilung des Lukullus* (1951) to a text by Brecht.

Gaetano Donizetti
(1797-1848)

250. Ashbrook, William. *Donizetti and His Operas.* New York: Cambridge University Press, 1982. viii, 744p. ISBN 0-521-23526-X ML 410 D68 A81 D6
This is a much-expanded revision of the author's *Donizetti* (1965). A footnoted biography; program notes and musical examples for each opera; plots and primary sources. Bibliography of about 150 items. This book provides sufficient guidance for anyone investigating Donizetti's works and the considerable literature about them. Ashbrook also co-authored (with Julian Budden) the substantial *New Grove* article. A conference on Donizetti was held in Bergamo, his birthplace, in 1975; the full list of papers presented is given in the *New Grove* bibliography.

For keeping current, there is a useful periodical:

251. Donizetti Society. *Journal of the Donizetti Society.* 1- . 1974- . London: The Society, 1974- . (Irregular.) ML 410 D7 A4
The only volumes in this proposed annual have been for 1974, 1975, 1977, and 1980 (i.e., 1981). They offer news of Donizetti performances, recordings, etc., and feature articles on many of the operas.
The Secretary of the Society, John R. Carter, has kindly responded to an inquiry about future publication of the *Journal*; volume 5 was expected in Spring 1984,

and Da Capo will reprint volumes 1 and 2 sometime in
1984. Volume 2 included diverse contributions concerning several operas: *Maria di Rohan*, *Les martyrs*, *La
favorite*, *Lucrezia Borgia*, *Don Pasquale*, and *Lucia*.
Volume 3 was devoted to essays on *Maria Stuarda*. Vol.
4, of varied content, includes a performance history of
L'esule di Roma. The promised fifth volume will carry
material on *Elisabeth d'Angleterre*, *Roberto Devereux*,
Lucrezia Borgia, and the incomplete *Le duc d'Albe*. A
listing of opera-house chronicles is also to appear in
this volume. The Donizetti Society publishes other
materials as well. Their newest book is *Donizetti's
Operas in Naples*, by John Black (1983), which is described
as "a statistical and chronological study of performances
of Donizetti's operas in Naples, from 1822 to 1848," with
an introductory discussion of the six theaters and their
administration. The 30th issue of the Society's *Newsletter* appeared in October 1982. Vocal scores, all with
essays and chronologies, have been published for *Maria
Stuarda*, *Roberto Devereux*, *Les martyrs*, *Caterina Cornaro*,
Maria di Rohan, *Lucrezia Borgia*, *Requiem*, and *L'esule
di Roma*. Other Donizetti materials are also distributed
by the Society, at 56 Harbut Road, London SW11 2RB.

A counterpart society in Italy has published three issues of:

252. *Studi Donizettiani*, 1- . 1962- . Bergamo: G. Seco-
        mandi, 1962- . ML 410 D56 A5
        Volume 1 published many Donizetti letters; volume 2
     included an essay by William Ashbrook on the genesis of
     La favorite.

*Bergamo was the site of an important conference on Donizetti
in 1975; Mr. Carter advises that the proceedings were to be
made available in late 1983 by the Azienda Autonoma di Turismo,
Bergamo, by presentation to major libraries and institutions
(not for sale); the document consists of 1,053 pages in two
volumes. A table of contents, provided by Mr. Carter, shows
a range of topics under consideration by principal authorities.
A 90-page "Contributo ad un catalogo Donizettiano," by Valeriano
Sacchiero, seems to be of special interest.*

Antonio Draghi
(1634 or 1635-1700)

There is little recent writing about Draghi, who composed 170
works between 1662 and 1699. An early study is still useful:

253. Neuhaus, Max. "Antonio Draghi." *Studien zur Musik-*
     wissenschaft, 1 (1913): 104-192.
     Gives his operas in chronological order, with casts
     required for performance; extended musical extracts;
     historical and structural analyses. No index.

This dissertation (not examined) seems to offer the latest
large-scale approach:

254. Schnitzler, Rudolf. "The Sacred-Dramatic Music of
     Antonio Draghi." Ph.D. dissertation. University of
     North Carolina, 1971.

Paul Dukas
(1865-1935)

255. Helbé, Jacques. *Paul Dukas (1865-1935)*. Paris: Ed.
     P.M.P., 1975. 87p. ML 410 D877 H46
     Ariane et Barbe-Bleue (1907), Dukas's only opera, is
     given program-note attention in this book, which is
     otherwise not useful. Fragmentary discography and
     bibliography; no index.

Antonín Dvořák
(1841-1904)

256. Clapham, John. *Dvořák*. 2d ed. New York and London:
     Norton, 1979. 238p. ISBN 0-3930-1204-2
     ML 410 D9 C58
     Dvořák's operas have attracted little attention; no
     substantial studies have been discovered. In this
     book, primarily a biography, there are some program
     notes. Bibliography of about 200 entries; work-list,
     chronology, name index.

Hanns Eisler
(1898-1962)

Several operas by Eisler, set to Brecht texts, are discussed in Nadar's dissertation, cited under Dessau.

William Henry Fry
(1810-1864)

Leonora (1845) was the first opera by a native American to receive public performance. It is discussed in Gombert's dissertation, cited under Bristow.

Johann Josef Fux
(1660-1741)

Although not remembered as an opera composer, Fux did write 18 or 19 of them. A good introduction to the man and the dramatic work is:

257.   Wellesz, Egon. *Fux.* New York and London: Oxford University Press, 1965. 54p. ML 410 F99 W45
          Essentially program notes, but with technical comments interspersed. Notes, musical examples.

The standard biography is a century old:

258.   Köchel, Ludwig Ritter von. *Johann Josef Fux.* Wien: Alfred Hölder, 1872. 584, 185p. ML 410 F99 K77
          (Reprint--Hildesheim and New York: Olms, 1974.)
          An excellent scholarly study, with documents and work-list, and an annotated thematic catalog (operas: pp. 127-147). Name and title index.

The recent biography, by Andreas Liess (1948), is superficial. There is one specific book about the operas:

259.   Meer, J.H. van der. *Johann Josef Fux als Opernkomponist.* Bilthoven: A.B. Creyghton, 1961. 3 vols. ML 410 F99 M4
          Detailed analyses of text, ballet, aria, orchestra, etc. in 16 operas, with backnotes, bibliography (about

400 entries), and name index. The final volume consists of 91 extended musical extracts.

Baldassare Galuppi
(1706-1785)

Popular and respected in his lifetime, Galuppi fell into immediate neglect when he died and is only now receiving some scholarly attention.

260. Muraro, Maria Teresa, ed. *Venezia e il melodramma nel seicento.* Firenze: Olschki, 1976. 400p.
ML 1733.8 V4 V45
————. *Venezia e il melodramma nel settecento.* Firenze: Olschki, 1978. 462p. ML 1733.8 V4 V457
Two volumes of conference papers on Venetian opera: the first on the 17th century, the second on the 18th century. In volume 2 there is an essay by Daniel Heartz on "Hasse, Galuppi, and Metastasio."

Mikhail Ivanovich Glinka
(1804-1857)

261. Brown, David. *Mikhail Glinka: A Biographical and Critical Study.* London and New York: Oxford University Press, 1974. 340p. ISBN 0-19-315311-4
ML 410 G56 B87
Glinka's important place in Russian music history has been extensively documented in his native language. (Brown refers to the "splendidly comprehensive bibliography of Glinka, listing nearly 3,500 Russian-language titles published up to 1956," by E. Gordeyeva: *M.I. Glinka--sbornik statei* [Moskva, 1958].) Brown's own bibliography is limited to about 60 unannotated titles; about half that number are listed in the same author's article on Glinka in *New Grove*. However, as a biography and introduction to the music this is a fine book--well documented, with musical examples, work-list, program notes on the operas (*Ruslan i Liùdmila* has 50 pages), and a name index.

262. Taruskin, Richard. "Glinka's Ambiguous Legacy and the Birth Pangs of Russian Opera." *19th Century Music*, 1-2 (November 1977): 142-162. ML 1 N714

Discusses the critical reception in Russia of Glinka's works and analyzes them in terms of the beginning of a national school of opera. 70 footnotes.

263.   Glinka, Mikhail Ivanovich. *Memoirs*. Trans. Richard B.
       Mudge. Norman: University of Oklahoma Press, 1963.
       264p. ML 410 G56 A22
       He traveled widely, studied constantly, and met in-
       teresting persons. The memoirs are given here in a
       well-documented annotated context, including a chronology
       of the life and of performances of his works. No bib-
       liography; index of names and titles. The original
       Russian version is available as part of the complete
       works, section on literary works and letters: *Polnoe
       sobranie sochinenii* (Moskva: Muzyka, 1975). A German
       translation was done by Ena von Baer (Wilhelmshaven:
       Heinrichshofen, 1969).

*Several useful essays by Gerald Abraham appear in two of his
collections:* Studies in Russian Music *(London: Reeves, 1935),
IOM-3129, has a general survey of the music;* On Russian Music
(London: Reeves, 1939), IOM-3130, includes a discussion of
A Life for the Czar. *Readers of Russian will find an elaborate
account of Glinka's music in volume 1 of* Izbrannye trudy, *by
Boris V. Asaf'ev (Moskva: Izd-vo Akademii Nauk SSSR, 1952-57),
IOM-3152. A monograph by the same author, on the life and
works, may also be useful:* M.I. Glinka *(Leningrad: Muzyka,
1950; reprinted 1978), 312p. About 90 pages are devoted to
a study of* Ruslan i Liudmila. *No bibliography; no index.*

Christoph Willibald Gluck
(1714-1787)

264.   Newman, Ernest. *Gluck and the Opera: A Study in Musical
       History*. London: Dobell, 1895. xx, 300p. (Reprints--
       London: Gollancz, 1967; Westport, Conn.: Greenwood,
       1976.) ISBN 0-8371-8849-0 (Westport) ML 410 G5 N3
       A valuable older study, including biography, program
       notes, letters, and consideration of Gluck's ideas.
       Footnotes; no bibliography. Index of names and topics.

265.   Howard, Patricia. *Gluck and the Birth of Modern Opera*.
       London: Barrie and Rockliff; New York: St. Martin,
       1963. 118p. ML 410 G5

A general survey of the operas and their background,
in program-note style; 40 short musical examples. Useful list of the operas and ballets, with facts about
the premieres. Bibliography of 21 items, with incomplete
data. Name index.

266. Berlioz, Hector. *Gluck and His Operas, with an Account
of Their Relation to Musical Art*. Trans. Edwin Evans.
London: Reeves, 1915. (Reprinted 1972.) xiv, 167p.
ML 410 B5 Ae
The French original was entitled *A travers chants,
études musicales, adorations, boutades et critiques*
(1862). Enlightened and perceptive reactions to *Orfeo*
(pp. 1-34) and *Alceste* (pp. 35-161). Without notes,
bibliography, or index.

267. Hopkinson, Cecil. *A Bibliography of the Printed Works
of C.W. von Gluck, 1714-1787*. Rev. ed. New York:
Broude, 1967. xiv, 96p. ML 134 G58 H7
First edition was 1959. Gives bibliographic descriptions of all the original scores, with locations,
variants, and later publications (full scores and
piano/vocals), including separate publications of
individual arias. Also a "comparative table of dates
of editions"; a strong bibliography of about 120 entries.
No index.

268. Kurth, Ernst. "Die Jungendopern Glucks bis Orfeo."
Studien zur Musikwissenschaft, 1 (1913): 193-277.
A thorough background study and technical analysis of
23 works, 1741-60. Notes and extended musical examples.
Reprinted from the 1908 edition of Gluck's works.

269. Mueller von Asow, Hedwig, and Erich Hermann Mueller von
Asow. *The Collected Correspondence of Christoph
Willibald Gluck*. New York: Random House; London:
Barrie and Rockliff, 1962. xi, 239p. ML 410 G5 A46
A well-annotated gathering of materials, with source-
list and index of names, titles, and topics.

Iphigénie en Tauride (See 362)

Orfeo ed Euridice

270. Heartz, Daniel. "Orfeo ed Euridice: Some Criticisms,
     Revisions, and Stage-Realizations During Gluck's
     Lifetime." *Chigiana*, 30 (1973): 383-394. (This issue
     of *Chigiana* presents papers read at the international
     conference on Gluck held in Siena, 1-4 September 1973.)
     Examines critical responses to the premiere (Vienna,
     1762) and later productions in London, Parma, Munich,
     and Stockholm; discusses revisions made in the score
     for those performances. The journal *Chigiana* (Firenze:
     Olschki, 1964-) carries many articles on Gluck; a
     number of citations appear in the *New Grove* bibliography.

271. Finscher, Ludwig. *Orphée et Euridice. Vorwort und
     kritischer Bericht.* Kassel: Bärenreiter, 1967.
     xxxviii, 367p. (Christoph Willibald Gluck. Sämtliche
     Werke, 1/6.)
     History of the Paris version (1774), with reviews
     reprinted, and of later performances to 1820. Questions
     of authenticity are taken up, with regard to ballet
     movements and other sections.

272. Robinson, Michael. "The 1774 S. Carlo Version of
     'Orfeo.'" *Chigiana*, 30 (1973): 395-413.
     ML 5 C48 v. 30
     A good account of the production, and of several
     others: Vienna, 1762; London, 1770 and 1771; Florence,
     1771; Naples, 1774. A table compares these productions
     in detail. Like the paper by Heartz (270), this was
     given at the international Gluck conference. Many other
     papers in the proceedings, printed in this volume of
     Chigiana, will be of interest; all are Italian except
     these two in English and one in French. There is no
     index to them in the volume.

273. Howard, Patricia. *C.W. von Gluck. Orfeo.* Cambridge,
     Eng.: Cambridge University Press, 1981. 143p. ISBN
     0-521-22827 ML 410 G5 H8
     One of the "Cambridge Opera Handbooks," containing
     essays by various writers. Topics include the Orfeo
     myth in operatic history; the libretto; reception of
     the premiere and of later productions into the 20th cen-
     tury; a comparison of the French and Italian versions;
     complete table of all the arias and numbers in all

versions. Bibliography of about 50 titles, incomplete
data. Discography, citing specific editions used.
Expansive index of names and topics.

Antonio Carlos Gomes
(1836-1896)

A standard older biography:

274. Gomes Vaz de Carvalho, Itala. *Vida de Carlos Gomes.*
3. ed. Rio de Janeiro: Editôra a Noite, 1946. 247p.
ML 410 G63 G63
First edition was 1935; an Italian translation appeared
in the same year. It presents a popular life account,
without footnotes, and some letters; it gives program
notes on the operas. No bibliography or index.

*What appears to be the newest study was not available for ex-
amination: Gaspare Nello Vetro, Antonio Carlos Gomes (Milano:
Nuove Edizioni, 1976).*

275. Ruberti, Salvatore. *O guarani e Colombo de Carlos Gomes.*
Rio de Janeiro: Editôra Laudes, 1972. 212p.
ML 410 G63 R8
Extended program notes on the major opera, *Il guarany
(O guaraní)*, and the 1892 Columbus Festival cantata,
Colombo. Without musical examples, notes, bibliography,
or index.

François-Joseph Gossec
(1734-1829)

275a. Thibaut, Walter. *François-Joseph Gossec, chantre de la
révolution française.* Gilly: Institut Jules Destrée,
1970. 79p. ML 410 G65 T5
A basic life story, with a few illustrations. Discography; bibliography of 13 items; no index.

Charles François Gounod
(1818-1893)

*There is a lack of recent scholarly writing on Gounod. The
standard biography is still that of Jacques-Gabriel Prod'homme*

and A. Dandelot, Gounod: sa vie et ses oeuvres *(Paris, 1911;
2 vols.).* Avant-scène opéra, 2 *(1976), has an extended treatment of* Faust. *The following will be of some use:*

276. Harding, James. *Gounod.* New York: Stein and Day, 1973.
      251p. ISBN 0-8128-1541-6 ML 410 G7 H4
      A popular biography, without notes, together with a
      program-note description of the operas. Work-list of
      titles only, giving no data. Name index, partly ex-
      pansive.

                    André Ernest Modeste Grétry

*Interest in Grétry seems to be reviving. There has been a
recent dissertation:*

277. Jobe, Robert. "The Operas of André Ernest Modeste
      Grétry." Ph.D. dissertation. University of Michigan,
      1965.
      Not examined.

The most useful biography:

278. Clercx, Suzanne. *Grétry, 1741-1813.* Bruxelles: La
      Renaissance du Livre, 1944. 139p. (Reprint--New
      York: AMS, 1978.) ML 410 G8 C62
      A general account, perceptive but undocumented. No
      musical examples, no index. Annotated bibliography
      of about 50 entries.

279. Pendle, Karin S. "The *Opéras Comiques* of Grétry and
      Marmontel." *Musical Quarterly,* 63-3 (July 1976):
      409-434.
      Discusses six operas written 1768-75 as illustrations
      of Grétry's maturing style. Marmontel was his librettist.

Le jugement de Midas

280. Culot, Paul, ed. *Le jugement de Midas....* Bruxelles:
      Bibliothèque Royale Albert Ier, 1978. 89p.
      ML 410 G8 C9

A facsimile of a contemporary score and libretto, with reviews and other documents relating to the performances (premiere, 1778) and relevant parts of Grétry's memoirs.

Lucile

281. Pendle, Karin. "*Les Philosophes* and *Opéra Comique*: The Case of Grétry's *Lucile*." *Music Review*, 38 (1977): 177-191. ML 5 M657
      Opinions on opera of Diderot and his associates; *Lucile* as a work favored by them. Program notes and some analysis of the opera; discussion of its pivotal place in the change from trivial comic opera to the more serious style preferred by the savants. Citations to earlier literature.

> *Jacques François Fromental Élie Halévy*
> (1799-1862)

There is some treatment of this now-neglected composer in Karin Pendle's study of Scribe, cited above under Auber (190).

> *Georg Friedrich Händel*
> (1685-1759)

His name is now usually written "Handel" in English-speaking countries, a form that he himself used in England; the Library of Congress continues with the umlaut form. The titles that follow will provide pathways into the extensive literature.

282. Mann, Alfred, and J. Merrill Knapp. "The Present State of Handel Research." *Acta musicologica*, 41 (1969): 4-26. ML 5 I6
      A splendid summary of the state of the art. Critical estimates of biographical writings, bibliographies, analytic studies, series, and collections. Despite the bulk of the literature, there are "only scattered contributions to the discussion of Handel's operatic style."

283. *Händel-Bibliographie*. Leipzig: VEB Deutscher Verlag für Musik, 1963. 356p. Nachtrag 1, 1965; 2, 1967. ML 134 H13 S25
      Konrad Sasse is editor of this compilation of about 7,000 titles. He began publishing Händel bibliography

with a supplement (1955) to an earlier inventory by Kurt
Taut (1933); in this work he combines the two earlier
lists and adds material published 1954-62. The aim is
comprehensiveness, so there is much trivial material
included; without annotations it is sometimes difficult
to determine whether a given citation is worth tracing.
In the section "Oper und szenische Kantate" there are
about 800 entries, including books and chapters from
books, articles, and dissertations. All languages are
represented. Complete bibliographic data are usually
given. Author index.

This is the major biographical study:

284.   Deutsch, Otto Erich. *Handel, A Documentary Biography.*
       London: Black; New York: Norton, 1955. xiv, 942p.
       (Reprint--New York: Da Capo, 1974.) ML 410 H13 D47
       "All known and many hitherto unknown or overlooked
       documents" form the basis for this indispensable work.
       Materials are reproduced in chronological order. News-
       paper comments and notices are included. The bibliog-
       raphy, being selective and partly annotated, may be more
       useful than that of Sasse (preceding item): it contains
       about 1,500 entries. Name, topic, and place index.

285.   Lang, Paul Henry. *George Frideric Handel.* New York:
       Norton, 1966. xviii, 731p. ML 410 H13 L26
       A semipopular study, written by a perceptive musicolo-
       gist, but sparsely footnoted and without bibliography.
       Lang shows special interest in cultural settings; his
       chapter on Baroque opera is interesting from this view-
       point. Partly expansive index of names, titles, and
       topics.

286.   *Händel-Handbuch. Band 1. Lebens- und Schaffensdaten.*
       Zusammengestellt von Siegfried Flesch. Kassel:
       Bärenreiter, 1978. ML 134 H13 E36
       A detailed chronology of his life and works. For each
       opera: premiere date and place; instrumentation and
       casting; thematic excerpts (three or four measures of
       each aria and number--e.g., 74 themes for *Almira*);
       sources; bibliography of writing about the opera;
       autographs; comments.

287. Dean, Winton. *Handel and the Opera Seria*. Berkeley and
     Los Angeles: University of California Press, 1969.
     220p. MT 100 H13 D28
     Holds that Händel's operas have been undervalued by
     posterity because of the 18th-century theatrical tradi-
     tions he had to confront. Good chapters on orchestra-
     tion and on modern revivals. The approach to the in-
     dividual operas is essentially program-note style; some
     general comments on structure are found (pp. 127-128).
     Footnotes, but no bibliography. Work-list; good ex-
     pansive index of names and topics.

288. *Handel, A Symposium*. Ed. Gerald Abraham. London, New
     York, and Toronto: Oxford University Press, 1954.
     334p. ML 410 H13 A66
     A number of interesting contributions appear in this
     volume, in particular the "Catalog of Works" by William C.
     Smith, the most thorough of its kind (for operas, gives
     premiere dates, autograph locations, and editions).
     Edward J. Dent's essay, "The Operas," is a useful intro-
     duction, with program notes and musical examples. The
     book has a poor bibliography, about 150 entries, in-
     complete data; and an index of names and titles.

289. Harris, Ellen. *Handel and the Pastoral Tradition*.
     London and New York: Oxford University Press, 1980.
     vii, 304p. ISBN 0-1931-52363 ML 410 H13 H31
     Demonstrates that the tradition of pastoral drama
     strongly influenced Händel's work, variously according
     to the country he was writing in. Good material on the
     pastoral dramas in Italy, Germany, and England; detailed
     attention to Händel's pastoral operas (*Florindo*, *Pastor
     fido*, *Acis and Galatea*); comprehensive chronology of
     Händel in Italy, 1706-10. Useful tables of harmonic
     structures, including works of other composers (*Cupid
     and Death*, *Venus and Adonis*, *Dido and Aeneas*). Bib-
     liography of about 250 titles. Index of names, titles,
     and topics.

290. Stompor, Stephan. "Die deutschen Aufführungen von Opern
     Händels in der ersten Hälfte des 18. Jahrhunderts."
     Ph.D. dissertation. Halle University, 1975. 3 vols.
     xiv, 257; 260; 89p.
     Not examined. Author summary in *RILM Abstracts*, 10-3
     (September-December 1976): 333-334, indicates that he

analyzed the Hamburg and Braunschweig versions of operas
presented there; these versions were considerably al-
tered in text and music. "Questions of aesthetics and
social functions are also addressed."

291. Poladian, Sirvart. "Handel as an Opera Composer."
     Ph.D. dissertation. Cornell University, 1946.
     Not examined.

292. Eisenschmidt, Joachim. *Die szenische Darstellung der*
     Opern Händels auf der Londoner Bühne seiner Zeit.
     Berlin and Wolfenbüttel: Kallmeyer, 1940. 2 vols.
     ML 5 H25 v. 5.
     Only the first volume was examined (77p.). Discusses
     the London setting for Händel's operas: the Haymarket
     and Covent Garden theaters, singers, critical reception.
     All quotes in German only. Notes; no index.

Giulio Cesare

293. Knapp, J. Merrill. "Handel's Giulio Cesare in Egitto."
     Studies in Music History; Essays for Oliver Strunk,
     ed. Harold S. Powers, pp. 389-403. Princeton, N.J.:
     Princeton University Press, 1968.
     Examines the four versions of the opera as performed
     in London between 1724 and 1732. Libretti and scores
     are compared through tabular presentation and placed
     in context of the characteristics of the work.

Johann Adolph Hasse
(1699-1783)

294. Millner, Frederick A. *The Operas of Johann Adolf Hasse.*
     Ann Arbor, Mich.: UMI Research, 1979. xxi, 405p.
     ISBN 0-8357-10068 ML 410 H348 M65
     The only modern study of substance. Considers the
     composer's life and work methods, revisions, etc.
     Examines each opera via program notes and critiques.
     Alphabetical list of works and chronological list.
     Performances grouped by city. Backnotes; bibliography
     of about 100 items, full data. Aria index; expansive
     general index of names, titles, and topics.

*The essay by Daniel Heartz on "Hasse, Galuppi, and Metastasio,"
in Muraro (260), offers some added perspectives. A fine work-
list of the operas is given in the New Grove article; it includes dates and places for premieres and other major performances and library locations for sources.*

Joseph Haydn
(1732-1809)

*Haydn's 15 surviving operas, overshadowed by his monumental
output in the instrumental genres, have received only modest
scholarly attention. There are only 75 entries for opera in
the comprehensive bibliography:*

295. Brown, A. Peter, and James T. Berkenstock. "Joseph
      Haydn in Literature: A Bibliography." *Haydn-Studien*,
      3-304 (July 1974): 173-352.
      Lists about 2,300 items through the end of 1972:
      books, articles, and dissertations. Criteria for in-
      clusion not stated, but "comprehensiveness is the
      ultimate aim." In author order, with topic index and
      index of works; name and place index, partly expansive.

296. Rossi, Nick. "Joseph Haydn and Opera." *Opera Quarterly*,
      1 (1983): 54-78.
      A historical review of Haydn's operatic writing at
      Esterháza, with good illustrations; an account of some
      recent productions and a discography; 28 footnotes.

*Information on the operas, and all Haydn subjects, is thoroughly
expounded by H.C. Robbins-Landon, in a number of landmark
works:* The Collected Correspondence and London Notebooks of
Joseph Haydn *(Fairlawn, N.J.: Essential Books, 1959);* Haydn
(New York: Praeger, 1972); and Haydn: Chronicle and Works
*(Bloomington: Indiana University Press, 1976). Karl Geirin-
ger's* Haydn, A Creative Life in Music *(3d ed.; Berkeley and
Los Angeles: University of California Press, 1982) has a
convenient guide to library locations of the autographs in
Budapest, Berlin, London, Harvard, and Marburg; however, its
approach to the operas is in program-note style, and its bib-
liography is out of date and presented with incomplete data.*
   *Two journals devoted to Haydn reveal only one major con-
tribution dealing with his operas:*

297.   "Kolloquium über Haydns Opern." *Haydn-Studien*, 2-2
       (May 1969): 113-118.
       Gives a list of the operas with facts on the premiere
       and other background data and a useful inventory of the
       singing roles. In other issues of *Haydn-Studien*
       (München: Henle, 1967-) a few short articles on opera
       appear. The *Haydn Jahrbuch* (Wien: Universal Edition,
       1962-) had nothing of interest through 1981.

                        Victor Herbert
                         (1859-1924)

298.   Waters, Edward N. *Victor Herbert*. *A Life in Music*.
       New York: Macmillan, 1955. 653p. (Reprint--New York:
       Da Capo, 1978.) ML 410 H
       A scholarly biography, though without bibliography.
       Work-list, with premiere information and publisher.
       Chapter on "The Grand Operas" gives good accounts of
       the writing and production of *Natoma* and *Madeleine*.
       Discography of his recordings; name and title index.

                 Louis Joseph Ferdinand Hérold
                         (1791-1833)

299.   Pougin, Arthur. *Hérold*. Paris: H. Laurens, 1906. 122p.
       ML 410 H56 P8
       This is the most recent book on the composer, who once
       occupied the first rank among French opera writers (with
       Zampa, 1831). It is a footnoted study of the life and a
       performance history of the operas. Good plates.
       Chronological work-list. No bibliography or index.

                        Juan Hidalgo
                       (ca. 1600-1685)

300.   Stevenson, Robert Murrell. "Espectáculos musicales en
       la España del siglo XVII." *Revista musica chilena*,
       27-121/122 (January-June 1973): 3-44. ML 5 R451
       One of the first great Spanish composers, Hidalgo
       produced the earliest surviving Spanish opera: *Celos
       aun del aire matan* (1660). This work is thoroughly
       discussed by Stevenson, in the context of a scholarly
       history of 17th-century opera and zarzuela; 168 foot-
       notes point to the earlier literature of importance.

Leoš Janáček
(1854-1928)

301. Vogel, Jaroslav. *Leoš Janáček, A Biography.* Rev. ed.
      London: Orbis; New York: Norton, 1981. 439p.
      ML 410 J18 V82
      A scholarly, amply footnoted biography, first issued
      in Prague (1962), followed by an English translation
      (London: Hamlyn, 1962). Detailed study of each opera,
      in the form of extended program notes: background,
      libretto, music examples. Work-list by genre, with
      title index. Name and title indexes, partly expansive.

302. Horsbrugh, Ian. *Leoš Janáček: The Field That Prospered.*
      New York: Scribner; London: David & Charles, 1981.
      327p. ISBN 0-684-17443-X (New York), 0-7153-8060-5
      (London) ML 410 J18 H81
      A useful biography, with footnotes, pictures, and
      musical examples; lengthy program notes on the operas.
      Appendix gives dates, premiere information, publishers,
      and other facts about operas and other stage works.
      Index of names and titles, expansive.

303. Hollander, Hans. *Leoš Janáček; His Life and Work.*
      Trans. Paul Hamburger. New York: St. Martin; London:
      Calder, 1963. 222p. ML 410 J18 H64
      Mostly biographical, with footnotes; about 30 pages
      of program notes on the operas. Bibliography, about 70
      entries. Work-list, with titles in both Czech and
      English, and publication dates. Index of names and
      titles, partly expansive. A German translation by Kurt
      Honolka (Stuttgart and Zürich: Belser, 1982) includes
      some updating of text and bibliography and adds a
      chronology, but omits the footnotes. In the work-list
      titles are in Czech and German. The index is to names
      only and is not expansive.

304. Štědroň, Bohumír. *Leoš Janáček in Letters and Reminis-
      cences.* Prague: Artia, 1946. 233p. ML 410 J18 A2 S8.
      In Czech: *Leoš Janáček: K jeho lidskému a uměleckému
      profilu* (Praha: Panton, 1976), with summary in German:
      and in German: *Leoš Janáček in Briefen und Errinerungen*
      (Praha: Artia, 1955).
      An annotated collection of 230 letters and other writings
      by and about the composer. Work-list; index of names.

*The nine operas have received much attention in the last 15
years or so. This is the most valuable study of them:*

305. Ewans, Michael. *Janáček's Tragic Operas.* London:
      Faber and Faber, 1977. 284p. ISBN 0-571-10959-4
      ML 410 J18 E9
      A German translation (Stuttgart: Reclam, 1981) was
      done by S. Vogt. Considers *Cunning Little Vixen,
      Destiny, The House of the Dead, Jenufa, Kát'a Kabanová,*
      and *The Makropoulos Affair.* Extended program notes,
      with some analytic observations. Comments on all edi-
      tions of each opera, noting that the continuing lack
      of adequate editions is "the most glaring deficiency
      of Janáček scholarship." Ewans also expresses dis-
      appointment over the English-language analyses of the
      operas; his comment is worth quoting: "I know only three
      works of interpretation which express deep understanding
      of Janáček's music. All are brief, but cogent and well-
      written; unfortunately, none has been translated into
      English. *Leoš Janáček* by Max Brod (in German; Universal
      Edition, Vienna, no. 8169); *Janáček,* by Daniel Muller
      (in French; Editions Rieder, Paris, 1934); and 'Umělecký
      profil Leoše Janáčka' (Artistic profile of Leoš Janáček)
      by Jan Kunc, in *Odkaz Leoše Janáčka české Opere,* by
      Leoš Firkušný (Brno, 1939)." Aside from a "Some Further
      Reading" page, from which the quotation is drawn, there
      is no bibliography. Expansive index of names, titles,
      and topics.

306. Chisholm, Erik. *The Operas of Leoš Janáček.* Oxford
      and New York: Pergamon, 1971. xxiv, 390p. ISBN
      0-8012-854-8 MT 100 J18 C5
      Identified as "the first comprehensive analysis in
      English," this is in fact a book of long program notes,
      with some thematic material discussed technically. It
      covers all nine operas but offers remarkably few facts
      about them. Many tiny music examples. No bibliography;
      no index.

307. Tyrrell, John R. "Janáček's Stylistic Development as
      an Operatic Composer as Evidenced in His Revisions
      of the First Five Operas." Ph.D. dissertation.
      Oxford University, 1969. 2 vols. 246p.
      Not examined. Tyrrell's summary, in *RILM Abstracts,*
      402 (May-August 1970): 158, says he has examined the

composer's revisions of *Šárka*, *The Beginning of a Romance*, *Jenufa*, *Fate (Destiny)*, and *Mr. Brouček's Ex-
cursion to the Moon*. Considers also the relationship
between voice and orchestra, and structural questions.

Kat'a Kabanová

308. Tyrrell, John. *Leoš Janáček. Káta Kabanová*. New York:
Cambridge University Press, 1982. xv, 234p. ISBN
0-521-23180-9 ML 410 J18 L58
One of the useful "Cambridge Opera Handbooks." Essays
by various writers, on the libretto and the play it is
based upon, reception of the Brno and Prague premieres,
and of performances in the United Kingdom and America,
text and orchestration problems; and several interpreta-
tions. Backnotes, photos, music examples. Bibliography of about 25 items, annotated; discography of four
albums; list of all productions of 1921-80, with casts;
index of names, expansive for Janáček only.

Niccolò Jommelli
(1714-1774)

*Highly successful composer of 82 operas, Jommelli is almost
entirely neglected by recent scholarship. The only biography,
by Hermann Abert, appeared in 1908. Two recent doctoral
dissertations may indicate a revival of interest. Audrey Lyn
Tolkoff, "The Stuttgart Operas of Niccolò Jommelli" (Yale
University, 1974), was followed in 1978 by a study that has
since been published:*

309. McClymonds, Marita P. *Niccolò Jommelli: The Last Years
1769-1774*. Ann Arbor, Mich.: UMI Research, 1980.
xix, 877p. ISBN 0-8357-1113-7 ML 410 J7 M14
Includes biographical material, based on 45 previously
unknown letters; an account of Italian opera at the
Portuguese court, 1750-80 (with plans and drawings of
the Tejo Theater and the Ajuda Theater in Lisbon); and
stylistic explorations of the late operas and sacred
music. An appendix offers a list of dramatic works by
composers active in Portugal, 1755-80, and another
presents titles of works produced at the Portuguese
court, 1752-92. Good bibliography of about 200 entries,
and discussion of major sources. Index (expansive) of
names, titles, and topics. The same author has an article

drawing on some of the dissertation research: "The Evolution of Jommelli's Operatic Style," *Journal of the
American Musicological Society*, 33-2 (Summer 1980: 326-
355.

Reinhard Keiser
(1674-1739)

*Here is another nearly forgotten composer who was of enormous
importance in his time. There is a strong presentation of
his work:*

310. Zelm, Klaus. *Die Opern Reinhard Keisers. Studien zur
        Chronologie, Überlieferung und Stilentwicklung.*
        München and Salzburg: Katzbichler, 1975. 246p.
        ISBN 3-87397-107-0 ML 410 K27 Z51
        Examination of sources and library locations; detailed
        analysis of aria, form, and scenic structure. Good
        plates and musical examples. Bibliography of about 150
        entries, incomplete data. Name index.

*Rosamond Brenner has written a recent dissertation: "The
Operas of Reinhard Keiser in Their Relationship to the
Affektenlehre" (Brandeis University, 1968), and an article:
"Emotional Expression in Keiser's Operas," Music Review, 33
(1972): 222-232.*

Ernst Křenek
(1900-   )

311. Rogge, Wolfgang. *Ernst Křeneks Opern: Spiegel der
        zwanziger Jahre.* Wolfenbüttel: Möseler, 1970.
        124p. ML 410 K77 R6
        A useful introduction to the composer's life, and some
        technical analysis of the works. No illustrations, no
        musical examples, and no bibliography. Index of names.

Michel-Richard Lalande (Delalande)
(1657-1726)

*Lalande's ballets are regarded as precursors of the later
opéra-ballet style; he did not write actual operas himself.*

312. Dufourcq, Norbert, et al. *Notes et références pour*
      servir à une histoire de Michel-Richard Delalande.
      Paris: Picard, 1957. 356p. ML 410 L19 D86
      Documents, letters, notices, and reviews of performances;
      detailed work-lists and a thematic incipit catalog. No
      bibliography; no index.

Stefano Landi
(ca. 1590-ca. 1655)

Sant' Alessio *(1632) was the first opera on a historical*
subject; the composer had some stature as an operatic pioneer.
However, he is largely forgotten today (no entry in the Concise Oxford Dictionary of Opera*), and the recent literature*
is limited to references in studies of other topics.   In
Murata (189) there is a treatment of Sant' Alessio, *because*
the librettist was Rospigliosi. And Pirrotta's essay in
New Looks at Italian Opera *(233), cited above under Caccini,*
gives him some attention.

Ferenc (Franz) Lehár
(1870-1948)

A useful guide to the available material:

313. Schönherr, Max. *Franz Lehár. Bibliographie zu Leben*
      und Werk. Wien: The Author, 1970. 161p.
      Lists all books, articles, and other writings about
      the composer. Also gives a corrected dating for all
      the operettas and discusses the place of the music in
      Vienna during the years of World War II. Index.

The Merry Widow

Avant-scène opéra, *45 (1982), 146p., offers a varied treatment*
of this work.

Leonardo Leo
(1694-1744)

314. Pastore, Giuseppe A. *Leonardo Leo.* Galatina: Pajano,
      1957. 159p. ML 410 L575 P29
      The composer, a founder of the so-called Neapolitan
      school, wrote 81 operas; none of them have received

recent scholarly attention. This book offers a brief
biography with backnotes and a list of all the operas,
with premiere data and librettists. No index, no bibliography.

Jean Baptiste Lully
(1632-1687)

*There is no important biography available; the one usually
cited is general and brief: Eugène Borrel, Jean Baptiste Lully
(Paris: La Colombe, 1949; 128p.). Lully's life is examined
as part of a major work on the operas:*

315. Newman, Joyce. *Jean-Baptiste de Lully and His Tragédies
      Lyriques*. Ann Arbor, Mich.: UMI Research, 1979.
      x, 266p. ISBN 0-8357-1002-5 ML 410 L95 N55
      As the first of the operatic "reformers" Lully created
      the distinctive French opera style, departing from the
      conventional Italian mode. Newman discusses the old
      and new traditions, gives biographical data, and then
      describes each of the operas in technical detail--music
      and libretto--with long musical examples. Footnotes,
      and useful bibliography of about 400 items, with com-
      plete information. Expansive index of names, titles,
      and topics.

316. Howard, Patricia. "The Operas of Jean Baptiste Lully."
      Ph.D. dissertation. University of Surrey, 1974.
      Not examined. According to the author's précis in
      RILM Abstracts, 9-1/2 (January-August 1975): 47, it
      includes a biographical sketch, an explanation of
      Lully's concept of drama and his style, and detailed
      studies of such components as recitative, aria, en-
      semble, and chorus. Work-list, bibliography, index.

317. Schneider, Herbert. *Chronologisch-thematisches Ver-
      zeichnis samtlicher Werke von Jean-Baptiste Lully*.
      Tutzing: Schneider, 1981. 570p. ML 134 L956 S3
      A work-list in date order, with thematic excerpts,
      information on manuscripts and printed sources,
      librettist, premiere facts, and citations of secondary
      literature. *Die Rezeption der Opern Lullys*, also by
      Schneider (Tutzing: Schneider, 1982), was not available
      for examination.

Marco Marazzoli
(ca. 1600-1662)

See notes under Abbatini and Mazzocchi.

Heinrich August Marschner
(1795-1861)

318. Palmer, A. Dean. *Heinrich August Marschner, 1795-1861:
His Life and Stage Works*. Ann Arbor, Mich.: UMI Research, 1980. xx, 591p. ISBN 8357-1114-5-S83
ML 410 M35 P3
A thorough study, with reference to all previous
literature. Includes biographical treatment (lists of
letters, archival inventory); synopses, program notes,
sources, and bibliography for each opera; illustrations
of productions; stylistic commentary. Bibliography
gives full data on about 600 books, journal and news-
paper articles, and other writings. Index of names and
titles.

Bohuslav Martinů
(1890-1959)

319. Halbreich, Harry. *Bohuslav Martinů, Werkverzeichnis,
Dokumentation, und Biographie*. Zürich: Atlantis
Verlag, 1968. 384p. ML 410 M39 H2
The most useful biography and study of the works.
For the 16 operas there is information on the premieres
(with casts), instrumentation, plot, and program notes.
The work-list is alphabetical, with titles in Czech and
in German. Annotated bibliography of about 25 entries,
giving complete data. Index.

*The papers given at an international conference on Martinů's
stage works (Brno, 1966) are listed in Tyrrell (703), p. 154.
They are in French, English, or German.*

Pietro Mascagni
(1863-1945)

320. Morini, Mario, ed. *Pietro Mascagni*. Milano: Sonzogno,
1964. 2 vols. 426, 349p. ML 410 M294 M6
A comprehensive musicological view of the composer,
including a collection of criticisms (Hanslick, Torchi,

Abbiati, Pizzetti, etc.); letters and documents; biography; an impressive list of premieres and important productions of all 15 operas in all principal cities, with casts; an immense bibliography, giving full information on about 1,000 publications; a discography for every aria. Elaborately footnoted. Index of names and titles.

Jules Massenet
(1842-1912)

321.   Irvine, Demar. *Massenet: A Chronicle of His Life and Times*. Seattle: The Author, 1974. 483p. (Typescript.) ML 410 M41 I72

Biography, letters, genealogy--a good footnoted introduction to the composer's life. Then, for 27 operas, plots, premiere data and reviews, editions. Table of Paris performances, 1867-1915. Bibliography of about 100 items, lacking publication details. Work-list; index of names (expansive).

322.   Harding, James. *Massenet*. London: Dent, 1970.   229p. ISBN 460-03928-8   ML 410 M41 H1

A popular biography, with program notes on the operas. Work-list; list of the operas, with premiere casts and other facts. Bibliography of about 100 works, with incomplete data. Name and title index.

323.   Finck, Henry T. *Massenet and His Operas*. London and New York: John Lane, 1910.   245p.   ML 410 M41 F4

Much detail on performance history makes this older book worth consulting. It also includes biographical information (without notes), and a good expansive index of names, titles, and topics.

Virgilio Mazzocchi
(1597-1646)

The first comic opera, Chi soffre, speri *(1639), was composed by Mazzocchi and Marazzoli. This work is discussed in Murata (189); see annotation at Abbatini.*

Étienne Nicolas Méhul
(1763-1817)

324. Pougin, Arthur. *Méhul, sa vie, son génie, son caractère.*
      Paris: Fischbacher, 1889. 309p. (Reprint--Genève:
      Minkoff, 1973.) ISBN 2-8266-0104-0 ML 410 M49 P8
      There was a second edition (not seen) in 1893. This
      is a dependable biography, well footnoted, with extensive
      quotations from correspondence. Detailed accounts of
      performances, but nothing about the music itself.
      Chronological list of the operas, with premiere dates
      and theaters. No bibliography; no index.

Gian Carlo Menotti
(1911-)

325. Grieb, Lyndal. *The Operas of Gian Carlo Menotti, 1937-*
      1972: A Selective Bibliography. Metuchen, N.J.:
      Scarecrow, 1974. 193p. ISBN 0-8108-0743-2
      ML 134 M533 G7
      A thorough, annotated list of more than 1,000 writings
      about Menotti, including books, articles, dissertations,
      and newspaper notices. Also a biographical sketch and
      work-list (with premiere data, editions published, and
      discography for each composition). Name index.

There is no scholarly biography. John Gruen's Menotti: A
Biography *(New York: Macmillan; London: Collier-Macmillan,
1978) is superficial and without documentation. A Ph.D. dissertation by Richard John Marriott, "Gian Carlo Menotti: Total
Musical Theatre, A Study of His Operas" (University of Illinois,
1975; 274p.), was not available for examination.*

Giacomo Meyerbeer
(1791-1864)

*Interest in Meyerbeer has fallen off; the only recent writings
of substance are dissertations:*

326. Gibson, Robert Wayne. "Meyerbeer's *Le prophète*: A Study
      in Operatic Style." Ph.D. dissertation. Northwestern
      University, 1972. 226p.
      Short biography; influences; analysis of *Le prophète*
      and some discussion of *Robert le diable* and *Les huguenots.*

Bibliography; no index. Not examined; information from *RILM Abstracts*, 10-4 (1976): 603.

327. Roberts, John Howell. "The Genesis of Meyerbeer's
     L'Africaine." Ph.D. dissertation. University of
     California, Berkeley, 1977. 233p.
     Not examined.

*Because Scribe was one of the librettists, there is some dis-
cussion of Meyerbeer operas in Pendle (190).*

Claudio Monteverdi
(1567-1643)

*"The founder of modern opera" (*Baker's Biographical Dictionary*), or even "The creator of modern music" (Schrade's title,
below), has given inspiration to many authors. The literature
is well summarized and criticized by one specialist:*

328. Abert, Anna Amalie. *Claudio Monteverdis Bedeutung für
     die Entstehung des musikalischen Dramas.* Darmstadt:
     Wissenschaftliche Buchgesellschaft, 1979. 103p.
     ISBN 3-5340-7614-1 ML 410 M7 A14 C6
     Discusses the state of research since 1920 on the life
     and on individual works, and comments on the editions of
     the music. Incomplete data on the writings that are
     cited: an infelicity in a valuable essay. Name index.
     The same author has also analyzed the operas:

329. Abert, Anna Amelie. *Claudio Monteverdi und das musikal-
     ische Drama.* Lippstadt: Kistner & Siegel, 1954.
     354p. ML 410 M7 A14
     Technical accounts of the operas, with musical examples
     and footnotes. Bibliography (incomplete data) of about
     200 books and articles. Name index.

330. Schrade, Leo. *Monteverdi, Creator of Modern Music.*
     New York: Norton, 1950. 384p. ML 410 M7 S37
     A scholarly biography, having little to say about the
     music itself. Chapter on *Orfeo* gives useful background
     information. Bibliography of about 150 entries, in-
     complete data. Index of names, titles, and topics.

331. Monteverdi, Claudio. *The Letters of Claudio Monteverdi*.
      Trans. and with introduction by Denis Stevens. Lon-
      don: Faber and Faber; New York: Cambridge University
      Press, 1980. 443p. ISBN 0-05-212359-1 (New York)
      ML 410 M7 A2 S82
      All the known letters, translated for the first time
      into English. (The standard collection in Italian is
      by Domenico de' Paoli: *Claudio Monteverdi, lettere,
      dediche, e prefazioni* [Roma, 1973].) Selected letters
      in English appear in the *Monteverdi Companion* (next
      entry below). This volume covers the years 1601-43
      with 126 letters, notes, and comments. Points of dif-
      ference in translation, or text, between the present
      edition and previous versions of the letters are not
      generally clarified--nor even mentioned. Index.

332. *The Monteverdi Companion*. Ed. Dennis Arnold and Nigel
      Fortune. London: Faber and Faber; New York: Norton,
      1968. 328p. ISBN 0-393-33636-0 (New York) (Reprint
      in paperback--Norton, 1972.) ML 410 M7 A75
      Essays by various writers. Most useful: Robert Doning-
      ton on *Orfeo* and Janet Beat on the operatic orchestra;
      both footnoted, with examples. Other topics covered
      are mostly biographical. Bibliography of about 300
      items, incomplete data. Name index.

*Two books cited earlier contain discussion of Monteverdi's
operas: René Leibowitz,* Les fantômes de l'opéra *(172); and*
New Looks at Italian Opera *(620), article by Pirrotta (233).
Tyrrell (703) gives a list of the papers read at a 1968 international conference on* Monteverdi e il suo tempo *(p. 176).*

            Wolfgang Amadeus (Johann Chrysostom) Mozart
                          (1756-1791)

*The literature is enormous. What follows is a very selective
group of titles, mostly quite recent works dealing directly
with the operas. One biography seems to stand out:*

333. Einstein, Alfred. *Mozart, His Character, His Work*.
      Trans. Arthur Mendel and Nathan Broder. New York and
      London: Oxford University Press, 1945. 492p.
      ML 410 M9 E4
      A thoughtful examination of Mozart's life, with general

observations on the music. Operas are discussed (program-note style), pp. 383-472. Work-list; name index.

334. Mann, William. *The Operas of Mozart.* London: Cassell;
     New York: Oxford University Press, 1977. ix, 656p.
     ISBN 0-304-29381-4 (London), 0-195198-913 (New York).
     MT 100 M93 M28
     Background, synopses, musical examples, and extended
     program notes on all the operas. References to earlier
     studies are incomplete. Bibliography of books only,
     about 120 titles. Index of names and titles, expansive.

335. Dent, Edward Joseph. *Mozart's Operas: A Critical Study.*
     2d ed. London: Oxford University Press, 1947. 276p.
     ML 410 M9 D32
     First edition was 1913; the intention of the second
     edition was to appeal more to "the general reader rather
     than ... the musicologist." However, the original edi-
     tion is not highly technical either; both editions offer
     sensible program notes, without analysis. Useful index
     (expansive) of names and titles.

336. Noske, Frits. *The Signifier and the Signified: Studies
     in the Operas of Mozart and Verdi.* The Hague: Nijhoff,
     1977. viii, 418p. ML 1700.1 N897
     An interesting attempt to apply semiotic critical
     method to the operatic genre. Finds "musical figure
     of death," "ironic signs," and other devices to indicate
     mood and situation. Aside from the thesis being pur-
     sued--which could be more clear in premise and execu-
     tion--there are good musical analyses of the operas,
     with references to earlier literature. No bibliography,
     however. Name and title index.

The Mozart-Jahrbuch *(new series, 1950-) offers many articles
on aspects of the operas, of which this essay--from a special
issue on* Idomeneo--*is a good representative:*

337. Federhofer, Hellmut, et al. "Tonartenplan und Motiv-
     struktur (Leitmotivtechnik?) in Mozarts Musik."
     Mozart-Jahrbuch 1973/74, pp. 82-144. ML 410 M8 A14
     A wide-ranging discussion by a working party, using
     Idomeneo as a point of departure. Considers questions

of tonal design and other unifying devices. Contributors were László Somfai, Janos Liebner, Daniel Heartz,
Frederich Neumann, Georg Feder, and Gernot Gruber. Not
indexed.

La clemenza di Tito

338. Tyson, Alan. "*La clemenza di Tito* and Its Chronology."
     Musical Times, 116-1585 (March 1975): 221-227.
     ML 5 M9863
     The techniques of paper and watermark analysis are
     used by Tyson to establish probable datings. He ex-
     amines the five types of paper used in the surviving
     parts of the *Tito* score and suggests a sequence of events
     in the composition. All recent literature on the opera
     is mentioned.

339. Lühning, Helga. "Zur Entstehungsgeschichte von Mozarts
     Titus." *Musikforschung*, 27-3 (July-September 1974):
     300-318. ML 5 M9437
     Considers the writing of the opera, using all sources
     and sketches. References to previous literature in 87
     footnotes.

Così fan tutte

Avant-scène opéra, *16/17 (1978), 178p., gives a good view of
the opera and its production history, with a libretto.*

Don Giovanni

340. Rushton, Julian. *W.A. Mozart; Don Giovanni.* New York:
     Cambridge University Press, 1981. 165p. ISBN
     0-521-22828-3 ML 410 M9
     A "Cambridge Opera Handbook." Gives the genesis of
     the opera, with production history, synopsis, and pro-
     gram notes. Bibliography of about 100 titles; incom-
     plete data. Discography; name index.

Avant-scène opéra, *24 (1979), 218p., presents its usual
format.*

La finta giardiniera

341. Angermüller, Rudolph. "Wer war der Librettist von *La
     finta giardiniera?*" *Mozart-Jahrbuch*, 1976/77, pp. 1-
     120. ML 410 M8 A14
     Argues that the supposed librettist, Raniero Calzabigi,
     did not in fact write the text. Suggests, on the basis
     of recently discovered material, that the real author
     was Abate Giuseppe Petrosellini.

Idomeneo

342. Heartz, Daniel. "The Genesis of Mozart's *Idomeneo.*"
     Mozart-Jahrbuch, 1967, pp. 150-164. Reprinted in
     Musical Quarterly, 55-1 (January 1969): 1-19.
     Shaping of the libretto, and background of the composi-
     tion.

*Discovery of a new version of the libretto had led to a better
idea of the original production. Another interesting article,
analyzing the arias and ensembles, is Jehoash Hirshberg,
"Formal and Dramatic Aspects of Sonata Form in Mozart's*
Idomeneo," Music Review, *38 (1977): 192-210.*

The Magic Flute

343. Schneider, Otto. "*Die Zauberflöte* in der Literatur;
     Ein bibliographisher Überblick." *Österreichische
     Muzikzeitschrift*, 22-8 (August 1967): 458-464.
     ML 5 0 1983
     An annotated list of 300 writings on the opera; useful
     despite the crowded narrative format. No bibliography.

344. Chailley, Jacques. *La flûte enchantée, opéra maçonnique.*
     Paris: Robert Laffort, 1968. 342p. (Reprint--Paris:
     Éditions d'Aujourd'hui, 1975.) ML 410 M8 C43. In
     English: *The Magic Flute; Masonic Opera.* Trans.
     Herbert Weinstock. New York: Knopf, 1971; London:
     Gollancz, 1972. xii, 336p. ISBN 0-575-01362 (London)
     ML 410 M8 C432
     A long account of the libretto, digging for the "hidden
     meaning" in Masonic symbolism. Whatever one may think
     of such endeavors, it is clear that the text of this
     opera does need an explanation. Bibliography of about
     75 titles. Index of names, titles, and topics.

Avant-scène opéra, 1 (1976), 130p., deals adequately with the
opera. There is also an "English National Opera Guide" (188).

The Marriage of Figaro

345. Levarie, Siegmund. *Mozart's Le nozze di Figaro. A
      Critical Analysis.* Chicago: University of Chicago
      Press, 1952. 268p. (Reprint--New York: Da Capo,
      1969.) ISBN 0-306-70897-3 MT 100 M78 L4
      An outstanding example of structural analysis, bring-
      ing the dramatic and musical elements into a convincing
      unity. Footnote references to earlier writers. No
      bibliography; no index.

A more traditional approach is available in the format of
Avant-scène opéra, 21 (1979), 170p.

There is a good "Rororo" guide for the opera: Attila Csampai
*and Dietmar Holland, W.A. Mozart. Die Zauberflöte (München:
Ricordi; Reinbek bei Hamburg: Rowohlt, 1982). Contents include essays on genesis, productions, and the symbolism; there
is a chronology and a discography, together with a bibliography
of about 100 items (incomplete data); no index.*

Modest Petrovich Musorgskiĭ (Musorgsky, Mussorgsky)
(1839-1881)

346. Orlova, Alexandra. *Musorgsky's Days and Works: A Biog-
      raphy in Documents.* Trans. and ed. Roy J. Guenther.
      Ann Arbor, Mich.: UMI Research, 1983. 650p. ISBN
      8357-1324-5-S83 ML 410 M97 O7
      Based on the Russian original (Moscow, 1963). A docu-
      mentary chronicle, drawing on all sources: letters,
      diaries, newspaper articles, writings of contemporaries.
      Includes details of composition and production of the
      operas.

347. Brown, Malcolm Hamrick, ed. *Musorgsky: In Memoriam,
      1881-1981.* Ann Arbor, Mich.: UMI Research, 1982.
      337p. ISBN 8357-1295-8-S83 ML 410 M97 M98
      A collection of essays by various specialists (Taruskin,
      Brown, Schwarz, Orlova, Oldani, Abraham, Stasov, etc.),
      on life, style, and individual works. "Editions of Boris

Godunov," by Robert William Oldani, gives library locations of all MSS; describes the composer's piano-vocal
score, Rimskiĭ-Korsakov's version, and the modern edition
of Lloyd-Jones. The essay by Alexandra Orlova and Maria
Schneerson examines the *Boris* libretto in terms of its
emergence from Pushkin's play and a history by Karamzin.
Expansive index of names, titles, and topics.

Boris Godunov

348. Fulle, Gerlinde. *Modest Mussorgskijs Boris Godunow:*
         Geschichte und Werk, Fassungen und Theaterpraxis.
         Wiesbaden: Breitkopf und Härtel, 1974. 357p. ISBN
         3-7651-0078-1 ML 410 M97 F84
         The libretto in all versions; performances and their
      critical reception in Western Europe, 1913-71. Good
      documentation throughout (600 footnotes). Musical ex-
      amples; bibliography of about 250 items (incomplete
      data). No index.

349. Oldani, Robert William. "Boris Godunov and the Censor."
         19th Century Music, 2-3 (March 1979): 245-253.
         ML 1 N714
         A fine review of the composer at work. Says the role
      of the censor in cuts and revisions has been exaggerated.
      Footnotes identify all the important literature on the
      opera.

350. Carr, Maureen A. "Keys and Modes, Functions and Progres-
         sions in Mussorgsky's Boris Godunov." Ph.D. disserta-
         tion. University of Wisconsin-Madison, 1972.
         Not examined. Description by the author in *RILM Ab-*
      stracts, 10-4 (1976): 599, indicates a highly technical
      approach. Keys and modes are distinguished, together
      with other harmonic features, and traced by category
      through the 1869 and 1872 versions. Finds the first
      version to have "more intense modal qualities." Bib-
      liography and index.

There is a fine critical and historical commentary by David
Lloyd-Jones in his edition of the opera: Boris Godunov *(New*
York: Oxford University Press, 1975). The annotations deal
with almost every measure of the score. Not indexed.

José de Nebra
(1702-1768)

*One of the most successful composers of opera and zarzuela
in the 18th-century Spanish theater. Best recent biographical
summary is Robert Stevenson's article in* New Grove *(with work-
list and bibliography). This item deals only with the life,
not the music:*

351. Solar-Quintes, Nicolás. "El compositor español José
     de Nebra." *Anuario musical*, 9 (1954): 179-206.
     ML 5 A636
     Letters, documents, commentary.

Jacques Offenbach
(1819-1880)

352. Faris, Alexander. *Jacques Offenbach*. New York: Scrib-
     ner, 1980. 275p. ISBN 0-684-16797-2 ML 410 041 F3
     A straightforward biography, with backnotes; program
     notes for the operas. Table of stage works, 1839-81,
     giving librettists and premiere dates and places. Also
     a work-list of the nonstage works, by genre. Pictures,
     musical examples. Bibliography of about 120 entries.
     Expansive index of names, titles, and topics. This
     biography is much to be preferred over James Harding's
     Jacques Offenbach: A Biography (London and New York,
     1980), a casual tract in popular style, without docu-
     mentation.

Les contes d'Hoffmann

353. Eisenberg, Anna. "Jacques Offenbach: Hoffmanns Erzähl-
     ungen. Analyse der szenischen Bearbeitung." Ph.D.
     dissertation. University of Köln, 1974. 380p.
     Not examined. From *RILM Abstracts*, 10-4 (1976): 601,
     we find that the study "endeavors to establish means of
     determining the planned, original form of the opera."
     Different settings and arrangements are compared in
     tabular form, and critical reactions in France and the
     Germanic cities are considered.

A good introduction to the opera appears in Avant-scène opéra,
25 (1980).

Giovanni Paisiello
(1740-1816)

354.   Hunt, Jno Leland. *Giovanni Paisiello: His Life as an
       Opera Composer*. New York: National Opera Association,
       1975. vii, 88p. ML 140 P149 H94
       (The author's first name is given here as it appears
       on the title page.) A footnoted bibliography, with a
       catalog of the dramatic works and a chronology. Letters
       and documents; bibliography of about 50 items, incomplete
       data; no index.

355.   Corte, Andrea della. *Paisiello*. Torino: Bocca, 1922.
       352p. ML 410 P149 C82
       The standard older biography. Includes program notes
       for major operas. No bibliography; name index.

Carlo Pallavicino
(1630-1688)

*The name also appears as Pallavicini; and the birthdate is
disputed.*

356.   Smith, Julian. "Carlo Pallavicino." *Proceedings of the
       Musical Association*, 96 (1969/70): 57-71. ML 28 L8 R85
       Brief biography with background on the times; useful
       comments on the style, with musical examples. Connec-
       tions to all earlier studies are made via 43 footnotes.

Bernardo Pasquini
(1637-1710)

*The only large-scale study of recent years seems to be this
one:*

357.   Crain, Gordon F. "The Operas of Bernardo Pasquini."
       Ph.D. dissertation. Yale University, 1965.
       Not examined.

Johann Christoph Pepusch
(1667-1752)

Pepusch composed only a part of the music for John Gay's very popular Beggar's Opera *(1728); most of the score consisted of adapted folksongs or borrowings from other composers.*

358. Kidson, Frank. *The Beggar's Opera; Its Predecessors and Successors.* Cambridge, Eng.: Cambridge University Press, 1922. 109p. ML 1731.3 K46
    A semischolarly consideration of sources, early publications, critiques of productions. Includes synopsis and pictures, but without notes or bibliography. Expansive index of names and titles.

See also discussions of the opera in Hogarth (179) and Aldrich (176). Two dissertations, not examined, are cited in the New Grove bibliography: J.G. Williams, "The Life, Work and Influence of J.C. Pepusch" (University of York, 1976); and D.F. Cook, "John Christopher Pepusch in London: His Vocal Music for the Theatre" (University of London, in progress).

Giovanni Battista Pergolesi
(1710-1736)

La serva padrona (1733) is probably the oldest opera in the modern repertoire; but no substantial study of the opera has been discovered.

359. Radiciotti, Giuseppe. *Giovanni Battista Pergolesi.* 2d ed. Milano: Fratelli Treves, 1935. 300p. ML 410 P43 R123
    The first edition was 1910. A German translation appeared in 1954: *Giovanni Battista Pergolesi: Leben und Werk* (trans., enl., and rev. Antoine E. Cherbuliez [Zürich: Pan, 1954]). A scholarly bibliography with footnotes; program notes on the operas, without musical examples. Work-list (titles only); bibliography of about 250 books, with incomplete data. Name index.

360. Hucke, Helmut. "Pergolesi: Probleme eines Werkverzeichnisses." *Acta musicologica,* 52-2 (1980): 195-225. ML 5 I6

A useful study of sources involved in preparing an
authentic work-list; valuable references to earlier
literature in 239 footnotes.

Jacopo Peri
(1561-1633)

*There is an extensive scholarly literature on Peri, especially
on his Euridice (1600), the earliest opera for which music
has survived. Rather than enumerate this literature here,
we may simply refer to an excellent critical summary of
scholarship, in:*

361. Peri, Jacopo. *Euridice: An Opera in One Act, Five
     Scenes*. Ed. Howard Mayer Brown. Madison, Wis.:
     A-R Editions, 1981. xxxvi, 211p. ISBN 0-89579-137-4
     M2 R238
     Brown's definitive edition, based on the 1600 score
     publîshed by Marescotti in Florence, is preceded by a
     valuable preface and critical notes on earlier writings.
     This would surely be the starting point for any research
     into Peri.

See also the article by Pirrotta, in New Looks *at Italian*
Opera *(620), already cited under Caccini.*

Niccolò Piccinni
(1728-1800)

362. Rushton, Julian. "Iphigénie en Tauride: The Operas of
     Gluck and Piccinni." *Music and Letters*, 53-4 (October
     1972): 411-430.
     The famous rivalry of these two composers is well
     represented by their settings of this libretto, pro-
     duced two years apart in the same theater. Rushton
     makes a detailed comparison, number by number, and
     declares Gluck to be the winner. Earlier literature
     is recalled through 20 footnotes. Contemporary reac-
     tions to the "querelle" are documented in Francesco
     Degrada, "Due volti di Ifigenia," *Chigiana*, 32 (1975):
     165-223.

Carlo Francesco Pollarolo
(1653-1722)

There seems to be only one active scholar concerned with Pollarolo:

363. Termini, Olga Ascher. "Carlo Francesco Pollarolo: His
      Life, Time, and Music, with Emphasis on the Operas."
      Ph.D. dissertation. University of Southern California,
      1970. 728p.
      Includes a work-list, thematic catalog, and bibliog-
      raphy. Termini also has an article: "Carlo Francesco
      Pollarolo: Follower or Leader in Venetian Opera?" *Studi
      musicali*, 8 (1979): 223-272; and the *New Grove* entry for
      the composer.

Amilcare Ponchielli
(1834-1886)

*There is no recent book-length study. Nicolaisen gives con-
sideration to the works in his* Italian Opera in Transition
(629), cited above under Catalani.

Sergeĭ Sergeevich Prokof'ev (Prokofiev)
(1891-1953)

364. Nestyev, Israel V. *Prokofiev*. Trans. Florence Jonas;
      foreword by Nicolas Slonimsky. Stanford, Calif:
      Stanford University Press, 1960. 528p. ML 410 P865 N4
      The only important biography, originally in Russian.
      (Moscow, 1957). Well documented, with program notes
      on the works. An anti-Western point of view is per-
      vasive but does not bias the facts. Work-list in
      chronological order, with dates of premieres and pub-
      lishers. Expansive name and title index.

365. Prokof'ev, Sergeĭ Sergeevich. *Avtobiografiiā*. Moskva:
      Sov. Kompozitor, 1973. 704p. ML 410 P865 A315.
      In English: *Prokofiev by Prokofiev, A Composer's
      Memoir*. Trans. Guy Daniels. Ed. David H. Appel.
      Garden City, N.Y.: Doubleday, 1979. xii, 370p.
      ISBN 0-385-09960-6.
      A youthful daily journal. Includes notes and expansive
      index of names and titles.

366. Seroff, Victor. *Sergei Prokofiev: A Soviet Tragedy.*
     New York: Funk & Wagnalls, 1968; London: Frewin,
     1969. 384p. ML 410 P865 S48
     A popular biography in political context, without
     footnotes (many undocumented quotations and invented
     conversations). Usefulness of the work-list is dimmed
     by the presentation of all titles in English only.
     Bibliography of about 20 entries; name index.

367. McAllister, Margaret. "The Operas of Sergei Prokofiev."
     Ph.D. dissertation. Cambridge University, 1970.
     Not examined. According to the summary in *RILM Ab-*
     stracts, 9-1/2 (January-August 1975): 102, it presents
     circumstances around the writing of all the operas,
     with premiere facts, sources of libretti, and comparison
     of various versions. Analyzes musical characterization
     and "thematic symbolism."

There is a report in RILM Abstracts, *10-3 (September-December*
1976): 376, of a detailed study of Voĭna i mir *(War and Peace):*

368. Volkov, Anatolij. *Voĭna i mir Prokof'eva.* Moskva:
     Muzyka, 1976. 135p.
     The abstract reads: "A monograph based on manuscript
     materials which deals with the operatic heritage of the
     composer. Discusses some general problems of dramaturgy
     and musical form; considers the variants in the overall
     composition of the opera and the general meaning of the
     changes. The formal design of the music is examined."

Giacomo Puccini
(1858-1924)

369. Carner, Mosco. *Puccini: A Critical Biography.* 2d ed.
     London: Duckworth, 1974. xvi, 520p.
     ISBN 0-7156-0795-2 ML 410 P89 C3
     First edition was 1958. A respectable biography,
     with footnotes; quotations from letters. Criticized
     by Greenfield (next entry) for a Freudian approach
     and mistranslations. Plots and program notes on the
     operas, occasionally marked by technical observations
     on tonality and structure. Bibliography of about 60
     titles; name and title index.

370. Greenfield, Howard. *Puccini*. New York: Putnam, 1980.
  299p. ISBN 0-399-12551-5 ML 410 P89 G73
  A popular biography, without footnotes. Includes
  comments on the earlier biographies, none of which appears satisfactory to Greenfield. Bibliography of about
  150 works. Index of names, theaters, and titles, partly
  expansive.

*Puccini's letters have attracted considerable interest for the
light they shed on his composing process and for his comments
on performances. Three collections stand out:*

371. Puccini, Giacomo. *Puccini, 276 lettere inedite: il
  fondo dell'Accademia d'Arte e Montecatini Terme*. Ed.
  Giuseppe Pintorno. Milano: Nuove Edizioni, 1974.
  223p. ML 410 P89 A36
  Presents 276 letters, many of them short and most
  having no musical content; but some offer comments on
  opera productions. Includes a chronology of Puccini's
  life and a glossary of personal names; also a name
  index.

372. *Puccini com'era*. Ed. Arnaldo Marchetti. Milano: Curci,
  1973. 495p. ML 410 P89 A35
  A good selection of 473 letters, to him and from him,
  with commentary. Some facsimiles and other illustrations. Both musical and personal in content; includes
  three letters from his lover, Josephine von Stängel.
  Name index.

373. Puccini, Giacomo. *Letters of Giacomo Puccini: Mainly
  Connected with the Composition and Production of His
  Operas*. Rev. ed. Ed. Giuseppe Adami. Trans. Ena
  Makin. London: Harrap, 1974. 341p.
  ISBN 1-245-52422-3 ML 410 P89 A23
  Published first in Italian (1928); first English edi-
  tion, 1931. A useful presentation, in which letters
  are put into context by running commentary. Footnoted.
  Index by name of addressee; general index of names,
  titles, and topics.

374. Hopkinson, Cecil. *A Bibliography of the Works of
  Giacomo Puccini, 1858-1924*. New York: Broude Brothers,

1968. xvii, 77p. ML 134 P94 H7
An annotated work-list, showing variant editions.
Appendixes give lists of extant manuscripts, dedicatees,
performances at leading houses to 1965 (Opéra-Comique
is the winner, with 3,862 performances of his operas),
Ricordi plate numbers, and textual variants in *Madama
Butterfly*.

375. Ashbrook, William. *The Operas of Puccini*. New York:
Oxford University Press, 1968. xv, 269p. MT 100 P95 A8
Program notes on all the operas, with footnotes and
musical examples. Sources discussed. Selective bibliography of about 60 entries. Index of names and
titles. *La Bohème* is the topic of *Avant-scène opéra*,
20 (1979), and of a "Rororo" handbook, 1981 (186).
Tosca is the concern of *Avant-scène opéra*, 11 (1977).

*Not much technical analysis of the operas has come to the
surface; these two studies are the only ones seen:*

376. Maisch, Walter. *Puccinis musikalische Formgebung,
untersucht an der Oper "La Bohème."* Neustadt: Schmidt,
1934. 90p. ML 3995 M23 P97
A publication of the author's dissertation (Friedrich-
Alexanders-Universität, Erlangen, 1933). Presents
elaborate micro- and macroanalyses of the score, taking
a Lorenzian approach (see 508). Notes, examples; no
bibliography and no index.

377. Winterhoff, Hans-Jürgen. *Analytische Untersuchungen
zu Puccinis Tosca*. Regensburg: Bosse, 1973. 136p.
ISBN 3-7649-2088-2 MT 100 P98 W5
A publication of the author's Ph.D. dissertation
(University of Köln, 1972). Studies the libretto, the
compositional process, the dramatic plan, motives,
formal structures, characterization through musical
style. Musical examples are handwritten and difficult
to decipher. No footnotes. Bibliography of 35 entries,
incomplete data. No index.

Another Ph.D. dissertation, not examined, deals with Il trittico*
Jürgen Leukel, "Puccinis Triptychon (Der Mantel, Schwester*

Angelica, Gianni Schicchi) und der italienische Verismo"
(University of Frankfurt, 1980). See also the chapters on
Puccini in Nicolaisen, Italian Opera in Transition *(629).*
A table of revisions for Edgar *is one useful feature.*

Henry Purcell
(1658 or 1659-1695)

378. Moore, Robert Etheridge. *Henry Purcell & the Restora-*
      tion Theatre. London: Heinemann, 1961. xv, 223p.
      (Reprint--Westport, Conn.: Greenwood, 1974.) ISBN
      0-8371-7155-5 ML 310 P93 M6
      A footnoted account of the stage works, with musical
      examples; program-note style. No bibliography. Name,
      title, and topic index.

Some modern ideas on staging are found in Roger Savage, "Pro-
ducing Dido and Aeneas," Early Music, 4 *(1976): 393-406. The*
author considers "16 problems," such as choice of edition,
decor, "who dances what?," and even "Is Dido a virgin queen
at the start and when does intimacy take place?"

Jean Philippe Rameau
(1683-1764)

379. Girdlestone, Cuthbert. *Jean-Philippe Rameau: His Life*
      and Work, 2d ed. London: Cassell, 1969. 631p.
      ML 410 R17 G5
      A documented account of considerable factual value.
      Footnotes, 312 musical examples, work-list (with premiere
      dates and places); bibliography of about 200 items;
      list of extant letters; name index.

380. Masson, Paul-Marie. *L'opéra de Rameau.* Paris: H.
      Laurens, 1930. 594p. (Reprint--New York: Da Capo,
      1972.) ISBN 0-306-70262-2 ML 410 R17 M41
      One of the classic music biographies. Considers both
      life and works, with footnotes, musical examples, and
      technical analyses of "l'expression dramatique et ses
      moyens." Bibliography of about 250 books (incomplete
      data); work-list with locations of manuscripts. Name
      index.

Nikolai Andreevich Rimskiĭ-Korsakov
(Rimsky-Korsakov)
(1844-1908)

The most accessible writings on the operas are various essays
by Gerald Abraham. In Studies in Russian Music *(263n) there*
are program notes on Pskovitiănka, Snow Maiden, Sadko, Czar's
Bride, Kitezh, *and* Le coq d'or. *See also his* "Pskovityanka:
The Original Version of Rimsky-Korsakov's First Opera."
Musical Quarterly, *54 (1968): 58-67; and* "Satire and Symbolism
in The Golden Cockerel," *Music and Letters, 52 (1971): 46-54.*
This item has some technical analysis:

381.   Pals, Nikolai van Gilse. *N.A. Rimsky-Korsakov. Opern-*
          Schaffen nebst Skizze über Leben und Wirken. Paris
          and Leipzig: W. Bessel, 1929. vii, 691p. (Reprint--
          Hildesheim: Olms, 1977.) ISNM 3-487-06427-8
          ML 410 R5 G48
          All the operas are closely analyzed in terms of har-
          mony, melody, form, relation of text to music, etc.,
          with many musical examples. Quotes from the opera
          libretti are in German translation only. No reference
          notes, no bibliography, no index.

Luigi Rossi
(1597-1653)

382.   Ghislanzoni, Alberto. *Luigi Rossi.* Milano: Bocca,
          1954. 321p. ML 410 R832 G42
          A scholarly treatment of the composer's life, with
          footnotes and documents. Useful thematic catalog of
          388 items, including individual arias. Some musical
          examples, but little actual discussion of the music.
          No bibliography, no index.

See also Murata (189) for a discussion of Rossi's opera Il
palazzo incantato.

Michelangelo Rossi
(ca. 1600-1656)

Murata (189) has a discussion of the opera Erminia sul
Giordano.

Gioacchino Antonio Rossini
(1792-1868)

383. Rognoni, Luigi. *Gioacchino Rossini*. 3d ed. Torino:
     Einaudi, 1977. 559p. ML 410 R8 R73
     First edition was 1956. The most useful biography,
     with ample notes and musical examples. Program notes
     on the operas; good study of the overtures. Important
     work-list compiled by Philip Gossett, with premiere
     data, editions, comments; discography; and bibliography,
     which is intended to supplement that of Radiciotti
     (1927-29), listing about 300 works (incomplete data).
     Index of names, titles, and topics.

384. Weinstock, Herbert. *Rossini: A Biography*. New York:
     Knopf; London: Oxford University Press, 1968. xviii,
     560p. ML 410 R8 W35
     A good, documented study of the composer's life and
     times, with program notes on each opera. Includes texts
     of his will, contract for *Barber of Seville*, etc.
     Chronological work-list of operas, with premiere in-
     formation. Bibliography of about 600 items; name and
     title index.

A steady source of major studies on Rossini is the Bollettino
*of the Centro Rossiniano di Studi (Pesaro: Fondazione Rossini,
1955-); ML 5 C42. Most of the substantial contributions
are by Philip Gossett, e.g. "The Tragic Finale of Tancredi"
(1976, pp. 9-172; text also in Italian); "Le sinfonie di
Rossini" (1979, pp. 7-123)--a detailed study of the overtures in
Italian and English, with tabular comparisons of characteristics
and 77 examples; and "La Gazza Ladra; Notes Toward a Critical
Edition" (1972, pp. 12-25), in which all editions and libretti
are studied and textual problems identified.*

   *Gossett's Ph.D. dissertation is indispensable: "The Operas
of Rossini: Problems of Textual Criticism in Nineteenth-
Century Opera" (Princeton University, 1970; 2 vols., 622p.).
It considers the printed scores and libretti, plus autographs
and manuscript sources, for 14 Rossini operas in an effort to
identify spurious material and to reconstruct authentic texts.
Gives information about publishers (including plate-number
lists). Bibliography; no index.*

385. Lippmann, Friedrich. "Per un esegesi dello stile
     rossiniano." *Nuova rivista musicale italiana*, 2-5

(September–October 1968): 813–856.

This issue of the journal is all about Rossini, and includes useful articles by Gossett (on the autographs), Rodolfo Celletti (on the vocal style), and Mila (see below). Lippmann offers perceptive observations on the nature of Rossini's style, with musical examples and good footnote references to earlier analysts. Emphasis is on melodic typology.

Il barbiere di Siviglia

No full-length scholarly work has been seen. Avant-scène opéra, *37 (1981), is a useful introduction.*

La cenerentola

386. Zedda, Alberto. "Problemi testuali della Cenerentola." *Bollettino*, Centro Rossiniano di Studi, 1971, pp. 29–51. ML 5 C42
     Examines the genesis of the libretto; cites earlier literature.

The opera is the topic of an "English National Opera Guide" (188).

La gazza ladra

See Gossett's article, cited above at 384n.

Tancredi

See Gossett's article cited above at 384n.

Il turco in Italia

387. Mila, Massimo. "Il turco in Italia, manifesto di dolce vita." *Nuova rivista musicale italiana*, 2–5 (September–October 1968): 857–1071.
     A program note, with discussion of the production history and critical comments over the years. Good footnotes identify all the earlier literature on the opera.

Camille Saint-Saëns
(1835-1921)

Samson et Dalila *(1877) is the only notable opera among 12 by
the composer. It is the subject of* Avant-scène opéra, *15
(1978), 122p.*

Giovanni Battista Sammartini
(1701-1775)

388. Jenkins, Newell, and Bathia Churgin. *Thematic Catalogue
      of the Works of Giovanni Battista Sammartini: Orches-
      tral and Vocal Music.* Cambridge, Mass.: Harvard Uni-
      versity Press, 1976. 315p. ISBN 0-674877-357
      ML 134 S189 J52
      Includes information on the operas, pp. 111-134: pre-
      miere date and place, casting, and instrumentation.
      Many thematic excerpts (30 are from *L'Agrippina*); manu-
      script sources and library locations. Comments on pub-
      lication history; references to secondary literature.
      Expansive index of names and titles.

389. Jenkins, Newell. "The Vocal Music of Giovanni Battista
      Sammartini." *Chigiana*, 32 (1977): 277-309. ML 5 C534
      The three operas--*Memet* (1732), *L'ambizione superata
      dalla virtù* (1734), and *L'Agrippina* (1743)--are thoroughly
      analyzed; the discussion proceeds from elaborate tonal-
      structure diagrams.

Alessandro Scarlatti
(1660-1725)

*An older work forms a useful introduction to this composer of
115 operas:*

390. Dent, Edward J. *Alessandro Scarlatti: His Life and
      Works.* 2d ed. London: Edward Arnold, 1960. 252p.
      ML 410 S218 D3
      This edition includes footnotes by Frank Walker;
      first edition was 1905. Biography; program notes on
      selected operas, with 94 musical examples. Work-list
      with library locations. No bibliography. Expansive
      index, names and titles.

391.   Grout, Donald Jay. *Alessandro Scarlatti: An Introduc-*
       tion to His Operas. Berkeley and Los Angeles: Uni-
       versity of California Press, 1979. vii, 154p.
       ML 410 S22 G7
       Texts of lectures given at the University of California
       in 1976, with some footnotes added. In general a casual
       presentation of the life, style, reputation, and con-
       temporaries of Scarlatti. Grout notes that only 30-35
       of the operas survive in "salvageable" form. He is
       editor of the series of critical editions issued by the
       Harvard University Press. There is an appendix of musical
       examples and a good expansive index of names, titles,
       and topics; no bibliography. The same author has an
       interesting article in *New Looks at Italian Opera* (620)
       on *Il Mitridate eupatore* (1707), and another study in
       Essays on Opera and English Music (648n). The latter
       is "The Original Version of Alessandro Scarlatti's
       Griselda"--a genesis account, noting revisions made
       before the official premiere.

                            Arnold Schoenberg
                              (1874-1951)

This is the spelling preferred by the composer in his later
years; however, the Library of Congress retains Schönberg,
as do most German writers.

392.   Reich, Willi. *Schoenberg: A Critical Biography.* Trans.
       Leo Black. New York: Praeger; London: Longman, 1971.
       xi, 268p. ISBN 0-582-12753-X (London)
       ML 410 S283 R43
       Originally: *Schönberg, oder der konservative Revolu-*
       tionär (Wien: Molden, 1968). A general biography, with
       footnotes; and program notes on the operas. Work-list
       in the translation has titles in English only; in the
       German edition the titles are in German. No information
       is provided about the compositions listed. Bibliography
       of about 25 books. Name index.

Erwartung

393.   Buchanan, Herbert H. "A Key to Schoenberg's 'Erwartung.'"
       Journal of the American Musicological Society, 20
       (1967): 434-449. ML 27 U5 M695
       Rejects the standard view that *Erwartung* is atonal
       and athematic; finds both thematic and tonal elements,

both related to one of the composer's early songs, "Am
Wegrand," op. 6 no. 6 (1905). Identifies motivic cells
that help to provide cohesion. Musical examples, and
references to earlier literature.

Erwartung and *Glückliche Hand*

394. Lessem, Alan Philip. *Music and Text in the Works of
Arnold Schoenberg: The Critical Years 1908-1922.*
Ann Arbor, Mich.: UMI Research, 1979. 247p. ISBN
0-8357-0994-9 ML 410 S283 L47
A general examination of "expressionisn, drama and
music" that includes detailed studies of the two early
operas. Extensive notes and musical examples. Bibliography of about 200 items. Expansive index of names,
titles, and topics.

*An article by John C. Crawford, "Die glückliche Hand: Schoen-
berg's Gesamtkunstwerk" (Musical Quarterly, 60 [1974]: 583-
601), explains how "every element of the text, setting, move-
ment, color, and music was conceived in great detail by
Schoenberg"; earlier writings are cited.*

Moses und Aron

395. Wörner, Karl Heinrich. *Schoenberg's Moses and Aron.*
Trans. Paul Hamburger. London: Faber and Faber, 1963.
208p. ML 410 S28 W613
The German title was *Gotteswort und Magie* (Heidelberg:
Schneider, 1959). This is a thorough historical and
technical study, offering details of the tone-rows as
well as a chronicle of productions with fine photos.
Emphasis on the religious ideas of the text. The
libretto in German/English is given in full; musical
examples; bibliography of about 30 entries; index of
names, titles, and topics.

Franz Peter Schubert
(1797-1828)

396. Hoorickx, P. Reinhard van. "Les opéras de Schubert."
Revue belge de musicologie, 28/30 (1974/76): 238-259.
ML 5 R292
A list of the ten complete operas and 11 that are in-
complete; plus 16 arias. Brief descriptive comments;
only two reference footnotes.

397. Cunningham, George R.   "Franz Schubert als Theater-
         komponist." Ph.D. dissertation. Albert-Ludwigs-
         Universität (Freiburg), 1974. 223p. ML 410 S3 C97
         Extended program notes, with some musical analysis,
      of all the operas. Backnotes; few musical examples.
      Bibliography of about 100 items, incomplete data. No
      index.

Another dissertation, not seen:

398. Citron, M.J.   "Schubert's Seven Complete Operas: A
         Musico-Dramatic Study." Ph.D. dissertation. Univer-
         sity of North Carolina, 1971.

Extended program notes on Fierrabras *and* Alfonso *and* Estrella
*are given by Maurice J.E. Brown, "Schubert's Two Major Operas--
A Consideration of the Possibility of Actual State Productions,"* Music Review, *20 (1959): 104-118.*

Dmitriĭ Dmitrievich Shostakovich
(1906-1975)

399. *Shostakovich: The Man and His Music.* Ed. Christopher
         Norris. Boston and London: Marion Boyars, 1982.
         233p. ML 410 S53 S5
         "The Operas," by Norris, pp. 105-124, offers a useful
      introduction and guidance to other literature through
      27 footnotes. Considers *The Nose*, *The Gamblers*, and
      especially *Lady Macbeth of Mtsensk*; all in program-
      note format.

400. Shostakovich, Dmitriĭ Dmitrievich. *Testimony: The
         Memoirs of Dmitriĭ Shostakovich.* Trans. Antonia W.
         Bouis. New York: Harper and Row, 1979. xli, 289p.
         ISBN 0-0601-4476-9 ML 410 S53 A3
         Of interest for background on the *Lady Macbeth* up-
      heavals. Includes a chronological work-list, all in
      English. Good expansive index of names and titles.

Bedrich Smetana
(1824-1884)

401. Large, Brian. *Smetana*. London: Duckworth; New York:
     Praeger, 1970. xvii, 473p. ML 410 S63 L4
     Biography and genealogy; good introduction to all the
     operas. Separate chapters on *Bartered Bride*, *Dalibor*,
     Two Widows, *The Kiss*, *The Secret*, and *The Devil's Wall*;
     style is program note, but primary sources are cited and
     there is some technical analysis. 26 plates and 112
     musical examples. An appendix gives detailed comparisons
     of the five versions of *Bartered Bride* and three versions
     of *Two Widows*. Chronological work-list; expansive index
     of names and titles.

Gasparo Spontini
(1774-1851)

The first name is also seen as Gaspare.

402. Ghislanzoni, Alberto. *Gasparo Spontini: studio storico-
     critico*. Roma: Edizioni dell'Ateneo, 1951. 281p.
     ML 410 S76 G45
     A footnoted biography, with some 50 photographs. Pro-
     gram notes and some technical observations on the operas.
     No bibliography. Name index.

403. Fragapane, Paolo. *Spontini*. Bologna: Sansoni, 1954.
     358p. ML 410 S76 F7
     A good biography, with footnotes. Work-list, giving
     publishers or library locations and instrumentations.
     Useful bibliographic essay (most of the writing on
     Spontini is old); name index.

Agostino Steffani
(1654-1728)

*Two dissertations (neither examined) seem to represent the
principal scholarly literature of our time:*

404. Baxter, W.H. "Agostino Steffani: A Study of the Man and
     His Work." Ph.D. dissertation. Eastman School of
     Music, University of Rochester, 1957.

405.   Croll, G. "Agostino Steffani (1654-1728): Studien zur
       Biographie, Bibliographie der Opern und Turnierspiele."
       Ph.D. dissertation. University of Münster, 1960.

Information on some operas of his middle period is given in:

406.   Keppler, Philip. "Agostino Steffani's Hannover Operas
       and a Rediscovered Catalogue." *Studies in Music
       History* (527n), pp. 341-355.
          Discusses stage works presented in Hannover, 1679-97,
       the nine operas of that period attributed to Steffani
       (six are said to be definitely genuine), and a manuscript
       catalog of the operas located by the author in the
       Hannover Landesbibliothek "in a mislabelled cardboard
       box."

                        Alessandro Stradella
                          (1664-1682)

*Much of the recent scholarly writing is by Carolyn Gianturco,
author of the* New Grove *article.*

407.   Gianturco, Carolyn M. "The Operas of Alessandro Stra-
       della (1644-1682)." Ph.D. dissertation. University
       of Oxford, 1970. 2 vols. 254, 121p.
          Not examined. The author summary in *RILM Abstracts*,
       4-2 (May-August 1970): 131, says she has made a "stylis-
       tic analysis of the works and an attempt to determine
       their chronology, with a comparison of the musical and
       textual sources." There are scene-by-scene studies of
       each opera. Bibliography; work-list; index.

Of several articles by Gianturco (cf. bibliography in New
Grove*), this offers the best factual and bibliographical
setting:*

408.   Gianturco, Carolyn. "Caratteri stilistici delle opere
       teatrali di Stradella." *Rivista italiana di musicologia*
       6 (1972): 211-245.
          Begins with a literature review; considers library
       locations of documents, then aria typology, use of basso
       ·ostinato, recitative, modulation, and orchestration.

Special attention to *Oratio*, *Corispero*, *Forza dell'amor paterno*.

Richard Strauss
(1864-1949)

409. Ortner, Oswald. *Richard Strauss Bibliographie. I. 1882-1944. II. 1944-1964.* Wien: C. Prachner, 1964-73. 2 vols. ISBN 3-8511-91102 ML 134 S93 O77
A thorough bibliography for the period covered, hailed by Del Mar (411 below) as "absolutely complete." Topical arrangement (each opera has a separate section) and then chronological. For books the publishers and pagination are given; for articles the pagination is not always given. Total of 3,463 items. Each volume has a name/title/topic/place index.

410. Brosche, Günter, and Karl Dachs. *Richard Strauss Autographen in München und Wien. Verzeichnis.* Tutzing: Schneider, 1979. xv, 378p. ML 134 S83 B87
An inventory of manuscripts and letters, arranged by library, in Munich and Vienna; full bibliographic descriptions. Also 31 letters printed in full for the first time. Index of works and names.

411. Del Mar, Norman. *Richard Strauss: A Critical Commentary on His Life and Works.* London: Barrie & Rockliff, 1969-1973. 3 vols. ISBN 0-8019-5700-1 ML 410 S93 D35
The standard biography; footnotes, quoted letters, and documents. Lengthy program notes on the operas, with particular detail for *Ariadne* and *Frau ohne Schatten*. Work-list gives titles in English only, and very little information (e.g., omits publishers). Discography has label numbers only. Bibliography of only about 70 titles, incomplete data. Good expansive index, names and titles, in the third volume.

412. Krause, Ernst. *Richard Strauss; The Man and His Work.* Boston: Crescendo, 1969. 588p. ISBN 8759-7024-9 ML 410 S93 K912
A popular biography; quotations but no footnotes. Chronological work-list, with many titles in English only (gives publisher, premiere date, instrumentation, and duration). Life chronology has much more detail

than others seen. Bibliography of only about 30 items,
with incomplete data. Name and title index. A work-
list with the German titles is found in the German
translation: *Richard Strauss. Gestalt und Werk* (Wies-
baden: Breitkopf und Härtel, 1980).

413. Schuh, Willi. *Richard Strauss: A Chronicle of the Early*
      Years, 1864-1898. Trans. Mary Whittall. New York:
      Cambridge University Press, 1982. 555p. ISBN
      0-5212-4104-9 ML 410 S93 S38 R52
        The original German edition: *Richard Strauss. Jugend*
      und frühe Meisterjahre. Lebenschronik, 1864-1898
      (Zürich: Atlantis, 1976). Useful for background only;
      there are only passing references to the major operas,
      all of which were written after the period covered. A
      weak bibliography, but good expansive index of names
      with titles.

414. Abert, Anna Amalie. *Richard Strauss--Die Opern.*
      Hannover: Friedrich, 1972. 133p. ML 410 S93 A52
        Technical analyses of each opera, in terms of libretto,
      compositional process, harmonic and melodic materials.
      Many long musical examples. Also a life chronology.
      No footnotes; bibliography of about 60 entries. No
      index.

415. Mann, William. *Richard Strauss: A Critical Study of*
      the Operas. London: Cassell, 1964; New York: Oxford
      University Press, 1966. 402p. MT 100 S93 M28. In
      German: *Richard Strauss; Das Opernwerk.* Trans. Willi
      Reich. München: Beck, 1967.
        Plots and program notes for all the stage works.
      Bibliography of about 75 items, incomplete data. Ex-
      pansive name and title index.

416. *Richard Strauss-Blätter.* 1- . June 1971- . Wien:
      International Richard Strauss Gesellschaft, 1971- .
      (Irregular.) ML 410 S93 R518
        Publisher varies. A new series began, with numbering
      from 1- , in June 1979. The earlier series, which
      ended December 1978, had articles in both German and
      English, in parallel columns. The "Neue Folge" articles
      are in either German or English, without translations.
      The content has been primarily made up of short notices,

discographies, and bibliographies, with feature articles
of a few pages in length. *RILM Abstracts*, 10-4 (1976):
516, 612-613, gives complete contents of volumes 1-8.
Volume 2 (1971) was devoted to *Die Frau ohne Schatten*,
volume 3 (1972) to *Daphne*. Later issues do not reveal
any special attention to the operas.

Ariadne auf Naxos

417. Daviau, Donald G., and George J. Buelow. *The Ariadne
auf Naxos of Hugo von Hofmannsthal and Richard Strauss*.
Chapel Hill: University of North Carolina Press,
1975. 269p. ISBN 0-8078-8080-9 ML 410 S93 D35
A scholarly study of the shaping of the libretto
(correspondence, revisions) and of the music. Technical
discussion of tonality and structure, with musical examples. Good bibliography of about 450 items, but data
are incomplete. No index.

418. Gräwe, Karl Dietrich. "Sprache, Musik und Szene in
'Ariadne auf Naxos' von Hugo von Hofmannsthal und
Richard Strauss." Ph.D. dissertation. Ludwig-Max-
imilians-Universität, München, 1969. 357p.
ML 410 S93 G73
Background of the libretto, with footnotes and docu-
ments; detailed musical analysis, with musical examples.
Bibliography of about 300 titles, incomplete data. No
index.

419. Forsyth, Karen. *Ariadne auf Naxos by Hugo von Hofmannsthal and Richard Strauss*. London and New York: Oxford
University Press, 1982. viii, 291p. ISBN 0-19-815536-0
ML 50 S93 A62 F7
Based on the author's Oxford dissertation. A thorough
background treatment, with footnotes: genesis of the
libretto and of the music; revisions; critical reception.
Analysis of the Vorspiel. Hofmannsthal's previously
unpublished notes; playbills; musical examples. Quotations from German are not translated. Bibliography of
about 90 items. Expansive index of names, titles, and
topics. Another Ph.D. dissertation, not examined, is
by Charlotte Elizabeth Erwin: "Richard Strauss's
'Ariadne auf Naxos': An Analysis of Musical Style Based
on a Study of Revisions" (Yale University, 1976; 265 p.).

Elektra

Three dissertations, not examined:

420. Hawkins, Jocelyn Hunter. "Hofmannsthal's 'Elektra':
      The Play and the Opera." Ph.D. dissertation. Indiana
      University, 1974. 326p.

421. McDonald, Lawrence Francis. "Compositional Procedures
      in Richard Strauss' 'Elektra.'" Ph.D. dissertation.
      University of Michigan, 1976. 196p.

422. Dinerstein, Norman Myron. "Polychordality in Salome and
      Elektra; A Study of the Application of Reinterpretation
      Technique." Ph.D. dissertation. Princeton University,
      1974. 170p.

Die Frau ohne Schatten

423. Knaus, Jakob. *Hofmannsthals Weg zur Oper Die Frau ohne
      Schatten.* Berlin: de Gruyter, 1971. 151p. ISBN
      3-11-001865-9 ML 423 H74 K6
      Originally the author's Ph.D. dissertation (Zürich,
      1971). A detailed study of the play and libretto; in-
      teractions between author and composer (many letters);
      the compositional process. Long footnotes; musical ex-
      amples. Attention to *Elektra*, *Rosenkavalier*, and
      Ariadne as well. Bibliography of about 120 entries,
      incomplete data. Name index.

424. Pantle, Sherrill Jean Hahn. "*Die Frau ohne Schatten*
      by Hugo von Hofmannsthal and Richard Strauss: An
      Analysis of Text, Music, and Their Relationship."
      Ph.D. dissertation. University of Colorado, 1976.
      310p.

Der Rosenkavalier

425. Schuh, Willi. *Der Rosenkavalier. Fassungen, Film-
      szenarium, Briefe.* Frankfurt: Fischer, 1972. 349p.
      ISBN 3-10-031533-2 ML 410 S93 A47

The complete German libretto (1910) is given, with a
full discussion of its emergence and several variants,
including the author's typescript. Staging directions
and diagrams. Correspondence among many persons concerned with the opera (1909-45). Description, with
photos, of Robert Wiene's 1926 film. Fine plates.
Bibliography; lists of editions, libretti, and letters.
No index.

*There is an "English National Opera Guide" (188) for the
opera.*

Salome

See Dinerstein (422).

Igor' Fedorovich Stravinskiĭ (Stravinsky)
(1882-1971)

426. White, Eric Walter. *Stravinsky--The Composer and His
Works*. 2d ed. London and Boston: Faber & Faber, 1979.
656p. ISBN 0-571-049230 (London) ML 410 S932 W58
A strong scholarly biography, with footnotes and
documents. Some letters in French, not translated.
Program notes on the stage works. Chronological work-
list, with titles in English only. Catalog of manuscripts
(1904-52) in Stravinsky's possession. Good annotated
bibliography of about 100 entries, including special
issues of journals. Name and title (English only)
index.

427. Stravinsky, Igor. *Selected Correspondence*. Vol. 1.
London: Faber & Faber, 1982. 471p.
ISBN 0-571-11724-4 ML 410 S932 A395
Annotated selection of letters by and to Stravinsky.
The correspondence with W.H. Auden, librettist for *The
Rake's Progress* (1947-65), gives some insights into the
collaborative process. Index of names and titles, ex-
pansive.

428. Schouvaloff, Alexander, and Victor Borovsky. *Stravinsky
on Stage*. London: Stainer & Bell, 1982. 226p.
ISBN 0-85249-604-4 ML 410 S9 S37

An attractive volume of photographs, many in color,
showing major productions worldwide. Premiere data,
including casts; synopses. Index of theaters, names,
and titles.

429. Griffiths, Paul. *Igor Stravinsky, The Rake's Progress.*
     Cambridge, Eng.: Cambridge University Press, 1982.
     xiv, 109p. ISBN 0-521-23746-7 ML 410 S932 G74
     One of the fine "Cambridge Opera Handbooks." Gives
     synopsis, sketches, performance history, and remarks
     by the composer. Bibliography of about 30 titles;
     discography of four albums; name index.

430. Lederman, Minna. *Stravinsky in the Theatre.* New York:
     Pellegrini & Cudahy, 1949. 228p. (Reprint--New York:
     Da Capo, 1975.) ML 410 S9 L47
     Discusses all the stage works; gives table of pre-
     mieres for major cities. Operas included are *Rossignol*,
     Histoire du soldat, *Mavra*, and *Oedipus rex*. An extensive
     bibliography of more than 600 citations, by Paul Magriel,
     is the most important feature: it lists, for each work,
     the books and articles about it (including parts of
     books); and provides abstracts for book entries. No
     index.

Sir Arthur Seymour Sullivan
(1842-1900)

431. Sullivan, Herbert, and Newman Flower. *Sir Arthur
     Sullivan; His Life, Letters & Diaries.* 2d ed. Lon-
     don: Cassell, 1950. 306p. ML 410 S95 S9
     First edition was 1927. A dependable biography, with
     some footnotes. Many letters. Good work-list, compiled
     by William C. Smith, pp. 268-283; in chronological
     order, with dates and publishers. Expansive index of
     names and titles.

432. Young, Percy M. *Sir Arthur Sullivan.* London: Dent;
     New York: Norton, 1971. xiii, 304p. ML 410 S95 Y7
     A useful life story, with footnotes and good plates.
     Program notes for the operas, with some technical ob-
     servations; musical examples. Chronological work-list,
     with premiere data and publishers. Bibliography of about
     125 items, incomplete information. Partly expansive
     name index.

433. Gilbert, William Schwenck. *The First Night Gilbert and
      Sullivan.* Ed. Reginald Allen. Rev. ed. London:
      Chappell, 1976. xxi, 465p. ML 49 S92 A1
      First edition was 1958. Texts of all the original
      libretti as given at the premieres, with contemporary
      reviews and drawings. Bibliography; index.

434. Helyar, James, ed. *Gilbert & Sullivan.* Papers pre-
      sented at the International Conference held at the
      University of Kansas, May 1970. Lawrence: University
      of Kansas, 1971. viii, 228p. ML 36 I584
      This was the first (and apparently the only) inter-
      national G&S conference. Of 19 papers two are of most
      interest: Roger Harris, "The Artistry and Authenticity
      of the Savoy Overtures"; and Colin Prestige, "D'Oyly
      Carte and the Pirates: The Original New York Productions
      of Gilbert & Sullivan" (all casts of New York performances,
      with facts and anecdotes).

There are three useful fact-books in dictionary style:

435. Ayre, Leslie. *The Gilbert and Sullivan Companion.* New
      York: Dodd, Mead, 1972. 485p. ISBN 0-306-06634-8
      ML 410 S95 A98
      A popular dictionary format, made up of short entries
      in alphabetical sequence. Covers songs, persons,
      characters, topics. Gives synopses of all the operas.
      No notes; no bibliography; no index.

436. *Crowell's Handbook of Gilbert & Sullivan.* Ed. Frank
      Ledlie Moore. New York: Crowell, 1962. 264p.
      MT 100 S9747 M7
      Historical/biographical essays on Gilbert, Sullivan,
      Richard D'Oyly Carte, the Savoy Company, etc. Synopses
      and program notes on each opera. Chronology; list of
      the roles; first lines and famous lines; themes and
      texts. Bibliography of about 35 items, annotated. No
      index.

437. Hardwick, Michael. *The Osprey Guide to Gilbert & Sul-
      livan.* Reading, Eng.: Osprey, 1972. 284p. ISBN
      85045-100-0 MT S9747 H31

Similar to Crowell (preceding entry): program notes, roles, etc. Also identifies famous quotations from each work, and gives a glossary of names and unusual expressions in the operas. Discography. No index.

The D'Oyly Carte Opera Company became known for its authentic productions. Their story is told by Cyril Rollins and R. John Witts, The D'Oyly Carte Opera Company in Gilbert & Sullivan Operas; A Record of Productions 1875-1961, *1962 (IOM-3488); it includes indexes of actors, actresses, composers, and theaters.*

Franz von Suppé
(1819-1895)

438. Schneiderheit, Otto. *Franz von Suppé: Der Wiener aus Dalmatien.* Berlin: VEB Lied der Zeit, 1977. 168p. ML 410 S9723 S4
      There is nothing about the music in this straightforward biography; nor are there footnotes, bibliography, or index. The only interest is in the illustrations: of theaters, scenes from the operas, floorplans, etc.

Deems Taylor
(1885-1966)

Taylor has had more Metropolitan performances than any other American composer, but it seems that the two operas responsible have not been staged elsewhere.

439. Brody, Elaine. "The King's Henchman: Fifty Years Later." *Notes,* 34-2 (December 1977): 319-322. ML 27 U5 M695
      The premiere date was 17 February 1927; it had 14 performances over three seasons. Brody discusses the opera in the light of a letter by Taylor that described his intentions for the work and gave his views on the function of opera.

Peter Ilyitch Tchaikovsky (See *Chaĭkovskiĭ*)

Georg Philipp Telemann
(1681-1767)

Telemann is not remembered for his operas, of which only seven survive. This is the only study of them:

440. Peckham, Mary Adelaide. "The Operas of Georg Philipp Telemann." Ph.D. dissertation. Columbia University, 1972. iv, 303p.
    Discusses the operas that have come down to us and the fragments of lost works; stylistic analysis and biographical/historical background. Bibliography and worklist; no index.

Sir Michael Tippett
(1905-)

441. White, Eric Walter. *Tippett and His Operas.* London: Barrie & Jenkins, 1979. 142p. ISBN 0-214-20573-8
    ML 410 T595 W58
    Begins with a 26-page biographical sketch; then offers synopses, premiere data, and program notes for the four operas. Letters from Tippett to White, regarding *Midsummer Marriage*, are quoted extensively. Without notes, musical examples, or bibliography. Index of names, titles, and topics.

Giuseppe Verdi
(1813-1901)

The scholarly literature on Verdi is increasing rapidly, in quantity and in quality. No comprehensive bibliography exists, although there has been recent discussion of the problems involved in compiling one (see notes under Atti, *below at 447). This is the most useful summary of Verdian research:*

442. Surian, Elvidio. "Lo stato attuale degli studi verdiani: appunti e bibliografia ragionata (1960-1975)." *Rivista italiana di musicologia,* 12 (1977): 305-329.
    ML 5 R624
    The literature survey begins with 1960, the year in which the Istituto di Studi Verdiani was established in Parma by the Italian government. Surian takes as

his starting point the several publication series of
the Istituto, noting the superficial, program-note level
of much that they include. He then laments the condi-
tion of printed sources; namely, that no critical
editions of the operas exist and that only nine of the
26 operas are even available in full score (he notes
the planned publication of critical scores by Ricordi
and the University of Chicago Press--see 477 below).
He then cites the principal efforts at Verdian bibliography, most of which are also mentioned below; and
submits observations on the leading biographies, collections of letters, and libretti publications. Taking
up analytical studies, he comments that this field is
of growing importance, and perceptively states that the
area of structural studies has presented some valuable
work that lacks, so far, "un principio costruttivo
generalmente operante." Analyses of specific operas
are noted; then material on Verdi in relation to musical
life of his time; and finally some contributions to
production, acting, staging, etc. This is the most
useful "gatekeeper" to the Verdi literature of the
period covered.

443.   Kämper, Dietrich. "Das deutsche Verdi-Schriftum."
       Analecta musicologica, 11 (1972): 185-197. ML 5 A532
       A bibliographic essay, summarizing major writings of
the 19th and 20th centuries by scholars of the Germanic
countries; 54 footnotes.

444.   *Verdi Companion*. Ed. William Weaver and Martin Chusid.
       New York: Norton, 1979. 366p. ISBN 0-393-01215-8
       ML 410 V4 V295
       Essays by various scholars, on Verdi and politics,
Verdi and his impresarios and publishers, his librettists
his treatment of the voice, his obscure contemporaries.
Several of the pieces had appeared elsewhere, or have
since. The most useful contribution is the selective
bibliography by Andrew Porter (who also did the bibliography for the *New Grove* article). It is a critical in-
ventory--many comments are indeed critical--of catalogs,
editions, biographies (none is satisfactory), and
analytical studies. The volume also has a valuable
chronology by Surian, pp. 255-324, and an index of
names, titles, and topics.

445. Istituto di Studi Verdiani, Parma. *Bollettini*. 1- .
1960- . Parma, 1960- . ML 410 V4 V3
This is the institute discussed at 442 above. *Bollettini* issued to date are: 1 (1960), *Un ballo in
maschera*; 3 parts. 2 (1961-1966), *La forza del destino*;
2 parts. 3 (1969, 1973-82), *Rigoletto*.

The Istituto also publishes two other series:

446. *Quaderni*. 1- . 1963- . Parma, 1963- . ML 410 V4 I87
These *Quaderni* have appeared: 1 (1963), *Il corsaro*.
2 (1963), *Jérusalem* and *I lombardi*. 3 (1968), *Stiffelio*
and *Aroldo*. 4 (1971), *Aida*.

447. Congresso Internazionale di Studi Verdiani, 1st- ,
1960- . *Atti del I [II, etc.] Congresso Internazionale di Studi Verdiani*.... Parma: Istituto di
Studi Verdiani, 1960- . ML 36 C769
Proceedings for these conferences have been published,
all under the title *Atti*: 1 (1960, Venice). 2 (1969,
Verona, Parma, Busseto), on *Don Carlos*. 3 (1972, Milan).
4 (1974, Chicago), mostly on *Simon Boccanegra*. 5 (1977,
Danville, Ky.), on *Macbeth*.

Notice will be taken below of various essays in these series.
Istituto publications may be ordered (in the Western Hemisphere,
Australia, and New Zealand) from Broude Brothers, 170 Varick
St., New York, N.Y. 10013.

In 1976 a second organization for Verdi scholarship was es-
tablished: The American Institute for Verdi Studies, with
office and archive in New York University. The AIVS News-
letter appeared in 1976, changing its name after two numbers
to Verdi Newsletter (semiannual; ML 410 V4 A64). Each issue
has a bibliography of new publications, including disserta-
tions and journal articles; reviews of books on Verdi; and
notices of performances in world opera houses. There are
also feature articles, one of which should be mentioned:
Martin Chusid's three-part series "Casts for Verdi Premieres
in London, 1845-1977," and "Casts for the Verdi Premieres in
the United States (1847-1976)"; these useful lists appeared
in numbers 2, 3, and 5. Issues 9-10 include a description of
the New York University Verdi Archive.

Biographies

*None is entirely satisfactory. The most important works are
given here in alphabetical order by author:*

448.   Abbiati, Franco. *Giuseppe Verdi*. Milano: Ricordi,
       1959. 4 vols. ML 410 V4 A52
       Described by Surian (442) as "monumentale, pero fan-
       tasiosa," this is a vast rambling account of Verdi's
       life, with extensive extracts from the letters. No
       footnotes and no bibliography; no musical examples and
       little said about the music. Name and title index.

449.   Baldini, Gabriele. *The Story of Giuseppe Verdi*. Trans.
       Roger Parker. Introduction by Julian Budden. New
       York: Cambridge University Press, 1980. xx, 296p.
       ISBN 0-521-29712 ML 410 V4 B172. Originally pub-
       lished as: *Abitare la battaglia* (Milano: Garzanti,
       1970).
       A sparsely footnoted biography, with some attempts
       at psychological analysis. Budden's laudatory introduc-
       tion may lead one to expect more than is actually pre-
       sented, which is (aside from the life story) a long
       program note. No musical examples, no technical analysis,
       no bibliography. Name and title index. Baldini died
       before completing the work.

450.   Kimbell, David R.B. *Verdi in the Age of Italian
       Romanticism*. Cambridge, Eng., and New York: Cambridge
       University Press, 1981. ix, 703p. ISBN 0-521-23052-7
       ML 410 V4 K49
       Material on Verdi's life is presented in topical
       contexts, such as political climate, censorship in the
       theater, business aspects. There are also sections on
       the arias, ensembles, recitatives, orchestration, etc.
       Period covered is from *Oberto* (1839) to *La traviata*
       (1853). Backnotes; musical examples; many documents
       and letters (not translated). The bibliography is de-
       fective: important items are missing and incomplete
       data are provided for the 100 or so entries. Good ex-
       pansive index of names, titles, and subjects.

451.   Martin, George Whitney. *Verdi; His Music, Life and
       Times*. New York: Dodd, Mead, 1963. xii, 633p.

(Reprint--New York: Da Capo, 1979.) ISBN 0-306-79549-3
ML 410 V4 M266
Could have been the preferred biography, except for
the absence of footnotes. A pleasing, straightforward
life story; good work-list, with premiere dates, casts,
and theaters; librettists and source plays for each
opera. Excellent selective, annotated bibliography of
about 100 titles, with full data. Ideal expansive
index of names, titles, and topics.

452. Walker, Frank. *The Man Verdi*. New York: Knopf, 1962.
526p. ML 410 V4 W2
A documentary biography, more than half consisting of
letters. Footnotes offer a guide to major primary
sources. All material is in English; for the originals
see the Italian translation of the book: *L'uomo Verdi*
(Milano, 1974). The music itself is not considered
here. Index of names and titles.

453. *Verdi: A Documentary Study*. Comp., ed., and trans.
William Weaver. London: Thames & Hudson, 1977.
256p. ISBN 0-500-01184-2 ML 410 V4 V29
A fine assemblage of 318 illustrations, 54 in color--
pages from scores, pictures of documents and of all
Verdi's persons and places, sets, and costumes. Also
an annotated collection of letters. Index of names,
partly expansive, and of titles.

Two other frequently cited works may be identified:

454. Hussey, Dyneley. *Verdi*. 5th ed., rev. Charles Osborne.
London: Dent, 1974. xiii, 365p. ISBN 0-460-03151-1
ML 410 V4 H8
A general study, with program notes on the operas.
May be useful for its good chronology. Name and title
index.

455. Toye, Francis. *Giuseppe Verdi, His Life and Works*.
New York: Knopf, 1946. 414p. (Reprint--New York:
Vienna House, 1972.) ISBN 0-8443-0067-5
ML 410 V4 T7
Once very popular, this older tract seems bland and
amateurish today. General program notes on each opera,

interlacing descriptions of Verdi's life, critical reception, etc. A few footnotes; no musical examples.
Expansive index of names and titles.

Correspondence

No adequate collection of all the letters has been issued.
Verdi wrote voluminously for most of his life; some of his
letters were drafted in notebooks (copialettere), that have
served as a source for some publications. But Philip Gossett
notes that to see all the published letters--many are not yet
published at all--would require consultation of hundreds of
books, periodicals, and newspapers. The principal gathering
is useful but has its shortcomings:

456.   Cesari, Gaetano, and Alessandro Luzio. *I copialettere*
          di Giuseppe Verdi. Bologna: Forni, 1968. xx, 759p.
          ML 410 V4 A3
          This is a reproduction of the Milan, 1913, edition.
       Consists of 386 letters with annotations. Criteria for
       the selection not given; Gossett notes the large gap
       without letters from 22 May 1858 to 20 September 1867
       and a second gap from 9 February 1875 to January 1877.
       (Gossett citations in this and the next entry are from
       Musical Quarterly, 59-4 [1973]: 633-639.) The editors
       chose letters as illustrations of aspects of Verdi's
       life and character, omitting portions they thought
       to be superfluous and suppressing information as they
       saw fit. There is an index of names, titles, and topics.

457.   Osborne, Charles. *The Letters of Giuseppe Verdi.* Lon-
          don: Gollancz, 1971. 280p. ISBN 0-575-00759-1
          ML 410 V4 A337
          A selection of 293 letters from the *Copialettere*
       (see preceding entry), translated into English and
       annotated. Gossett cites an "enormous number of errors
       in translation and commentary" in this work. Bio-
       graphical sketches for persons addressed or mentioned;
       index of names, titles, letters (by recipient).

458.   Verdi, Giuseppe. *Verdi, The Man in His Letters.* Ed.
          Franz Werfel and Paul Stefan. Trans. Edward Downes.
          New York: L.B. Fischer, 1942. 469p. (Reprint--New
          York: Vienna House, 1973.) ISBN 0-8443-0088-8
          ML 410 V4 A385

A selection from 1880 to 1901, with brief comments.
Also a work-list and an expansive index of names, topics,
and places.

459. *Carteggio Verdi-Boito.* Ed. Mario Medici and Marcello
Conati. Parma: Istituto di Studi Verdiani, 1978.
2 vols. ML 410 V4 A43
The first publication of the complete correspondence,
consisting of 301 letters with detailed comments. Bibliography, about 100 items (incomplete data). Index of
names, titles, and topics. Note that Boito invariably
addresses Verdi in the most formal style ("Lei"), while
Verdi addresses Boito in the semiformal manner ("voi").

*Other collections of letters are cited by Surian (442) and
Porter (444), and in Porter's* New Grove *bibliography.*

Work-lists

New Grove *and many other reference books will provide a basic
enumeration of the operas, with their librettists and premiere
information. For greater detail these two compilations will
be needed:*

460. Chusid, Martin. *A Catalog of Verdi's Operas.* Hacken-
sack, N.J.: J. Boonin, 1974. xi, 201p. ISBN
0-913574-05-8 ML 134 V47 C5
The standard bibliography, containing much useful
material: premiere dates and casts, autographs, early
scores, locations of sources, arias and numbers of each
work with alternatives and variants from different versions, and lists of full scores and piano-vocal scores.
Bibliography of about 180 entries. Name index with
identifiers: "tenor," "librettist," etc. Generally well
received by critics; but see comment in next entry.

461. Hopkinson, Cecil. *A Bibliography of the Works of Giuseppe Verdi, 1813-1901. 1: Vocal and Instrumental
Works. 2: Operas.* New York: Broude Brothers, 1973-
78. 2 vols. xi, 108, 191p.
An attempt to record all editions in all formats of
all the works of Verdi. Gives incipits, publishing
histories, locations, plate numbers, bibliographic

descriptions, background comments. In the "List of
Works Consulted" (2, 190) he observes that Chusid's
Catalog (preceding entry) "presents to a bibliographer
something of a problem, as it does not pretend to be
anything more than an incomplete catalogue of Verdi's
works with the appearance of only 'selected editions of
some early piano-vocal scores,' so that the reader is
quite unaware how many have been omitted." On the other
hand, Porter in *Verdi Companion*, above, is puzzled by
Hopkinson's "detailed and curious publication" and notes
omissions even there. The bibliographer's dilemma is
vividly presented: if you are selective, they will
wonder about your criteria; if you try to be comprehensive, they will always find something you left out.

The Operas

462. Budden, Julian. *The Operas of Verdi*. London: Cassell;
      New York: Oxford University Press, 1973-81. 3 vols.
      ISBN 0-19-520030-6, 0-19-520068-3, 0-19-520254-6
      (New York) ML 410 V4 B88
      The most satisfactory commentary on the operas, pre-
      senting historical and technical viewpoints in great
      detail, with ample reference to earlier research.
      Strong sections on opera of the times (e.g., "collapse
      of a tradition" in 2, 1-32). Relevant letters are given
      (in English only); about 1,000 musical examples illu-
      minate the arguments. On the negative side, Budden re-
      veals a blind spot toward macroanalysis (tonal, struc-
      tural) that leaves him more or less in a position of
      uncertainty over a formal plan for an opera. And his
      bibliography of about 400 entries is a disappointing
      presentation in *New Grove* style: articles unpaginated,
      authors identified by initials instead of first names,
      lack of publishers, etc. Name, title, and topic in-
      dexes, partly expansive.

463. Osborne, Charles. *The Complete Operas of Verdi*. Lon-
      don: Gollancz; New York: Knopf, 1969. 486p. (Re-
      print--New York: Da Capo, 1977.) ISBN 0-306-80072-1
      (Da Capo) MT 100 V4708
      Program notes on the 26 operas, placing them in his-
      torical context. Footnotes; musical examples. Bib-
      liography of about 40 items. Index of names.

464. Godefroy, Vincent. *The Dramatic Genius of Verdi. Studies of Selected Operas.* Vol. 1. New York: St. Martin, 1975. 287p. ML 410 V4 G

An attempt to "examine Verdi's methods of construction and portrayal" in the early works plus *Rigoletto* and *Trovatore*. Relates the music to the source plays. Musical examples, footnotes. No index.

A number of dissertations should be mentioned:

465. Jablonsky, Stephen. "The Development of Tonal Coherence as Evidenced in the Revised Operas of Giuseppe Verdi." Ph.D. dissertation. New York University, 1973. 465p.

The author's imaginative approach--as indicated in his summary for *RILM Abstracts*, 9-1/2 (January-August 1975): 79--was to compare "the original and revised versions of twelve pairs of musical numbers taken from six pairs of operas revised by Verdi...." He found that there was increased tonal coherence, and more logical coherence among key centers, in the revisions.

466. Lawton, David. "Tonality and Drama in Verdi's Early Operas." Ph.D. dissertation. University of California, Berkeley, 1973. 2 vols. 333, 343p.

The operas up to and including *Rigoletto* are examined from the viewpoint of tonal structure, both micro- and macrolevels. Up to *Macbeth*, Verdi may have changed keys to satisfy singers; thus tonal design was obscured. But with *Macbeth* and after he did not make such alterations, so his intentions are clear. Various devices are identified: referential use of keys, repeated series of keys in cadential patterns, and the shaping of large forms through key relations. Although convincing answers are not found here--Lawton is unable to determine a key center for *Rigoletto*, for example; he seems to find it in a mystic point between D-major and D^b-major--the questions raised are stimulating and the analyses are exacting. Bibliography of 39 items; no index.

467. Moreen, Robert Anthony. "Integration of Text Forms and Musical Forms in Verdi's Early Operas." Ph.D. dissertation. Princeton University, 1975. 338p.

A unique approach, examining the "relationship of the prosodic forms of the libretti of Verdi's operas to the

musical and dramatic shape of the operas." Takes as
point of departure Abramo Basevi's *Studio sulle opere
di Giuseppe Verdi* (Firenze: Tofani, 1859), and the fact
that Verdi requested specific poetic forms in his
libretti. Finds that the division of the numbers of
the early operas, and other patterns, grow out of
poetic-structural demands as explicated by Basevi.
Both micro- and macrolevel consequences are discussed.
Operas through *Traviata* are covered. Bibliography of
about 25 entries; no index.

468. Parker, Roger. "Studies in Early Verdi." Ph.D. dis-
     sertation. University of London, 1981.
     An extract is cited below, under Ernani.

Aida

469. Busch, Hans. *Verdi's Aida: The History of the Opera in
     Letters and Documents*. Minneapolis: University of
     Minnesota Press, 1978. 1v, 688p. ISBN 0-8166-07982
     ML 410 V4 V312
     An impressive gathering of letters, contracts, sketches,
     stage directions, drawings, and other documents, spanning
     23 years. All materials are annotated and unified into
     a result "as vivid and enthralling as a novel" (Julian
     Budden's review). Includes original production notes
     by Verdi, Giulio Ricordi, and Franco Faccio. Bibliog-
     raphy of 250 items; expansive index to the letters;
     index of names, titles, and topics.

Other useful publications on Aida *include* Avant-scène opéra,
4 (1976), 130p., and Quaderni, *4 (446 above). There is also
an "English National Opera Guide" (188).*

Aroldo

*This title was given to a revised version (1857) of the un-
successful* Stiffelio *(1850).* Quaderni, *3 (1968; see 446
above), was devoted to the opera. The changes are described
in V. Levi's "Stiffelio e il suo rifacimento Aroldo," in*
Atti, *1 (1960): 172-175.*

Un ballo in maschera

Bollettino, 1 (1960), offers various approaches. An exchange of ideas on the opera's tonal macrostructure appeared in 19th Century Music: *Siegmund Levarie, "Key Relations in Verdi's Un Ballo in maschera," 2 (1978/79): 143-147; Joseph Kerman, "Viewpoint," ibid., 186-191; Guy A. Marco, "On Key Relations in Opera," 3 (1979): 83-88; and a last word by Levarie, ibid., 88-89. In quick synopsis of the exchange: Levarie offers an explication of Ballo's macrostructure based on the interplay of dramatic situations and key patterns; Kerman takes issue with the basic notion and with details of execution; Marco looks at a basis for a general theory of operatic structure that stems from key relations; Levarie sums up with a state-ment distinguishing his own "ontic" (being) orientation from Kerman's "gignetic" (becoming) position. The debate was pursued by Roger Parker and Matthew Brown, in "Motivic and Tonal Interaction in Verdi's Un ballo in maschera,"* Journal of the American Musicological Society, *36-2 (Summer 1983): 243-265. They present some useful schematics that elucidate many structural features but find themselves unable to dis-cover any tonal or motivic pattern that unifies the entire work and conclude with some murky grumbles about the danger of "organicism." See also Siegmund Levarie, "A Pitch Cell in Verdi's Un ballo in maschera,"* Journal of Musicological Re-search, *3 (1981): 399-409.*

Il corsaro

Quaderni, 1 (1963), consists of several articles on the opera.

Don Carlos

470. Günther, Ursula. "La genèse de *Don Carlos* ..." *Revue de musicologie*, 58-1 (1972): 16-64; 60-1/2 (1974): 87-158. ML 5 R32

Supplementary information was given in Günther's "Zur Revision des Don Carlos; Postscriptum zu Teil II." *Analecta musicologica*, 19 (1979): 373-377. The author gives a thorough elucidation of the emergence of the opera, based partly on newly discovered sources (letters, libretti, etc.). The composer's changes and corrections are discussed; rehearsals are dated. References to pre-vious writings are cited, with original source material, in 286 footnotes. Various disagreements with Anthony Porter ("The Making of Don Carlos," *Proceedings of the*

Royal Musical Association, 98 (1971/72). It is curious
that Budden, in the second volume of *The Operas of
Verdi*, makes only four passing references in footnotes
to this monumental study.

*Leibowitz (172) has some useful observations on the opera;
and it was the subject of Atti, 2.*

I due Foscari

471. Petrobelli, Pierluigi. "Osservazioni sul processo com-
          positivo in Verdi." *Acta musicologica*, 43 (1971):
          125-142. ML 5 I6
          An examination of draft fragments for *I due Foscari*
      and the sketch for *Rigoletto*, offering what Surian
      describes (442) as the only study that tries to tell
      why Verdi made specific changes in the final versions.
      His conclusion is most interesting: the sketch is a
      concentrated nucleus of the musical ideas; those ideas
      expand into the revised score.

Ernani

*A part of Roger Parker's dissertation (468) was the basis for
his "Levels of Motivic Definition in Verdi's Ernani," 19th
Century Music, 6-2 (Fall 1982): 141-150. ML 1 N714. He "owes
much" to Noske (336) in his approach. Finds internal coherence
in Verdi's use of a "recurring melodic contour, the rising
sixth from dominant to mediant." He feels it is "unfortunate
that a good deal of the close analytic work of recent years
has concerned itself with the contentious topic of overall
key relationships."*

Falstaff

*No comprehensive study has been seen. This dissertation sounds
promising, but it was not available for examination:*

472. Sabbeth, Daniel Paul. "Principles of Tonal and Dramatic
          Organization in Verdi's Falstaff." Ph.D. dissertation.
          City University of New York, 1976. 234p.
          The same author contributed to *Atti*, 3 (pp. 415-442),
      an essay entitled "Dramatic and Musical Organization in

'Falstaff.'" Another article from *Atti*, this from volume 1: Guglielmo Barblan: "Spunti rivelatori nella genesi del 'Falstaff.'"

La forza del destino

Bollettino, *2, is devoted to* Forza.

Jérusalem (See *I lombardi alla prima crociata*)

I lombardi alla prima crociata

See Quaderni, *2 (1963). Given in Paris with revisions and the title* Jérusalem.

Macbeth

473.   Osthoff, Wolfgang. "Die beiden Fassungen von Verdis 'Macbeth.'" *Archiv für Musikwissenschaft*, 29 (1972): 17-44. ML 5 A632
A genesis study, with program notes and musical examples.

474.   Degrada, Francesco. "Lettura di *Macbeth* di Verdi." *Studi musicali*, 6 (1977): 207-267. ML 5 S9331
A well-documented genesis study. Texts of letters; text changes by Piave; references to earlier literature.

475.   Goldin, Daniela. "Il Macbeth verdiano: genesi e linguaggio di un libretto." *Analecta musicologica*, 19 (1979): 336-372. ML 5 A532
A fine review of previous writings (130 notes) makes this genesis account particularly useful.

See also Avant-scène opéra, *40 (1982), 143p.; and* Atti, *5 (1977).*

Otello

476. Archibald, Bruce. "Tonality in *Otello*." *Music Review*,
      35 (1974): 23-28. ML 5 M657
      An imaginative approach to tonal structure, taking
      the key of F major as the tonic of Act I, from which
      prior and later keys are said to "radiate" in the form
      of a star.

*Avant-scène opéra, 3 (1976), is on Otello, and there are
volumes of the "Rororo" series (186) and "English National
Opera Guides" (188).*

Rigoletto

477. Gallico, Claudio. "Ricognizione di Rigoletto." *Nuova
      rivista musicale italiana*, 3 (1969): 855-901.
      ML 5 N973
      An extended program note with 40 musical examples.
      No references.

*The draft of Rigoletto is the only one available for study.
It was published (Milano, 1941) with an introduction by
Carlo Gatti. The comments of Gino Roncaglia, "L'abbozzo del
Rigoletto," Rivista musicale italiana, 48 (1946): 112-129,
do not seem to add anything useful but do offer a basic
description of the draft, with notes and musical examples.
Bollettino, 3 (1969, 1973-82), is devoted to the opera. It
includes a chronology of premieres in various theaters of the
world, an article by Lawton on the tonal structure (see 466),
and an important bibliography of the critical literature
from 1851, by Corte. The volume has a list of libretto
editions and a discography.*

*An event of great consequence for Verdi research is the
appearance of the first volume in "The Works of Giuseppe
Verdi": it is Rigoletto, in a critical edition of the orchestra
score with annotations and a 100-page commentary by Martin
Chusid. Planned as a 30-volume set, to be issued one volume
per year, this edition is published by the University of
Chicago Press in collaboration with Ricordi of Milan.*

Simon Boccanegra

478. Osthoff, Wolfgang. "Die beiden 'Boccanegra'--Fassungen
und der Beginn von Verdis Spätwerk." *Analecta musicologica*, 1 (1963): 70-89. ML 5 A532
A technical comparison of the two versions, with notes
and examples.

Atti, *4 (1974), and* Avant-scène opéra, *19 (1979), 137p., are
on Boccanegra. There is also an essay by Frank Walker, "Verdi,
Giuseppe Montanelli and the Libretto of Simon Boccanegra," in
Bolletino, 1 (1960): 1373-1390. See also the dissertation
cited under* Les vêpres siciliennes *(482).*

La traviata

479. Chusid, Martin. "Drama and the Key of F major in 'La
traviata.'" *Atti*, 3 (1972): 89-121. ML 36 C769
Discusses the role of the key of F in association with
aspects of the romance of Violetta and Alfredo.

There is an "English National Opera Guide" for the opera (188).

Il trovatore

480. Petrobelli, Pietro. "Per un' esegesi della struttura
drammatica del *Trovatore*." *Atti,* 3 (1972): 387-400.
ML 36 C769
Program notes; attention to genesis. Good footnote
review of the literature.

Les vêpres siciliennes

481. Vlad, Roman. "Unità strutturale dei *Vespri siciliani*."
*Il melodramma italiano dell'ottocento: studi e
ricerche per Massimo Mila*, pp. 45-90. Torino: G.
Einaudi, 1977. ML 1733.4 M5
Differs with Baldini (449), an extreme nonstructural-
ist; finds formal coherence in the opera based on re-
currence of melodic motives.

482. Neuls-Bates, Carol. "Verdi's Les vêpres siciliennes
         (1855) and Simon Boccanegra (1857)." Ph.D. disserta-
         tion. Yale University, 1970. 470p.
      Not seen. In *RILM Abstracts*, 4-3 (September-December
      1970): 247, the author summarizes: derivation of the
      libretti, critical and popular reception in the early
      years, and a chronology of Verdi's projects in the late
      1850s. Bibliography; no index.

483. Porter, Andrew. "*Les vêpres siciliennes*: New Letters
         from Verdi to Scribe." *19th Century Music*, 2 (1978/
         79): 95-109. ML 1 N714
      Argues that Verdi did influence the shaping of the
      libretto, contrary to the accepted view that the com-
      poser was dissatisfied with the text but let it stand.

*The opera is the subject of a volume in the Collana series
(1973).*

Antonio Vivaldi
(1678-1741)

484. Pincherle, Marc. *Vivaldi*. Paris: Éditions de Bon
         Plaisir, Librairie Plon, 1955. 278p. ML 410 V82 P532.
      In English: *Vivaldi, Genius of the Baroque*. New
      York: Norton, 1957.
      A popular-style biography (no footnotes), with thin
      program notes on the operas. Useful list of the
      dramatic works, with librettists and place and year
      of premiere, but this information is also available
      in *New Grove*. Weak bibliography of about 25 items, in-
      complete data. Index of names.

485. Rinaldo, Mario. *Il teatro musicale di Antonio Vivaldi*.
         Firenze: Olschki, 1979. vii, 279p. ML 410 V82 R57
      This is the first book to deal exclusively with the
      operas. Unfortunately, it presents little more than
      program notes with musical examples. There is a vague
      chronology of events and writings, 1899-1979 (new pro-
      ductions, etc.); name index.

The first major study in English:

486. Cross, Eric. *The Late Operas of Antonio Vivaldi, 1727-
      1738.* Ann Arbor, Mich.: UMI Research, 1981. 2 vols.
      277, 320p. ISBN 0-8357-1158-7 ML 410 V82 C8
      Background material on Venice and the opera seria;
      then detailed technical examination of the Vivaldi works,
      emphasizing *Griselda.* Attention to characterization and
      overall structure. Chronology of operas, with casts and
      notes. Volume 2 is made up of musical examples. Bib-
      liography of about 150 entries, incomplete data. Ex-
      pansive index of names, titles, and topics; separate
      index of works.

This dissertation was not examined:

487. Rowell, L.E. "Four Operas of Antonio Vivaldi." Ph.D.
      dissertation. University of Rochester, 1958.

Two essays on the comic operas appear in Muraro (260).

                    Richard Wagner
                     (1813-1883)

*It is said that the literature about Wagner is greater than
that on any other musician; indeed, it has been claimed that
only Lincoln and Napoleon have had more written about them.
There are several guides to this bibliography, of which the
following appear to be the most useful.*

488. Oesterlein, Nikolaus. *Katalog einer Richard Wagner-
      Bibliothek.* Leipzig: Breitkopf und Härtel, 1882.
      4 vols. (Reprint--Wiesbaden: Sändig, 1970.) ISBN
      3-500-21920-9 ML 134 W134 O29
      Consists of 10,180 numbered entries: the writings of
      Wagner himself (including letters and documents as well
      as prose works) and most of what was written about him
      and his music during his lifetime. Covers translations,
      photos and portraits, books, articles, reviews of
      performances, etc. Some of the books are annotated,
      and periodical articles are summarized. Name index in
      each volume.

489. *Internationale Wagner-Bibliographie, 1944-55-* . Hrsg.
        Herbert Barth. Bayreuth: Edition Musica, 1956- .
        56p. ML 134 W134 I6. Continuations, ed. Herbert
        Barth, or by his son Henrik: 1956-60 (142p.); 1961-
        66 (99p.); 1967-78 (175p.). Publisher varies.
        Selective lists of writings in French, German, and
        English, grouped by language, with name indexes. Special
        features in the various volumes; e.g., 1945-55 has an
        international discography, performance statistics for
        the Wagner operas by major opera companies, and descrip-
        tions of important collections; 1956-60 includes per-
        formance data for all the Bayreuth Festival performances,
        1876-1960, with names of all singers in each role.

*Wagner's prose writings have attracted much scholarly atten-
tion. A collective publication was issued under his direction
as* Gesammelte Schriften und Dichtungen *(Leipzig: Breitkopf
und Härtel, 1871-73; 9 vols.), and in a revised edition with
an additional volume--also supervised by Wagner--in 1883.
Reprints of 1887 and 1897 were identified as the 3d and 4th
editions; but the next issue with new material was the*
Sämtliche Schriften und Dichtungen, *hrsg. Hans von Wolzogen
and Richard Sternfeld (1911; 12 vols.). This edition was
translated into English by W.A. Ellis as* Richard Wagner's
Prose Works *(London, 1892-1900; 8 vols.). Details on the
contents of these editions are summarized clearly in* Baker's
(103). The New Grove *account could hardly be more obscure.*
        Wagner's tale of his own life is inscribed in two works:
Mein Leben *(München: Bruckmann, 1911; 2 vols.)--best presented
in Martin Gregor-Dellin's critical edition (München: List,
1969; 2 vols.; reprinted 1976). This autobiography covers
the years 1813-64. Later years are treated in* Das braune
Buch, *published in complete form under editorship of Joachim
Bergfeld (Zürich: Atlantis, 1975) and in English translation
by George Bird:* The Diary of Richard Wagner, 1865-1882; The
Brown Book *(London: Cambridge University Press, 1980). Contents include diary entries for 1865-68, and sketches for
works--some later completed, like* Parsifal, *others abandoned--
with philosophic notes and miscellaneous telegraphic comments.
The English version has 202 footnotes and an index of names,
topics, and titles.*
        *Recently there have been some useful presentations of
Wagner's ideas in topical/historical formats:*

490. Wagner, Richard. *Wagner on Music and Drama; A Com-
        pendium of Richard Wagner's Prose Works*. Sel. and

arr. Albert Goldman and Evert Sprinchorn. Trans. H.
Ashton Ellis. New York: Dutton, 1964. 447p.
ML 410 W1 A134
Described in the introduction as "an integrated presentation of the whole of Wagner's thought by means of an
arrangement of key pieces in passages drawn from many
sources ... fitted together so that they can be read as
continuous systematic exposition." The concept is
reasonably well implemented; but the effort is flawed
by the paucity of notes and lack of an index.

491. Hürlimann, Martin. *Richard Wagner in Selbstzeugnissen
    und im Urteil der Zeitgenossen*. Zürich: Manesse,
    1972. 412p. ML 410 W2 H89
    Offers Wagner's opinions and recollections of events
    in contrast with views by contemporary critics and
    musicians (Schumann, Berlioz, Hanslick, etc.), as well
    as observations by Minna and Mathilde. Weak bibliog-
    raphy of about 20 items, incomplete data. Name and
    title index.

492. Glass, Frank W. *The Fertilizing Seed: Wagner's Concept
    of the Poetic Intent*. Ann Arbor, Mich.: UMI Research,
    1983. xi, 320p. ML 410 W19 G46
    Not seen. Publisher's announcement describes it as
    the "first in-depth study in English of all of Wagner's
    writings dealing with the relationship between text
    and music." A "new understanding" of Wagner's "concept
    of the poetic intent" is proposed.

The principal biography is:

493. Newman, Ernest. *Life of Richard Wagner*. New York:
    Knopf, 1933-46. 4 vols. (Reprint--New York: Cam-
    bridge University Press, 1976.) ML 410 W1 N52
    A well-documented, interesting account. Quotations
    from letters and other materials are given in English
    translation only. The bibliography is poor; about 150
    items with incomplete data. Expansive index of names,
    titles, and topics in each volume.

A more recent biography of substance is not entirely satis-
factory:

494.   Westernhagen, Curt von. *Wagner*. 2. Aufl. Zürich:
       Atlantis, 1979. 601p. ISBN 3-7611-0287-9
       ML 410 W1 W52 W1. In English: *Wagner: A Biography*.
       Trans. Mary Whittall. New York: Cambridge University
       Press, 1978. 2 vols. xiii, 327; x, 325p.
       ML 410 W1 W52 W12
          First edition was 1968. A scholarly, footnoted work,
       citing letters and primary documents. Detailed life-
       chronology; a plain work-list, with page references
       but no facts. Meager bibliography of about 150 items,
       incomplete data. Name index only (the English edition
       has an expansive index of names and titles). Problems
       with Westernhagen's book are that it does not account
       for much recent scholarship, although it does advance
       beyond Newman in some respects (e.g., coverage of
       Cosima's diaries); and it is frequently unreliable re-
       garding facts. Compared with Newman's detached manner,
       Westernhagen appears more than a little adulatory about
       his subject.

Of a fairly large number of shorter biographies published
lately, a few seem worth mentioning:

495.   Chancellor, John. *Wagner*. Boston: Little, Brown;
       London: Weidenfeld & Nicolson, 1978. x, 310p. ISBN
       0-316-13622-0 (Boston), 0-29777-4298 (London)
       ML 410 W1 C43
          An adequate narrative in short, informal format.
       A few footnotes. A life chronology is the main reference
       feature. Weak bibliography of some 30 items, incom-
       plete data. Good expansive index of names and titles.

496.   Watson, Derek. *Richard Wagner: A Biography*. London:
       Dent, 1979. 352p. ISBN 0-460-03166-X ML 410 W1 W338
          A general work, without footnotes, presenting a dis-
       passionate view of Wagner's personality. Considerable
       commentary on the prose writings; nothing about the
       music. Appendix of biographical sketches describing
       persons of consequence in the narrative. Bibliography
       of about 120 entries, incomplete data. Partly expansive
       index of names and titles.

497. Taylor, Ronald. *Richard Wagner: His Life, Art and Thought*. London: Paul Elek, 1979. 285p. ISBN 0-2364-0071 ML 410 W13 T24

A good introduction: sympathetic to Wagner but not adulatory. Strong in background matters, such as the 1848 Revolution and its consequences, Bavarian politics, etc.

A biography that rests on the intellectual currents of the times:

498. Gutman, Robert W. *Richard Wagner: The Man, His Mind, and His Music*. London: Secker & Warburg; New York: Harcourt, 1968. xx, 490p. ML 410 W1 G83

The author states his purpose: "to see Wagner in terms of ideas--of cultural history." He aims at laypeople, however, and offers what is essentially a chronological life story, without reference footnotes, with discussion of Wagner's prose work dominating. Gutman is uneasy in the face of macrostructural questions; "one can feel, not demonstrate, the strength of his formal logic." The Lorenz demonstrations are set aside as "protracted and tortuous." Excellent bibliography of about 500 items; a good expansive index.

This is a useful supplement to the regular biographies:

499. Mack, Dietrich, and Egon Voss. *Richard Wagner. Leben und Werk in Daten und Bildern*. Frankfurt: Insel, 1978. 271p. ISBN 345-8320-342 ML 410 W196 R51

A picture book, consisting of 206 plates, with commentary. Shows Wagner's scores, manuscripts, places, programs, and persons. Good detailed chronology; list of the prose writings. No index.

Wagner's wife, Cosima, sheds important light on his life as much as on her own, in diaries published recently for the first time:

500. Wagner, Cosima. *Cosima Wagner's Diaries*. Ed. and annotated Martin Gregor-Dellin and Dietrich Mack. Trans. with an Introduction by Geoffrey Skelton. New York

and London: Harcourt Brace Jovanovich, 1977-78.   2
vols.   ISBN 0-15-122635-0   ML 410 W11 C5253
     The original German: *Cosima Wagner. Die Tagebücher,
1869-1877, 1878-1883* (München and Zürich: Piper, 1976-
77).   Her daily jottings concern domestic matters to
some degree, but also bring hundreds of vignettes and
remarks of Richard--giving a highly personal impression
of his contorted character and extravagant biases.   The
English version benefits from extensive annotations by
Skelton.   List of works cited; name index.

*The literature on Wagner's music may be divided into two
categories: material on history and production of the operas,
and analytical studies.   In the first category four books
are of special interest:*

501.   Osborne, Charles.   *The World Theater of Wagner.   A Cele-
          bration of 150 Years of Wagner Productions.*   New York:
          Macmillan, 1982.   224p.   ISBN 0-02-594050-3   MT 100 W208
          An illustrated narrative account of production in
       Vienna, Bayreuth, Hamburg, Berlin, New York, London,
       San Francisco, Buenos Aires, etc.   Biographical sketches
       of important individuals.   Name and title index.

502.   Petzet, Michael, and Detta Petzet.   *Die Richard Wagner
          Bühne König Ludwigs II.*   München: Prestel, 1970.
          840p.   ML 410 W11 P5
          Documents on the Munich premieres and early stagings
       of nine operas and of *Parsifal* at Bayreuth, with much
       production detail.   Views of King Ludwig; correspondence
       and miscellaneous essays.   Features 771 fine plates.
       Name index.

503.   Jung, Ute.   *Die Rezeption der Kunst Richard Wagners in
          Italien.*   Regensburg: Bosse, 1974.   524p.   ISBN
          3-7649-2076-9   ML 410 W1 J95
          A thorough description of productions at Bologna,
       La Scala, and elsewhere in Italy, with critical recep-
       tion and other contemporary writing about the music.
       Extends from early performances to our own time.   Ex-
       cellent footnotes lead into the entire relevant litera-
       ture, which is enumerated in a 700-item bibliography
       (unfortunately giving incomplete data).   Partly ex-
       pansive index of names, titles, and topics.

504. Bauer, Oswald Georg. *Richard Wagner: Die Bühnenwerke
      von der Uraufführung bis Heute*. Frankfurt: Propyläen,
      1982. 288p. ISBN 3-549-06658-9 ML 410 W19 B38
      Presents illustrated production histories for all the
      music dramas. Bibliography on production matters, about
      75 entries, incomplete data. Index of names and places.

*Two works cited earlier give information on the Festival at
Bayreuth: 73 and 167. These full-length studies offer richer
detail:*

505. Mayer, Hans. *Richard Wagner in Bayreuth, 1876-1976.*
      Stuttgart: Belser, 1976. 248p. ISBN 3-7630-9018-5
      ML 410 W2 M46
      An English translation by Jack Zipes, with the same
      title, is available (New York: Rizzoli, 1976). It is
      a large photobook, with ample commentary in historical
      sequence. Some comments on previous writings, but no
      notes. Name index.

506. Karbaum, Michael. *Studien zur Geschichte der Bayreuther
      Festspiele. Hundert Jahre Bayreuth.* Regensburg:
      Bosse, 1976. 106, 158p. ISBN 3-7649-2060-2
      ML 410 W15 K18
      A thorough, footnoted history of the Festival, with
      pertinent documents reprinted. Bibliography of about
      50 items, incomplete data. No index.

507. Skelton, Geoffrey. *Wagner at Bayreuth.* 2d ed. London
      and New York: White Lion, 1976. 251p. ML 410 W2 S55
      (Reprint--New York: Da Capo, 1983.) ISBN 0-306-76157-2
      A popular history, without notes. Useful list of
      productions, singers, and their roles, 1876-1975. Bib-
      liography of about 50 entries, incomplete data. Ex-
      pansive index of names and titles.

In the large category of musical analyses the seminal work is:

508. Lorenz, Alfred Ottokar. *Das Geheimnis der Form bei
      Richard Wagner.* Berlin: Hesse, 1924-33. 4 vols.
      (Reprint--Tutzing: Schneider, 1966.) ML 410 W22 L86
      It was Lorenz who pioneered the concept that large-
      scale works are built from the same formal patterns as

small works; that the simple ABA and AAB forms are
found, extended over long time spans, in operatic structures. His ideas, and his imaginative application of
them to the Wagner music dramas, have aroused much con-
troversy. Modern scholarship seems to be turning away
from Lorenzian analytic technique, while embracing his
fundamental view that structure can be discovered in
large works. One scholar who has modeled his approach
on Lorenz is Siegmund Levarie (cf. 345). A negative
appraisal appears in Bailey's study of the *Ring* (527).
See also Abraham (531n), Coren (532n), and Parker and
Brown (469n).

509.   Newman, Ernest. *The Wagner Operas*. New York: Knopf,
         1949. xii, 724p. MT 100 W2 N53
         British title: *Wagner Nights*. Detailed program notes
       on all the post-*Rienzi* works. Much attention to the
       Leitmotive; many musical examples (198 of them for the
       Ring). Does not attempt structural analysis. No bib-
       liography; index of names and titles.

510.   Dahlhaus, Carl. *Wagners Konzeption des musikalischen
         Dramas*. Regensburg: Bosse, 1971. 124p. ISBN 3-764-920
         610 ML 410 W13 D13
         A useful introduction to Wagner's intentions regarding
       music drama; form and motives in the *Ring* (taking up
       micro- and macrostructure, with attention to Lorenz,
       who is denounced as unconvincing); and the music as
       drama. Footnotes; no index.

511.   ————. *Richard Wagners Musikdramen*. Velber: Friedrich,
         1971. 163p. ML 410 W13 D153 Also in English:
         Richard Wagner's Music Dramas. Trans. Mary Whittall.
         New York: Cambridge University Press, 1979. 161p.
         ISBN 0-521-22397-0
         Concise essays on the motives and structures of the
       operas, relying much on the Lorenzian idea of large
       forms based on the AAB and ABA principles. Considerable
       character analysis, of Siegfried, Brünnhilde, etc., done
       with great insight. No footnotes, bibliography, or
       index.

512.   Bailey, Robert. "The Evolution of Wagner's Compositional
         Procedure After *Lohengrin*." *Proceedings* of the Elevent

Congress of the International Musicological Society,
Copenhagen, 1972, pp. 240-245. Copenhagen: Hansen,
1974. ISBN 87-7455-026-8 ML 26 I61
Considers changes in interrelations between drafts
and final full scores. Beginning in 1856, with *Siegfried*, Wagner added second drafts before going to the
full score.

513. Mander, Raymond, and Joe Mitchenson. *The Wagner Com-
        panion*. London: Allen; New York: Hawthorn, 1978.
        x, 265p. ISBN 0-8015-8356-X (New York) ML 410 W13 M27
        Production histories, with good illustrations; glos-
    sary of the names of the characters; discography of all
    complete recordings in print. Name and title index;
    useless bibliography of about 30 titles, incomplete
    data. Note that the next entry has the same name.

514. *The Wagner Companion*. Ed. Peter Burbidge and Richard
        Sutton. London: Faber and Faber; New York: Cambridge
        University Press, 1979. 462p. ISBN 0-521-227879
        ML 410 W13 W137
        Essays by various scholars, dealing with the literary
    and musical background for the operas, the Leitmotiv
    and some of the less-obvious elements of the musical
    language, the music drama as total work of art, etc.
    Robert Bailey makes an important contribution with
    "The Method of Composition," continuing the line of
    thought in his "Siegfrieds Tod" article (527n). A
    useful study by Geoffrey Skelton on the founding of
    Bayreuth is also worth noticing; but most of the content
    of this volume is derivative or otherwise unsatisfying.
    Backnotes; bibliography of about 350 entries, incomplete
    data, some annotations; good expansive index of names
    and subjects.

*The remaining citations in this section deal with individual
works.*

The Flying Dutchman

515. Machlin, Paul Stuart. "Genesis, Revisions and Publica-
        tions History of Wagner's Flying Dutchman." Ph.D.

dissertation. University of California, Berkeley,
1975. 233p.
  Not examined. In *RILM Abstracts*, 9-1/2 (January-
August 1975): 82, the author summary states that he has
compared all the sketches in order to "reconstruct the
work's genesis." He also compares the printed editions,
concluding that a new one is needed. Machlin also has
an important article: "Wagner, Durand and 'The Flying
Dutchman': The 1852 Revisions of the Overture." *Music
and Letters*, 55-4 (October 1974): 410-428.

Lohengrin

*What appears to be an important dissertation was not available
for appraisal:*

516. Cramer, Thomas. "Lohengrin, Edition und Untersuchung."
        Habilitationschrift, Karlsruhe Universität, 1971.
        598p. Published--München: Fink, 1971.
          The *RILM Abstracts* account by the author (10-2, May-
        August 1976: 177) describes it as "a critical edition
        of Lohengrin based on all available manuscripts. Dis-
        proves the theory that the story stems from two authors.
        Traces the legend of the swan children and the knight
        of the swan in France, Flanders, and the Lower Rhine
        and in Germany. Discusses the question of dates....
        Investigates the allegory...."

Die Meistersinger

517. Csampai, Attila, and Dietmar Holland, eds. *Die Meister-
        singer von Nürnberg: Texte, Materialen, Kommentare.*
        Reinbeck: Rowohlt Taschenbuch, 1981. 281p. ISBN
        3-499-17419-7 ML 50 W13 M5 C9
          One of the "Rororo Opernbücher." It gives the German
        libretto; genesis of the work; letters (Wagner to
        Mathilde Wesendonk); premiere and production history
        to 1960; essays by Hanslick, Thomas Mann, Carl Dahlhaus,
        and others. Chronology, 1813-88; discography; bibliog-
        raphy of about 50 items; no index.

518. Mey, Curt. *Der Meistergesang in Geschichte und Kunst.*
        2. Aufl. Leipzig: H. Seeman, 1901. xvi, 392p.
        (Reprint--Walluf: Sändig, 1973.) ISBN 3-500-27350-5
        ML 183 M61

A general study of Meistersingers in history and art,
with a long section (pp. 271-390) on the opera; covers
poetic and metrical form, appearance of motives, text
problems, sources, and other aspects. No index.

519. McDonald, William E. "Words, Music, and Dramatic Development in *Die Meistersinger*." *19th Century Music*, 1-3
(March 1978): 246-260.
A useful examination of the story and personages, most
interesting for a character appraisal of Hans Sachs.

Parsifal

520. Beckett, Lucy. *Richard Wagner: Parsifal*. New York:
Cambridge University Press, 1981. viii, 163p.
ISBN 0-521-22825-5 ML 410 W17 B37
One of the "Cambridge Opera Handbooks," in their
usual format: synopsis, program notes, sources, production history, critical opinions. Discography, giving
label numbers and principal singers; bibliography of
incomplete data on 19 titles. Name and topic index.

521. Geck, Martin, and Egon Voss. *Dokumente zur Entstehung
und ersten Aufführung des Bühnenweihfestspiels Parsifal*.
Mainz: Schott, 1970. 261p. ML 410 W145 G44 (Richard
Wagner. Sämtliche Werke, 30.)
Presents the source material on the opera: the musical
and prose sketches; and documents concerning the 1882
performances. Index.

Avant-scène opéra, 38/39 (1982), is about Parsifal.

Rienzi

522. Deathridge, John. *Wagner's Rienzi: A Reappraisal Based
on a Study of Sketches and Drafts*. Oxford: Clarendon
Press, 1977. xvii, 199p. ISBN 0-19-816131-X
ML 410 W132 D28
Based on his Oxford dissertation (1974). A thorough
discussion of all sources: sketches, drafts, fragments
(with clear distinctions among categories; a useful
approach to terminological consistency), with their
library locations. Comparison of the draft with the

vocal score of Gustav Klink (1844). All previous
literature is considered; there are 199 backnotes in
the main text and 29 in the appendix. German passages
are not translated. Bibliography of about 75 entries;
name and title index.

Der Ring des Nibelungen

The writings mentioned first deal with the Ring *cycle as a
whole; discussions of the individual operas follow.*

523. Cord, William O. *An Introduction to Richard Wagner's
        Der Ring des Nibelungen: A Handbook.* Athens: Ohio
        University Press, 1983. 163p. ISBN 0-8214-0648-5
        ML 410 W1 A289
        A convenient general introduction in popular style;
        sensible program notes on each opera; no musical examples
        or analysis. Chronological table for Wagner's works,
        with dates of literary sources, sketches, premieres,
        etc. Discography of complete recordings; bibliography
        of English writings, about 150 entries. No index.

524. Donington, Robert. *Wagner's "Ring" and Its Symbols;
        the Music and the Myth.* Rev. ed. New York: St.
        Martin, 1974. 342p. ML 410 W15 D6. In German:
        *Richard Wagners Ring des Nibelungen und seine Symbole.
        Musik und Mythos.* Stuttgart: Reclam, 1976.
        First published 1963. One of the most controversial
        books in modern opera literature. Donington presents
        an ingenious interpretation of the story and characters
        in Jungian terms (e.g., Fricka is said to function as
        if she were [Wotan's] super-ego personified). See also
        comments above in the annotation for Donington's *The
        Opera* (21n). Provocative musical analyses follow from
        the author's premises; there are 91 examples of motives
        with discussion. Annotated bibliography of about 150
        items. Index of names, characters, themes, and topics.

525. Cooke, Deryck. *I Saw the World End: A Study of Wagner's
        Ring.* London: Oxford University Press, 1979. 360p.
        ISBN 0-193153181 ML 410 W15 C77
        The theme of this book is the mythological base for
        the story; the approach includes serious attention to
        Wagner's intent, as well as the resulting "overt meaning

Cooke--who died before completing this work--examines
the characters and their motivations, relating all to
the sagas. He reviews the previous literature very
critically, taking issue with Donington in particular.
Bibliography is rudimentary: about 35 entries, with
incomplete data. Expansive index of names, titles,
topics, and characters.

526. Westernhagen, Curt von. *Die Entstehung des Ring*. Zürich:
     Atlantis, 1973. 294p. ML 410 W15 W1853. In English:
     The Forging of the Ring. Trans. Mary Whittall. New
     York: Cambridge University Press, 1976. viii, 248p.
     ISBN 0-5212-12936.
     An important study of Wagner's sketches--more than 800
     pages--with all passages compared with final versions
     of the score. Modifications are dated and analyzed.
     Bibliography of works consulted gives incomplete data
     for about 70 items. Name index.

527. Bailey, Robert. "The Structure of the *Ring* and Its
     Evolution." *19th Century Music*, 1-1 (July 1977):
     48-61. ML 1 N714
     A fine, brief account of the composer at work. Con-
     sideration of tonal planning in terms of associative
     keys and macrostructure; presents an anti-Lorenz point
     of view. An earlier contribution by Bailey, "Wagner's
     Musical Sketches for *Siegfried's Tod*," *Studies in Music
     History: Essays for Oliver Strunk*, ed. Harold Powers
     (Princeton, N.J.: Princeton University Press, 1968),
     pp. 459-494, clarifies the relation between sketches
     and the final version of *Siegfried's Tod*--Wagner's first
     name for the *Ring*--and parallel segments of the *Ring*
     sketches and last version. One of Bailey's observa-
     tions--about the time interval between *Siegfried* and
     Götterdammerung--inspired a most interesting study by
     Kenneth G. Chapman: "Siegfried and Brünnhilde and the
     Passage of Time in Wagner's Ring," *Current Musicology*,
     32 (1981): 43-58.

528. Deathridge, John. "Wagner's Sketches for the 'Ring';
     Some Recent Studies." *Musical Times*, 118 (May 1977):
     383-389. ML 5 M9863
     Primarily a commentary on the work of Westernhagen,
     with attention to analyses by Robert Bailey and others.
     He faults Westernhagen for claiming to have examined all

the sketches, observing that certain categories were
omitted. (Deathridge has made a useful contribution
in this regard by defining the diverse types of drafts
and sketches in the Wagnerian sources; cf. his article,
"The Nomenclature of Wagner's Sketches," *Proceedings of
the Royal Musical Association*, 101 [1974-1975], and his
book on *Rienzi*, 522 above.) He concludes that no study
has yet presented an overall convincing account of how
the *Ring* evolved.

*For a less erudite, but valuable and interesting, approach to
the cycle we have the volumes of Avant-scène opéra (6, 7, 8,
12, 13, and 14), which present their usual varied format.*
*A well-known older commentary is still of interest, perhaps
mostly for its style and vigor.*

529.   Shaw, George Bernard. *The Perfect Wagnerite; A Commen-
           tary on the Niblung's Ring*. London: Richards, 1898.
           xviii, 151p. MT 100 W25 S53
           A clever socialist interpretation, aimed at general
       readers. Without notes or index.

Das Rheingold

530.   Knapp, J. Merrill. "The Instrumentation Draft of
           Wagner's *Das Rheingold*." *Journal of the American
           Musicological Society*, 30-2 (Summer 1977): 272-295.
           ML 27 U5 A83363
           Describes and discusses the Wagner manuscript at
       Princeton University in the light of materials at Bay-
       reuth. Compares the format and details with the full
       score. Useful footnote references on the terminology
       of drafts and on the validity of the collections of
       letters.

Die Walküre

This dissertation was not seen:

531.   Jenkins, John Edward. "The Leitmotiv 'Sword' in 'Die
           Walküre.'" Ph.D. dissertation. University of Souther
           Mississippi, 1978. 160p.

Number 8 of Avant-scène opéra is on this work. In his A Hundred Years of Music *(3d ed.; Chicago: Aldine, 1964) Gerald*

Abraham presents a readable technical introduction to Wag-
nerian procedures, with detailed analyses--following Lorenz
closely--of Walküre. *The picture given of Lorenz is very*
positive.

Siegfried

532. McCreless, Patrick Phillip. *Wagner's Siegfried.* Ann
     Arbor, Mich.: UMI Research, 1981. 248p. ISBN
     0-8357-1361-X ML 410 W15 M35
     Based on the author's dissertation (University of
     Rochester, 1981). A thorough analysis of the work's
     genesis and musical structure at micro- and macrolevels.
     85 notes. Bibliography of about 125 entries. Name,
     title, and topic index in expansive form.

A curious dissertation by Daniel Henry Coren, "A Study of
Richard Wagner's Siegfried" (University of California, Berkeley,
1971), seems based on a determination to show that "the Ring
is not a vast organic entity" but a collection of internally
unified discrete scenes. He has strongly negative views of
the Lorenz school (Levarie's approach to Marriage of Figaro
is classified as "wrong-headed"), but his own attempts at
analysis are indeed rather Lorenzian.

Götterdämmerung

Avant-scène opéra, *13-14, give a good treatment of this work.*

Tannhäuser

533. Abbate, Carolyn. "The Parisian 'Vénus' and the 'Paris'
     Tannhäuser." *Journal of the American Musicological*
     Society, 36-1 (Spring 1983): 73-123. ML 27 U5 A83363
     The two versions discussed are the Dresden (1845;
     revised 1845-47) and Paris (1861). What is now known as
     the Paris version is what was given in Munich in 1867
     and Vienna in 1875. Differences are analyzed closely,
     with details of the revision process. Full of valuable
     insights into the compositional act and into structural
     questions. All important editions and secondary litera-
     ture are cited in 42 footnotes. Texts of 11 letters
     are in an appendix.

Tristan und Isolde

534. Bailey, Robert. "The Genesis of Tristan and Isolde,
        and a Study of Wagner's Sketches and Drafts for the
        First Act." Ph.D. dissertation. Princeton University,
        1969. 390p.
            Not seen. According to the author, in *RILM Abstracts*,
        3-3 (September-December 1969): 52, he examined the musical
        and prose sketches, plus all drafts and worksheets,
        and was able to derive "the full story of how *Tristan*
        was put together act by act." He also offered a contri-
        bution toward "a new musical and dramatic analysis of
        the first act."

535. Zuckerman, Elliott. *The First Hundred Years of Tristan.*
        New York: Columbia University Press, 1964. xiv, 235p.
        ML 410 W1 Z8
            Deals with various topics: sources of the music and of
        the legend; the impact of early performances; Nietzsche;
        influence on symbolist poets and novelists; 20th-century
        analytic approaches. An appendix gives the premiere
        dates of *Tristan* and the other operas in major cities.
        Notes, but no bibliography. Expansive index of names,
        titles, and topics.

Avant-scène opéra, *34-35, give many perspectives on* Tristan.
There is also an "English National Opera Guide" (188).

Carl Maria von Weber
(1786-1826)

536. Warrack, John Hamilton. *Carl Maria von Weber.* 2d ed.
        Cambridge, Eng.: Cambridge University Press, 1976.
        411p. ISBN 0-5212-13541 ML 410 Ws W26
            First edition was 1968. German translation of that
        edition as *Carl Maria von Weber. Eine Biographie*
        (Hamburg: Claassen, 1972). A useful life story,
        citing major documents, letters, and other primary
        sources; bibliographic essay on the sources and on
        critical studies. Program notes on the six major
        operas, with attention to genesis and reception. Work-
        list; a chapter (second edition only) on Weber's style
        and historical significance. Musical examples. Poor
        bibliography detracts from the value of this work: it
        has about 100 incomplete entries, many of them trivial,

and omits important writing, such as the Gras dissertation (540 below). Index of names, titles, and places.

537. Weber, Carl Maria von. *Writings on Music.* Trans. Martin Cooper. Ed. John Warrack. Cambridge, Eng.: Cambridge University Press, 1981. 402p. ISBN 0-521-22892-1
     ML 410 W3 A37
     A collection of reviews, articles, and open letters to journals; interesting insights and critical opinions. Biographical glossary, footnote comments, and name index.

538. Hürlimann, Martin. *Carl Maria von Weber in seinen Schriften und in zeitgenössichen Dokumenten.* Zürich: Manesse, 1973. 301p.
     Weber's own writings, in German only; and views of contemporaries--Meyerbeer, Spohr, Goethe, Rossini, etc.-- on Weber.

539. Jones, Gaynor G. "Backgrounds and Themes of the Operas of Carl Maria von Weber." Ph.D. dissertation. Cornell University, 1972. 369p.
     Not available for examination.

540. Gras, Alfred H. "A Study of Der Freischütz by Carl Maria von Weber." Ph.D. dissertation. Northwestern University, 1968. 321p.
     This fine study seems to be the only modern full-length examination of a Weber opera. It takes up the background of the German romantic tradition, and matters of genesis, and goes on to a perceptive technical analysis. There is special attention to tonal structure. Music examples; bibliography; no index.

Kurt Weill
(1900-1950)

541. Kowalke, Kim H. *Kurt Weill in Europe.* Ann Arbor, Mich.: UMI Research, 1979. 600p. ISBN 0-8357-1076-9
     ML 410 W395 K7
     A thorough, scholarly examination of the early Weill (to 1935), concentrating on biographical and background matters. Some attention to *Dreigroschenoper* and

Mahagonny. Work-list through 1935, including literary
writings; extensive bibliography of more than 300 entries.
Expansive index of names, titles, and topics. Based on
Kowalke's Ph.D. dissertation (Yale University, 1977).

XV. OPERA IN SPECIFIC COUNTRIES AND REGIONS

*Listed in this chapter are works that provide information about
operatic composition and operatic performance, arranged geo-
graphically. The intention is to describe those works that
are specifically or primarily concerned with opera. Other
works of a more general nature, in which some operatic facts
may be found, are in most cases given only a brief citation
and a reference to the location of a full description in*
Information on Music. *To conserve space, citations are usually
omitted entirely for works in these categories, for a given
country: introductions to the music of the country; histories
of music in the country and in its cities or other subdivisions;
biographies; bibliographies and indexes. Articles in* New Grove
and in MGG *are cited only when they present some special features or otherwise require comment.*

*The reader is reminded that the content of many general
histories and other general reference works, already described
or cited in earlier chapters, includes attention to individual
countries; the annotations of those works were written with
the aim of bringing out such coverage. Cross-references from
the specific countries in the present chapter to such general
works in the earlier chapters are made only in unusual cases.*

*Names of countries are rendered in the native spelling
first, transliterated if necessary into Roman script, with
English and other names following if such forms appear in the
important literature. The names are in alphabetical order
under their English forms.*

*Before proceeding to the separate countries, it is best to
note certain works that concern several nations, i.e., Latin
America. Material presented here is not cross-referenced from
the individual countries as they appear later in the chapter.*

Latin America

This designation includes Mexico, Central America, South America, and the Caribbean.

542. Günther, Robert. *Die Musikkulturen Lateinamerikas im 19. Jahrhundert.* Regensburg: Bosse, 1982. 464p. ISBN 3-7649-2208-7 ML 199 M987
      Essays by many scholars, on individual countries (Argentina, Bolivia, Brazil, Chile, Costa Rica, Jamaica, Mexico, Puerto Rico, and Uruguay) and certain cities (Santiago de Chile, Valparaíso) and some more general studies. Long English summaries are given for each chapter. There are good footnotes, illustrations, and musical examples. Much biographical information throughout; 19th-century operatic life is well covered. Name index.

543. "Caribbean Music History. A Selective Annotated Bibliography with Musical Supplement." *Inter-American Music Review*, 4-1 (Fall 1981): 1-112. ML 1 I613
      Covers to 1975. Richly developed annotations make this list very useful, even without access to the works described. Valuable data appear passim (e.g., list of opera premieres in Haiti).

544. Stevenson, Robert Murrell. "The South American Lyric Stage (to 1800)." *Inter-American Music Bulletin*, 87 (July-October 1973): 1-27. ML 1 I57
      A scholarly account (164 footnotes), packed with useful data. Much attention to early opera in Peru. Gives synopses of major works, details of production, lists of operas by major composers.

Current periodicals that deal with Latin American music are the Inter-American Music Review, *1978- (IOM-1332j) and the* Latin American Music Review, *1980- (IOM-1332k). Noncurrent but useful periodicals are listed in IOM-0880/0883.*

Important guides to Latin American library resources are described at IOM-0897/0901.

Argentina

Two essential histories of music in the country are: Rodolfo
Arizaga, Enciclopedia de la música argentina, *1971 (IOM-0919),*
which includes an appendix list of Argentine operas; and
Vicente Gesualdo, Historia de la música en la Argentina,
1961 (IOM-0920), which gives strong coverage to opera in Buenos
Aires and presents a list of scores published in the country,
1830-1900. Operatic life has been centered in the Teatro
Colón of Buenos Aires, which opened in 1857, was destroyed in
1889, and rebuilt for a performance of Aida *on May 25, 1908.*
The most comprehensive story of the new Teatro Colón is:

545. Caamaño, Roberto. *La historia del Teatro Colón, 1908-*
       1968. Buenos Aires: Editorial Cinetea, 1969. 3 vols.
       349, 613, 503p. IOM-0941 ML 1717.8 B9 C3
       Excellent color plates make up most of the content:
       artists, scenes, costumes, and stage designs; but there
       is a useful text in the form of essays by various
       scholars. Coverage of the building itself, personnel,
       performances (all casts given), critics, etc. Composer
       and artist indexes. The same author has written several
       brief accounts of the theater (IOM-0942, 0942a, 0942b).
       A collection of documents on the theater was assembled
       by Ernesto de la Guardia and Roberto Herrera, *El arte*
       lírico en el Teatro Colón (1908-1933), 1933 (IOM-0943).

An important dissertation describes works performed:

546. Kuss, Malena. "Nativistic Strains in Argentine Operas
       Premiered at the Teatro Colón (1908-1972)." Ph.D.
       dissertation. University of California, Los Angeles,
       1976. xii, 523p.
       Considers the operas of 12 composers: Hector Panizza
       (1875-1967), Eduardo García-Mansilla (1871-1930),
       Arturo Beruti (1862-1938), Carlos López Buchardo
       (1881-1948), Floro M. Ugarte (1884-1975), Gilardo Gilardi
       (1889-1963), Athos Palma (1891-1951), Pascual de
       Rogatis (1880-   ), Felipe Boero (1884-1958), Juan José
       Castro (1895-1968), Valdo Sciamarella (1924-   ), and
       Alberto Ginastera (1916-   ). Gives a history of opera
       in Argentina, as well as technical analyses of in-
       dividual works. Musical examples; footnotes; quotations
       in Spanish with English translations. Discussion of
       opera in other Latin countries, pp. 373-386. Work-

lists of composers; bibliography of about 350 titles.
No index.

The most comprehensive chronology:

547. Fiorda Kelly, Alfredo. *Cronología de las óperas,*
      dramas líricos, oratorios, himnos, etc., cantados
      en Buenos Aires. Buenos Aires: Riera, 1934. 83p.
      IOM-0945 ML 1717.8 B9 F5
      Covers performances in all theaters, 1825-1933; ar-
      ranged by date, with lists also by composer and title;
      cast and performer information. Another useful treatise
      is Mariano Bosch, *Historia del teatro en Buenos Aires,*
      1910 (IOM-0944).

A collection of recent opera criticisms:

548. D'Urbano, Jorge. *Música en Buenos Aires.* Prefacio de
      Virgil Thomson. Buenos Aires: Editorial Sudamericana,
      1966.
      Presents the author's critiques of performances from
      1950 to 1965. Name index, with works listed under
      composer.

An interesting short study of the earliest days:

549. Gesualdo, Vicente. *Pablo Rosquellas y los orígenes de*
      la ópera en Buenos Aires. Buenos Aires: Artes en
      América, 1962. 55p. ML 1717.8 B9 G4
      Rosquellas was a singer, composer, and violinist who
      lived in the city from 1823 to 1833; he organized the
      first opera performances there. The book gives casts
      and production information on the early stagings, with
      biographical sketches of the singers and critical re-
      views; thoroughly footnoted, but without bibliography
      or index.

Australia

No literature of substance on Australian opera has been seen.
The following titles may be of some use:

550.   Cargher, John. *Opera and Ballet in Australia.*   Stanmore:
          Cassell Australia, 1977. xiii, 352p.
          ISBN 0-7269-1360-X   ML 1751 A9 C37
          Primarily a photo book, with an earthy popular commen-
          tary. Historical summary and discussion of recent per-
          formances in Melbourne and Sydney. Name and title index.

551.   *Opera and the Australian Composer.*   Ed. Kay Dreyfus.
          Camberwell, Victoria: K. Dreyfus, 1973. iv, 102p.
          ISBN 0-9598595-0   ML 1751 A9 06
          Reports on a symposium sponsored by the International
          Society for Contemporary Music. A chatty view of the
          "current scene" is too vague to be of use. An essay
          by Elizabeth Wood, "1840-1965: Precedents and Problems
          for the Australian Opera Composers," includes a few
          facts. No index.

There is a good chapter on opera in Australia in the Mackenzie
book Singers of Australia, *cited above (121).*
     The Australian Opera has issued annual reports since 1972
that give details on all productions, with photos and financial
data; none has been available for examination. During the
same period a publication entitled Sydney Opera House Monthly
Diary *was issued; it would appear to be a chronicle of events*
(none seen). On the new opera house itself there have been
numerous articles published (see list in Stoddard, 53); this
one seems to cover the main points:

552.   Hubble, Ava. *More than an Opera House.*   Sydney: Sydney
          Opera House, 1978. 67p.
          Not seen; described in *RILM Abstracts*, 12-2 (1978),
          as an illustrated booklet on "planning, design, con-
          struction, decoration, management, financing, organiza-
          tion and uses" of the center; with dimensions, facili-
          ties, photographs, and notes on artists and others
          associated with the complex.

Austria

The vast literature on opera in Austria, especially in Vienna, can be represented here by only a few useful works. A larger selection, including materials of wider scope in which opera has its place, will be found in IOM-1576/1643. This handbook forms a convenient entry point:

553. Goertz, Harald. *Österreichisches Musikhandbuch.* Wien:
      Jugend & Volk, 1971. 349p. IOM-1625 ISBN
      3-7141-6910-5 ML 21 G6
      A guidebook presentation of organizations and events,
      including opera houses and companies, artists, and
      festivals. Locations of memorials to musicians. Index
      of topics and organizations. See also the guidebook
      by Brody and Brook (67).

Concert and opera reviews are found in several periodicals (see list in Brody), of which this is the best known:

554. *Österreichische Musikzeitschrift.* 1- . January
      1946- . Wien: H. Bauer, 1946- . (Monthly.)
      ML 5 0 1983
      Includes some scholarly articles as well as short
      feature articles; all musical topics are covered, with
      emphasis on Austria. Calendars and reviews of per-
      formances in Austria and neighboring countries; reviews
      of books and discs.

Three scholarly histories of opera in Vienna:

555. Pirchan, Emil, et al. *300 Jahre Wiener Operntheater;
      Werk und Werden.* Wien: Fortuna, 1953. 312p.
      IOM-1592. ML 1723.8
      Covers all stage presentations from the Baroque
      onward. Biographies; bibliography of about 120 items;
      233 plates; name index.

556. Witeschnik, Alexander. *Wiener Opernkunst von den
      Anfängen bis zu Karajan.* Wien: Kremayr & Scherian,
      1959. 332p. IOM-1953 ML 1723.8 V6 W55

Surveys operatic history from the beginnings; illustrated with nine plates and black-and-white photos and
drawings. Bibliography, index.

557. Wallaschek, Richard. *Das K.K. Hofoperntheater. Die
Theater Wiens*, v. 4. Wien: Gesellschaft für Verviel-
fältigende Kunst, 1899-1909. 4 vols. in 6. IOM-1594
PN 2216 V5 T4
The fourth volume of a general history of Viennese
theater is about opera and musical life. Includes
narrative account and performance chronologies for the
Kärtnerthortheater, 1763-1870; Hofoperntheater, 1869-94.
List of operas and the number of their performances,
1869-94. Bibliography of about 130 titles; name and
title index.

A long scholarly study of early opera in the city:

558. Wellesz, Egon. "Die Opern und Oratorien in Wien von
1600-1708." *Studien zur Musikwissenschaft* 6 (1919):
5:138. M2 D42
A narrative account, with a list of about 60 operas
given and their dates. Chapters on instrumental music
in the operas, on individual composers (Badia, Ziani,
the Bononcinis), vocal forms, libretti, and structure
of the aria. Musical examples; notes; no index.

*The Hofoper became the Staatsoper in 1918. This is the famous
Vienna Opera, Das Wiener Opernhaus. It was destroyed in a
bombing raid on 12 March 1945; rebuilt and opened again on
5 November 1955. The principal histories of the house and
its productions are:*

559. Beetz, Wilhelm. *Das Wiener Opernhaus, 1869 bis 1945.*
2. Aufl. Wien: Panorama, 1955. 288p. IOM-1597
ML 1723.8 V62 0 73
First edition (only one seen) was 1949. A statistical
history, with many lists and tables: complete record of
performances of 337 German operas and Singspiele; 42
Italian and French operas; ballets and other stage
works, 1869-1919. Lists of directors and performers,
including orchestral musicians, by nationality and by
instrument or specialty. Table of titles of all works

given, with premiere and later productions of each year,
1869-1944; chronology of notable performances, 1926-44.
80 plates, showing interior and exterior of the building.
Access to all the data is slow, since there is no index.

560.   Haas, Robert. *Die Wiener Oper*. Wien and Budapest:
          Eligius, 1926. 70p. and plates. ML 1723.8 V62 S825
          A useful concise history in narrative style. Much in-
       formation on design and construction of the 1869
       building, including names of painters and sculptors,
       etc. The architects, August Siccard von Siccardsburg
       and Eduard van der Null, receive considerable attention.
       59 plates show much detail of doorways, statuary, salons,
       lunettes, and exteriors. No index.

561.   Hadamowsky, Franz. *Die Wiener Hoftheater (Staatstheater)*,
          1776-1966. Wien: G. Prachner, 1966-75. 2 vols.
          PN 2616 W7 H2
          A well-documented narrative account of the Oper and
       its predecessor, the Hoftheater. Includes a list of
       performances from 1811 to 1974, with staff--but not the
       casts--identified. Name indexes.

*Three popular histories of the Oper have been translated into
English:*

562.   Klein, Rudolf. *Die Wiener Staatsoper*. Wien: Lafite,
          1967. 80p. IOM-1589 ML 1723.8 V62 S83. In English:
          The Vienna State Opera. Vienna: Lafite, 1969.
          Well illustrated; includes a list of premieres, 1869-
       1969, and a list of the opera directors.

563.   Kralik, Heinrich. *Die Wiener Oper*. Wien: Brüder
          Rosenbaum, 1962. 189p. IOM-1590 ML 1723.8 V6 K7.
          In English: *The Vienna Opera*. Vienna: Brüder Rosen-
          baum; dist. in New York by Heinman, 1963.
          A narrative history with fine illustrations, including
       drawings and watercolors of the star singers. Name
       index.

564.   Prawy, Marcel. *Die Wiener Oper*. Zürich: Molden, 1969.
          228p. IOM-1591 ML 1723.8 V62 O 775. In English:

The Vienna Opera. New York: Praeger; Wien: Molden,
1969.
Emphasizes 20th-century personalities; portraits of
about 150 of them. Lavishly illustrated. Name index.

*Vienna is well supplied with other theaters and concert halls.
An inventory of 576 larger auditoriums is given in Georg Butter-
weck,* Veranstaltungssäle in Wien, 1973 *(IOM-1600). Aside from
the Oper, the principal houses are the Kärtnerthortheater
(see item 557 above), the Burgtheater, and the Theater an
der Wien; there is a good history of the last named:*

565. Bauer, Anton. *150 Jahre Theater an der Wien.* Zürich:
        Amalthea, 1952. 515p. IOM-1598 ML 1723.8 V62 O 72
        The Theater opened 13 June 1801. From late 1945 to
      1954 it housed the productions of the Wiener Oper,
      while that building was being reconstructed. This is
      a scholarly narrative history, with a large foldout
      plan and other good illustrations. Performance chronology,
      1801-1939 and 1945-51, without casts. Name and topic
      index.

Some updating of Bauer is provided by:

566. Lang, Attila. *Das Theater an der Wien. Vom Singspiel
        zum Musical.* 2. Aufl. Wien and München: Jugend und
        Volk, 1977. 134p. ISBN 3-7141-6096-5
        ML 1723.8 V6 T55 L2
        A footnoted review of light opera (Lortzing, Kálmán,
      Offenbach, and other standard composers, plus recent
      works like *Gigi* and *Pippin*), with a chronology of pre-
      mieres; a chronology of all performances 6 October 1945
      to 11 March 1976; and a list of directors, 1801-1965.
      No bibliography. Name index.

There is an interesting article on the Burgtheater:

567. Heartz, Daniel. "Nicolas Jadot and the Building of
        the Burgtheater." *Musical Quarterly,* 68-1 (January
        1982): 1-31. ML 5 M98
        The theater opened 14 May 1748; opera flourished there
      throughout the 18th century. After 1801, and the opening

of Theater an der Wien, the Burgtheater began to be used
more for spoken drama (it is now the State Theater for
that genre) but was still the site of many important
productions in the 19th century until the opening of
the Hofoper (i.e., the Wiener Staatsoper of today) in
1869. Jean Nicolas Jadot was the architect. The article
gives pictures and floor plans, plus useful notes on
early works performed.

*Many writers have been inspired to compile lists of opera
premieres and other performances in Vienna's history. The
most comprehensive seems to be:*

568. Bauer, Anton. *Opern und Operetten in Wien; Verzeichnis
ihrer Erstaufführungern in der Zeit von 1629 bis zur
Gegenwart.* Graz: H. Böhlars Nachf., 1955. xii, 156p.
IOM-1595　ML 1723.8 V6 B22
All stage works performed from 1629 are listed in
title order; the total is 4,856. Indexed by date,
composer, and librettist. A map shows locations of
the theaters. Bibliography of about 100 items. Gruber
(48) provides a useful update to Bauer.

*Comic opera and operetta is well treated in a history by Otto
Rommel, Die alt-Wiener Volkskomödie, 1952 (IOM-1599). Attention to opera in Austria's second city is provided by Rudolf
List, Oper und Operette in Graz, 1974 (IOM-1601). Theaters
in and outside of Vienna are described in:*

569. Dace, Wallace. *National Theaters in Larger German and
Austrian Cities.* New York: Richards Rosen, 1980.
468p.　ISBN 0-8239-0527-6　PN 2044 G4 D3
A book of photographs and floor plans, plus names of
operas given with performance information, and financial
statistics; covers Vienna, Linz, West Berlin, Nuremberg,
Stuttgart, Düsseldorf, Frankfurt, Cologne, Munich, and
Hamburg. Institutions for research and library collections in Austria and Germany are surveyed. Glossary;
bibliography of about 150 items; name and title index.
See also Vaughan (73).

*Other material on aspects of opera in Austrian cities appears
in various local histories; a selection of these is given in
IOM-1608/1620. See also Brockpähler (609).*

Belgium

French: *Belgique;* Dutch: *België:* German: *Belgien.* The country
became independent of the Netherlands in 1831; it remains bi-
lingual, with Dutch (Flemish) spoken in Flanders (Vlaanderen)
and French spoken elsewhere. A good orientation to operatic
institutions is found in Brody (68). For current information
on opera and concert events there is a musical bulletin: La
vie musicale belge, *1961-* (IOM-1666a). The scholarly literature on opera is slight; these works are useful:

570. Renieu, Lionel. *Histoire des théâtres de Bruxelles
      depuis leur origine jusqu'à ce jour.* Paris: Duchartre
      & Van Buggenhoudt, 1928. 2 vols. IOM-1648
      PN 2706 B7 R4 or ML 1726.8 B7 R4
      First performances and historical accounts of the
      major theaters in Brussels; includes all forms of stage
      works. Bibliography of about 300 titles; no index.

571. Salès, Jules. *Théâtre Royal de la Monnaie, 1856-1970.*
      Nivelles: Havaux, 1971. 454, xi p. IOM-1649
      ML 1726.8 B7 T43
      The first Monnaie was built in 1700; the present
      structure dates from 1856. Renamed the Opéra National
      in 1963, it is the major opera house of the country.
      This is a chronology of performances, with casts and a
      title index. Bibliography of only six items.

572. Pols, André. *Vijftig jaar vlaamsche opera.* Antwerp:
      Pierre Dirix, 1943. 63p. and picture section.
      IOM-1650 ML 1726.8 A7 P6
      The Royal Flemish Opera (Vlaamsche Opera) opened in
      1893; this is a chronology of works performed through
      1942/43, with historical narrative. All operas in the
      house are sung in Flemish. No index.

573. Sanders, L. *Onderzoek opera en publiek te Antwerpen.*
      Antwerpen: Dienst Sociologie, 1974. 2 vols.
      ML 1726.8 A7 S25
      Essentially a statistical study of opera-going and
      financial-sociological considerations, but does give
      some facts on several Belgian opera companies. Bibliog-
      raphy may be helpful (about 100 entries), though supplied
      with incomplete data. No index.

Brazil

*Portuguese: Brasil; Spanish: Brasil; Italian: Brasile. A
rather old introduction to opera in the country is found in
150 anos de música no Brasil, 1800-1950, by Luis Heitor
Corrêa de Azevedo, 1956 (IOM-0976); the same author has a
chapter on opera in his Música e músicos do Brasil, 1950
(IOM-0986). Even older is the reliable history by Renato
Almeida, História da música brasileira, 1942 (IOM-0975).
A recent work with a promising title (not available for
examination) is the Enciclopédia da música brasileira (São
Paulo: Art Editora, 1977; 2 vols.). The following studies
are entirely about opera:*

574.   Lange, Francisco Curt. "La ópera y las casas de ópera
          en Brasil colonial." *Boletín interamericano de música*,
          44 (November 1964): 3-11. IOM-1019.
          An illustrated footnoted account of opera in Rio de
       Janeiro, Vila Rica, and Cuyaba, 1770-95; list of works.

575.   Corrêa de Azevedo, Luiz Heitor. *Relaçao das óperas de
          autores brasileiros.* Rio de Janeiro: Ministério de
          Educação e Saude, 1938. 116p. IOM-1017 ML 1717 B8 C6
          A chronological list of 97 operas by Brazilian com-
       posers, with historical and biographical information.

576.   Chaves Júnior, Edgard de Brito. *Memórias e glórias de
          um teatro: sessenta anos de história do Teatro
          Municipal de Rio de Janeiro.* Rio de Janeiro: Com-
          panhia Editora Americana, 1971. 683p. IOM-1018
          ML 232.8 R5 T43
          The Teatro Municipal, principal opera house of Rio,
       opened in 1909. This book gives a daily chronology
       of works performed to 1970, and discussions of the
       various genres: opera, operetta, ballet, etc. Illus-
       trated, but no bibliography or index.

577.   Pena, Luiz Carlos Martins. *Folhetins, a semana lírica.*
          Rio de Janeiro: Instituto Nacional do Livro, 1965.
          387p. ML 1717.8 R5 P5
          Consists of long reviews of the season 1846/47 in Rio,
       originally published in the *Jornal do Comérico*. Name
       and title index.

578. Cerquera, Paulo de Oliveira Castro. *Um século de ópera em São Paulo*. São Paulo: Editória Guia Fiscal, 1954. 327p. ML 1717 C44
    A discussion of each season, 1874-1951, in each theater, with all casts given; then a title list of all operas performed, with dates and casts. Photos of singers; index of names.

Bulgaria

Bulgarian: Bǔlgariia; French: Bulgarie; German: Bulgarien; Italian: Bulgaria; Russian: Bulgariia. The best introduction to Bulgarian art music in a Western language is the MGG article (IOM-1679); it covers only to 1950. The New Grove gives only one and a half columns to art music, with a six-item bibliography. A University of Vienna dissertation, not examined, appears valuable: "Die Entwicklung der Oper in Bulgarien von ihren Anfängen bis 1915 ...," by Eugenie Pantschewa, 1950 (IOM-1688). A factual treatment in English is available:

579. Seaman, Gerald. "The Rise of Slavonic Opera." *New Zealand Slavonic Journal*, 2 (1978): 1-16. PG 1 N53
    It is less than brief: one paragraph only on Bulgaria. (The article will be cited later for its more extended coverage of other Slavic countries.) A longer presentation is found in the *Concise Oxford Dictionary of Opera* (5).

Writings in Bulgarian offer a range of approaches. The Entsiklopediia na bǔlgarskata muzikalna kultura, 1967 (IOM-1680), includes chronologies and composer work-lists as well as topical articles. Rozaliia Aleksandrova Biks has a scholarly history of Bulgarian opera: Bǔlgarski operen teatǔr, 1976 (IOM-1690). Stories and backgrounds of 23 native works are found in Liubomir Sagaev, Sǔvremennoto bǔlgarsko operno tvorchestvo, 1974 (IOM-1689). A history of the national opera theater includes a chronology, 1909-53/54: Zlata Bozhkova, Sofiiska Narodna Opera memoari, 1975 (IOM-1691); this chronology is updated in Narodna Opera Sofiia, 1944-1969, issued by the Opera (IOM-1692).
    Two valuable contributions in German are found in Oper Heute (75), vol. 2: "Opern bulgarischer Komponisten, 1900-1978" (a chronology of about 60 works); and Maria Kostakewa, "Entwicklungs Prozesse in der bulgarischen Oper," which is a general survey of recent writing.

Canada

The useful survey in the Concise Oxford Dictionary of Opera
*says that "permanent companies had no lasting success until
the middle of the 20th century." In 1950 the Canadian Opera
Company was established in Toronto; it now performs regularly
in many Canadian cities as well as outside the country. Two
general histories offer some attention to opera: Ernest Mac-
Millan, Music in Canada, 1955 (IOM-1544); and Arnold Walter,
Aspects of Music in Canada, 1969 (IOM-0545). Discographies
of native singers and composers, with useful background information, are available in this important book: Edward B. Moogk,
Roll Back the Years ..., 1975 (IOM-0554). A list of operas
by Canadians appears in* Canadian Vocal Music Available for
Perusal from the Library of the Canadian Music Centre, 1971
*(IOM-0604). Current news of national and international
operatic life, with calendars, is given in* Opera Canada,
1960-   , a quarterly journal (IOM-0568).

Chile

580. Cánepa Guzmán, Mario. *La ópera en Chile, 1839-1930.*
      Santiago de Chile: Alonso Ovalle, 1976.   305p.
      ML 1717 C5 C3
      A straightforward general history with some footnotes.
      Good portraits of the singers. Bibliography of about
      50 items, incomplete data. No index.

*Opera is covered adequately in two general histories: Eugenio
Pereira Salas,* Historia de la música en Chile, 1850-1900,
*1957 (IOM-1051); and Samuel Claro Valdés and Jorge Urrutia
Blondel,* Historia de la música en Chile, 1973 (IOM-1052),
*with a useful chronology, 1940-71. One book is entirely
about light opera:*

581. Abascal Brunet, Manuel. *Apuntes para la historia del
      teatro en Chile: la zarzuela grande.* Santiago: Im-
      prenta Universitaria, 1941, 1951. 2 vols. IOM-1064
      ML 1717 A25
      A footnoted historical study, with facts about singers
      and performances. Includes chronology of performances.
      Period covered is 1628-1882. Bibliography of 20
      entries; name indexes.

Colombia

582. Perdomo Escobar, José Ignacio. *La ópera en Colombia.*
      Bogotá: Litografía Arco, 1979. 107p. ML 1717 C6 P43
      A fine account of native opera composers, singers
      and companies, theaters, and periodicals. A list of
      operas performed in the country, by composer, shows
      primarily the standard European works; but a number of
      Latin composers are included: Escobar, Falla, Gomes,
      Ricci, Rossi Guerra, Serra de Oxlo, Uriber Holguin, etc.
      Good color plates; partly annotated bibliography of
      about 50 items. No index.

*Operatic topics are also covered in the same author's His-
toria de la música en Colombia, 1963 (IOM-1083). Another
useful general history is Andrés Pardo Tovar, La cultura
musical en Colombia, 1966 (IOM-1082).*

Cuba

583. Tolón, Edwin Teurbe, and Jorge A. Gonzáles. *Óperas
      cubanos y sus autores.* Habana: Ucar, 1943. 472p.
      ML 1714 T6 IOM-1122
      A scholarly study of 12 composers, with portraits.
      No bibliography or index. The same two authors wrote
      also: *Historia del teatro en La Habana*, 1961 (IOM-1123),
      which covers opera to 1850.

Czechoslovakia

*The official name is Československá Socialistická Republika,
or ČSSR, but the former name is also in use: Československo.
French: Tchecoslovaquie; German: Tschechoslowakei; Russian:
Chekhoslovakiia. There is little scholarly writing about
operatic matters in Western European languages. Brian Large
has a useful overview of modern works in Sternfeld (17); he
lists about 80 operas and gives a discography of nine composers. Another good summary is found in Seaman (579). Some
interesting observations on recent opera, from a rigid
socialist point of view, are found in the program of the
1975 Brno festival (IOM-1723); the text is in four languages.
These books are in popular format, but do include names of
operas and certain other information:*

584. Eckstein, Pavel. *A Brief Outline of Czechoslovak Opera.*
      Prague: Theatre Institute, 1964. 115p. IOM-1740
      ML 1724 E3
      Following a historical survey, there is a list of
      operas with name of librettist, premiere data, re-
      cordings, and photos. No index.

585. ————. *The Czechoslovak Contemporary Opera: Pictures
      and Information.* Praha: Panton, 1967. 50p. IOM-1741
      ML 1724.5 E26
      Title also in German; text in both English and German.
      Photos and brief descriptions of 50 operas premiered
      between 1921 and 1966.

586. "Tschechische und slowakische Opern seit 1946." *Musik-
      bühne* 1975, pp. 141-151. IOM-1742 ML 1700.1 M8
      A list of 125 operas in chronological order, with
      librettists and premiere information. Titles are in
      the original languages, with German translation. In
      the same issue of the journal there is a list of about
      125 operettas written since 1946. The list of pre-
      mieres is carried through 1979 in volume 4 of *Oper
      Heute* (74).

Even in the Eastern languages there seems to be just one history of early opera in Czechoslovakia: *Igor' Fedorovich Belza,*
Cheshskaĭia opernaĭa klassika, 1951 (IOM-1737). For Slovakia
alone there is an extended account: *Štefan Hoza*, Opera na
Slovensku, 1953-54 (IOM-1743). Several detailed histories
of performance in the national theater are available in
Czech:

587. Němeček, Jan. *Opera Národního Divadla v období Karla
      Kovařovice 1900-1920.* Praha: Divadelní Ústav, 1968.
      2 vols. 262, 331p. ML 1724.8 P9 N43
      Karel Kovařovic was director of the national theater
      from 1900 to 1920. His biography is given here, with a
      survey of Bohemian opera of his time. The repertoire
      of the theater is presented in tabular form, and through
      seasonal chronologies. Well documented with 745 foot-
      notes, but without bibliography. Indexed.

588. Pala, František. *Opera Národního Divadla v období
      otakara ostrčila.* Praha: Ústav, 1962-1970. 4 vols.
      ML 1724.8 P9 N18

A narrative of each season in the theater from 1918/19 through 1928/29. Well documented, but not indexed. Attention to notable personalities.

589. Volek, Tomislav. *Repertoir Nosticovského Divadla v Praze z let 1794, 1796-8*. Praha, 1961. 191p.
ML 1724.8 P9 V9
Mostly a narrative account of four early years of opera in Prague, with tables of works performed and personnel lists. No index. Another study of early Prague: Otakar Kamper, *Hudební Praha v XVIII věku*, 1936 (IOM-1780), deals with the 18th century; it includes a chronology of operas performed. The *MGG* article on "Prag" offers a thorough history of musical life, with opera given full attention. See also Brockpähler (609).

Some information on opera in other Czechoslovakian cities is found in the local histories cited in IOM, beginning at 1772a. For the preceding era there is Zdeněk Nejedlý, Dějiny opery Národního Divadla, 1949 (IOM-1738), covering 1881-1920; it includes lists of works performed, but no chronology.

No up-to-date directories have been discovered. Two titles are described in IOM: Kulturní adresář, 1973 (IOM-1780a), and Československý hudební adresář 69, 1969 (IOM-1781). Both give identifications of opera houses, companies, and artists.

Several periodicals are of use for current information: Hudební rozhledy (IOM-1786), Music News from Prague (IOM-1788), and Opus musicum (IOM-1790).

Finally, there is a publisher's catalog of interest: Catalogue of Selected Music-Dramatical Works, by Dilia in Prague, 1971 (IOM-1823); it lists about 450 operas and ballets, with librettist, instrumentation, cast, and voice types.

Denmark

Danish: Danmark; French: Danemark; German: Dänemark. An essay by Svend Kragh-Jacobsen, "Le théâtre musical depuis 1931," La vie musicale au Danemark, pp. 97-128, 1962 (IOM-1838), lists and discusses operas performed 1931-61. A chronology of all opera and stage performances in the national theater, 1889-1975, is given in Georg Leicht and Marianne Hallar, Det Kongelige Teaters repertoire, 1977 (IOM-1841), with many indexes. A scholarly history of the opera house in Copenhagen, emphasizing architectural features: Thorkild Roepstorff,

Operahuset i København, *1970 (IOM-1840)*. Gerhard Schepelern,
Italienerne paa Hofteateret, *1976 (IOM-1842) describes
Italian touring opera companies that performed in Copenhagen,
1841-54, and gives lists of Danish operas premiered 1789-
1899; summary in German; indexes. A history and chronology
of operatic life in the city of Aarhus: Gustav Albeck and
Gerhard Schepelern, Opera i Aarhus ..., 1972 (IOM-1839).
Both MGG and New Grove give useful accounts of operatic activity in their articles on Copenhagen. A thorough musical
directory, covering all of Scandinavia:*

590. Olt, Harry. *Musiklivet i Norden.* København: Minis-
      teriet for Kulturelle Anliggender, 1969. IOM-1860
      ML 310.5 O 47
      Covers institutions and events, with lists of per-
      forming groups, libraries, periodicals, etc. A loose-
      leaf update is available in the *Nomus katalog*, Stock-
      holm, 1979- (IOM-1862).

*Three periodicals offer coverage of current concerts and
opera, with articles on performers, reviews, discographies,
etc.:* Musical Denmark, *1952- (IOM-1867);* Dansk musiker
tidende, *1911- (IOM-1868);* Dansk musiktidsskrift, *1925-
(IOM-1869). Recent compositions by Danes are carefully in-
ventoried:*

591. *Danske komponister af i dag; en vaerfortegnelse. Danish
      Composers of Today: A Catalogue of Works....* Køben-
      havn: Dansk Komponistforening, 1980- . 1 vol.
      (looseleaf). ISBN 87-981001-0-6 IOM-1890a
      ML 106 D46 D3
      As of July 1982 this catalog contained 368 pages,
      listing 4,693 works by 94 composers; revised and addi-
      tional pages are sent to subscribers. Information
      given: number of movements or acts, instrumentation,
      premiere data, publisher, and duration.

Finland

*Finnish: Suomen; French: Finlande; German: Finnland. No
scholarly writing about opera in Finland exists in a common
language. The best approaches seem to be these popular
surveys in English. The journal* Musikrevy *(IOM-3038) had a
special issue on Finland in 1975; it included an illustrated*

*history of opera in the country, composer work-lists, and
biographies of singers (IOM-1903). Denby Richards, The Music
of Finland, 1968 (IOM-1904), is a chatty survey, with work-
lists. Musica Fennica, by Timo Mäkinen and Seppo Nummi,
1965 (IOM-1906), has survey information and some attention to
performers and festivals. See also general Scandinavian
material listed under Denmark.*

France

*German: Frankreich; Italian: Francia. The literature is ex-
tensive. Several general histories of certain periods--with
attention to opera--are important.* James Anthony, **French
Baroque Music** *from Beaujoyeulx to Rameau, 1978 (IOM-1984);
and Robert M. Isherwood,* Music in the Service of the King ...,
*1973 (IOM-1990), offer strong coverage of the Baroque back-
ground. Ursula Bäcker,* Frankreichs Musik zwischen Romantik
und Moderne, *1965, covers the period 1848-1914, emphasizing
the place of Wagner; it has a bibliography of more than 1,000
items (IOM-1993). Short scholarly introductions to French
opera appear in the* New Oxford History of Music; *the articles
of each volume are noted above (15). The predecessor and
companion form to French opera was the ballet de cour, which
is the topic of two valuable books:*

592. McGowan, Margaret M. *L'art du ballet de cour en France,
      1581-1643.* Paris: Centre National de la Recherche
      Scientifique, 1963. 351p. ML 3460 M146
      A narrative history, footnoted, with 24 plates.
      Description and location of all source materials;
      references to contemporary criticism. Bibliography of
      about 300 items, incomplete data. Name and title index.

593. Christout, Marie-Françoise. *Le ballet de cour de Louis
      XIV, 1643-1672.* Paris: Picard, 1967. 276p.
      ML 270 A1 V5 vol. 12
      Scholarly history with 24 plates; much attention to
      costume, music, and scenography. Chronology of ballets,
      with bibliographic references. The bibliography of
      primary and secondary materials has about 200 entries.
      Name and title index.

*The principal histories of opera are given next; each covers
only a limited period.*

594. Crozet, Félix. *Revue de la musique dramatique en
     France....* Grenoble: Prudhomme, 1866. 477p. Sup-
     plément, 1872. 39p. ML 1727.4 C7
     Consists of premiere data and plot synopses for about
     1,000 works, with notes; and a chronology of 386 works
     presented 1671-1842. No bibliography; no index.

595. Demuth, Norman. *French Opera; Its Development to the
     Revolution.* Sussex: Artemis, 1963. xii, 337p.
     (Reprint--New York: Da Capo, 1982.)
     ISBN 0-306-77576-X (New York) ML 1727 D44
     A historical survey with useful lists: documents held
     by the Académie Royale de Musique 1669-1802, all theaters
     occupied by the Académie 1671-1794, etc. Musical ex-
     amples; 19 plates and other illustrations; bibliography;
     index.

596. Prunières, Henry. *L'opéra italien en France avant Lulli.*
     Paris: Champion, 1913. 512p. IOM-1950 ML 1727.2 P9
     Italian opera at the French court, and its influence.
     Letters and documents, performance chronology. Bibliog-
     raphy and index.

597. Lesure, François. *L'opéra classique français, 17e et
     18e siècles.* Genève: Minkoff, 1972. vi, 121p.
     ISBN 2-8266-0000-1 IOM-1951 ML 89 L285 L7
     This is volume 1 of the series "Iconographie musicale"
     (IOM-0125). It consists of 93 plates, illustrating
     stage design and machinery, with an introduction and
     commentary. Bibliography; no index.

598. Bruyas, Florian. *Histoire de l'operette en France,
     1855-1965.* Lyon: Vitte, 1974. 693p. IOM-1952
     ML 1727 B78
     A historical narrative. Interesting descriptions of
     Parisian musical life in the years 1850, 1871, 1900,
     and 1945. Bibliography of about 30 items; names and
     title index. For another approach to the 19th century
     see 190.

There are two useful articles in Oper Heute *(74), vol. 3:*
"Opern, Operetten und Musicals, Ballette französischer

Komponisten seit 1945" (a chronology of about 300 works), and
"Opernbühnen in Frankreich" (a directory of opera companies).
Opera in Paris is the subject of the next group. Three
permanent companies were active in the 17th century: the
Académie Royale de Musique, the Comédie-Française, and the
Comédie-Italienne. The Academie, directed by Lully, opened
in 1672; it enjoyed royal privileges and dominated the others.
The familiar name "L'Opéra" has remained the common designa-
tion, while the formal name has varied; at present it is
officially the Théâtre National de Musique. Its present
structure, Le Palais Garnier (1875), is the 13th to house
the Opéra.

599. Paris. Opéra. *Petite encyclopédie illustrée de l'Opéra*
     de Paris. Paris: Théâtre National de l'Opéra, 1974.
     160p. IOM-1953 ML 1727.8 P2 P284
     Dictionary entries, covering architecture and dimen-
     sions of the Palais Garnier; its library, museum, ward-
     robe, artworks, electrical equipment; stage machinery;
     and the great staircase. Also material on administra-
     tion of the enterprise, with financial data, and on the
     ballet. Excellent illustrations; no bibliography or
     index.

Various historical approaches to L'Opéra are available; most
are described in IOM. The basic work is F.H. Castil Blaze,
L'Académie Impériale de Musique ..., *1855 (IOM-1956); it in-*
cludes lists of singers and staff; a chronology of 647 per-
formances, and a general narrative of events from 1645 to
1855. A brief history, covering into the 20th century, is
Jacques-Gabriel Prod'homme, L'Opéra (1669-1925), *1925 (IOM-*
1955); includes details on the Palais Garnier and a performance
chronology, 1671-1925. Nérée Desarbres, Deux siècles à l'Opéra
(1669-1868) ..., *1868 (IOM-1958), offers biographical informa-*
tion on performers and staff, together with a chronology of
performances, 1671-1868. Operas performed since 1645, with
their casts and biographical notices, are included in a docu-
mentary history by Jacques-Bernard Durey de Noinville and
Louis-Antoine Travenol, Histoire du théâtre de l'Académie
Royale de Musique ..., *1757 (IOM-1959). Dependable coverage*
of the period 1671-1876 is given in Théodore Dufaure de Lajarte,
Bibliothèque musicale du Théâtre de l'Opéra, *1878, reprint*
1969 (IOM-1957); it contains a descriptive chronology of 241
operas, 110 ballets and 243 other works, with biographical
sketches and indexes by composer and title. Archival docu-
ments relating to the Opéra and its personalities are assembled

in Émile Campardon, L'Académie Royale de Musique au XVIIIe
siècle ..., *1884, reprints 1970 and 1971 (IOM-1960).*
    *Albert Soubies has prepared extensive chronologies in
tabular format, covering the four major houses; his* Soixante-
sept ans à l'Opéra *... (Paris: Fischbacher, 1893) gives premiere dates for all works and shows number of performances
by season for each opera, 1826-93. The book includes a narrative history and various documents.*
    An intensive view of a brief period:

600.   Ducrot, Ariane. "Les répresentations de l'Académie
            Royale de Musique à Paris au temps de Louis XIV
            (1671-1715)." *Recherches*, 10 (1970): 19-55.
        ML 270 R297
        Describes the typical "season": days and hours of
        performances, etc. Table of premieres at the court
        and in Paris; chronology of all works. Has 105 foot-
        notes.

The period immediately following is well presented in:

601.   Lagrave, Henri. *Le théâtre et le public à Paris de
            1715 à 1750.* Paris: Klincksieck, 1972. 717p.
        ISBN 2-252-01434-2   PC 13 B6 ser. C vol. 37
        An expansive table of contents makes access convenient
        to this imposing work. It covers the halls, the public,
        seasons, programs, finances, and critical reception;
        also discusses taste of the times and administrative
        matters. With 22 plates (including plans); a strong
        bibliography of about 400 items; name and title index.

*Julian Gordon Rushton's dissertation, "Music and Drama at the
Académie Royale de Musique, Paris, 1774-1789" (Ph.D., Oxford
University, 1969), gives particular attention to the Gluck-
Piccinni rivalry of the time.*
    A useful fact-book on the Palais Garnier:

602.   Wolff, Stéphane. *L'Opéra au Palais Garnier, 1875-1961.*
            Paris: "L'Entr'acte," 1962. 565p.   IOM-1962
        ML 1727.8 P2 W8
        Performance chronology for the period, with total
        number of presentations in Paris. Information on about
        3,000 artists.

There is a scholarly older study of the Opéra-Comique:

603. Soubies, Albert, and Charles Malherbe. *Histoire de
     l'Opéra-Comique....* Paris: Flammarion, 1892-93.
     799 cols. (Reprint--Genève: Minkoff, 1974.) ISBN
     2-8266-0629-8 IOM-1964 ML 1727.8 P2 S6
     Details on the repertoire, personnel, finances, docu-
     ments, and the building.

*Soubies also has a tabular presentation of the repertoire,
with premiere dates and number of performances by season for
all works 1825-94: Soixante-neuf ans à l'Opéra Comique ...
Paris: Fischbacher, 1894). For an earlier era:*

604. Pougin, Arthur. *L'Opéra-Comique pendant la Révolution
     de 1788 à 1801.* Paris, 1891. 337p. (Reprint--
     Genève: Minkoff, 1973.) ISBN 2-8266-0656-7
     ML 1727.3 P85
     A year-by-year record of performances, business trans-
     actions, and official documents. The approach was
     scholarly, but notes are not given. No index.

Recent performances are listed in Stéphane Wolff, Un demi-
siècle d'Opéra-Comique (1900-1950) ..., *1953 (IOM-1963);
401 works are listed, with casts, total number of performances,
and facts on 2,500 artists. The complex history of the company
is well summarized in the article in* Concise Oxford Dictionary
of Opera *(5), which also has useful entries on the other Paris
theaters. On the other theaters documentation is less complete. These accounts are useful:*

605. Soubies, Albert. *Le Théâtre-Italien de 1801 à 1913.*
     Paris: Fischbacher, 1913. iv, 186, iv p. IOM-1965
     ML 1727.8 P3 T3
     Features a vast foldout chart: "Tableau des pièces
     représentées," which shows performances by season of
     each work. Also letters, documents, pictures, and a
     narrative of each season; without notes, index, or
     bibliography.

606. Walsh, T.J. *Second Empire Opera: The Théâtre Lyrique,
     Paris 1851-1870.* New York: Riverrun; London: Calder,

1981. x, 384p. ML 1727 W227
A thorough history, with much information on finances
and audiences. Lacks attention to concurrent activity
in the Opéra and other Parisian houses, thus offering
a curiously isolated view of operatic life. Poorly
printed illustrations; backnotes; bibliography of about
100 entries, data incomplete; partly expansive index of
names and titles.

Further details on the Théâtre-Lyrique are given in an older
work:

607. LaSalle, Albert de. *Mémorial du Théâtre-Lyrique....*
      Paris: Lecuir, 1877. 107p. ML 1727.8 P2 L33
      Covers 1847-70. Chronology of performances with casts
      and comments; various statistical tables. Index of names
      and titles.

The repertoire, with premiere dates of all works, and number
of performances by season of each opera, will be found in
Albert Soubies, Histoire du Théâtre-Lyrique, 1851-1870
(Paris: Fischbacher, 1899); data are on a foldout chart, in
tabular format.
     Local histories of French cities and regions provide infor-
mation on opera outside Paris. Principal local histories are
described in IOM-2000/2012.
     A valuable annual directory: Annuaire du spectacle;
théâtre, cinéma, musique, radio, television, *1942/43- (IOM-*
1966), identifies groups and individual artists and describes
theaters in France and neighboring countries. Two journals
present opera and concert news: Le guide du concert, *1910-*
(weekly; IOM-2031); and Le courrier musical de France, *1904-*
(3 per year; IOM-2032).
     Further bibliography on French opera is available:

608. Surian, Elvidio. *A Checklist of Writings on 18th-Century*
      French and Italian Opera (Excluding Mozart). Hacken-
      sack, N.J.: J. Boonin, 1970. xiv, 121p. IOM-2045
      ML 128 O4 S9
      Lists 1,501 books and articles, including dictionaries,
      chronologies, contemporary writings, material on in-
      dividuals, and the literature on each city. No annota-
      tions or index.

Germany

German: *Deutschland;* French: *Allemande;* Italian: *Germania.*
The correct names of the present German states are Bundes-
republik Deutschland (BRD) or the Federal Republic of Germany,
also known as West Germany; and Deutsche Demokratische Repub-
lik (DDR) or the German Democratic Republic, also known as
East Germany. Principal cities of BRD are Hamburg, München
(Munich), Köln (Cologne), Frankfurt, Dortmund, Essen, Düssel-
dorf, Bremen, Stuttgart, and the capital, Bonn. In DDR the
major centers are Leipzig, Dresden, and Weimar; the capital is
East Berlin. Since the end of World War II Berlin has been
divided into two zones: West Berlin (under BRD) and East
Berlin (DDR). Two of the major opera houses in Berlin are
in the East zone: Die Staatsoper and Die Komische Oper. Die
Deutsche Oper is in West Berlin.
A good general history of German music, with a fine over-
view of operatic topics, is found in the MGG article "Deutsch-
land" (IOM-2111). Two histories by Hans Joachim Moser,
Geschichte der deutschen Musik, *1930 (IOM-2112), and* Kleine
deutsche Musikgeschichte ..., *1949 (IOM-2113), offer valuable*
background. For English readers the preferred history is
found in a collection of essays entitled Of German Music: A
Symposium, *1976 (IOM-2114). No scholarly study devoted en-*
tirely to the history of German opera has been seen, but there
are many examinations of specific periods and localities.
An excellent starting point is this bibliography/fact-book:

609. Brockpähler, Renate. *Handbuch zur Geschichte der*
     Barockoper in Deutschland. Emsdetten: Lechte, 1964.
     394p. IOM-2076 ML 1729.3 B78
     A documentation of operatic life in 48 German cities,
     plus Vienna and Prague. Includes bibliographies, his-
     torical summaries, names of persons and institutions,
     and opera performances in chronological order. Name
     index.

A history in English is available as a dissertation: Sheila
Marie Allen, "German Baroque Opera (1678-1740) with a Practical
Edition of Selected Soprano Arias" (Eastman School of Music,
University of Rochester, 1974; IOM-2075). Opera in the
second half of the 19th century is analyzed in Siegfried
Goslich, Die deutsche romantische Oper, *1975 (IOM-2077).*
Modern works are listed in "Musikbühnen-Uraufführungen in
der DDR seit 1945," Musikbühne, *1977 (IOM-2077a), which gives*
premiere data on about 250 operas and operettas.

*The German equivalent of opéra-comique is the Singspiel, well
discussed in:*

610. Schletterer, Hans Michel. *Das deutsche Singspiel von
      seinen ersten Anfängen bis auf die neueste Zeit.*
      Hildesheim and New York: Olms, 1975. x, 340p.
      ISBN 3-487-05577-5 ML 1729.3 S34
      Analyzes the works of Opitz, Rebhun, Betuleium, Ruff,
      von Braunschweig, Kirchmeyr, and other leading figures,
      in a historical context. Footnotes; list of sources.
      No index.

*The famous Staatsoper in East Berlin, also known as Die Linden-
oper because of its location on Unter den Linden, is the subject of a useful recent survey:*

611. Otto, Werner. *Die Lindenoper.* Berlin: Henschel, 1977.
      347p. ML 1729.8 B53 S955
      A general account, without footnotes, of the theater
      and its performance history from 1742 to 1975. No bib-
      liography; no index.

More scholarly approaches are older:

612. Kapp, Julius. *Geschichte der Staatsoper Berlin.*   Berlin:
      Hesse, 1937. 264p. (Reprint 1942.) IOM-2079
      ML 1729.8 B53 S93
      Examines early opera in the city; gives a list of
      works performed 1786-1942; tables of operas with number
      of performances for each; staff lists. Without foot-
      notes or bibliography; has 600 illustrations and a
      name index.

613. Fetting, Hugo. *Die Geschichte der deutschen Staatsoper.*
      Berlin: Henschelverlag, 1955. 283p. IOM-2080
      ML 1729.8 B53 S914
      A footnoted history from 1741 to 1954. Includes names
      of operas performed, about 200 photographs of scenes,
      artists, and the building (destroyed 1941, rebuilt and
      again destroyed 1945, rebuilt again according to original
      plans 1955). No index.

614. Schäffer, Carl, and Carl Hartmann. *Die Königlichen*
       Theater in Berlin.... Berlin: Comtoir, 1886. 304p.
       IOM-2078 ML 1729.8 B52 K68
       Until 1919 the Staatsoper was known as the Königlichen
       Theater. This is a fact-book covering 1786-1885, in-
       cluding a list of about 2,500 works performed, with
       dates and total number of performances. Also seasonal
       chronologies, lists of all performers and their seasons,
       and accounts of the buildings that had housed the opera.

Two informative articles appeared in Oper Heute *(74), vol. 1:*
"Uraufführungen der Deutschen Staatsoper, 1945-1977" (a chron-
ology of 18 premieres); and "Daten und Fakten zur Geschichte
des Opernhauses Unter den Linden" (a chronology of events--
not operas--from 1742 to 1974.

     For East Berlin's other famous company there was a useful
annual: Jahrbuch der Komischen Oper Berlin, *1960/61-1971/72.*
This became Musikbühne, *with added scope, and then* Oper Heute
(see 74). In volume 2 of Oper Heute *there is a useful descrip-*
tive article on the Komische Oper; in volume 3 there is a
chronology of productions, 1947-79. The items on Walter
Felsenstein, cited above at 155 and 156, contain further
material.

     Until 1945 opera in Dresden centered on the famous Staats-
oper building designed by Gottfried Semper in 1841. With the
destruction of that structure, performances were held in other
halls; it has not been rebuilt. Two worthy histories of opera
in the city cover much the same ground: Hans Schnoor, Dresden:
Vierhundert Jahre deutsche Musikkultur...., *1948 (IOM-2082);*
and Schnoor's Die Stunde des Rosenkavaliers, *1968 (IOM-2083).*
Both works include a chronology of performances, 1548-1948.
The first book has good bibliography of some 500 titles; the
second book has no bibliography but gives more information on
20th-century activity. Both have name indexes. A useful
popular summary of historical highlights appeared in Oper
Heute *(74), volumes 2 and 3: "Leitmotive der Dresdner Opern-*
geschichte," by Mathias Rank and Horst Seeger.

     The long operatic history of Frankfurt was focused in
1880 with the opening of its new theater, the Opernhaus; it
was destroyed in 1943, rebuilt in 1951. Albert Richard Mohr
has two books: Frankfurter Opernhaus 1880-1980 *... (Frankfurt:*
Kramer, 1980; 372p.), which includes reconstruction details
and a general history of productions and conductors, with a
name index; and Die Frankfurter Oper 1924-44 *(Frankfurt:*
Kramer, 1971; 752p.), which is a review of seasons with
chronology and press notices, with name index.

*Hamburg was the site of the first public opera house in
Germany, the "Gänsemarkt," 1678. Its history, repertoire,
audiences, and final decline (it closed in 1738) are told in
Hans Joachim Marx, "Geschichte der Hamburger Barockoper.* Ein
Forschungsbericht," Hamburger Jahrbuch für Musikwissenschaft,
*3 (1978): 7-34. Details on the original plans and structure
are found in Dennis R. Martin, "Germany's First Major Opera
House: A Reassessment of Its Design,"* Current Musicology, *31
(1981): 55-64. The most detailed story of early opera in the
city:*

615.   Wolff, Hellmuth C. *Die Barockoper in Hamburg: 1678-
       1738.* Wolfenbüttel: Möseler, 1957. 2 vols.   IOM-2085
       ML 1729.8 H19 W6
       Full coverage of the Gänsemarkt opera house: rooms,
       artworks, stage, machinery, etc. Discussion of operas
       performed; a chapter on ballet. 38 plates. Bibliog-
       raphy of about 300 items. Index of operas and names.

A shorter report is provided by a collection of essays: 300
Jahre Oper in Hamburg: 1687-1978, *1977 (IOM-2086).*
      *The old Staatstheater in Kassel was destroyed in 1943;
a new building replaced it in 1959. For that occasion a useful collection of studies was published:* Theater in Kassel;
Aus der Geschichte des Staatstheaters Kassel von den Anfängen
bis zur Gegenwart, *1959 (IOM-2087). It includes a list of
most-performed operas since 1814 and a bibliography of about
100 entries.*
      *There are several good chronicles of the operatic history
of Munich. Recent times are covered by Hans Wagner,* 200 Jahre
Münchener Theaterchronik 1750-1950, *1958, with a supplement
for 1957-60 (IOM-2090); it gives histories and chronologies
for 12 theaters, with composer and performer indexes. For
the early days there is Max Zenger,* Geschichte der Münchener
Oper, *1923 (IOM-2088), and also Hubertus Bolongaro-Crevenna,*
L'arpa festante, *1963 (IOM-2089). The title of the latter
work is that of the first opera performed in the city, in
August 1653. While the principal theater is the National-
theater--destroyed in 1943, rebuilt in 1963--the architectural gem is the Residenztheater, described in this little
book:*

616.   Brunner, Herbert. *Altes Residenztheater in Munich.*
       München: Bayerische Verwaltung der Staatlichen
       Schlösser, Gärten und Seen, 1972. 47p.
       ML 1729.8 M962 R52

A narrative and chronology of events, with much detail on the plan, decor, and artwork of the structure. François Cuvilliés was the architect; the building opened in 1753, was destroyed in the Second World War, and was reconstructed 1958.

The Fürstbischöfliches Opernhaus, in Passau, is the topic of a recent study:

617. Schäffer, Gottfried. *Das Fürstbischöfliche und Königliche Theater zu Passau (1783-1883)*.... Passau: Vereins für Ostbairische Heimatforschung, 1973. xvii, 193p. ML 1729.8 P3 F8
    Foldout plans are included in this general history, together with 18th-century staff lists, and performance chronologies with casts. Name index.

Weimar's Hoftheater had a number of distinguished directors and conductors, among them Goethe, Liszt, Hummel, von Bülow, and Richard Strauss. Its golden age is recounted in:

618. Huschke, Wolfram. *Musik im klassischen und nach-klassischen Weimar, 1756-1861*. Weimar: Böhlaus, 1982. 240p. ML 284.8 W34 H96
    A narrative history, with valuable reference features; chronology of all performances 1848-58; general musical chronology 1756-1861; table of Mozart performances (280 of them), 1791-1817; etc. Bibliography of about 200 entries; name index; 36 plates. This is updated by: Adolf Bartels, *Chronik des Weimarischen Hoftheaters, 1817-1907* (Weimar: Bohlaus, 1908); it has chronologies with complete casts.

Current information on operatic institutions and activity is found in several directories. Brody has been cited above (67). Music in Germany, *1965 (IOM-2057), presents much information but is not well organized.* Alles über Musik. *by Friedrich Herzfeld, 1959, is an interesting assemblage of facts on the BRD, including chronologies of opera and operetta productions (IOM-2163). Brief accounts of musical life in about 50 cities are found in* Studying Music in the Federal Republic of Germany, *1980 (IOM-2165). For the DDR there is Karl Laux,* Das Musikleben in der Deutschen Demokratischen Republik, 1945-1959, *1963*

(IOM-2166). It lists halls, festivals, composers, opera com-
panies, etc.; includes 281 photos, plus an index of names and
subjects.
    Several periodicals report on operatic activity in BRD.
The famous old Neue Zeitschrift für Musik, *established by*
Robert Schumann in 1834, offers opera reviews for all major
German cities (IOM-2167). Details of opera productions in
Germany, Austria, and Switzerland appear in Orpheus, *1973-*
(IOM-2168), and in Die deutsche Bühne, *1930- (IOM-2169).*
Music events in DDR are reported in Musik und Gesellschaft,
1951- (IOM-2178).

Hungary

Hungarian: Magyarország; *French:* Hongrie; *German:* Ungarn;
Italian: Ungheria. *There are good summaries of musical life,*
including the past and present of opera, in three encyclo-
pedias: La musica *(IOM-0081),* "Ungheria"; *MGG,* "Ungarn";
and New Grove, *"Hungary." The newest history of the national*
opera:

619.   Kertész, Iván. *A Magyar Állami Operaház.* Budapest:
          Magyar Állami Operaház, 1975. ML 1725.8 B82 063
          A narrative account with color photographs of the
          Magyar Állami Operaház, dating from 1884; formerly
          known (1884-1909) as the Magyar Királyi Operaház (Royal
          Opera). Without index, chronologies, or other reference
          features. Text is in five langusges.

A hetvenötéves Magyar Állami Operaház, 1884-1959, 1969 (IOM-
2309), commemorates the 75th anniversary of the theater; it
includes a list of works performed there and in the earlier
Nemzeti Szinház; and it gives the number of times each work
was performed. Also portraits and staff lists. A chronologica
list of 675 operas and other events is given in Lajos Koch,
A Budapesti Operaház musora, 1884-1959, 1959 (IOM-2310). The
principal opera center outside Budapest is the subject of
Mátyás Horányi, The Magnificence of Eszterháza, *1962 (IOM-2311)*
it includes a chronology of the opera repertoire; 113 works.
Singers are listed and discussed.
    About 25 recent Hungarian operas are listed in volume 1
of Oper Heute *(74):* "Opern ungarischer Komponisten seit 1948";
titles are in Hungarian and German. Current information on
operatic activity, and musical life in general, is found in
two English periodicals: Hungarian Music News, *1969- (IOM-232*

and Hungarian Musical Guide, *1966- (IOM-2328). A concert
chronicle in Hungarian is* Muzsika, *1958- (IOM-2325). There
is no recent musical directory.*

Ireland

*The Republic of Ireland, or Eire, comprises the 26 southern
counties of the island; it has been independent of Great
Britain since 1949. Dublin is the only city with an important
operatic history. Its chronicler has been T.J. Walsh, in*
Opera in Dublin, 1705-1797 *..., 1973 (IOM-2372), and* Opera
in Old Dublin, 1819-1838, *1952 (IOM-2373). An article by
W.J. Lawrence, "Early Irish Ballad Opera and Comic Opera,"*
Musical Quarterly, *8 (1922): 397-412 (IOM-2371), is a useful
supplement.*

Italy

*Italian: Italia; French: Italie; German: Italien. A good
introduction to opera and other musical activity in Italy is
the article "Italien" in MGG, by Bruno Stäblein et al.
The bibliography, by Claudio Sartori, is the most comprehensive available. Of the entries in other musical encyclopedias,* New Grove *offers respectable coverage up to the 20th
century, while Michel (IOM-0072) and* La musica *(IOM-0081)
give useful summaries of later trends and activities. A
collective volume with varied approaches:*

620. Austin, William W., ed. *New Looks at Italian Opera:
      Essays in Honor of Donald J. Grout.* Ithaca, N.Y.:
      Cornell University Press, 1968. ix, 290p. (Reprint--
      Westport, Conn.: Greenwood, 1976.) ISBN 0-8371-8761-3
      ML 1733.1 A92
      Consists of eight contributions, of which the most
      useful are Claude Palisca, "The Alterati of Florence,
      Pioneers in the Theory of Dramatic Music" (describes a
      group that had priority over the Camerata in approach
      to the music drama); Nino Pirrotta, "Early Opera and
      Aria" (discusses the definition of aria and its manifes-
      tation in Peri, Caccini, and Monteverdi); and William
      Carl Holmes, "Giacinto Andrea Cicognini's and Antonio
      Cesti's Orontea, 1649" (cited above under Cesti [242]).
      The volume is indexed by name and title.

*Important historical studies are listed next. The first item
is widest in scope; succeeding entries are in sequence according to the periods they discuss.*

621.   Bonaventura, Arnaldo. *Saggio storico sul teatro
        musicale italiano.* Livorno: Raffaello Giusti, 1913.
        xii, 414p. IOM-2406 ML 1733 B77
        Considers the antecedents of opera, then the 16th
        and 17th centuries by city, and general trends to 1910.
        A footnoted narrative, with some photos of theaters,
        a 12-page bibliography, and index of names and titles.

622.   Solerti, Angelo. *Gli albori del melodramma.* Milano:
        R. Sandron, 1904. 3 vols. IOM-2407 ML 1702 S68
        A scholarly study of ballets, masques, and other pre-
        cursors of opera up to the early 17th century. Docu-
        ments, and complete texts of many works. No index.

623.   ————. *Le origini del melodramma; testimonianze dei
        contemporanei....* Torino: Bocca, 1903. vi, 262p.
        (Reprint--Hildesheim: Olms, 1969.) IOM-2408
        ML 1702 S682
        Discusses 54 operas from 1600 to 1664, with full bib-
        liographic detail on publications, and gives a general
        bibliography on the period (about 100 items). No index.

624.   Goldschmidt, Hugo. *Studien zur Geschichte der italian-
        ischen Oper im 17. Jahrhundert.* Leipzig: Breitkopf
        und Härtel, 1901-04. 2 vols. (Reprints--Hildesheim:
        Olms; Wiesbaden: Breitkopf und Härtel, 1967.)
        IOM-2409 ML 1733.2 G62
        Scholarly study of Baroque opera, stressing Monte-
        verdi, opera in Rome, the opera orchestra, and comic
        opera. The entire score of *L'incoronazione di Poppea*
        is among the musical examples. Bibliography and index.

625.   Pirrotta, Nino, and Elena Povoledo. *Music and Theater
        from Poliziano to Monteverdi.* New York: Cambridge
        University Press, 1981. xi, 382p. ISBN 0-521-23259-7
        ML 1733 P5713
        An English version of *Li due Orfei, da Poliziano a
        Monteverdi* (Torino: ERI, 1969). Essays on preopera
        genres (strambotti, intermedie, pastoral, etc.); early

aria and recitative (reprinted from 620; see 233); with
fine notes and musical examples. No bibliography; no
index.

626. Strohm, Reinhard. *Die italienische Oper im 18. Jahr-
     hundert*. Wilhelmshaven: Heinrichshofen, 1979. 398p.
     ISBN 3-7959-0110-3 IOM-2409a ML 1703 S87
     Discusses 24 operas, "commedie per musica," and opere
     buffe. Cites editions and secondary literature. Bib-
     liography of 261 items; name and topic index.

627. Grout, Donald J. "Some Desiderata and Goals for the
     Study of 18th-century Italian Opera." *Current
     Musicology*, 9 (1969): 88-91. ML 1 C98
     Among the needs mentioned are: style histories, a
     history of the libretto, and studies of the relation
     of opera to social conditions. The major lack is of
     modern editions of scores; an approach to the prepara-
     tion of such editions is suggested.

628. Corte, Andrea della. *L'opera comica italiana nel '700*.
     Bari: Laterza, 1923. 2 vols. IOM-2411 ML 1733.3 C68
     Considers the antecedents of comic opera, such as
     comic parts in serious opera, and the fully developed
     comic works of all the important composers in the 18th
     century. Footnoted, but without musical examples or
     bibliography. Name and title index.

629. Nicolaisen, Jay. *Italian Opera in Transition, 1871-
     1893*. Ann Arbor, Mich.: UMI Research, 1980. 315p.
     ISBN 8357-1121-8-S83 ML 1733 N5
     Based on the author's dissertation (University of
     California, Berkeley, 1977). A thorough, interesting
     examination of a period that is receiving belated
     scholarly attention. Some citations to the book have
     been made above (under Catalani, Ponchielli, etc.).
     Concentrates on the development of the dramatic poten-
     tial in compositions that followed the period of Rossini.
     Combines historical and analytic modes; well documented
     with footnotes, musical examples, list of scores con-
     sulted (with full data), and list of writings consulted
     (about 120 items). There is a list of all reviews for
     each opera and a list of operas most performed at La
     Scala, 1870-90 (leaders were *Aida*, *L'ebrea [La juive]*,

Gli ugonotti, and *Faust*), and other theaters. An appendix gives a table of revisions Puccini made for *Edgar*. Texts are quoted in Italian only, without translations. Expansive name, title, and topic index.

A basic list of about 200 operas by Italians that were performed between 1946 and 1975 appears in Musikbühne, *76 (1976), pp. 186-202.* IOM-2410 ML 1700.1 M8

The next group of titles consists of studies of individual cities. A list of 215 operas and stage works given in 20 theaters of Bari, totaling 4,080 performances, is the main feature of Alfredo Giovine, L'opera in musica in teatri di Bari. Statistica delle rappresentazioni dal 1830 al 1969, *1969 (IOM-2412). It also includes discussion of opera houses and tabulations of performances by season. More detail on several theaters of Bari may be found in other books by Giovine:* Teatro Margherita di Bari *(1967),* Teatro Petruzzelli *(1971), and* Teatro Piccinni *(1970). They all give narrative accounts plus chronologies and indexes.*

Bologna's operatic history is detailed in several works.

630. Trezzini, Lamberto, and Sergio Pagnelli. *Due secoli di vita musicale. Storia del Teatro Comunale di Bologna.* Bologna: Alfa, 1966. 2 vols. xv, 249p.; xix, 263p. ML 290.8 B68 T74

A narrative history with footnotes occupies the first volume. In volume 2 there is a detailed chronology of productions from 1763 to 1966; it gives casts, publications, and references to secondary literature. Name and title index.

Supplementary chronologies and facts on the Teatro Comunale (opened 1763) are found in Luigi Bignami, Chronologia di tutti gli spettacoli rappresentati nel Gran Teatro Comunale di Bologna...., *1880 (IOM-2413), useful for its identification of all the singers and other artists--even orchestral players; and in Renzo Giacomelli,* Il Teatro Comunale di Bologna ..., *1965 (IOM-2414), which provides documents, letters and anecdotes for the period 1763-1963. Opera was offered in the city as early as 1600; documentation is available in Alessandro Machiavelli,* Serie cronologica de' drammi recitati su de' pubblici teatri di Bologna dall' anno ... 1600 sino al corrente 1727 *(Bologna: Soci Filopatri, 1737; 94p. ML 1733.8 B7).*

*Opera in Cremona is well covered by Elia Santoro, Il teatro
di Cremona, 1969-1972, 4 vols. (IOM-2415); it gives a history
of performances from 1747 to 1972, with name and title indexing.*

*Florence (Firenze) is distinguished as the birthplace of
opera. In 1597 Peri's Dafne was performed; in 1656 the Teatro
della Pergola, which still stands, was opened. The modern
Teatro Comunale opened in 1864. A basic document is:*

631.   Weaver, Robert Lamar, and Norma Wright Weaver. *A
       Chronology of Music in the Florentine Theater, 1590-
       1750.* Detroit: Information Coordinators, 1978. 421p.
       ISBN 0-911772-89-8   IOM-2417   ML 1733.8 F6 W4
       A footnoted history with chronological lists of stage
       works performed; casts are given, and library locations
       of scores and libretti. Bibliography; name and title
       index. An article by Robert Weaver, "Opera in Florence,
       1646-1731," *Studies in Musicology: Essays in the History,
       Style, and Bibliography of Music in Memory of Glenn
       Haydon* (Chapel Hill: University of North Carolina Press,
       1969), pp. 60-71, discusses 41 comic operas of the
       period.

*Other historical and chronological data are given in Ugo
Morini, La R. Accademia degli Immobili ed il suo teatro "La
Pergola," 1649-1925, 1926 (IOM-2416); Giuseppe Pavan,
Saggio di cronistoria teatrale fiorentina, 1901 (IOM-2418);
Leonardo Pinzauti, Il maggio musicale fiorentino (Firenze:
Valecchi, 1967); 501p. (gives casts for spring seasons 1928-
67, with 109 photographs and 20 color plates); and Marcello
de Angelis, La musica del Granduca. Vita musicale e correnti
critiche a Firenze 1800-1855 (Firenze: Vallecchi, 1978;
225p.) (a description of musical life drawn from contemporary
periodical reviews).*

*In Genoa (Genova) the great theater is the Carlo Felice,
named for King Charles Felix--Charles the Happy--who was responsible for the structure; it opened in 1828, was destroyed
in the Second World War and later reconstructed. An interesting
account of the reconstruction appears in:*

632.   Teatro Comunale dell' Opera. *Teatro Comunale dell'
       Opera di Genova.* Genova: Il Teatro, 1973. [not
       paged]   IOM-2420   ML 1733.8 G3 B8
       A popular history of opera in the city, with many
       fine photographs. Lists of singers and their roles,
       with performance dates, 1900-30. No index.

*A scholarly history of the theater is available: G.B. Valle-
bona,* Il teatro Carlo Felice; cronistoria di un secolo, 1828–
1928, *1928 (IOM-2419); it has an informative chronology of
the 15,776 performances in the century studied. The title
index provides the total number of stagings for each work.
Some added facts are available in Ambrogio Brocca,* Il teatro
Carlo Felice; cronistoria dal 7 aprile 1828 al 27 febbraio
1898, *1898 (IOM-2421); and in Remo Giazotto,* La musica a
Genova nella vita pubblica e privata dal XIII al XVIII
secolo *(Genova: Società Industrie Grafiche e Lavorazioni
Affini, 1951), 371p.*

   *A history of opera in Lucca, with chronology, 1819-1936,
and a description of the theater, is given in:*

633.   Paoli Catelani, Bice. *Il Teatro Comunale del "Giglio"
      di Lucca.* Pescia: Artidoro Benedetti, 1941. 111p.
      IOM-2422 ML 1733.8 L8 P4
      Describes the theater and gives the history of opera
      in the city; presents a chronology of performances,
      1819-1936, with casts.

For Mantua we have Giuseppe Amadei, I centocinquant'anni del
Sociale nella storia dei teatri di Mantova, *1973 (IOM-2423),
which offers chronologies for the two major houses: the
Sociale (opened 1822) and the Andreani (opened 1862).*

   *Most of the writing on opera in Milan (Milano) concen-
trates rightly on its renowned Teatro alla Scala, but there
are many other houses; a good illustrated account of them
is given in:*

634.   Manzella, Domenico, and Emilio Pozzi. *I teatri di Milano.*
      Milano: Mursia, 1971. 306p. IOM-2424 PN 2686 M5 M3
      Histories of all theaters, including cabarets; well
      illustrated, but without chronologies. Bibliography;
      index of theaters and of names.

*For the great La Scala--which opened 1778, was nearly destroyed
in a bombing raid in 1943, and was rebuilt in 1946--there are
many books from which to choose. For English readers the
best available is a popular, illustrated history: Lorenzo
Arruga,* La Scala, *1975 (IOM-2426b). The most complete La
Scala chronology is found in Giampiero Tintori,* Cronologia:
opere, balletti, concerti 1778-1977, *1979 (IOM-2426a); it
names all performers for all stage events in the main theater*

*and in the adjunct Piccola Scala, which opened in 1955. The
best description:*

635. Cambiasi, Pompeo. *La Scala: 1778-1889*. 5. ed. Milano:
     Ricordi, 1906. xli, 523p. IOM-2426 ML 1733.3 M5 C2
     Dimensions and documents of the theater; chronology
     of all seasons, with casts and contemporary judgments
     of the performances. Supplementary list of performances
     at the Teatro della Canobbiana, 1779-1889. No index.

*Yet another chronology, with a fine narrative history, is
given in Carlo Gatti, Il Teatro alla Scala nella storia e
nell' arte (1778-1963), 1964 (IOM-2425).*
  *Operatic life in Modena has been chronicled by several
authors; one appears to have covered the most ground:*

636. Tardini, Vincenzo. *I teatri di Modena*. Modena:
     Forghieri, Pellequi, 1899-1902. 3 vols. 1903 suppl.
     bound in vol. 3. IOM-2427 ML 1733.8 M6 T2
     Only volume 3 is about opera. It has a chronology
     of performances from 1594 to 1903, beginning with Orazio
     Vecchi's madrigal-comedy *L'amfiparnaso*. Casts are
     given. Name and title index. Earlier years are tabu-
     lated in Alessandro Gandini, *Cronistoria dei teatri di
     Modena dal 1539 al 1871* (Modena: Tipografia Sociale,
     1873; 3 vols.).

*The idea of a distinct "Neapolitan opera" style is losing
popularity among musicologists, but there was certainly a
flourishing operatic school there in the 18th century, pro-
ducing "opera seria." Writing about Naples (Napoli) centers
on that period, and on the great San Carlo theater. These
seem to be the most useful works in a large literature:*

637. Robinson, Michael F. *Naples and Neapolitan Opera*.
     Oxford: Clarendon Press, 1972. ix, 281p. ISBN
     0-19-816124-7 IOM-2438 ML 1733.8 N3 R6
     Valuable examination of texts and scores, with extended
     musical examples. Also a study of overtures and other
     orchestral pieces. Bibliography and index.

638. Tintori, Giampiero. *L'opera napoletana*. Milano:
      Ricordi, 1958. 301p. IOM-2429 ML 1733.8 N3 T5
      Most useful for a list of about 2,000 operas, arranged
      by composer, with librettists and premiere data. Index
      to persons and theaters.

*Graham Hardie, "Neapolitan Comic Opera 1707-1750: Some Addenda
and Corrigenda for the* New Grove," *Journal of the American
Musicological Society, 36 (Spring 1983): 124-127, provides
bibliographic data for operas omitted in the* New Grove *work-
lists and offers added commentaries for certain pieces that
are cited in those lists. A dissertation by William Park
Stalnaker, "The Beginnings of Opera in Naples" (Princeton
University, 1968) should be of interest; it has not been
examined. On the San Carlo theater (opened, 1737; burned in
1816 and rebuilt in six months; damaged but not destroyed in
the Second World War) the principal study is Felice de
Filippis and R. Arnese,* Cronache del Teatro di S. *Carlo (1737-
1960), 1961-63 (IOM-2430); it has a chronology of performed
works, with illustrations, composer work-lists, and indexes
of librettists and singers. A good collection of essays:
Ente Autonomo del Teatro di San Carlo,* Cento anni di vita
del Teatro di San Carlo, *1848-1948, 1948 (IOM-2431); includes
details on the building, documents, list of impresarios,
and a chronology for the period. 95 illustrations; no index.*
     *The other theaters of Naples are covered by Francesco
Florimo,* La scuola musicale di Napoli *... (Napoli: Morano,
1880-82), 4 vols. in 3. All performers and performances
in the city, from 1651 to 1881, are included in the chronology.*
     *A scholarly narrative history of opera in Padua (Padova):
Bruno Brunelli Bonetti,* I teatri di Padova dalle origini alla
fine del secolo XIX, *1921 (IOM-2432), includes descriptions
of the theaters and many of the works performed, but has no
chronology. A partial chronology appears in:*

639. Pallerotti, A. *Spettacoli melodrammatici e coreografici
      rappresentati in Padova nei teatri Obizzi, Nuovo e del
      Prato della Valle dal 1751 al 1892*. Padova: Prosperini,
      1892. 72p. ML 1733.8 P2 P15
      A list of about 750 productions, by date, with names
      of artists. No index.

*For Palermo there is a fine study of 19th-century musical
life: Ottavio Tiby,* Il Real Teatro Carolino e l'ottocento
musicale palermitano, *1957 (IOM-2433). The Carolino theater*

opened in 1809 as an enlarged reconstruction of a building
that had housed opera since 1726. (The Teatro Massimo,
opened 1897, is now the principal house.) A chronology for
the Carolino, 1808/09-1896/97, is given; with lists of works,
composers, impresarios, directors, and singers. No book about
the Massimo has been seen.

Parma has a distinguished operatic past, boasting one of
the oldest extant theaters, the Farnese (opened 1628), and
later associations with Verdi--it is the home of the Istituto
di Studi Verdiani--and Toscanini. The present center for
opera is the Teatro Regio, which opened 1829. Tabular
chronologies for the pre-Regio period appear in:

640. Ferrari, Paolo-Emilio. *Spettacoli drammatico-musicali*
      e coreografici in Parma dal' anno 1628 all' anno 1883.
      Parma: Aderni, 1884. 383p. (Reprint--Bologna: Forni,
      1969.) ML 1733.8 P28 F375
      Gives tabular chronologies of performances, by theater,
      with casts of singers, dancers, conductors, etc. Commen-
      taries and notes; detailed index to all persons, titles,
      and topics.

A good account of the Teatro Regio: Il Teatro Regio di Parma
nella sua storia dal 1883 al 1929, *1929 (IOM-2434), discusses*
the building, personalities, and performances; there is a
chronology, and an index that identifies the singers of
leading roles. Some updating is available in Maurizio
Corradi-Cervi, Cronologia del Teatro Regio di Parma, 1928-
1948, *1955 (IOM-2435).*

Operatic life in Rome displays an unsteady past. There
were performances as early as 1606, and the first comic opera
was given there in 1639 (see Mazzocchi, above), but there was
sporadic papal opposition to opera (Pope Innocent had the
Teatro Torinona demolished in 1697), and the city never
reached the distinction of other centers in Italy. The Teatro
Argentina opened in 1732; its history is thoroughly presented
in Mario Rinaldi, Due secoli di musica al Teatro Argentina
(Firenze: Olschki, 1978; 3 vols.). A chronology to 1978 is
included, and there is an exhaustive bibliography of more
than 500 primary and secondary sources. Names and titles
are indexed. No comparable study of the newer Teatro
Costanzi, 1880, renovated as the Teatro Reale dell' Opera in
1928, has been seen. One Pope was an opera patron: Clement IX;
he was in fact a librettist of 12 operas, under the name
Giulio Rospigliosi. An important study of his work has
already been cited (189).

The lively operatic history of Turin (Torino) was concen-
trated on the great Teatro Regio from its opening in 1740 until
its destruction by fire in 1936. (It was finally rebuilt and
reopened in 1973.) An excellent work offers a full range of
facts:

641.   Bouquet, Marie-Thérese, and Alberto Basso. *Storia del*
       Teatro Regio di Torino. Torino: Cassa di Risparmio
       di Torino, 1976. 2 vols.   561, 856p.   PN 2686 T82 R437
       A scholarly history, with thousands of footnotes and
       presentation of all relevant documents; outstanding
       color plates, chronology of performances with casts,
       chronological tables. A great deal of detail is offered--
       e.g., the salaries paid to singers for most performances.
       Each volume has a name and title index.

In Venice (Venezia) opera became a public rather than private
spectacle. The first public opera house in the world opened
in 1637, followed quickly by many others in that city (there
is a convenient list in the Concise Oxford Dictionary of
Opera*). In 1792 the famous theater La Fenice opened; it is*
thought by many to be the most beautiful of the world's opera
houses. A scholarly account of the early period is Simon
Towneley Worsthorne, Venetian Opera in the Seventeenth Century,
1954 (IOM-2436).
    Chronologies of all performances in 16 theaters, with
casts and commentaries, are given by Giovanni Salvioli, I
teatri musicali di Venezia nel secolo XVII (1637-1700) ...,
1879 (IOM-2438). For the next century the principal study is
Taddeo Wiel, I teatri musicali veneziani del settecento,
1897 (IOM-2439); a chronology of 1,274 performances in all
theaters is offered; with indexes to titles, librettists,
musicians, singers, dancers, and choreographers. A collec-
tion of essays on La Fenice: Mario Nani Mocenigo, Il teatro
La Fenice: notizie storiche e artistiche, *1926 (IOM-2437);*
a chronology of operas and ballets produced 1792-1925 is
included, with names of artists, commentaries, and critical
reception.
    Other works on the operatic life of individual cities
are cited in Surian (608). Further titles are also noted in
the section "Regional and Local Histories" of the Italian
chapter in IOM (items 2469-2493); and at the beginning of
that section the most important articles on cities from MGG
and New Grove are identified.
    The most useful directory is Brody (70). An informative
adjunct is Siegmund Levarie, Musical Italy Revisited ...,

1963 (IOM-2390). Current notices of operatic performances
in Italian cities are found in the quarterly journal L'opera.
Rivista trimestrale della lirica e della concertistica internazionale, 1965- (Milano: Fenarete, 1965-).

Mexico

Spanish: México. The most useful treatise:

642. Stevenson, Robert Murrell. Music in Mexico: A Historical
        Survey. New York: Crowell, 1952. 300p. IOM-1193
        ML 210 S8
        A scholarly, comprehensive study covering all periods
        and genres. The operatic 19th century is thoroughly
        discussed in a 50-page chapter with 92 footnotes.
        Musical examples; 11-page bibliography; index of names,
        titles, and topics.

Extended treatment of opera is also found in:

643. Olavarria y Ferrari, Enrique de. Reseña histórica del
        teatro en México.... 3d ed. México: Porrua, 1961.
        6 vols. IOM-1212 PN 2311 043
        The sixth volume is an index of names, organizations,
        theaters, places, and publications. Coverage is 1538-
        1961, with opera and other stage works discussed. A
        chronology of performances, 1911-61, appears in volume 5.

A more recent study, not seen, is Carlos Du-Pond Díaz, Cinquenta
años de ópera en México (México: UNAM, 1978), 326p. The review
in Inter-American Music Review, 5-1 (Fall 1982); 118-121,
makes favorable comments but observes that the book should be
"reedited with careful insertion or confirmation of dates,
places, and names. Footnotes should be added, identifying
persons and places casually mentioned. Above all an index
is needed."
    Current concert and opera news is found in Heterofonía:
revista musical bimestral, 1968- (IOM-1226).

Monaco

644. Walsh, T.J. Monte Carlo Opera, 1879-1909. Dublin: Gill
        and Macmillan, 1975. xix, 321p. ISBN 0-7171-0725-6

IOM-2528   ML 1751 M66 W3

The basic study: a scholarly narrative, well documented and illustrated. Includes a chronology of operas performed, with casts; performances by the company abroad; number of performances of each opera; seasonal reports. Bibliography; name and title index. Updating is given by Georges Favre, *Histoire musicale de la Principauté de Monaco du XVIe au XXe siècle*, 1973 (IOM-2527); 20th-century opera performances are discussed.

Netherlands

Dutch: Nederland, or Holland; French: Hollande; German: Niederlande. The basic writings are in Dutch.

645. Monnikendam, Marius. *Nederlands componisten van heden
      en verleden*. Amsterdam: A.J.G. Strengholt, 1968.
      280p. IOM-2534   ML 390 M658 N4
      A strong introduction to past and present musical
life, including a chapter on opera. Name index.

De opera in Nederland, *1946, by S.A.M. Bottenheim (IOM-2539),
is the only full-length history of opera. A yearly tabulation
of concert and opera activity is issued by the government:*
Statistiek van het concert- opera/operetta- en ballet-bezoek,
1973/74- (IOM-2533). Daniel François Scheurleer, Het muziek-
leven in Nederland ..., *1909 (IOM-2551), is a scholarly account
of musical life in the Hague and Amsterdam in the second part
of the 18th century. The* MGG *and* New Grove *articles on Amsterdam are both strong, and give useful facts on opera in
the city.* Het toonkunstenaarboek, *1956- (IOM-2564) is a
frequently revised directory of all Dutch music organizations.
Brody (68) also gives directory coverage. Current performances
are noted in* Key Notes: Musical Life in the Netherlands,
*1975- (IOM-2565), a semiannual journal published in English;
and in the annual* Nederlands theater-en televisie jaarboek,
1951- (IOM-2566). Another periodical, Opera journaal, *began
in 1972 (continuing* Opera: periodiek voor muziekdramatische
kunst, *1967-1971); it published monthly until 1979 (latest
issues at Library of Congress).*

New Zealand

646. Brusey, Phyllis Wilkins. *Ring Down the Curtain*. Wellington: C. Rex Monigatti, 1973. xii, 192 [48]p. of plates. ML 1751 N5 N56
A well-illustrated popular history of opera in the country. Includes a list of productions of the New Zealand Opera Company from 1954 to 1971. No bibliography; no index.

Peru

Spanish: Perú. The basic general history is:

647. Stevenson, Robert Murrell. *The Music of Peru: Aboriginal and Viceroyal Epochs*. Washington, D.C.: Pan American Union, 1960. xii, 331p. IOM-1256 ML 236 S8
Thoroughly documented, detailed account of all musical topics, with consideration of early opera. Bibliography, musical examples; index.

The same author also has a major study of opera: Foundations of New World Opera, *with a Transcription of the Earliest Extant American Opera, 1701, 1973 (IOM-1260). It is the definitive historical study, including the music of Tomás de Torrejón y Velasco's* La púrpura de la rosa, *the first Western Hemisphere opera for which music has survived. A chronological list of operas, ballets, and other dramatic works with Peruvian subject matter, 1658-1927, is given in Juan Sixto Prieto, "El Perú en la música escénica,"* Fénix, Revista de la Biblioteca Nacional, *9 (1953): 278-351 (IOM-1270).*

Poland

Polish: Polska; French: Pologne; German: Polen. The major literature concerning opera is in Polish. This essay collection in English provides some useful background:

648. Jarociński, Stefan. *Polish Music*. Warsaw: PWN, 1965. viii, 327p. IOM-2615 ML 306 J28
Includes essays on various aspects of musical culture, among them opera statistics, 1949-62, and a historical

chronology through 1963.   Excellent bibliography of
musical literature; about 200 items.   Name index.

*An excellent historical study is also in English: John M.
Glowacki, "The History of Polish Opera: (Ph.D. dissertation.
Boston University, 1952); it discusses early opera in the
country and works by Polish composers, and gives a list of
all Polish operas with premiere dates (IOM-2622).   A good
short summary by Gerald Abraham, "The Early Development of
Opera in Poland,"* Essays on Opera and English Music: in
Honour of Sir Jack Westrup *(Oxford: Blackwell, 1975), pp.
148-165, notes the first performance in 1628, and the
earliest Polish opera in 1778.   Titles of works are given in
Polish; there are 40 reference footnotes.   The longest list
of Polish operas, about 750 works, is found in Kornel
Michalowski,* Opery polskie; katalog, *1954 (IOM-2689).   A
collection of studies on opera in old Poland: Julian Lewanski,*
Opera w dawnej Polsce na dworze Wldayslawa IV i królów
saskich *(Warszawa: Ossolineum, 1973; 201p.), includes 63
pictures of theaters and stage scenes.   The period covered
is 1635-1762.   Three articles by Józef Kański in* Musikbühne,
76, *give some views of recent work: "Die neue polnischer
Oper," "Opern polnischer Komponisten seit 1951," and "Ballette
polnischer Komponisten seit 1947" (IOM-2623).   Another work
by Kański,* Przewodnik operowy, *1978 (IOM-2624) is a general
opera guide, with Polish composers well represented.*
    *Several books deal with opera in individual cities.   For
Danzig (Gdańsk):*

649.   *Państwowa Opera i Filharmonia Baltycka w Gdańsku....*
        Gdańsk: Wydawn. Morskie, 1971.   162p.   IOM-2648
        ML 1740.8 D3 P3
        Miscellaneous essays on concert and ballet activity
        in the city.   Gives repertoire of operas performed
        1950-70, with casts and illustrations.   Names of artists
        in the opera company are listed.   No bibliography; no
        index.

For Poznań: Jerzy Waldorff, Opera Poznańska, 1919-1969, *1970
(IOM-2626), gives a history of opera in the city, with biographies and a chronology of 412 performances.   Warsaw is
covered by these studies: Józef Kański,* Teatr Wielki w
Warszawie, *1965 (IOM-2627), a picture book issued on the
reopening of the Teatr Wielki (Grand Theater), originally
built 1833 and destroyed 1939.   Preface is in five languages,*

*but the main text is in Polish only. A list of 230 operas
and ballets given in the Teatr, and in the earlier house, from
1778 to 1965, is a very useful feature. Another book of
photographs of the new theater is:*

650. *Dwadzieścia piec lat opery Warszawskiej w Polsce Ludowej,
       1945-1970.* Warszawa: Teatr Wielki, 1970. 339p.
       IOM-2628. ML 1740.8 W4 T446
       Although this is primarily a photo-book, showing scenes,
       posters, portraits, and many views of the Grand Theater,
       it does include a chronological list of performances from
       1945 to 1970, with directors (not the singers) named.
       No index.

*Another chronology appears in Witold Filler, Rendez-vous z
warszawska operetka, 1961 (IOM-2629), a history of light opera
by Poles and others that have been given in Warsaw; list of
works performed, 1859-1939. Concert and operatic life in
Warsaw during specific periods is examined in two articles
by Hanna Pukińska-Szepietowska, in Szkice o kulturze muzycznej
XIX wieku, 1971-76 (IOM-2653/2654). Musical life in 18th-
century Warsaw is the subject of Jan Prosnak, Kultura muzyczna
Warszawy, XVIII w., 1955 (IOM-2652).*

*Two of the news journals are published in common languages:
Polish Music, 1966- (IOM-2659), in English and German, gives
notices of concert and opera, with short feature articles;
Music in Poland, 1966- (IOM-2660), is a chronicle of events,
with book reviews and articles. Both of these are published
quarterly. A Polish news periodical appears twice a month:
Ruch muzyczny, 1945- (IOM-2661). There is also a yearly
review of plays and operas performed in the country, listed
by city: Almanach sceny polskiej, 1959/60- (IOM-2625).*

Portugal

*Several general works on Portuguese music form a valuable
basis for study of opera. Not many libraries have the first
item, but it is worth searching out as the most dependable
brief review:*

651. Stevenson, Robert. "Portuguese Music: A Historical
       Résumé." *Journal of the American Portuguese Cultural
       Society,* 4 (Summer-Fall 1970): 1-13. IOM-2706a
       DP 501 A5

An excellent summary, beginning in the early sixth
century. Opera in the 18th century has considerable
attention, and modern works are discussed.

*Six monographs by one of the most important Portuguese scholars
are found in Mário de Sampayo Ribeiro, Achegas para a história
da música em Portugal, 1932-61 (IOM-2709). Francisco Marques
de Sousa Viterbo, Subsídios para a história da música em
Portugal, 1932 (IOM-2710), presents historical data in the
form of a biographical dictionary. Another biographical work,
Os músicos portuguezes: biographia-bibliographia, by Joaquim
Antonio da Fonseca E. Vasconcellos (1870; IOM-2722), is useful for work-lists and historical context; it includes a
chronology of performances of operas by Marcos Portugal
(1762-1830), one of Europe's leading composers in the genre.
Ernesto Vieira, Diccionário biográphico de músicos portu-
guezes; história e bibliographia da música em Portugal, 1900
(IOM-2723), is a dependable source. Michelangelo Lambertini,
"Portugal," Encyclopédie de la musique et dictionnaire du
Conservatoire (IOM-2694), gives a much less reliable general
impression, but does provide valuable data on 18th-century
opera.*
   Specific studies of opera produce only a partial picture:

652. Marques, José Joaquim. *Cronologia da ópera em Portugal...*
     Lisboa: Artística, 1947. 159p. IOM-2701
     Although most of this volume concerns a form of can-
     tata called vilhancico, it does include a chronology
     of operatic and other dramatic performances in Portugal,
     1640-1793. No bibliography; no index.

*Francisco da Fonseca Benevides, O Real Theatro de S. Carlos
de Lisboa ..., 1883 (IOM-2702), presents a chronology for
Lisbon's principal theater from 1793 to 1883. Some updating
is given in the same author's O Real Theatro de S. Carlos de
Lisboa: memorias, 1883-1902, 1902 (IOM-2703).*

Romania

*The spelling "Rumania" is also used. French: Roumanie; German:
Rumänien. Since 1965 the official name of the country has
been Republica Socialista România. A recent book of essays
on music forms a useful starting point:*

653. Cosma, Viorel. *România muzicală*. Bucureşti: Editura
     Muzicală, 1980. 131p. IOM-2730 ML 258 C7
     Includes essays on opera companies and other musical
     institutions. Bibliography; no index.

*An earlier review of the musical situation: Petre Nitulescu,
Muzica românească de azi, 1939 (IOM-2729), has considerable
detail on the operatic institutions. Petre Brâncusi, Muzica
în România socialistă, 1973 (IOM-2728), is a popular introduction to operatic and other musical activities, stressing
socialist values.*

*A scholarly history of opera, emphasizing the 19th and
20th centuries:*

654. Massoff, Ioan. *Teatrul romînesc; privire istorică.*
     Bucureşti: Editura Pentru Literatură, 1961- .
     IOM-2742 PN 2841 M3
     Only one volume has been seen, in what was planned
     as a multivolume history. It gives details on opera
     houses, companies, and individuals. The only actual
     chronology is for 1852-60 in one theater. Bibliography
     of about 600 entries; no index. The next item is a
     good supplement:

655. Cosma, Octavian L. *Opera romînească: privire istorica
     asupra creatiei lirico-dramatice.* Bucureşti:
     Editura Muzicală, 1962. 332p. IOM-2743
     ML 1751 R8 C68
     Considers opera and ballet after the First World War;
     well illustrated and footnoted. List of opera composers
     and their works: about 300 operas. Chronology of per-
     forming groups in Bucharest, 1772-1921. Bibliography
     of about 200 titles; index of persons and titles.

*A universal opera guide is useful for program notes and synop-
ses of about 40 Romanian operas: Gabriela Constantinescu, et
al., Ghid de opera, 1971 (IOM-2744); and a similar guide to
operetta is also informative: Titus Moisescu and Miltiade
Păun, Opereta. Ghid, 1969 (IOM-2745). Performing groups and
theaters are identified in the New Grove article on Bucharest.
The most useful periodical for news about opera is Muzica,
1951- (IOM-2860), a monthly review of concert and opera life,
with articles, interviews, and notices; recent issues in French
and Romanian.*

Spain

*Spanish: España; French: Espagne; German: Spanien. A fine
introduction to all forms of Spanish music is given in the
New Grove article, by Robert Stevenson et al.; Stevenson's
entry for Madrid is also informative. MGG offers thorough
coverage in "Spanien," an article of multiple authorship,
and in articles by José Subirá on Barcelona and Madrid.
    This is the great general history:*

656. Subirá, José. *Historia de la música española e hispano-
         americana.* Barcelona: Salvat Editores, 1953. 1,003p.
         IOM-2928
         A comprehensive account of opera and other forms;
         with biographical data, many illustrations and examples.
         No bibliography; index.

Other general histories of value are Adolfo Salazar, La música
de España, *1972 (IOM-2922);* Gilbert Chase, *The Music of Spain,
1959 (IOM-2935);* Mary Neal Hamilton, *Music in Eighteenth-
Century Spain, 1937 (IOM-2949);* Frederico Sopeña Ibáñez,
*Historia de la música española contemporanea, 1958 (IOM-2953);
and Manuel Valls,* La música española despues de Manuel de
Falla, *1962 (IOM-2954).*
    *A useful brief survey of operatic history is offered by
José Subirá,* Historia de la música teatral en España, *1945
(IOM-2905). The zarzuela, an operatic form in which spoken
dialogue and music are mingled, is given a concise historical
account by Jack Sage and Lionel Salter in their New Grove
article. Details are found in Roger Mindlin,* Die Zarzuela:
das spanische Singspiel im 19. und 20. Jahrhundert, *1965
(IOM-2911), and Emilio Cotarelo y Mori,* Historia de la zarzuela ..., *1934 (IOM-2909). This is a special approach:*

657. Bussey, William M. *French and Italian Influence on the
         Zarzuela 1700-1770.* Ann Arbor, Mich.: UMI Research,
         1982. 297p. ISBN 0-8357-1285-0 ML 1950 B87
         A scholarly account of the era, with musical examples,
         production histories, structural analyses, and notes on
         the primary and secondary sources. A useful glossary
         of terms; bibliography of about 500 items; index of
         names, titles, and topics.

Specific time periods in operatic history are treated in many studies. Emilio Cotarelo y Mori, Orígenes y establecimiento de la ópera en España hasta 1800, *1917 (IOM-2912), is a detailed, documented story of the 16th and 17th centuries. Robert Stevenson, "Espectáculos musicales en la España del siglo XVII," is an important discussion, already cited (300). An anthology of music with comments offers a good view of early writing: Felipe Pedrell,* Teatro lírico español anterior al siglo XIX *(La Coruña: Berea, 1897-98; 5 vols.). A later epoch treated in Antonio Pena y Goni,* La ópera española y la música dramática en España en el siglo XIX; apuntes históricos, *1881 (IOM-2913).*

The recent century is discussed in:

658.   Fernández-Cid, Antonio. *Cien años de teatro musical en España, 1875-1975.* Madrid: Real Musical, 1975.   610p.
ISBN 84-387-0021-7   IOM-2906   ML 1747 F47
Includes a useful narrative survey of opera, zarzuela, and other stage music for the century, and a list of librettists; also a biographical section for composers. No bibliography.   Photographs; index.

Since operatic life has been focused on Madrid and Barcelona, the accounts limited to those cities also have general application. These are the basic works on Barcelona: José Subirá, La ópera en los teatros de Barcelona, *1960 (IOM-2916); covering 18th century to 1936; Francisco Virella Cassañes,* La ópera en Barcelona; estudio histórico-crítico, *1888 (IOM-2917), with a chronology of performances, 1788-1888; and Juan Mestres Calvert,* El gran Teatro del Liceo visto por su empresario *(Barcelona: Vergara, n.d.), 269p., covering to 1945 in narrative style. The Liceo opened 1847, burned 1861, was rebuilt and repoened 1862. In Madrid the Teatro Real opened 1850 and had a distinguished history in the 19th century. The first opera "broadcast" originated there, in 1896/97--the transmission being by telephone. This interesting fact is given in:*

659.   Gómez de la Serna, Gaspar. *Gracias y desgracias del Teatro Real.* 2. ed. Madrid: Ministerio de Educación y Ciencia, 1975.   viii, 78p.   ISBN 8436904559
ML 1747.8 M32 T44
Begins with a useful review of theaters in Madrid in 1850, when the Teatro Real opened. Gives a general account of each season 1868-1924/25, without chronological

lists or casts. The Teatro closed after 1925 and was
not reopened until October 1966. Illustrations; no
notes, bibliography, or index.

*Chronologies and alphabetical lists of works performed are
presented in José Subirá, Historia y anecdotario del Teatro
Real, 1949 (IOM-2915). News of current activities is found
in the quarterly journal Ritmo, 1929- (IOM-2975).*

Sweden

*Swedish: Sverige; German: Schweden. The New Grove article
forms a useful introduction. A survey of musical life in
recent years covers operatic activity:*

660. Prieberg, Fred K. *Musik und Musikpolitik in Schweden.*
      Herrenberg: Döring, 1976. 112, [12]p. IOM-3012a
      Describes the Institutet för Rikskonserter and other
      state institutions for the dissemination of musical
      performances, covering the 1960s and early 1970s.
      Name index.

*An earlier publication by the Institutet för Rikskonserter
gave names of opera houses and listed opera performances:
Music for Sweden, 1972 (IOM-3013). A special issue of the
journal Musikrevy (IOM-3038) was published in English:
Swedish Music Past and Present, 1976 (IOM-3016). It includes a good summary of the operatic situation. Directories
of Scandinavia, already cited (71n), contain facts on Swedish
operatic life.*
    *Major opera productions have taken place in Stockholm
since the mid-18th century. The first permanent theater was
built in the suburb Drottningholm in 1754 (burned 1762; rebuilt 1766 and still in use). Its story is told in Agne
Beijer, Drottningholms slottsteater pa Lovisa Ulrikas och
Gustaf IIIs tid, 1981 (IOM-3023a). The principal house today
is the Kungliga Teatern (Royal Opera House), opened 1898.
A useful book was published by the Teatern for the 200th
anniversary of the company, which had occupied various sites
since 1773: Kungliga Teatern: repertoar 1773-1973, 1974
(IOM-3022). It names all the works performed in chronological
order; the title index includes about 1,400 names. Some updating and extra information is given in the popular, illustrated history by Ake Sällström, Opera pa Stockholmsoperan,
1977 (IOM-3023).*

An inventory of modern Swedish operas is available: Swedish
Music Information Center, Fran Sveagaldrar till Reliken: svenska
musikdramatiska verk 1890-1975, *1977 (IOM-3061); it lists
about 150 works, with cast needed, instrumentation, duration,
premiere data, and publisher.*

Switzerland

*French: Suisse; German: Der Schweiz; Italian: Svizzera.   Two
articles provide an introduction to Swiss operatic writings:*

661.   Gaillard, Paul-André. "Les compositeurs suisses et
       l'opéra." *Schweizerische Musikzeitung*, 114 (July-
       August 1974): 219-225; 114 (September-October 1974):
       280-286. IOM-3080 ML 5 S34
       Consists of interviews with opera composers and com-
       ments on their works. Gaillard states that there is no
       specifically Swiss style of opera. Footnotes lead to
       important earlier literature, and there is a 15-item
       bibliography.

*An older review of the operatic scene is by Edgar Refardt,
"Schweizer Opern und Opernkomponister," Schweizerische Musikzeitung, 85 (1945): 385-389 (IOM-3081).   Operatic life is
best approached by individual city.   For Basel: Wilhelm
Merian, Basels Musikleben im XIX. Jahrhundert, 1920 (IOM-3087a);
a general narrative, without footnotes, covering opera and
other musical activity.   Geneva (Genève) is discussed in Roger
de Candolle, Histoire du théâtre de Genève, 1978 (IOM-3081a);
it includes chronologies for the Grand Casino (1952/53-
1961/62) and the new Grand-Théâtre (1962/63-1978/79).
Further information on the 19th century is found in Claude
Tappolet, La vie musicale à Genève au dix-neuvième siècle
(1814-1918), 1972 (IOM-3094).   Vaud is the southwestern canton
that includes Lausanne, Geneva, and Montreux; a documented
history of early music there is available: Jacques Burdet,
La musique dans le pays de Vaud sous le régime Bernois (1536-
1798), (IOM-3098).   For Zürich there is a good introduction
in Rudolf Schoch, Hundert Jahre Tonhalle Zürich, 1968 (IOM-
3103), the title of which fails to suggest its wide scope as
a history of musical life.   The Tonhalle is used for concerts,
the Stadttheater for opera.   On the latter there is Martin
Hürliman and Harry Olt, Theater in Zürich--125 Jahre Stadttheater.*

Directory information is given in Thomas Adank, Schweizer Musik-Handbuch, *1979 (IOM-3105), and in Brody (68). Current events are noted in the bimonthly* Schweizerische Musikzeitung, *1942- (IOM-3107), which has published under various names since 1862.*

Union of Soviet Socialist Republics

The Soîuz Sovetskikh Sotŝialisticheskikh Respublik (SSSR) is known in English as the Union of Soviet Socialist Republics (USSR) or the Soviet Union. French: Union des Républiques Socialistes Soviétiques (URSS); German: Sowjetunion. Before the 1917 Revolution the area was named Rossiîa (Russia; Russie; Russland); the name has remained in use as an easy designation for the present USSR, although it is no longer correct. USSR comprises 15 republics: Armenia, Azerbaidjan, Belorussia (White Russia), Estonia, Georgia, Kazakhstan, Kirghizia, Latvia, Lithuania, Moldavia, Russia (the largest republic, covering much of the territory of prerevolutionary Russia), Tadjikistan, Turkmenistan, Ukraine, and Uzbekistan. The official names of these units carry the words "Soviet Socialist Republic" (SSR); e.g. Uzbekskaîa SSR. Moskva is the capital of the Soviet Union, and of the Russian republic: Russian Socialist Federal Soviet Republic (RSFSR); it is Moscow in English, Moscou in French, and Moskau in German. Leningrad was known as St. Petersburg to 1914, and Petrograd to 1924.

These explications of terminology are offered to simplify the task of those who wish to study Russian opera. The task requires at least a basic knowledge of the Russian language as well, as there is hardly any research literature in Western tongues. In the present book Russian is transliterated to the Roman alphabet according to the Library of Congress system, the system that will be encountered in most American research libraries. But there are many other transliterations in use--a fact that should be borne in mind when approaching indexes and other alphabetical arrangements of material.

A further complication in the life of the researcher is that library research collections have demonstrated extremely vague acquisition practice for books and journals published in the USSR. Neither the Library of Congress nor any other great library consulted in the preparation of this volume gave evidence of a coherent collection policy; it may well be that important items are missing from this inventory, and that certain items cited have been superseded by later editions of new titles.

IOM offers a full view of the available literature on all the Soviet republics. In the present volume only these republi are considered (after the general section): Belorussia, Estonia, Latvia, Lithuania, and Ukraine.

Unfortunately, the articles on the USSR in the Western musical encyclopedias are all uneven, and vague in their approaches to opera. The most useful encyclopedias are in Russian: Muzykal'naîa entsiklopediîa, 1973- (IOM-3125), and:

662.   Bol'shaîa sovetskaîa entsiklopediîa.3. izd.   Moskva:
       Izd. Sovetskaîa Entsiklopediîa, 1970-78.   30 vols.
       IOM-3126   AE 55 B62
       Consists of about 100,000 articles on all subjects,
       emphasizing Soviet matters.   Signed scholarly essays
       with bibliographies.   Good musical coverage; e.g.,
       individual articles on European opera houses, with
       photos and floor plans.   Fortunately, this important
       work is available in English translation as the *Great
       Soviet Encyclopedia*, 1973-80 (IOM-3126).   Another
       valuable encyclopedia: *Teatral'naîa entsiklopediîa*,
       1967 (IOM-3163), features long articles on opera in
       each republic, with chronologies and casts, and details
       on the theaters.

*Gerald Abraham has made some important contributions to Russian
studies; most of them appear in three essay collections:*
Slavonic and Romantic Music, *1968 (IOM-3128);* Studies in
Russian Music *(263n), and* On Russian Music *(263n).   Another
essential gathering of essays: Boris V. Asaf'ev,* Izbrannye
trudy *(263n), gives extensive detail on Glinka (all of
volume i), Tchaikovsky, Musorgskiî, and Rimskiî-Korsakov.
The principal general history of music: Moscow.   Institut
Istorii Iskusstv.* Istoriîa muzyki narodov SSSR, *196-   (IOM-
3183), is a series of volumes by various authors, edited by
îûriî Keldysh.   Basic arrangement is chronological; latest
volume seen is the fifth, covering 1956-67.   The preferred
general history in English is:*

663.   Leonard, Richard Anthony.   *A History of Russian Music.*
       New York: Macmillan, 1957; London: Jarrolds, 1956.
       Reissued--New York: Funk & Wagnalls, 1968.   395p.
       (Reprint--Westport, Conn.: Greenwood, 1977.   ISBN
       0-8371-9658-2), IOM-3190   ML 300 L45
       A useful survey of main trends, drawn from secondary
       sources in Western languages.   Good summary of operatic
       development.   Bibliography of about 100 titles; expansive
       index of names and titles.

*Significant studies are available on specific periods. Iʉriĭ
Keldysh, Russkaĩa muzyka XVIII veka, 1965 (IOM-3193), gives
scholarly attention to opera and all genres. An earlier work
is still useful: Nikolaĭ Findeizen, Ocherki po istorii muzyki
v Rossii ..., 1928-29 (IOM-3194); it includes lists of operas
performed to the end of the 18th century. The preferred
Western account of the 18th century is:*

664.   Mooser, Robert Aloys. *Annales de la musique et des
       musiciens en Russie au XVIIIe siècle.* Genève: Mont-
       Blanc, 1948-51. 3 vols. IOM-3195 ML 300 M84
       Based on primary documents, which are quoted extensive-
       ly. Includes much biographical detail. Appendixes
       of letters, programs, and other contemporary materials.
       Impressive bibliography of about 800 titles, unfor-
       tunately in French translation only. Name and title
       indexes.

*For the 19th century the most esteemed writers are Asaf'ev
and Stasov. The main works are: Boris V. Asaf'ev, Russkaĩa
muzyka ot nachala XIX stoletiĩa, 1930 (IOM-3197); this has
been translated: Russian Music from the Beginning of the
Nineteenth Century, 1953 (IOM-3197). Vladimir V. Stasov,
Selected Essays on Music, 1968 (IOM-3198), offers in English
seven principal essays; Stasov was an influential critic and
advocate of young composers.
    There is a useful English account of 20th-century trends:*

665.   Schwarz, Boris. *Music and Musical Life in Soviet
       Russia, 1917-1970.* New York: Norton, 1972. 550p.
       ISBN 0-393-02152 IOM-3202 ML 300.5 S37
       Trends and principal figures are thoroughly discussed
       in this well-documented study. Bibliography of about
       250 entries; name and topic index.

*On opera specifically, the most important work is a series of
volumes by Abram A. Gozenpud: Muzykal'nyĭ teatr v Rossii; ot
istokov do Glinki, 1959 (IOM-3160), covering to the mid-19th
century; Russkiĭ opernyĭ teatr XIX veka, 1969-73 (IOM-3161),
covering 1836-89 in three volumes; Russkiĭ opernyĭ teatr na
rubezhe XIX-XX vekov i F.I. Shalĩapin, 1974, covering the
turn of the century; Russkiĭ opernyĭ teatr mezhdu dvukh
revoliũtsii, 1975, covering 1905-17; and Russkiĭ sovetskiĭ
opernyĭ teatr, 1917-1941, 1963 (IOM-3162). These are scholarly*

volumes, with much detail on individual works and name in-
dexes; but bibliographies are weak and musical examples lack-
ing; and there are no chronologies. An alphabetical list of
about 700 opera titles is a useful feature of the shorter
history by Vsevolod E. Cheshikhin, Istoriı͡a russkoı̆ opery s
1674 do 1903 g., *1905 (IOM-3159). This is a valuable hand-*
book:

666. Bernandt, Grigoriı̆ Borisovich. *Slovar' oper....* Moskva:
     Sovetskiı̆ Kompozitor, 1962. 554p. IOM-3164
     ML 102 06 B45
     Includes program notes on major operas; a chronology
     of premieres by city; and indexes to composers, libret-
     tists, conductors, ballet masters, stage managers, etc.

An important study in English:

667. Taruskin, Richard. *Opera and Drama in Russia as*
     Preached and Practiced in the 1860's. Ann Arbor,
     Mich.: UMI Research, 1981. xvii, 560p. ISBN
     0-8357-1245-1 IOM-3164a ML 1737 T37
     An exhaustive analysis of the period, emphasizing
     Glinka, Serov, and Cui. Works are identified in both
     Russian and English. Footnotes, extended musical ex-
     amples in score, pp. 451-541. Index of names and
     topics.

A useful study in French concerns the 18th century: Robert
Aloys Mooser, Opéras, intermezzos, ballets, cantates,
oratorios joués en Russie durant le XVIIIe siècle ...,
1955 (IOM-3165). For recent times there is a convenient
chronological list of about 350 Soviet operas (titles in
German only) in "Sowjetische Opern seit 1945," Musikbühne,
74, pp. 174-197 (IOM-3164b).
   Russkiı̆ sovetskiı̆ teatr, *1975 (IOM-3169), is an interest-*
ing collection of essays on the theaters of Leningrad and
Moscow, with lists of all performances and casts, 1917-26;
index of theaters and personal names.
   In Leningrad, then St. Petersburg, the first opera per-
formance occurred in 1736. The principal opera houses were
the Mariinskiı̆ Teatr (1860, replacing an earlier structure;
renamed the Kirov--see full title below--in 1935) and the
Mikhailovskiı̆ (1833; rebuilt 1859; renamed the Malyı̆ Opernyı̆
Teatr after the Revolution). A theater for comic opera opened

in 1927. *The* New Grove *article on the city is informative
with regard to history of these theaters. For details there
are several useful works: Leningrad. Gosudarstvennyĭ
Akademischeskiĭ Teatr Opery i Baleta.* Leningradskiĭ
Gosudarstvennyĭ Ordena Lenina Akademichskiĭ Teatr Opery i
Baleta Imeni S.M. Kirova, 1917-1967, *1967 (IOM-3166); includes
a chronology of performances 1917-67 and staff-lists. A brief
historical survey of the Kirov: Mihail Matveev,* Leningradskiĭ
Teatr Opery i Baleta Im. S.M. Kirova, *1973 (IOM-3167), gives
descriptions of major productions and biographies of singers;
also staff-lists and a repertoire-list, but no chronologies.
For the comic-opera house: Leningrad. Gosudarstvennyĭ Teatr
Komedii.* Leningradskiĭ Teatr Muzykal'noĭ Komedii, *1972 (IOM-
3168), is a narrative history, with chronology from 1929-71
and a staff-list.*

*Moscow developed as a major opera center only in the later
19th century, though it had an opera house as early as 1742.
The famous Bol'shoĭ Teatr opened in 1825, burned in 1853, was
rebuilt in 1856; it has been the subject of many books, of
which the following seems to be the most informative:* Bol'shoĭ
Teatr SSSR: opera, balet, *1958 (IOM-3710); an oversized book
of color pictures with a historical narrative and a bibliography of more than 1,000 entries. Another fine book of color
plates is: Moscow. Gosudarstvennyĭ Akademicheskiĭ Bol'shoĭ
Teatr.* Bol'shoĭ Teatr SSSR: fotoalbom *(Moskva: Planeta, 1976;
2 vols. ML 1741.8 M72 G75).*

A useful book in English is available:

668.   Pokrovsky, Boris Alexandrovich, and Yuri Nikolayevich
        Grigorovich. *The Bolshoi; Opera and Ballet at the
        Greatest Theater in Russia.* New York: Morrow, 1979.
        238p. ML 1741.8 M7 P762
        A large photo-book, with historical summary; includes
        a repertoire-list that shows only 42 operas presented
        since 1842 (only eight composers were foreigners;
        Wagner has never been produced). Index of opera titles.

There is also a list of Bol'shoĭ premieres, 1917-80, in Oper
Heute, *4 (74). The* New Grove *article on the city is a good
one.*

Notices about operatic activity are found in Sovetskaĭa
muzyka, *1933- (IOM-3218), a monthly; and in* Teatral'no-
kontsertnaĭa, *1971- (IOM-3220), a weekly. Writings on opera,
and other musical topics, are indexed in* Sovetskaĭa literatura
o muzyke ..., *1948/53- (IOM-3250); it is published ir-
regularly, with the periods covered far behind the publication
date.*

The next group of titles deals with opera in certain re-
publics of the USSR. On Belorussia the most informative in-
troduction is Muzykal'naîa kultura Belorusskoĭ SSR, *1977
(IOM-3306), which includes an essay on opera.* There is also
a scholarly narrative history of opera and operetta: Bronislav
Sil'vestrovich Smol'skiĭ, Belorusskiĭ muzykal'nyĭ teatr, *1963
(IOM-3310); and an account of the Bol'shoĭ Teatr in Minsk,
with a chronology 1852-1961: Beloruskiĭ Gosudarstvennyĭ Ordena
Lenina Bol'shoĭ Teatr Opery i Baleta, 1963, also by Smol'skiĭ
(IOM-3311).*

For Estonia there is a photo-book about the *Riiklik
Akadeemiline Ooperi- ja Balleti Teatr,* entitled Estonia (1906-
1966), *1969 (IOM-3325); it includes staff-rosters and lists
of operas that have been performed.*

A short introduction in English to opera in Latvia is
found in:

669. Rutkis, Jānis. *Latvia; Country and People.* Stockholm:
Latvian National Foundation, 1967. xv, 683p. IOM-
3355 DK 511 L16 R848
A general encyclopedia, with chapters on musical
topics. "Opera and Ballet" has four pages.

*German readers will find some useful segments in Longīns
Apkalns, Lettische Musik, 1977 (IOM-3356). But the best
history of opera in Latvia is Vija Briede-Bulāvinova,*
Opernoe tvorchestvo latyshskikh kompozitorov, *1979 (IOM-3358);
it gives facts about leading composers and the principal
operas.* A more extended history by the same author, in Latvian, is Latviešu opera: lidz 1940 g., *1975 (IOM-3359). It
contains a chronology of performances at the Latvijas
Nacionalas Operas, 1920-40.* Another work, not examined,
should be of interest: Sofiîa Fridrikhovna Verinîa,
Muzikal'nyĭ teatr Latvii ... *(Leningrad: "Muzyka," 1973;
184p. ML 1738 L4 V5).*

A useful introduction to Lithuanian music, including
opera, is:

670. Tauragis, Adeodatas. *Lithuanian Music; Past and Present.*
Vilnius: Gintaras, 1971. 223p. IOM-3368
ML 309 L5 T43
A survey beginning in the 14th century; includes a
chapter on opera. Profiles of 15 composers and brief
studies of 40 others. Bibliography of about 80 entries;
discography of about 50 items. No index.

*Something of a directory, in popular idiom, appears
under the name* The Lithuanian Musical Scene, *by Jonas Bagdan-
skis, 1974 (IOM-3369); it is informative on institutions and
individuals. All the scholarly writing on opera is in Lithuanian, except a Master's thesis: Vytas Nakas, "Jurgis Karnavičius: Gražina, the First Lithuanian Opera" (Indiana University, 1974); not examined, but the entry in RILM Abstracts,
8-2/3 (May-December 1974): 209, indicates the content covers
Lithuanian opera in general. The Lithuanian writings about
opera are Vytautas Mažeika,* Opera ... 1940-1965, *1967 (IOM-
3377), a popular narrative history, with a chronology of premieres;* Muzika ir teatras: almanachas, 1962- *(IOM-3378), an
annual review of opera and theater;* Stasys Yla, *Lietuvių
nacionalinė opera, 1960 (IOM-3379), a collection of essays
about the national opera, composers, and works.*

*Ukrainian opera is one of the topics in a recent essay
collection:*

671.   Soĩuz Kompozitorov Ukrainskoĩ SSR. *Muzykal'naĩa kul'tura
       Ukrainskoĩ SSR. Sbornik stateĩ.* Moskva: "Muzyka,"
       1979. 462p.   IOM-3409a ML 308 M994

*Lidiĩa Borysivna Arkhymovych has written two studies of the
national opera, discussing individual works:* Shĩakhy rozvytku
ukraïns'koï radĩans'koï opery, *1970 (IOM-3413), and* Ukraïns'ka
klasychna opera; istory'chnyĩ narys, *1957 (IOM-3414). Probably
the most informative single volume is Mykhaĩlo Pavlovych
Stefanovych,* Kyïvs'kyi Derzhavnyĩ Ordena Lenina Akademichnyĩ
Teatr Opery ta Baletu URSR Imeni T.G. Shevchenka, *1966 (IOM-
3415); it discusses musical life in Kiev during the 19th
century; opera in Ukraine, 1867-1917; the Akademichnyĩ Teatr
(Shevchenko State Academic Theater of Opera and Ballet), 1917-
67; gives a chronology of performances, 1917-67; and staff-
lists. For Khar'kov, the second city, there is a brief history
of musical life:* Ĩosyp Mykhaĩlovych Myklashevs'kyĩ, *Muzychna
i teatral'na kul'tura Kharkova, 1967 (IOM-3422). Current
events are chronicled in* Muzyka/zhurnal, 1972- *(IOM-3426),
published bimonthly.*

United Kingdom

*The United Kingdom (UK) comprises England, Scotland, Wales,
and Northern Ireland. Great Britain, the larger of the two
principal islands, includes England, Scotland, and Wales.
All the significant writing on music is in English. This is
the standard study of the earliest period in opera:*

672. Dent, Edward Joseph. *Foundations of English Opera: A Study of Musical Drama in England During the Seventeenth Century.* Cambridge, Eng.: Cambridge University Press, 1928. xv, lx, 241p. (Reprint--New York: Da Capo, 1965.) IOM-3476 ML 1731.2 D4
Examines predecessor forms, continental influences, chamber opera, and other developments up to and including Purcell. Footnotes and musical examples; no bibliography. Name, title, and topic index. Dent's evidence and conclusions are critically assessed in:

673. Buttrey, John. "The Evolution of English Opera Between 1656 and 1695: A Re-Investigation." Ph.D. dissertation. University of Cambridge, 1967. 2 vols. 579p.
Not seen. Author's entry in *RILM Abstracts*, 4-2 (May-August 1970): 129, suggests a wide range of corrections to Dent. Says that opera in England did not begin until 1674. Discusses all subsequent operas to 1695, with particular attention to *Dido and Aeneas*. Bibliography; work-lists; no index.

A useful survey of the entire history of English opera:

674. White, Eric Walter. *The Rise of English Opera.* New York: Philosophical Library; London: Lehmann, 1951, vi, 355p. (Reprint--New York: Da Capo, 1972.) IOM-3477 ML 1731 W6
Examines the development of opera in Britain up to *Billy Budd* (1951); treats composers, librettists, management, and organizations. List of about 750 works, with premiere dates; list of operas produced in English translation; list of operas given in London at half-century intervals: 1732, 1791, 1851, 1891, 1948. Bibliography of about 75 titles; name, title, and theater index. A revision, as *A History of English Opera*, was announced for late 1983 by Faber & Faber.

This study, not seen, would seem to be of interest: Lawrence Stuart Rinkel, "The Forms of English Opera: Literary and Musical Responses to a Continental Genre" (Ph.D. dissertation, Rutgers University, 1977).
A monumental reference work, for opera and other theatrical presentations:

675. *The London Stage 1660-1800: A Calendar of Plays, Enter-*
        tainments and Afterpieces.... Carbondale: Southern
        Illinois Press; London: Transatlantic Book Service,
        1960-79. 11 vols. IOM-3478 PN 2592 L6
        All stage productions are listed, by date, with their
        casts; financial data and critical reviews are given.
        The place of music and dancing is stated for each work.
        The 11th volume is a vast index of more than a half-
        million references, citing all titles, and all persons.

A companion work by the same publisher: Philip H. Highfill, Jr.,
et al., A Biographical Dictionary of Actors, Actresses,
Musicians, Dancers, Managers, and Other Stage Personnel in
London, 1660-1880, *1973- (IOM-3552). Biographical informa-*
tion on about 8,500 persons--half of them musicians--will be
included in the completed set.
    Studies of the major theaters and companies in London are
good avenues into the history of opera. The Concise Oxford
Dictionary of Opera *has excellent articles on all the opera*
houses. This summary of the most important institutions may
be useful:
    Drury Lane. Four buildings have occupied the site, dating
from 1663, 1674, 1794, and 1812 (the present theater). Impor-
tant in the 19th century, the theater is no longer used regu-
larly for opera.
    Her Majesty's Theatre. This is the theater in the Hay-
market, opened in 1705 as the Queen's Theatre, renamed the
King's Theatre in 1714, given present name in 1837. It was
the exclusive home of Italian opera. Demolished 1891. A new
building went up in 1897, but it is no longer used for opera.
A scholarly history of the theater: Daniel Nalbach, The
King's Theatre, 1704-1867: London's First Italian Opera House
(London: Society for Theatre Research, 1972), xii, 164p.
    An important recent study:

676. Petty, Frederick C. *Italian Opera in London, 1760-1800.*
        Ann Arbor, Mich.: UMI Research, 1980. xi, 426p.
        ISBN 8357-1073-4-S83 ML 1731.8 L7 P512
        Based on the author's dissertation (Yale University,
        1971). A scholarly documentary account of operas, per-
        formers, productions, institutions, audiences, critical
        reactions, and miscellaneous facts. Includes chronology
        of the 1760-1800 seasons in the King's Theatre and a
        table of performances of the operas of each composer.
        The most popular opera was Piccinni's *La buona figliuola*
        (112 times), followed by three of Paisiello's. Only two

works of importance in the period remain in the repertoire: *Alceste* and *Il matrimonio segreto*. Excellent
bibliography of about 500 entries; name index and index
to operas and arias.

William Charles Smith, The Italian Opera and Contemporary
Ballet in London, 1789-1820, *1955 (IOM-3479), carries the
story ahead two decades. It gives discussions of each season,
with casts; it has a useful index of works and artists. The
memoirs of Lumley (162) and Mapleson (163) contribute some
added information.*

*The Royal Opera House, Covent Garden, has had three
buildings: 1732 (burned 1808), 1809 (burned 1856), and the
present structure, 1858. The principal history is:*

677. Rosenthal, Harold D. *Two Centuries of Opera at Covent
     Garden.* London: Putnam, 1958; Chester Springs, Pa.:
     Dufour, 1964. xiv, 849p. IOM-3482 ML 1731.8 L72 C67
     A well-illustrated popular account; useful for "analy-
     sis of seasons" 1847-1956/57, which gives casts of all
     performances. For 1947-57 there are lists of all solo-
     ists and conductors. Index of names (including operatic
     characters), operas, and topics.

Some updating is provided by Ellenor Handley and Martin Kinna,
Royal Opera House Covent Garden: A History from 1732 *(West
Wickham: Fourlance, 1978; 64p.). An anecdotal older volume
may be of interest: Henry Saxe Wyndham,* The Annals of Covent
Garden Theatre from 1732 to 1897, *1906 (IOM-3483).*

*Sadler's Wells. The first house opened 1765 and was the
site of occasional opera until it fell into disuse in the
late 19th century. It was renovated in 1931; moved to the
Coliseum Theatre in 1968; was renamed the English National
Opera in 1974. There are two popular accounts of its history:
Dennis Arundell,* The Story of Sadler's Wells *(2d ed.; London:
Hamish Hamilton, 1977); and Richard Jarman,* A History of Sad-
ler's Wells Opera ... *(London: English National Opera, 1974).
Jarman's work is an illustrated booklet, with seasonal
chronologies to 1974.*

*Outside London the most notable opera life has been in the
John Christie estate "Glyndebourne," near Lewes, Sussex.
Christie built a festival opera house there in 1934, leading
to a long series of distinguished productions.*

678.   Hughes, Patrick Cairns (Spike). *Glyndebourne.* New ed.
        London and North Pomfret, Vt.: David & Charles, 1981.
        388p.   ISBN 0-7153-7891-0   ML 1731.8 G63 H89
        Updates the first edition of 1965, extending the
        chronology with a 1964-79 supplement; operas, casts,
        artists and their roles, and recordings are given. There
        is also a popular narrative history of the festival,
        without notes. Well illustrated. Index of names and
        titles.

Information on the other London theaters is given in Diana
Howard, London Theatres and Music Halls, *1970 (IOM-3489); it*
gives descriptive/historical notes on 910 theaters.
     A number of works give details on shorter periods.

679.   Fiske, Roger. *English Theatre Music in the Eighteenth*
        Century. London: Oxford University Press, 1973.
        xiv, 684p.   ISBN 0-19-316402-7   IOM-3480
        ML 1731.8 F38
        A scholarly study of all stage genres: masque, pan-
        tomime, ballad opera, etc. Includes biographies of
        about 50 singers, musical examples, a bibliography of
        about 250 entries. An important index of titles gives
        the names of all works that have survived in full score
        or vocal score; also a name index, with works under
        composers.

For the period 1830-59 there is a book of reviews by the
critic of the Athenaeum: *Henry F. Chorley,* Thirty Years'
Musical Recollections *(New York: Knopf, 1926; xxv, 411p.),*
originally published in 1862. Chorley was a good observer
of Italian opera, though he did not appreciate Wagner.   Index
of names and titles.
     An anecdotal picture of the later Victorian era is given
in Herman Klein, The Golden Age of Opera *(London: Routledge,*
1933), and in Thirty Years of Musical Life in London *(180)*
by the same author. He was a Sunday Times *critic who covered*
all the debuts, premieres, and operatic activity in London.
Further critical opinions are gathered in Percy Alfred Scholes,
The Mirror of Music, 1844-1944; A Century of Musical Life in
Britain in the Pages of the Musical Times, *1947 (IOM-3518).*
     Some facts on 20th-century opera are found in:

680.   Northouse, Cameron. *Twentieth-Century Opera in England*

and the United States. Boston: G.K. Hall, 1976. viii,
400p. ISBN 0-8161-7896-8 ML 128 O4 N87
Comprises several lists: 1) First performances of
20th-century English and American operas, 1900-74;
arranged by year, with city, date, and librettist;
total of 1,612 works. 2) Additional 941 operas for
which complete performance information is lacking.
3) Operas based on literary works. 4) List of published
operas. Indexing provides access by composer, librettist,
title, literary title, and literary author.

*For recent operatic composition and performance two items are
of special interest. Rodney Milnes, "Die Entwicklung der
Oper in Grossbritannien seit 1945," Musikbühne, 74, pp. 208-
224 (IOM-3482a), a discussion of trends. In the same issue
of the journal there is a chronology of operas by English
composers since 1945, originally printed in the Music Yearbook (see below). Arts Council of Great Britain, A Report
on Opera and Ballet in the United Kingdom, 1966-69, 1969
(IOM-3481), is an official publication that gives many facts
about the operatic situation. Discusses the major theaters
and their staff, singers, repertoire, and audiences. An
appendix identifies the most-performed operas (Aida was most
frequently heard).*
*Material on Gilbert and Sullivan operas and their produc-
tions has been presented above under Sullivan (431 to 437n).*
*Brody (69) is the most useful directory for the UK. The
British Music Yearbook, 1975- (IOM-3537), also gives directory
information; and it names the operas performed by all the
British companies. In the 5th ed., 1977/78, there was a
list of 800 operas with published English translations;
this has been supplemented in later editions.*
*Several other periodical publications provide news and
reports. London Musical Events, 1946- (IOM-2536), is a
monthly calendar of performances. The Year's Work in Music,
1947/48- (IOM-3538), summarizes the highlights of opera and
concert life and other musical activity. British Federation
of Music Festivals, Yearbook, 1933- (IOM-3539), gives lists
and calendars for festivals of opera and other music.*
*Opera in Scotland is described in Conrad Wilson, Scottish
Opera: The First Ten Years, 1972 (IOM-3581), outlining each
season of the Scottish Opera since it was founded in 1961.
Opera performances are among the events treated in George
Bruce, Festival in the North; The Story of the Edinburgh Festival, 1975 (IOM-3587).*

United States of America

*In the United States opera has flourished through performances
rather than through composition. No American work forms part
of the standard repertoire, although the American musical--
emerging from the operetta--has become universally admired.
For about 100 years American composers produced ballad operas
only; William Henry Fry's* Leonora *(1845) was the first pub-
licly performed grand opera by a native. Accordingly, most
of the literature on opera is about companies and singers as
they interacted with the European masterpieces. Much of the
research writing concerns operatic life in the individual
cities.*

*A scholarly introduction to operatic and other musical
activity is given by John Tasker Howard,* Our American Music;
A Comprehensive History from 1620 to the Present, *1965 (IOM-
0707). Another fine history is Gilbert Chase,* America's Music;
From the Pilgrims to the Present, *1966 (IOM-0710). The preferred brief survey is H. Wiley Hitchcock,* Music in the United
States: A Historical Introduction, *1974 (IOM-0709). A useful
chronology: Henry Charles Lahee,* Annals of Music in America ...,
*1922 (IOM-0713). As guides to the extensive literature, IOM,
volume 2, will be useful, as well as David Horn,* The Literature of American Music in Books and Folk Music Collections: A
Fully Annotated Bibliography, *1977 (IOM-1332i); Richard Jackson,*
United States Music; Sources of Bibliography and Collective
Biography *(100); and* United States. Library of Congress, *A
Guide to the Study of the United States of America ..., 1960,
supplement 1976 (IOM-0790).*

*Specifically on operatic history, the basic work is Oscar
G.T. Sonneck,* Early Opera in America, *1915 (IOM-0695). Coverage
extends from 1703 through the 19th century; primary source
materials used and cited. Much detail on performances in New
York, Philadelphia, Boston, and New England, Baltimore, Charles-
ton, and the South. Another useful study is Henry Charles
Lahee,* Grand Opera in America, *1902 (IOM-0692f). A recent
treatise deals with the early period:*

681. Virga, Patricia H. *The American Opera to 1790.* Ann
      Arbor, Mich.: UMI Research, 1982. xix, 393p. ISBN
      8357-1374-1-S83 ML 1711 V816
      Discusses the first music-stage works written in
America, the ballad and comic operas. Special attention
to *The Disappointment* (1767). Includes musical analyses
and comments on productions. The backnotes are informative. Bibliography of about 400 items; expansive
index of names, titles, and topics.

Another useful account:

682. Davis, Ronald L. *A History of Opera in the American West.* Englewood Cliffs, N.J.: Prentice-Hall, 1965. 178p. ML 1711 D4

    The title is misleading, as the coverage includes Chicago and New Orleans as well as states from Texas to California. A documented story of stage activity from the beginnings to recent times, in all the major cities and in important smaller centers like Central City and Santa Fe. Well illustrated; name and title index, but no bibliography.

This dissertation was not available for examination: Molly Sue Nelson, "Operas Composed in America in the Nineteenth Century" (Ph.D dissertation. University of North Carolina 1976). A mixture of genres is discussed in the oddly titled American Operetta from H.M.S. Pinafore to Sweeney Todd, *by G. Bordman (New York: Oxford University Press, 1981). The main topic is the musical, for which a range of facts is given on about 80 specimens, but some inclusions are indeed light operas. Without notes or bibliography; index of names and titles.*

There are various lists of American operas. Central Opera Service has issued a Directory of American Contemporary Operas, 1967 *(IOM-0690), and a supplementary* Directory of American and Foreign Contemporary Operas and American Opera Premieres, 1975 *(IOM-0691). H. Earle Johnson,* Operas on American Subjects, 1964 *(IOM-0692b), is a useful inventory of operas having any subject matter related to North or South America, whatever the composer's nationality; it also has an interesting list of American and British literary works that have been adapted as opera libretti. Andrew H. Drummond,* American Opera Librettos, 1973 *(IOM-0692), examines 40 libretti, for works that were performed at the New York City Opera, 1948-71. There is a good bibliography and a chronology for the NYCO for the period. The study by Northouse has been cited above (680).*

The next group of titles is concerned with individual cities. Only works devoted to opera are mentioned; but some information on opera will be found in the more generalized city and regional histories identified in IOM, volume 2. Treatises on the "stage" history of particular cities are often useful for operatic studies; citations are given in IOM and in Sheehy's Guide to Reference Books, *and in the* Guide to the Study of the United States of America, *mentioned above.*

Boston has had an unsteady operatic history. Until the foundation in 1958 of the Opera Company of Boston, under Sarah Caldwell, there had been only one resident company of consequence, and it lasted just five years:

683.   Eaton, Quaintance. *The Boston Opera Company.* New York:
       Appleton-Century-Crofts, 1965. xiv, 338p.
       ML 1711.8 B7 E14
       A popular, undocumented narrative, with 55 illustra-
       tions. Gives complete casts for all performances,
       material on the singers, and a chapter on the Boston
       critics. Strong expansive index of names and titles.

Chicago, the so-called Second City, takes that position also in American opera. A performance was heard as early as 1850; and an opera house was constructed in 1865 (the Crosby Opera House, burned in the great fire of 1871). The superb Audi-torium, designed by Louis Sullivan and Dankmar Adler, was the home of visiting companies from 1889 to 1910, then of the new Chicago Grand Opera Company. In 1929 opera moved to the new Civic Opera House, but the depression of the 1930s put an end to the local company. In 1954 the Lyric Theater, later the Lyric Opera, began its highly successful seasons. The literature is not very satisfactory; Ronald Davis, Opera in Chicago; A Social and Cultural History, *1966 (IOM-0689a), is a popular undocumented survey, emphasizing the personal lives of singers; it does give casts for the performances of 1910-65. An earlier work by Edward C. Moore,* Forty Years of Opera in Chicago *(New York: Liveright, 1930), is without documentation or index but does give yearly staff-lists and many illustrations; it is limited to activity in the Audi-torium.*

Los Angeles has had resident companies from time to time, but none has enjoyed long success. The story is told by Neil E. Wilson, "A History of Opera Activities in Los Angeles, 1887-1965," Ph.D. dissertation. Indiana University, 1967.

Ballad operas and similar works were heard in New York in the early 18th century; the first Italian company came in 1825. Two books by Henry Edward Krehbiel give the best view of the period up to 1918: Chapters of Opera ..., *1911 (IOM-0692d), and* More Chapters of Opera ..., *1919 (IOM-0692e). Another study that seems apropos is Jay Robert Teran, "The New York Opera Audience, 1825-1974" (Ph.D. dissertation. New York University, 1974), was not examined. Various houses and companies competed for audiences through the 19th century, among them the Astor Place Opera, under Maretzek (164), 1847-*

52, and the Academy of Music, under Mapleson (163), 1854-
1925, but not used for opera after the turn of the century.
A dissertation by Michael Joseph Pisoni, "Operatic War in
New York City, 1883-84 ..." (Ph.D. dissertation. Indiana
University, 1975), describes the stormy birth of the Metropolitan Opera, which opened 22 October 1883, with Campanini
and Nilsson singing Faust.

684. Kolodin, Irving. The Metropolitan Opera, 1883-1966: A
      Candid History. 4th ed. New York: Knopf, 1966.
      xxi, 762, xlvii p. IOM-0692c ML 1711.8 N3 M44
      First edition was 1953. A narrative survey with
      documentation. Useful list of works performed to 1952,
      with dates and number of performances. Index.

685. Seltsam, William H. Metropolitan Opera Annals; A Chron-
      icle of Artists and Performances. New York: Wilson,
      1947. 751p. IOM-0694** ML 1711.8 N32 M48
      Three supplements have brought the record to 1976.
      Casts and selected press notices are given for all per-
      formances. Portraits; artist and title indexes.

686. Eaton, Quaintance. Opera Caravan. Adventures of the
      Metropolitan on Tour, 1883-1956. New York: Farrar,
      Straus, and Cudahy, 1957. (Reprint--New York: Da
      Capo, 1978.) ML 1711.8 N3 M425
      A chronology of all tours, by city; gives all casts.
      Many interesting photographs en route. But the main
      text is in highly popular style, without notes, and
      with some invented conversations. Partly expansive
      index of names, titles, and cities.

687. Heylbut, Rose, and Aimé Gerber. Backstage at the Opera.
      New York: Crowell, 1937. ix, 325p.
      ML 1711.8 N5 M59 H6 (Reprint, as Backstage at the
      Metropolitan Opera--New York: Arno, 1977.) ISBN
      0-4050-96836
      An informal look at the stage procedures, dressing
      rooms, administration, broadcasting, maintenance, etc.,
      with some facts on leading personalities. The style
      is chatty, and there are imaginary dialogues. Name
      and title index.

*The original building of the Metropolitan stood on Broadway,
between 39th and 40th streets. In 1966 the company moved to
new quarters at Lincoln Center. Photos of the old and new
houses are found in:*

688. Seligman, Paul. *Debuts and Farewells: A Two-decade
      Photographic Chronicle of the Metropolitan Opera.*
      New York: Knopf, 1972. 180p. ISBN 0-394-47983-1
      ML 1711.8 N3 M597
      There are pictures of the singers, on stage and off,
      as well as of the buildings.

*Collections of critical reviews from newspapers and magazines
offer useful approaches to Metropolitan performances. Volumes
already cited: Aldrich (176), Henderson (178), and Porter
(183). A new view of one season--not examined--has been re-
leased: Patrick J. Smith,* A Year at the Met *(New York: Knopf,
1983); it is described by a reviewer as a "blend of praise and
criticism." Another source of information is the memoir of
an impresario. Those cited above are Bing (152, 153) and
Gatti-Casazza (158). See also 164.*

*New York's other important company is the New York City
Opera, founded in 1944. It is chronicled in:*

689. Sokol, Martin. *The New York City Opera: An American
      Adventure.* New York: Macmillan, 1981. xiv, 562p.
      ISBN 0-02-612280 ML 1711.8 N3 N58 S6
      The narrative account is general and sparsely foot-
      noted. But the "annals" section, modeled after Seltsam's
      treatment of the Metropolitan, is a useful chronology
      of each season with all casts (no reviews, however).
      There are good photographs, and tables of broadcasts,
      TV appearances, films, and recordings. Index of names,
      titles, and topics. See also 682n.

The Metropolitan had another rival company for several years:

690. Cone, John Frederick. *Oscar Hammerstein's Manhattan
      Opera Company.* Norman: University of Oklahoma Press,
      1966. 399p. ML 1711.8 N3 M153
      The company operated 1906-10. This is an illustrated
      narrative account, with an appendix that gives all casts
      of all performances. Bibliography of about 200 books
      and articles; index of names, titles, and topics.

Philadelphia is the home of the oldest opera house in continu-
ous use in the United States, the Academy of Music (1857);
however, resident companies have not shown comparable longevity.
There is no comprehensive history, but two writers have
addressed the earlier days:

691. Albrecht, Otto. "Opera in Philadelphia, 1800-1830."
      Journal of the American Musicological Society, 32-3
      (Fall 1979): 499-515. ML 27 A83363
      A brief narrative of the period, with a list of all
      operas performed and references to the other literature
      on Philadelphia opera.

692. Armstrong, William G. *A Record of the Opera in Phila-*
      delphia. Philadelphia: Porter & Coates, 1884. 274p.
      (Reprint--New York: AMS, 1976.) ISBN 0-404-12853-X
      ML 1711.8 P5 A7
      A historical review, with list of operas produced by
      all major companies, 1827-83. Considerable detail on
      the Academy building and some interesting comparative
      information on other world opera houses. (Capacities
      are given, with internal dimensions and colors of the
      interiors. Prague is white, Moscow amber; Philadelphia,
      like most of the great houses, was crimson.) Lists of
      Academy directors, 1853-83. No bibliography. Name and
      title index.

There is a thorough study of musical-stage activity in Puerto
Rico: Emilio Pasarell, Orígenes y desarrollo de la afición
teatral en Puerto Rico, 1969 (IOM-1282). It includes lists
of works performed in alphabetical and chronological order.
  The first opera performance in San Francisco took place
in 1852; within a few years 11 theaters were involved in
presentations by many visiting companies. Carmen was sung--
by Caruso, Fremstad, and Journet--on the day of the great
1906 earthquake. The San Francisco Opera was founded in
1923; since 1932 its home has been the War Memorial Opera
House. This is the only history:

693. Bloomfield, Arthur J. *The San Francisco Opera, 1922-78*.
      Sausalito, Calif.: Comstock Editions, 1978. 552p.
      ISBN 0-89174-032-5 ML 1711.8 S2 B65
      An earlier edition, covering 1923-61, appeared in
      1961. Bloomfield is critic for the local newspaper;
      his account is popular and journalistic. Casts for

each season are given; and the repertoire is arrayed
by composer. Conductors, designers, choreographers,
etc., are identified. Name and topic index.

The Seattle Opera Association dates from 1964:

694. Salem, Mahmoud M. *Organizational Survival in the Per-*
         forming Arts. The Making of the Seattle Opera. New
         York: Praeger, 1976. 210p. ISBN 0-275-05670-8
         ML 1711.8 S4 S47
         Primarily a story of financial problems and successes;
      some reference to the opera performances passim. Ex-
      pansive index of names, titles, and topics.

Operas performed in Washington, D.C., are listed in:

695. Squares, Roy. "The Washington Opera, Inc., 1956-1977."
         Master's thesis. American University, 1977. 112p.
         Not examined. According to *RILM Abstracts*, 11-2
      (May-August 1977): 198, it includes names of works
      offered at Kennedy Center, 1971-77; Wolf Trap Farm
      Park, 1971-78; and by the Opera Society of Washington,
      1956-77.

Directories that cover American operatic institutions have
been cited above: The Musician's Guide, *which identifies*
600 U.S. and Canadian opera companies (64); Musical America:
Directory Issue *(65), and* Musical Courier Annual Directory ...
(66). The major news journal is Opera News *(79).*

Uruguay

696. Ayestarán, Lauro. *La música en el Uruguay.* Montevideo:
         Servicio Oficial de Difusión Radio Elétrica, 1953.
         817p. IOM-1294 ML 237 A9
         The standard history for the country, giving a scholar-
      ly account of all genres to 1860. Operatic-performance
      chronologies are included. Illustrations, musical ex-
      amples; name index. The same author's *Crónica de una*
      temporada musical en el Montevideo de 1830, 1943 (IOM-
      1299), provides a cross-section of a single season,
      covering opera and other musical life.

Venezuela

697. Calcaño, José Antonio. *400 años de música caraqueña.*
Caracas: Círculo Musical, 1967. 98p. IOM-1309
ML 238.8 C3 C34
A lavishly illustrated volume that gives a good view
of musical life in Caracas from 1567. The same author
has a more detailed history also: *La ciudad y su música,*
1958 (IOM-1308). A brief history of opera to 1881 is
part of Juan José Churión, *El teatro en Caracas,* 1924
(IOM-1322).

Yugoslavia

The official name is Socijalistička Federativna Republika
Jugoslavija. English: Yugoslavia or Jugoslavia; French:
Yougoslave; German: Jugoslawien. Since the First World War
the country has been a federation comprising the republics
of Serbia (capital Belgrade, or Beograd), Croatia (Zagreb),
Slovenia (Ljubljana), Montenegro (Titograd), Bosnia and
Herzegovina (Sarajevo), and Macedonia (Skopje). The official
language is Serbo-Croat. Latin alphabet is used in Croatia,
Slovenia, Bosnia, and Herzegovina; Cyrillic is predominant
in Serbia, Montenegro, and Macedonia.
Italian opera was brought to Ljubljana as early as 1652,
and native composing in Slovenia began in the late 18th cen-
tury. In Zagreb a German company arrived in 1797; Croatian
national opera writing began a half-century later. Serbian
operatic activity was later to start, but the Belgrade national
theater has achieved the highest place in recent years. There
are several good introductions in Western languages to the
music and operatic traditions:

698. *Yugoslav music....* Sarajevo: Zvuk, 1967. 154p.
IOM-3611 ML 260 Y83
Title and text in English, French, and German. A
useful collection of essays by topic and locality;
musical and operatic life of each major city is discussed.

699. Andreis, Josip, and Slavko Zlatić. *Yugoslav Music.*
Trans. Karla Kunc. Beograd: Edition Jugoslavija, 1959.
158p. IOM-3612 ML 260 A5
The history and current musical scene in each republic,
including an account of opera in the important cities.

An important book by Andreis has been partly translated, as
Music in Croatia, 1974 (IOM-3645); it is thorough and well
documented, with musical examples, bibliography, and name
index. The translation is taken from the most comprehensive
treatise on music of the country: Josip Andreis et al.,
Historijski razvoj muzičke kulture u Jugoslaviji, *1962 (IOM-*
3644). Seaman (579) offers a good background summary of
operatic landmarks.
    The chapter on music in Croatia: Land, People, Culture,
1964 (IOM-3617), gives names of leading opera singers and
identifies institutions in Zagreb. The MGG Article "Jugo-
slawien" gives good coverage to opera in past and present
(IOM-3614). There is a fine encyclopedia of music written
in Serbo-Croat: Muzička enciklopedija, *1971-77 (IOM-3618),*
3 vols. Bibliographies and work-lists will be accessible
even to those who do not read the language.
    The standard history of Serbian music, Stana Djurić-Klajn,
Istorijski razvoj muzičke kulture u Srbiji, *1971 (IOM-3648),*
has been translated as A Survey of Serbian Music Through the
Ages, *1972. It is well documented and illustrated, with*
good detail on operatic development. Program notes for
major works; name index. Dragotin Cvetko's standard history
of music in Slovenia is available in French translation as
Histoire de la musique slovène, *1967 (IOM-3651).*
    Specific studies of opera are all in native languages.
These are useful:

700.   Sivec, Jože. *Opera v Stanovskem gledališču v Ljubljani*
       od let 1790 do 1861. Ljubljana: Slovenska Matica,
       1971. 236p. IOM-3629 ML 1724.8 L6 S6
       A scholarly narrative approach, without chronologies
       or other lists. Summary in German; name index.

701.   Narodno Pozorište Sarajevo. Opera. *Jubilarna godina*
       Sarajevske opere, 1946-1966. Sarajevo: Sarajevska
       Opera Narodnog Pozorišta, 1967. 64p. IOM-3630
       ML 1751.8 S27 N4
       An illustrated history with chronologies of performances
       for the period.

702.   Zagreb. Hrvatsko Narodno Kazalište. *Sto godina opere,*
       1870/71-1970/71. Zabreb: Grafički Zavod Hrvatske,
       1971. [not paged] IOM-3631 ML 1751.8 Z3
       Commemorates the first centennial of the national

theater; includes a historical text, illustrations, and
a chronology. Also portraits of current artists; composer index.

*The periodical that offers current information on operatic
activity is Zvuk, 1955- (IOM-3658).*

XVI. FURTHER BIBLIOGRAPHY

While the preceding pages have presented the core literature on opera, as well as guidance to more specialized writings, researchers may have need for more remote publications. In this concluding chapter several useful sources for further information on opera will be cited.

It may be well to remind the reader of the substantial bibliographies to be found in works already mentioned. Grout's Short History of Opera *(20) and his* History of Western Music *(17n) provide thousands of citations. The* New Oxford History *(15) is a valuable resource. Other general histories named at 17n should be kept in mind. Library catalogs listed at 44-47 are of great importance. For singers we have the Farkas bibliography mentioned in the Introduction and the NATS lists (97).*

The numerous general indexes and bibliographies of musical literature are described in Information on Music, *especially in volume 1.*

This is a key to a class of publication that is easily overlooked:

703. Tyrrell, John, and Rosemary Wise. *A Guide to International Congress Reports in Musicology, 1900-1975.* New York: Garland, 1979. 353p. ISBN 0-8240-9839-0
ML 113 T95
Lists about 10,000 papers included in published proceedings for international conferences in music and related subjects. Well indexed, by place, title, series, sponsor, author, editor, and subject. "Opera" has about one and a half columns of entries in the subject index; Wagner, a half-column; etc.

Reviews of the state of research can be highly valuable   Some of these relate to individual composers, such as Holoman's for Berlioz (206) and Surian's for Verdi (442). Others are more general, like this one:

704. Abert, Anna Amalie. "Die Oper zwischen Barock und
      Romantik. Ein Bericht über die Forschung seit dem
      zweiten Weltkrieg." *Acta musicologica* 49 (1977):
      137-193. ML 5 I6
      A thorough listing of publications dealing with 18th-
      and 19th-century opera, arranged by country, then by
      genre; limited to post-1945 research. Brief annotations
      and unifying commentaries make this a useful guide to a
      large body of literature. A similar essay by Heinz
      Becker, "Zur Situation der Opernforschung" (*Musik-
      forschung*, 27 [1974]: 153-165), is shorter and more
      tightly focused; the author concentrates on the status
      of editions and mentions neglected areas of score pub-
      lication and of research.

A CHECKLIST OF OPERA COMPOSERS
AND THEIR MAJOR WORKS

While writing this book I became aware of the need for a basic list of significant operas, one which would extend beyond the usual barriers of time and nationality. What follows is an attempt at such a list. It includes composers and operas of our own time (among others, I have named all the operas in the current repertoires of the leading American and European companies), or in earlier centuries; it gives a place to the work of landmark status: the work that had some historic identity, the work that enjoyed vast popularity, the work that--for whatever reason--has been the subject of extensive scholarly attention. All together I have identified 1,051 works. They are given in their original titles, with common alternative titles, and with English titles for works that have become familiar in English translation.

In compiling the list I have sought to meet a subsidiary need: that for correctness and consistency of identification. It has been the custom among opera publishers, and among those who write about opera, to apply multiple titles to the same work, to shorten titles, and to translate foreign titles into various disguises. Using for the most part the authority of the Library of Congress, I have offered standardized renditions of composers' names and of opera titles. Transliterations from Cyrillic follow the Library of Congress system, the system used by most American research libraries. (I have applied the system consistently, even where the Library of Congress has not; e.g., in such cases as Stravinskiĭ and Prokof'ev). The date given for each opera is that of the premiere, unless otherwise noted.

Abbatini, Antonio Maria, 1609 or 1610-1677 or ca. 1679.
Dal male il bene, 1653.
Ione, 1664 or 1666.
La comica del cielo, 1668.

Adam, Adolphe Charles, 1803-1856.
Le chalet, 1834.
Le postillon de Longjumeau, 1836.

Albéniz, Isaac Manuel Fran-
    cisco, 1860-1909.
  La sortija (The Magic Opal;
    The Magic Ring), 1893.
  San Antonio de la Flórida
    (L'hermitage fleuri), 1894.
  Pepita Jiménez, 1896.

Albert, Eugen d', 1864-1932.
  Die Abreise, 1898.
  Tiefland, 1903.
  Flauto solo, 1905.
  Die toten Augen, 1916.

Albinioni, Tomaso, 1671-1750.
  Zenobia, regina di Palmireni,
    1694.

Alfano, Franco, 1876-1954.
  Risurezzione, 1904.
  L'ombra di Don Giovanni,
    1914.
  La leggenda di Sakuntala,
    1921.

Anfossi, Pasquale, 1727-1797.
  L'incognita perseguitata,
    1773.
  I viaggiatori felici, 1780.
  Zenobia di Palmira, 1789.

Antheil, George, 1900-1959.
  Transatlantic, 1930.

Araia, Francesco, 1709-1770.
  La forza dell' amore e dell'
    odio, 1736. (First opera
    given in Russia.)
  Tsefal i Prokris, 1755.
    (First opera in Russian.)

Arenskiǐ, Antonii Stepanovich,
    1861-1906.
  Son na Volge (A Dream on
    the Volga), 1891.

Arne, Thomas Augustine, 1710-
    1778.
  Comus, 1738.

Thomas and Sally, 1760.
Artaxerxes, 1762.
Love in a Village, 1762.
Olimpiade, 1764.

Arrieta, Emilio (Pascual),
    1823-1894.
  Marina (L'orfana di Lloret),
    1871.

Atanasov, Georgy, 1882-1931.
  (Founder of Bulgarian
    opera.)
  Borislav, 1911.
  Gergana, 1917.
  Zapustyalata vodenitsa, 1923.
  Tsveta, 1925.
  Kosara, 1927.
  Altsek, 1930.

Auber, Daniel François
    Esprit, 1782-1871.
  Le maçon, 1825.
  La muette de Portici, 1828.
  La fiançée, 1829.
  Fra diavolo, 1830.
  Gustave III, 1833.
  Le domino noir, 1837.
  La part du diable, 1843.
  Haydée, 1847.
  Le premier jour de bonheur,
    1868.

Audran, Edmond, 1840-1901.
  La mascotte, 1880.
  Le cigale et la fourmi,
    1886.
  Miss Hélyet, 1890.
  La poupée, 1896.

Bach, Johann Christian, 1735-
    1782.
  Orione, 1763.
  Zanaida, 1763.
  Carattaco, 1767.
  Le clemenza di Scipione,
    1778.
  Amadis des Gaules, 1779.

Balfe, Michael William, 1808–
1870.
The Siege of Rochelle, 1835.
The Maid of Artois, 1837.
The Bohemian Girl, 1843.
The Rose of Castille, 1857.

Bantock, Granville, *Sir*,
1868–1946.
The Pearl of Iran, 1894.

Barber, Samuel, 1910–1981.
Vanessa, 1958.
Antony and Cleopatra, 1966.
(Premiered on opening
night of the new Metro-
politan Opera house.)

Barbieri, Francisco Asenjo,
1823–1894.
Jugar con fuego, 1851.
Pan y toros, 1864.

Bartók, Béla, 1881–1945.
A Kékszakállú herceg vára
(Duke Bluebeard's Castle),
1918.

Bazin, François Emmanuel
Joseph, 1816–1878.
Maître Pathelin, 1856.

Beethoven, Ludwig van, 1770–
1837.
Fidelio, 1805.

Bellini, Vincenzo, 1801–1835.
Il pirata, 1827.
I Capuletti [or Capuleti] e
[or ed] i Montecchi, 1830.
Norma, 1831.
La sonnambula, 1831.
Beatrice di Tenda, 1833.
I puritani di Scozia, 1835.

Benda, Georg (Jiří Antonín),
1722–1795.
Der Dorfjahrmarkt, 1775

Ariadne auf Naxos, 1775.
Medea, 1775.
Romeo und Juliet, 1776.
(Earliest opera based
on this story.)
Pygmalion, 1779.

Benjamin, Arthur, 1893–1960.
Mañana, 1956. (First opera
commissioned for BBC
television.)

Berg, Alban, 1885–1935.
Wozzeck, 1925.
Lulu, 1937.

Berkeley, Lennox, *Sir*, 1903– .
A Dinner Engagement, 1954.
Ruth, 1956.
Castaway, 1967.

Berlioz, Hector, 1803–1869.
Benvenuto Cellini, 1838.
Béatrice et Bénédict,
1862.
Les troyens, 1890.
La damnation de Faust,
1893.

Bernstein, Leonard, 1918– .
Trouble in Tahiti, 1952.
Candide, 1956.

Berton, Henri Montan, 1767–
1844.
Les rigeuers du cloitre,
1790.
Montano et Stéphanie, 1799.
Le délire, 1799.
Aline, reine de Golconde,
1803.

Berutti, Arturo, 1862–1938.
Vendetta, 1892.
Evangelina, 1893.
Tarass Bulba, 1895.
Pampa, 1897.
Yupanki, 1899.

Berwald, Franz Adolf, 1796-
   1868.
Ein ländisches Verlobungs-
   fest in Schweden, 1847.
Estrella di Soria, 1862.
Drottningen av Golconda,
   1868.

Birtwistle, Harrison, 1934- .
Punch and Judy, 1968.
Down by the the Greenwood
   Side, 1969.

Bizet, Georges, 1838-1875.
Les pêcheurs de perles,
   1863.
Le jolie fille de Perth,
   1867.
Djamileh, 1872.
Carmen, 1875.

Blake, David, 1936- .
Toussaint, 1976.

Bliss, Arthur, *Sir*, 1891-1975.
Tobias and the Angel, 1960.

Blitzstein, Marc, 1905-1964.
The Cradle Will Rock, 1937.
No for an Answer, 1940.
Regina, 1949.

Blockx, Jan, 1851-1912.
Herbergprinses, 1896.
Thyl Uylenspiegel, 1900.
De bruid der zee, 1901.

Blomdahl, Karl-Birger, 1916-
   1968.
Aniara, 1958.

Blow, John, 1649-1708.
Venus and Adonis, ca. 1684.

Boero, Felipe, 1885-1958.
El matrero, 1929.

Boieldieu, François Adrien,
   1775-1834.
Le calife de Bagdad, 1800.
Ma tante Aurore, 1803.
Les voitures versées, 1808.
Jean de Paris, 1812.
La dame blanche, 1825.
Les deux nuits, 1829.

Boito, Arrigo, 1842-1918.
Mefistofele, 1868.

Bononcini, Giovanni, 1670-
   1747.
Il trionfo di Camilla,
   1696.
Crispo, 1721.
Astianatte, 1727.

Boretti, Giovanni Antonio,
   ca. 1640-ca. 1673.
Eliogabalo, 1668.

Borodin, Aleksandr Porfir'evich,
   1833-1887.
Kniāz' Igor' (Prince Igor),
   1890.

Bréton y Hernández, Tomás,
   1850-1923
La Dolores, 1895.

Bristow, George, 1825-1898.
Rip van Winkle, 1855.

Britten, Benjamin, 1913-
   1976.
Peter Grimes, 1945.
The Rape of Lucretia, 1946.
Albert Herring, 1947.
Billy Budd, 1951.
The Turn of the Screw, 1954.
A Midsummer Night's Dream,
   1960.
Curlew River, 1964.
Owen Wingrave, 1971.
Death in Venice, 1973.

Busoni, Ferruccio Benvenuto,
    1866-1924.
  Die Brautwahl, 1912.
  Arlecchino, 1917.
  Turandot, 1917.
  Doktor Faust, 1925.

Caccini, Francesca, 1588-ca.
    1640.
  La liberazione di Ruggiero
    dall' isola d'Alcina, 1625.
    (First opera by a woman;
    first Italian opera staged
    outside Italy, Warsaw,
    1682.)

Caccini, Giulio, 1545-1618.
    (See note at Jacopo Peri.)
  La Dafne (lost; but "might
    have been used at a per-
    formance in August 1600,"
    according to Loewenberg.)
  Il rapimento di Cefalo, 1600.
  L'Euridice, 1602.

Cadman, Charles Wakefield,
    1881-1946.
  Shanewis, 1918.

Caldara, Antonio, ca. 1670-
    1736.
  Olimpiade, 1733.

Cambert, Robert, 1628-1677
    (The first French opera
    composer.)
  Pomone, 1671.
  Ariane, 1674.

Campra, André, 1660-1744.
  L'Europe galante, 1697.
  Tancrède, 1702.
  Les festes vénitiennes, 1710.

Carafa di Colobrano, Michele
    Enrico, 1787-1872.
  Le solitaire, 1822.
  Le valet de chambre, 1823.
  Masaniello, 1827.

Carnicer, Ramon, 1789-1855.
  Elena e Malvina, 1829.
  Cristoforo Colombo, 1831.
  Eufemio di Messina, 1832.
  Ismalia, 1838.

Carr, Benjamin, 1768-1831.
  The Archers, 1796. (The
    first American opera for
    which some music survives.)

Casella, Alfredo, 1883-1947.
  La donna serpente, 1932.

Castro, Juan José, 1895-
    1968.
  La zapatera prodigiosa,
    1949.
  Proserpina y el extranjero,
    1952.
  Bodas de sangre, 1956.

Catalani, Alfredo, 1854-1893.
  La Wally, 1852.
  Edmea, 1886.

Caudella, Eduard, 1841-1924.
  Petru rares, 1900. (The
    first important Romanian
    opera.)

Cavalli, Pier Francesco,
    1602-1676.
  La Didone, 1641.
  L'Egisto, 1643.
  Giasone, 1649.
  Calisto, 1651 or 1652.
  Xerse, 1654.
  L'Erismena, 1655.
  Ercole amante, 1662.

Cavos, Catterino, 1776-1840.
  Kníaz' nevídimka (The In-
    visible Prince), 1805.
  Ilya Bogatir, 1807.
  Kazak' stikhotvorefs' (The
    Cossack Poet), 1812.
  Ivan' Susanin', 1815.

Cesti, Antonio, 1623-1669.
  Orontea, 1649.
  L'argia, 1655.
  La Dori, 1661.
  Il pomo d'oro, 1667.

Chabrier, Emmanuel, 1841-1894.
  L'étoile, 1877.
  Gwendoline, 1886.
  Le roi malgré lui, 1887.

Chaĭkovskiĭ, Petr Il'ich,
    1840-1893.
  Oprichnik, 1874.
  Evgeniĭ Onegin (Eugene
    Onegin), 1879.
  Orleanskaĭà deva (The Maid
    of Orleans), 1881.
  Mazepa (Mazeppa), 1884.
  Charodyĭka (The Sorceress),
    1887.
  Pikovaĭà dama (Pique dame;
    Queen of Spades), 1890.

Charpentier, Gustave, 1860-
    1956.
  Louise, 1900.

Chávez, Carlos, 1899-1978.
  Panfilo and Lauretta (The
    Visitors), 1957.

Cherubini, Luigi, 1760-1842.
  Démophoön, 1788.
  Lodoïska, 1791.
  Élisa, 1794.
  Medée, 1797.
  Les deux journées, 1800.
  Faniska, 1806.
  Pimmaglione, 1809.
  Les abencérages, 1813.

Chueca, Federico, 1846-1908.
  La gran via [with Valverde],
    1886.

Cilèa, Francesco, 1866-1950.
  La Tilda, 1892.

  Adriana Lecouvreur, 1902.
  Gloria, 1907.

Cimarosa, Domenico, 1749-
    1801.
  L'italiana in Londra, 1778.
  Giannina e Bernadone, 1781.
  Il matrimoniu segreto,
    1792.

Coates, Albert, 1882-1953.
  Pickwick, 1936. (First
    opera to be televised--
    in part--BBC, 1936.)

Coccia, Carlo, 1782-1873.
  Clotilda, 1815.
  Caterina di Guise, 1833.

Colasse, Pascal, 1649-1709.
  Achile et Polixéne, 1687.
  Thétis et Pélée, 1689.

Constantinescu, Paul, 1908-
    1963.
  O noapte furtunoasă (A
    Stormy Night), 1935.

Converse, Frederick Shepherd,
    1871-1940.
  The Pipe of Desire, 1906.
    (First American opera
    given at the Metropolitan
    Opera, 1910.)

Copland, Aaron, 1900- .
  The Tender Land, 1954.

Cornelius, Peter, 1824-1874.
  Der Barbier von Bagdad,
    1858.
  Der Cid, 1865.
  Gunlöd, 1891.

Corsi, Jacopo, ca. 1560-1604.
  See note at Peri.

Cui, César, 1835-1918.
 Vil'iam Ratklif (William
  Ratcliff), 1869
 Kavkazskiǐ plennik (The
  Captive in the Caucasus),
  1883.
 Saraťsin (Saracen), 1899.
 Kapitanskaǐa dochka (The
  Captain's Daughter), 1911.

Dalayrac, Nicolas-Marie, 1753-
  1809.
 Nina, 1786.
 Azémia, 1786.
 Les deux petits savoyards,
  1789.
 Adolphe et Clara, 1799.
 Maison à vendre, 1800.
 Léhéman, 1801.
 Gulistan, 1805.
 Deux mots, 1806.

Dallapiccola, Luigi, 1904-
  1975.
 Volo di notte, 1940.
 Il prigioniero, 1949.
 Ulisse, 1968.

Damrosch, Walter Johannes,
  1862-1950.
 The Scarlet Letter, 1896.
 Cyrano de Bergerac, 1913.
 The Man Without a Country,
  1937.

Dargomyzhskiǐ, Aleksandr
  Sergeevich, 1813-1869.
 Rusalka, 1856.
 Kammenyǐ gost' (The Stone
  Guest), 1872.

David, Félicien César, 1810-
  1876.
 La perle du Brésil, 1851.
 Herculanum, 1859.
 Lalla Roukh, 1862.

Davies, Peter Maxwell, 1934- .
 Taverner, 1972.

Debussy, Claude, 1862-1918.
 Pelléas et Mélisande, 1902.

De Koven, Reginald, 1859-
  1920.
 Robin Hood, 1890.
 The Canterbury Pilgrim,
  1917.

Delibes, Léo, 1836-1891.
 Le roi l'a dit, 1873.
 Jean de Nivelle, 1880.
 Lakmé, 1883.

Delius, Frederick, 1862-1934.
 Koanga, 1904.
 Romeo und Julia auf dem
  Dorfe (A Village Romeo
  and Juliet), 1907.

Dessau, Paul, 1894-1979.
 Die Verurteilung des
  Lukullus (Das Verhör des
  Lukullus), 1951.
 Puntila, 1966.
 Lanzelot, 1969.
 Einstein, 1973.

Destouches, André Cardinal,
  1672-1749.
 Issé, 1697.
 Amadis de Grèce, 1699.
 Omphale, 1700.
 Callirhoé, 1712.

Dibdin, Charles, 1745-1814.
 The Padlock, 1768.
 The Waterman, 1774.

Ditters von Dittersdorf,
  Karl, 1739-1799.
 Doctor und Apotheker,
  1786.

Donizetti, Gaetano, 1797-1848.
 L'esule di Roma, 1828.
 La regina di Golconda, 1828.
 Anna Bolena, 1830.
 L'elisir d'amore, 1832.

Donizetti, Gaetano (cont'd)
  Lucrezia Borgia, 1833.
  Gemma di Vergy, 1834.
  Lucia di Lammermoor, 1835.
  Belisario, 1836.
  Il campanello di notte,
    1836.
  Roberto Devereux, 1836.
  La fille du régiment, 1840.
  Les martyrs, 1840.
  La favorite (La favorita),
    1840
  Maria Padilla, 1841.
  Linda di Chamounix, 1842.
  Don Pasquale, 1843.
  Maria di Rohan, 1843.
  Rita, 1860.

Draghi, Antonio, 1635-1700.
    (As resident composer in
    the Vienna court, Draghi
    wrote more than 170 stage
    works--authorities differ
    on the exact number--be-
    tween 1661 and 1699. Only
    five premieres are listed
    by Loewenberg; they are
    given here as examples of
    his work.)
  Achille in Sciro, 1663.
  Leonida in Tegea, 1670.
  La lanterna di Diogene,
    1674.
  La patienza, di Socrate,
    1680. (First opera given
    in Prague.)
  La chimera, 1682.

Dukas, Paul, 1865-1935.
  Ariane et Barbe-bleue,
    1907.

Duni, Egidio Romualdo, 1709-
    1715.
  Ninette à la cour (Caprice
    amoureux), 1755.
  Le peintre amoureux de son
    modèle, 1757.

  La fille mal gardée, 1758.
  Nina et Lindor, 1758.
  L'isle des foux, 1760.
  Les deux chasseurs et la
    laitière, 1763.
  La fée Urgèle, 1765.
  La clochette, 1766.
  Les moissonneurs, 1768.
  Les sabots, 1768.
  Thémire, 1770.

Dvořák, Antonín, 1841-1904.
  Šelma sedlák, 1878.
  Jakobín, 1889.
  Čert a Káča (The Devil and
    Kate), 1899.
  Rusalka, 1901.

Dzerzhinskiĭ, Ivan Ivanovich,
    1909-1978.
  Tikhiĭ Don (The Quiet Don),
    1935.
  Sud'ba cheloveka (Fate of a
    Man), 1962.

Egk, Werner, 1901- .
  Die Zaubergeige, 1935.
  Peer Gynt, 1938.
  Circe, 1948. (Revised as
    17 Tage und 4 Minuten,
    1966.)
  Irische Legende, 1955.
  Der Revisor, 1957.
  Verlobung in San Domingo,
    1963.
  17 Tage und 4 Minuten, 1966.
    (Revision of Circe.)

Einem, Gottfried von, 1918- .
  Dantons Tod, 1947.
  Der Prozess, 1953.

Elsner, Józef Antoni Fran-
    ciszek, 1769-1854.
  Andromeda, 1807.
  Leszak bialy, 1809.
  Król Lokietek, 1818.

Enesco, Georges, 1881–1955.
  Oedipe, 1936.

Enna, August, 1860–1939.
  Heksen, 1892.

Erkel, Ferenc, 1810–1893.
  Báthory Mária, 1840.
  Hunyady László, 1844.
  Két pisztoly, 1844.
  Bánk-bán, 1861.

Fall, Leo, 1873–1925.
  Die Dollarprinzessin, 1907.

Falla, Manuel de, 1876–1946.
  La vida breve (La vie brève),
    1905.
  El retablo del Maese Pedro,
    1923.
  Atlántida, 1961.

Fauré, Gabriel Urbain, 1845–
    1924.
  Pénélope, 1913.

Fioravanti, Vincenzo, 1799–
    1877.
  Le cantatrici villane, 1799.
  I virtuosi ambulanti, 1807.

Flotow, Friedrich von, 1812–
    1883.
  Alessandro Stradella, 1844.
  Martha, 1847.

Floyd, Carlisle, 1926– .
  Susannah, 1955.

Foerster, Anton, 1837–1926.
  Gorenjski slavček, 1872.

Foerster, Joseph Bohuslav,
    1859–1951.
  Eva, 1889.
  Jessika, 1905.

Fomin, Evstigneĭ Ipatovich,
    1761–1800.
  Ĭamshchiki na podstave,
    1787.
  Amerikantsy, 1800.

Foss, Lukas, 1922– .
  The Jumping Frog of Cala-
    veras County, 1950.
  Griffelkin, 1955.

Franck, César, 1822–1890.
  Hulda, 1894.

Freschi, Domenico, 1640–
    1690.
  Helena rapita da Paride,
    1677.

Fry, William Henry, 1813–
    1864.
  Leonora, 1845. (First
    publicly performed opera
    with continuous music by
    an American.)

Fux, Johann Josef, 1660–1741.
  Orfeo ed Euridice, 1715.
  Costanza e fortezza, 1723.

Gagliano, Marco da, ca. 1575–
    1642.
  La Dafne, 1608.

Gaito, Constantino, 1878–
    1945.
  Ollantay, 1925.
  Lázaro, 1929.
  La sangre de las guitarras,
    1932.

Galuppi, Baldassare, 1706–
    1785.
  L'Olimpiade, 1747.
  Il mondo della luna, 1750.
  Il mondo all roversa, 1750.
  Le virtuose ridicole, 1752.

Galuppi, Baldassare (cont'd)
Il filosofo di campagna,
1754.
L'amante di tutte, 1760.

Gasparini, Francesco, 1668-
1727.
Il più fedel frà i vassalli,
1703.
La fede tradita e vendicata,
1704.

Gazzaniga, Giuseppe, 1743-
1818.
Don Giovanni Tenorio, 1787.

Genée, Richard, 1823-1895.
Nanon, die Wirtin vom
Goldenen Lamm, 1877.

Gershwin, George, 1898-1937.
Porgy and Bess, 1935.

Giannini, Vittorio, 1903-1966.
The Taming of the Shrew,
1953.

Gibbons, Christopher, 1615-
1676.
Cupid and Death, 1653 (with
Matthew Locke).

Ginastera, Alberto Evaristo,
1916- .
Don Rodrigo, 1964.
Bomarzo, 1967.
Beatrix Cenci, 1971. (First
opera performed at Kennedy
Center, Washington.)

Giordano, Umberto, 1867-1948.
Andrea Chénier, 1896.
Fedora, 1898.
Siberia, 1903.

Glinka, Mikhail Ivanovich,
1804-1857.
Zhizn' za tsaria (Ivan'

sussanin'; A Life for
the Tsar), 1836.
Ruslan' i Liudmila, 1842.

Gluck, Christoph Willibald,
Ritter von, 1714-1787.
Orfeo ed Euridice, 1762.
La rencontre imprévue,
1764.
Alceste, 1767.
Paride ed Elena, 1770.
Iphigénie en Aulide, 1773.
Armide, 1777.
Iphigénie en Tauride, 1779.

Gobatti, Stefano, 1852-1913.
I goti, 1873.

Godard, Benjamin Louis Paul,
1849-1895.
Jocelyn, 1888.
La vivandière, 1895.

Goehr, Alexander, 1932- .
Arden muss sterben, 1967.
Naboth's Vineyard, 1968.
Shadowplay, 1970.

Goetz, Hermann, 1840-1876.
Der widerspänstigen
Zähmung, 1874.

Goldmark, Karl, 1830-1915.
Die Königen von Saba (The
Queen of Sheba), 1875.

Gomes, Antonio Carlos, 1836-
1896.
O guaraní (Il guarany),
1870.
Salvator Rosa, 1874.
Maria Tudor, 1879.
O escravo (Lo schiavo),
1889.

Gossec, François Joseph,
1734-1829.
Le pêcheurs, 1766.
Toinin et Toinette, 1767.

Gorovac, Jakov, 1895– .
Ero s onoga svijeta, 1935.

Gounod, Charles, 1818–1893.
Le médecin malgré lui, 1858.
Faust, 1859.
Philémon et Baucis, 1860.
La colombe, 1860.
Mireille, 1864.
Roméo et Juliette, 1867.

Granados y Campina, Enrique,
1867–1916.
María del Carmen, 1898.
Goyescas, 1916.

Greber, Jakob, 16??–1731.
The Loves of Ergasto (Gli
amori di Ergasto), 1705.
(First Italian opera given
in London.)

Grétry, André Ernest Modeste,
1741–1813.
Le tableau parlant, 1769.
Lucile, 1769.
Les deux avares, 1770.
L'ami de la maison, 1771.
Zemire et Azor, 1771.
Le jugement de Midas, 1778.
Le caravane, du Caire, 1783.
Richard Coeur de Lion, 1784.
Panurge dans l'isle des lan-
ternes, 1785.

Gruenberg, Louis, 1884–1964.
The Emperor Jones, 1933.

Gulak-Artemovsky, Semyon,
1813–1873.
Zaporozhets a Dunayem, 1863.
(First Ukrainian opera.)

Gyrowetz, Adalbert, 1763–1850.
Agnes Sorel, 1806.
Der Augenarzt, 1811.

Haarklou, Johannes, 1847–
1925.
Fra gamle dage, 1894.
(First Norwegian opera.)

Hába, Alois, 1893–1973.
Die Mutter, 1931. (First
quarter-tone opera to
be produced.)

Hadley, Henry Kimball, 1871–
1937.
Azora, 1917.
Cleopatra's Night, 1920.

Hageman, Richard, 1882–1966.
Caponsacchi (Tragödie in
Arezzo), 1932.

Hahn, Reynaldo, 1875–1947.
Ciboulette, 1923.
Le marchand de Venise,
1935.
Halévy, Jacques François
Fromental Élie, 1799–
1862
La juive, 1835.
L'éclair, 1835.
La reine de Chypre, 1841.

Hallström, Ivar, 1826–1901.
Den bergtagna, 1874.

Händel, Georg Friedrich
(George Frideric Handel),
1685–1759.
Rinaldo, 1711.
Il pastor fido, 1712.
Radamisto, 1720.
Tamerlano, 1724.
Giulio Cesare, 1724.
Rodelinda, 1725.
Admeto, 1727.
Acis and Galatea, 1731.
Orlando, 1733.
Alcina, 1735.
Ariodante, 1735.
Serse (Xerxes), 1738.

Hanson, Howard, 1896-   .
  Merry Mount, 1934.

Hartmann, Johan Ernst, 1726-
  1793.
  Fiskerne, 1780.

Hasse, Johann Adolph, 1699-
  1783.
  Sesostrate, 1726.
  Artaterse, 1730.
  Siroe, 1733.

Haydn, Joseph, 1732-1809.
  Der Apotheker (Lo speziale),
  1768.
  Il mondo della luna, 1777.
  Armida, 1784.

Henze, Hans Werner, 1926-   .
  Boulevard solitude, 1952.
  König Hirsch, 1956.
  Der Prinz von Homburg, 1960.
  Elegie für Junge Liebende,
  1961.
  The Bassarids, 1966.
  La chatte anglaise, 1983.

Herbert, Victor, 1859-1924.
  Babes in Toyland, 1903.
  Natoma, 1911.
  Madeleine, 1914.

Hernando, Rafael José Maria,
  1822-1888.
  Colegialas y soldados,
  1849.

Hérold, Louis Joseph Ferdinand,
  1791-1833.
  Les rosières, 1817.
  La clochette, 1817.
  Marie, 1826.
  Zampa, 1831.
  Le pré aux clercs, 1832.

Hervé, Florimond Ronger,
  1825-1892.
  Chilpéric, 1868.
  Le petit Faust, 1868.
  Mam'zelle Nitouche, 1883.

Hewitt, James, 1770-1827.
  Tammany, 1794.

Hidalgo, Juan, ca. 1600-1685.
  Ni amor se libra da amor,
  1640.
  Los celos hacen estrellas,
  1644. (First zarzuela
  whose composer is known.)
  Celos aun del aire matan,
  1660. (Earliest Spanish
  opera.)

Hiller, Johann Adam, 1728-
  1804.
  Der Teufel is los (Die
  werwandelten Weiber)
  1766.
  Die Jagd, 1770.

Hindemith, Paul, 1895-1963.
  Cardillac, 1926.
  Hin und zurück, 1927.
  Neues vom Tage, 1929.
  Mathis der Maler, 1938.
  Die Harmonie der Welt,
  1957.
  Der lange Weihnachtsmahl,
  1961.

Hoffmann, E.T.A., 1776-1822.
  Undine, 1816.

Holst, Gustav, 1874-1934.
  Savitri, 1916.
  The Perfect Fool, 1923.
  At the Boar's Head, 1925.
  The Wandering Scholar, 1934.

Honegger, Arthur, 1892-1955.
  Le Roi David, 1921.

Antigone, 1927.
Jeanne d'Arc au bucher, 1936.
L'aiglon, 1937 (with Jacques
    Ibert).

Hopkinson, Francis, 1737-1791.
The Temple of Minerva, 1781.

Horký, Karel, 1909- .
Atlántida, 1983.

Howland, William Legrand,
    1873-1915.
Sarrona, 1903. (First
    American opera staged in
    Europe.)

Hubay, Jenő, 1858-1937.
A Cremonai hegedűs, 1894.

Humperdinck, Engelbert, 1854-
    1921.
Hänsel und Gretel, 1893.
Königskinder, 1897.

Ibert, Jacques, 1890-1962.
Angélique, 1927.
Le roi d'Yvetot, 1930.
Gonzague, 1933.
L'aiglon, 1937 (with Arthur
    Honegger).

Indy, Vincent d', 1851-1931.
Fervaal, 1897.
L'étranger, 1903.

Isouard, Niccolò, 1775-1818.
Les rendez-vous bourgeois,
    1807.
Cendrillon, 1810.
Joconde, 1814.

Janáček, Leoš, 1854-1928.
Počátek románu (The Beginning
    of a Romance), 1894.
Osud (Fate; Destiny), 1903.
Její pastorkyňa (later
    Jenufa), 1904.

Jenufa, 1916.
Výlety páně Broučkovy (Mr.
    Brouček's Excursions),
    1920.
Kat'a Kabanová, 1921.
Lišky příhody Bystroušky
    (The Sly Little Fox; The
    Cunning Little Vixen),
    1924.
Šárka, 1925.
Věc Makropoulos (The
    Makropoulos Affair),
    1926.
Z mrtvého domu (The House
    of the Dead), 1930.

Jommelli, Niccolò, 1714-1774
Demofoonte, 1743.
Artaterse, 1749.
L'Ifigenia, 1751.
Fetonte, 1753.
L'Olimpiade, 1761.

Jones, Sidney, 1861-1946.
The Geisha, 1896.

Joplin, Scott, 1868-1917.
Treemonisha, 1915.

Josephs, Wilfred, 1927- .
Rebecca, 1983.

Kabalevskiĭ, Dmitrii Borisovich,
    1904- .
Kola Briun'on (Colas Breugnon),
    1938.
Sem'ía Tarasa (The Family of
    Taras), 1947.
Nikita Vershinin, 1955.

Kálmán, Imre, 1882-1953.
Die Csárdás Fürstin, 1915.
Gräfin, Mariza (Countess
    Maritza), 1924.
Die Zirkusprinzessin, 1926.

Kalnipš, Alfreds, 1879-1951.
Banuta, 1920 (First Latvian
    opera).

Kalomiris, Manolis, 1883–
     1962.
  Ho prōtomastoras, 1916.
  Tō dakhtilidi tis manas,
     1917.
  Anatoli, 1945.
  Ta xotika nera, 1950.

Kamieński, Maciej (Mathias),
     1734–1821.
  Nędza uszcaęśliwiona, 1778.
     (First Polish opera to be
     performed.)
  Zoška czyli wiejskie zaloty,
     1779.

Karnavičius, Georgy, 1884–1931.
  Gražina, 1933. (First
     Lithuanian opera.)

Kastle, Leonard, 1929– .
  Deseret, 1961.

Kauer, Ferdinand, 1751–1831.
  Das Donauweibchen, 1798.

Keiser, Reinhard, 1674–1739.
  Störtebecker, 1701.
  Der angenehme Betrug, 1707.
  Croesus, 1711.
  Die grossmüthige Tomyris,
     1717.

Kern, Jerome, 1885–1945.
  Show Boat, 1927. (Might
     be classed as a musical;
     but performed at New York
     City Opera in 1954.)

Khrennikov, Tikhon Nikolaevich,
     1913– .
  V buriū, 1939.
  Mat' (Mother), 1958.

Kienzl, Wilhelm, 1857–1941.
  Der Evangelimann, 1895.

Kodály, Zoltán, 1882–1967.
  Háry János, 1926.
  Székely fonó, 1932.
  Czinka panna, 1948.

Korngold, Erich, 1897–1957.
  Die tote Stadt, 1920.

Kovařovic, Karel, 1862–
     1920.
  Psohlavci (The Dogheads),
     1898.
  Na starém bělidle (At the
     Old Bleaching Ground),
     1901.

Křenek, Ernst, 1900– .
  Jonny spielt auf, 1927.
  Karl V, 1938.
  Der goldene Bock, 1964.

Kreutzer, Konradin, 1780–
     1849.
  Das Nachtlager von Granada,
     1834.

Kreutzer, Rodolphe, 1766–
     1831.
  Paul et Virginie, 1791.
  Lodoïska, 1791.
  Astianax, 1801.
  Aristippe, 1808.
  Abel, 1810.

Kurka, Robert Frank, 1921–
     1957.
  The Good Soldier Schweik,
     1958.

Kurpiński, Karol, 1785–1857.
  Jadwiga, 1814.
  Zabobon, 1816.
  Zamek na Czorsztynie, 1819.

Laguerre, Elisabeth Claude
     de, 1659–1729.
  Céphale et Procris, 1694.
     (First opera by a woman

to be staged at the Paris
Opéra.)

La Guerre, Michel de, ca.
1605-1679.
La triomphe de l'amour,
1655. (First French
opera; music lost.)

Lalo, Édouard, 1823-1892.
Le roi d'Ys, 1888.

Landi, Stefano, ca. 1590-ca.
1655.
La morte d'Orfeo, 1619.
Sant' Alessio, 1632.

Laparra, Raoul, 1876-1943.
La habanera, 1908.
Le joueur de viole, 1925.

Lecocq, Alexandre Charles,
1832-1918.
Fleur-de-thé, 1868.
La fille de Madame Angot,
1872.
Giroflé-girofla, 1874.
Le petit duc, 1878.

Legrenzi, Giovanni, 1626-
1690.
Totila, 1677.
Il Giustino, 1683.

Lehár, Ferenc (Franz), 1870-
1948.
Die lustige Witwe (The
Merry Widow), 1905.
Der Graf von Luxembourg,
1909.
Zigeunerliebe (Gypsy Love),
1910.
Eva, 1911.
Frasquita, 1922.
Paganini, 1925.
Frederica, 1928.
Das Land des Lächelns, 1929.
Giuditta, 1934.

Leo, Leonardo Oronzo Salva-
tore de, 1694-1744.
L'Olimpiade, 1737.
Amor vuol sofferenza,
1739.
L'Andromaca, 1742.

Leoncavallo, Ruggiero, 1857-
1919.
I pagliacci, 1892.
La bohème, 1897.
Zaza, 1900.

Le Sueur, Jean François,
1760-1837.
La caverne, 1793.
Paul et Virginie, 1794.
Ossian, 1804.

Linley, Thomas, 1733-1795.
The Duenna, 1775.

Lisinski, Vatroslav, 1819-
1854.
Ljubav i Zloba, 1845.
(First Croatian opera.)
Porin, 1897.

Locke, Matthew, ca. 1630-
1677.
Cupid and Death, 1653.
(With Christopher Gib-
bons.)
The Siege of Rhodes, 1656.
(First English opera;
lost.)
Psyche, 1675. (First sur-
viving example of an
English opera.)

Lortzing, Albert, 1801-1851.
Die beiden Schützen, 1837.
Czaar und Zimmermann, 1837.
Der Wildschütz, 1842.
Undine, 1845.
Der Waffenschmied, 1846.
Zum Grossadmiral, 1847.

Lotti, Antonio, 1667-1740.
  Alessandro Severo, 1716.

Lully, Jean Baptiste, 1632-
    1687.
  Cadmus et Hermione, 1673.
  Alceste, 1674.
  Thésée, 1675.
  Atys, 1676.
  Isis, 1677.
  Psyché, 1678.
  Bellérophon, 1679.
  Proserpine, 1680.
  Persée, 1682.
  Phaéton, 1683.
  Amadis, 1684.
  Roland, 1685.
  Armide, 1686. (First French
    opera staged in Italy.)
  Acis et Galatée, 1686.

Lysenko, Mykola Vitaliĭovych,
    1842-1912.
  Risdivyana nich (Christmas
    Eve), 1883.
  Natalka Poltavka, 1889.
  Taras Bul'ba, 1924.

Madetoja, Leevi, 1887-1947.
  Pohjalaisia, 1924.

Maillart, Louis Aimé, 1817-
    1871.
  Les dragons de Villars, 1856.

Majo, Gian Francesco de, 1732-
    1770.
  Ifigenia in Tauride, 1764.
  Adriano in Siria, 1769.

Malipiero, Gian Francesco,
    1882-1973.
  L'Orfeide, 1925.
  Il mistero di Venezia, 1932.

Mancini, Francesco, 1679-1739.
  Gli amanti generosi, 1704;
    revised as L'idaspe fedele,
    1710.

Manelli, Francesco, 1595-
    1667.
  Andromeda, 1637. (First
    opera given in the first
    opera house, Teatro San
    Cassiano, Venice.)

Marais, Marin, 1656-1728.
  Alcione, 1706.

Marazzoli, Marco, ca. 1619-
    1662.
  Dal male il bene, 1653.
    (With Antonio Abbatini.)
  La vita humana, 1656.

Marchetti, Filippo, 1831-
    1902.
  Ruy Blas, 1869.

Marschner, Heinrich August,
    1795-1861.
  Der Vampyr, 1828.
  Der Templer und die Jüdin,
    1829.
  Hans Heiling, 1833.

Martin, Frank, 1890-1974.
  Le vin herbé, 1941.
  Der Sturm, 1956.

Martín y Soler, Vicente, ca.
    1756-1806.
  Una cosa rara, 1768.
  L'arbore di Diana, 1787.
  Il burbero di buon cuore,
    1787.
  La capricciosa corretta
    (La scola de maritati),
    1795.

Martinů, Bohuslav, 1890-1959.
  Julietta, 1938.
  Veselohra na mostě (Comedy
    on a Bridge), 1952.
  Griechische Passion (Greek
    Passion), 1961.

Mascagni, Pietro, 1863-1945.
Cavalleria rusticana, 1890.
L'amico Fritz, 1891.
Iris, 1898.
Le maschere, 1901.
Il piccolo Marat, 1921.

Massé, Victor, 1822-1884.
Galatée, 1852.
Les noces de Jeannette,
1853.
La reine Topaze, 1856.
Paul et Virginie, 1876.

Massenet, Jules Émile
Frédéric, 1842-1912.
Hérodiade, 1881.
Manon, 1884.
Werther, 1892.
Thaïs, 1894.
La navarraise, 1894.
Cendrillon, 1899.
Le jongleur de Notre Dame,
1902.
Don Quichotte, 1910.

Mayr, Johann Simon, 1763-
1845.
Che originali!, 1798.
Medea in Corinto, 1813.

Mazzocchi, Virgilio, 1597-
1646.
La catena d'Adone, 1626.
Chi soffre speri, 1639.
(First comic opera.)

Méhul, Étienne Nicolas, 1763-
1817.
Euphrosine, 1790.
Ariodant, 1798.
L'irato, 1801.
Une folie, 1802.
Le trésor supposé, 1802.
Héléna, 1803.
Uthal, 1806. (Scored with-
out violins.)
Joseph, 1807.

Melani, Jacopo, 1623-1676.
Ercole in Tebe, 1661.

Menotti, Gian Carlo, 1911- .
Amelia Goes to the Ball,
1937.
The Old Maid and the Thief,
1939.
The Island God, 1942.
The Medium, 1946.
The Telephone, 1947.
The Consul, 1950.
Amahl and the Night Visitors,
1951.
The Saint of Bleeker Street,
1954.
Maria Golovin, 1958.
The Last Savage (L'ultimo
selvaggio), 1963.
Help! Help! The Globolinks!,
1968.

Mercadante, Saverio, 1795-
1870.
Elisa e Claudio, 1821.
Amleto, 1822.
I normanni a Parigi, 1832.
Il giuramento, 1837.

Merikanto, Oscar, 1868-1924.
Pohjan neito, 1908. (First
opera with Finnish text.)

Messager, André Charles
Prosper, 1853-1929.
La basoche, 1890.
Madame Chrysanthème, 1893.
Les p'tites Michu, 1897.
Véronique, 1898.
Fortunio, 1907.
Monsieur Beaucaire, 1919.

Meyerbeer, Giacomo, 1791-
1864.
Robert le diable, 1831.
Les huguenots, 1836.
Le prophète, 1849.
L'étoile du nord, 1854.

Meyerbeer, Giacomo (cont'd)
  Le pardon de Ploërmel
    (Dinorah), 1859.
  L'africaine, 1865.

Meytus, Yuly, 1903- .
  Molodaya gvardia, 1947.

Milhaud, Darius, 1892-1974.
  Le pauvre matelot, 1927.
  Christophe Columbus, 1930.
  David, 1954.

Millöcker, Karl, 1842-1899.
  Apajune, 1880.
  Der Bettelstudent, 1882.

Moniuszko, Stanisław, 1819-
    1872.
  Halka, 1848.
  Straszny dwór (The Haunted
    Manor), 1865.

Monsigny, Pierre Alexandre de,
    1729-1817.
  La cadi dupé, 1761.
  Le roi et le fermier, 1762.
  Rose et Colas, 1764.
  Le déserteur, 1769.
  La belle Arsène, 1773.

Montemezzi, Italo, 1875-1952.
  L'amore dei tre re, 1913.
  La nave, 1918.

Monteverdi, Claudio, 1567-
    1643.
  L'Orfeo (La favola d'Orfeo),
    1607.
  Arianna, 1608.
  Il combattimento di Tancredi
    e Clorinda, 1624.
  Il ritorno d'Ulisse in
    patria, 1641.
  L'incoronazione di Poppea,
    1642. (First opera on an
    historical subject.)

Moore, Douglas, 1893-1969.
  The Devil and Daniel Web-
    ster, 1938.
  Giants in the Earth, 1951.
  The Ballad of Baby Doe,
    1956.
  Wings of the Dove, 1961.

Morales, Melesio, 1838-1908.
  Romeo y Julieta, 1863.
  Ildegonda, 1865. (Given in
    Florence, 1868; first
    Mexican opera staged in
    Europe.)

Mosonyi, Michael, 1815-1870.
  Szép Ilonka, 1861.

Mouret, Jean Joseph, 1682-
    1738.
  Les festes de Thalie, 1714.

Mozart, Wolfgang Amadeus
    (Johann Chrysostom),
    1756-1791.
  Bastien und Bastienne,
    1768.
  La finta giardiniera, 1775.
  Il re pastore, 1775.
  Idomeneo, 1781.
  Die Entführung aus dem
    Serail (The Abduction
    from the Seraglio), 1782.
  Le nozze di Figaro (The
    Marriage of Figaro),
    1786.
  Don Giovanni (Il dissoluto
    punito), 1787.
  Così fan tutte, 1790.
  La clemenza di Tito, 1791.
  Die Zauberflöte (The Magic
    Flute), 1791.

Musgrave, Thea, 1928- .
  The Decision, 1867.
  Mary, Queen of Scots,
    1977.

Müller, Wenzel, 1767-1835.
Das Neusonntagskind, 1793.
Die Schwestern von Prag,
1794.
Die Teufelsmühle am Wiener-
berg, 1799.

Musorgskiĭ, Modest Petrovich,
1839-1881.
Boris Godunov, 1870.
Khovanshchina, 1886.
Sorochinskaĭa ĭarmaka (The
Fair of Sorochinsk), 1917.

Mysliveczek, Joseph, 1737-
1781.
Olimpiade, 1778.

Napravnik, Eduard Frantsevich,
1839-1916.
Dubrovskiĭ, 1895.

Naumann, Johann Gottlieb,
1741-1801.
Orpheus og Euridice, 1786.
(First grand opera in
Danish.)
La dama soldato, 1791.

Nessler, Viktor, 1841-1890.
Der Trompeter von Säckingen,
1884.

Nicolai, Otto, 1810-1849.
Die lustigen Weiber von
Windsor (The Merry Wives
of Windsor), 1849.
Il templario, 1840.

Nielsen, Carl, 1865-1931.
Saul og David, 1902.
Maskarade, 1906.

Nouguès, Jean, 1875-1932.
Quo vadis, 1909.

Offenbach, Jacques, 1819-1880.
Orphée aux enfers, 1858.

La belle Hélène, 1864.
Barbe-bleue, 1866.
La vie parisienne, 1866.
La grand-duchesse de
Gérolstein, 1867.
La périchole, 1868.
Les contes d'Hoffmann (The
Tales of Hoffmann),
1881.

Orff, Carl, 1895- .
Carmina burana, 1937.
Der Mond, 1939.
Die Kluge, 1943.
Antigonae, 1949.
Oedipus der Tyrann, 1959.

Orlandini, Giuseppe Maria,
1688-ca. 1750.
Il marito giogatore, 1718.

Pacini, Giovanni, 1796-1867.
L'ultimo giorno di Pompei,
1825.
Saffo, 1840.
Medea, 1843.

Paër, Ferdinando, 1771-1839.
Griselda (La virtù al
cimento), 1798.
Camilla, 1799.
Achille, 1801.
Le maître de chapelle,
1821.

Paine, John Knowles, 1839-
1906.
Azara, 1907.

Paisiello, Giovanni, 1740-
1816.
Le finte contesse, 1766.
Socrate immaginario, 1775.
Gli astrologi immaginari,
1779.
La serva padrona, 1781.
Il barbiere di Siviglia,
1782.

Paisiello, Giovanni (cont'd)
  Pirro, 1787.
  L'amor contrastato (La
    molinara), 1788.
  Nina, 1789.
  I zingari in fiera, 1789.

Pallavicino, Carlo, 1630-1688.
  Massimo Puppieno, 1684.
  L'amazone corsara, 1686.
  La Gierusalemme liberata,
    1687.

Paniagua y Vasques, Cenobia,
  1821-1882.
  Catalina de Guisa, 1859.
    (First opera by a Mexican
    to be staged; sung in
    Italian.)

Panizza, Ettore (Héctor),
  1875-1967.
  Il fidanzato del mare, 1897.
  Medio evo latino, 1900.
  Aurora, 1908.
  Bisanzio, 1939.

Parker, Horatio William,
  1863-1919.
  Mona, 1912.

Pasquini, Bernardo, 1637-1710.
  L'Idalma, 1680.

Pedrell, Felipe, 1841-1922.
  Los Pirineos (I Pirenei),
    1902.

Penderecki, Krzysztof, 1933- .
  Diably z Loudun (Die Teufel
    von Loudon; The Devils of
    Loudun), 1969.

Pepusch, John Christopher,
  1667-1752.
  The Beggar's Opera, 1728.
  Polly, 1777 (published
    1729).

Pérez, Davide, 1711-1778.
  Demetrio, 1741.
  Solimano, 1757.

Pergolesi, Giovanni Battista,
  1710-1736.
  Lo frate 'nnamorato, 1732.
  La serva padrona, 1733.
  Olimpiade, 1735.

Peri, Jacopo, 1561-1633.
  La Dafne, 1597 or 1598.
    (The first opera. Music
    mostly lost; of six
    surviving excerpts, two
    are attributed to Jacopo
    Corsi.)
  L'Euridice, 1600. (Earliest
    opera for which complete
    music survives. Several
    arias and choruses are by
    Giulio Caccini.)

Petrauskas, Mikas, 1873-1937.
  Birute, 1906. (First
    Lithuanian opera.)

Pfitzner, Hans Erich, 1869-
  1949.
  Palestrina, 1917.

Philidor, François André
  Danican, 1726-1795.
  Blaise le savetier, 1759.
  Le soldat magicien, 1760.
  Le maréchal ferrant, 1761.
  Le sorcier, 1764.
  Tom Jones, 1765.

Piccini, Niccolò, 1728-1800.
  Le cecchina (La buona
    figliuola), 1760. (First
    opera staged in Africa
    and Asia.)
  Iphigénie en Tauride, 1781.
  Didon, 1783.
  Le faux lord, 1783.

Pizzetti, Ildebrando, 1880–
1968.
Debora e Jaéle, 1922.
Figlia di Jorio, 1954.
L'assassinio nella catte-
drale, 1958.

Planquette, Robert, 1848–1903.
Les cloches de Corneville,
1877.
Rip van Winkle, 1882.

Pollarolo, Carlo Francesco,
ca. 1653–1722.
Gl'inganni felici, 1695.

Ponchielli, Amilcare, 1834–
1886.
La gioconda, 1876.

Porpora, Nicola Antonio, 1686–
1768.
Semiramide riconosciuta,
1729.

Portugal, Marcos Antônio da
Fonseca, 1762–1830.
La confusione nata dalla
somiglianza, 1793.
Fernando nel Messico, 1797
or 1798.
Le donne cambiate, 1797.
Lo spazzacamino principe,
1794.

Poulenc, Francis, 1899–1963.
Les mamelles de Tirésias,
1944.
Dialogues des carmélites,
1957.
La voix humaine, 1958.

Prokof'ev, Sergeĭ Sergeevich,
1891–1953.
Liubov k trem apelsinam
(The Love for Three
Oranges), 1921.

Igrok (The Gambler), 1929
(composed 1917).
Semyon Kotko, 1940.
Voina i mir (War and Peace),
1946.
Obruchenie v monastyre
(Betrothal in a Monas-
tery; The Duenna), 1946.
Povest' o nastoíaschchem
cheloveke (The Story of
a Real Man), 1948.
Ognennie angel (The Flaming
Angel), 1954.

Puccini, Giacomo, 1858–1924.
Le villi, 1884.
Edgar, 1889.
Manon Lescaut, 1893.
La Bohème. 1896.
La Tosca, 1900.
Madama Butterfly, 1904.
La fanciulla del west,
1910.
La rondine, 1917.
Il trittico (Il tabarro;
Suor Angelica, Gianni
Schicchi), 1918.
Turandot, 1926.

Purcell, Henry, ca. 1659–
1695.
Dido and Aeneas, 1689.
The Fairy Queen, 1692.

Rabaud, Henri, 1873–1949.
Mârouf, savetier de Caire,
1914.

Rachmaninoff, Sergei, 1873–
1943.
Aleko, 1893.
Skupoĭ rytšar' (The Miserly
Knight), 1906.
Francesca da Rimini, 1906.

Rameau, Jean Philippe, 1683–
1764.
Hippolyte et Aricie, 1733.

Rameau, Jean Philippe (cont'd)
  Les indes galantes, 1735.
  Castor et Pollux, 1737.
  Dardanus, 1737.

Ravel, Maurice, 1875-1937.
  L'heure espagnole, 1907.
  L'enfant et les sortilèges,
    1925.

Rebikov, Vladimir Ivanovich,
    1866-1920.
  Yelka (The Christmas Tree),
    1903.

Respighi, Ottorino, 1879-
    1936.
  La bella addormentata nel
    bosco, 1922.
  Belfagor, 1923.
  La campana sommersa, 1927.
  Maria Egiziaca, 1932.
  La fiamma, 1934.
  Lucrezia, 1937.

Reyer, Ernest [Louis-
    Étienne Rey], 1823-1909.
  Sigurd, 1884.
  Salammbô, 1890.

Rezniček, Emil Nikolaus
    Joseph, *Freiherr von*,
    1860-1945.
  Donna Diana, 1894.
  Till Eulenspiegel, 1902.

Rimskiĭ-Korsakov, Nikolai
    Andreevich, 1844-1908.
  Pskovitîanka (The Maid of
    Pskov), 1873.
  Maĭskaîa noch' (May Night),
    1880.
  Snegurochka (The Snow
    Maiden), 1882.
  Sadko, 1898.
  Tsarskaîa nevesta (The Tsar's
    Bride), 1899.
  Skazka o Tsare Saltane, 1900.

Skazanie o nevidimom gradie
    Kitezhie (The Invisible
    City of Kitezh), 1907.
Zolotoĭ petushok (Le coq
    d'or; The Golden Cock-
    erel), 1909.

Rinaldo di Capua, ca. 1705-
    ca. 1780. [This is the
    form of name given in
    all books of reference.]
  La zingara, 1753.

Ristori, Giovanni Alberto,
    1692-1753.
  Calandro, 1731. (First
    opera staged in Russia:
    11 Dec. 1731.)

Rosenberg, Hilding, 1892- .
  Resa till Amerika, 1932.
  Marionetter, 1939.
  Lycksalighetens ö, 1945.
  Hus med dubbel ingang,
    1970.

Rossi, Luigi, ca. 1598-1653.
  Il palazzo d'Atlante
    incantato, 1642.
  L'Orfeo, 1647.

Rossi, Michelangelo, 1601 or
    1602-1656.
  Erminia sul Giordano,
    1633.

Rossini, Gioacchino, 1792-
    1868.
  La cambiale di matrimonio,
    1810.
  L'inganno felice, 1812.
  La scala di seta, 1812.
  La pietra del paragone,
    1812.
  Il signor Bruschino, 1813.
  Tancredi, 1813.
  L'italiana in Algeri, 1813.
  Il turco in Italia, 1814.

Elisabetta, regina d'In-
ghilterra, 1815.
Almaviva (Il barbiere di
Siviglia; The Barber of
Seville), 1816.
Otello, 1816.
La cenerentola, 1817.
La gazza ladra, 1817.
Armida, 1817.
Mosè in Egitto, 1818. (Re-
vised as Moïse, 1827.)
Ricciardo e Zoraide, 1818.
La donna del lago, 1819.
Maometto II, 1820. (Re-
vised as La siège de
Corinthe, 1826.)
Zelmira, 1822.
Semiramide, 1823.
Le Comte Ory, 1828.
Guillaume Tell (William
Tell), 1829.

Rota, Nino, 1911-1979.
Il cappello di paglia di
Firenze, 1955.
La notte di un nevrastenico,
1960.
Aladino e la lampada magica,
1968.
La visita meravigliosa,
1970.

Rousseau, Jean Jacques, 1712-
1778.
Le devin du village, 1752.

Roussel, Albert, 1869-1937.
Padmâvatî, 1923.

Rubinstein, Anton, 1830-1894.
Demon, 1875.

Ruzitska, Jószef, ca. 1755-
after 1823.
Béla futása, 1822. (Earliest
extant Hungarian opera.)

Sacchini, Antonio Maria Gaspere,
1730-1786.
L'isola d'amore, 1766.
Oedipe à Colone, 1786.

Sacrati, Francesco Paolo,
d. 1650.
La finta pazza, 1641.
(First known Italian
opera staged in Paris.)

Saint-Saëns, Camille, 1835-
1921.
Samson et Dalila, 1877.

Salieri, Antonio, 1750-1825.
Europa riconosciuta, 1778.
(Performed at the opening
of La Scala.)
Les danaïdes, 1784.
La grotta di Trofonio,
1785.
Tarare, 1787.

Sammartini, Giovanni Battista,
1700 or 1701-1775.
Memet, 1732.
L'ambizione superata dalla
virtù, 1734.
L'Agrippina, 1743.

Sarti, Giuseppe, 1729-1802.
Giulio Sabino, 1781.
Fra due litiganti il terzo
goda, 1782.

Sartorio, Antonio, ca. 1630-
1680.
L'Adelaide, 1672.

Satie, Erik, 1866-1925.
Socrate, 1925.

Scarlatti, Alessandro, 1660-
1725.
Pirro, e Demetrio, 1694.
Massimo Puppieno, 1695.
L'Eraclea, 1700.
Il Mitridate eupatore,
1707.
Tigrane, 1715.
Marco Attilio Regulo, 1719.
La Griselda, 1721.

Schillings, Max von, 1868-1933.
Mona Lisa, 1915.

Schoenberg, Arnold, 1874-1951.
Erwartung, 1924.
Die glückliche Hand, 1924.
Von Heute auf Morgen, 1930.
(Earliest atonal opera.)
Moses und Aron, 1957.

Schreker, Franz, 1878-1934.
Der Schatzgräber, 1920.

Schubert, Franz, 1797-1828.
Alfonso und Estrella, 1854.
Die Verschworenen, 1861.
Fierrabras, 1897.

Schütz, Heinrich, 1585-1672.
Dafne, 1627. (The earliest
opera in German; lost.)

Šebor, Karel, 1843-1903.
Husitská nevešta, 1868.

Serov, Alexander, 1820-1871.
Îudith (Judith), 1863.
Rogneda, 1865.
Vrazh'îa sila, 1871.

Shaporin, Îuriĭ, 1887-1966.
Dekabristi, 1953.

Shield, William, 1748-1829.
The Shamrock, 1783.
Robin Hood, 1784.

Shostakovich, Dmitriĭ
Dmitrievich, 1906-1975.
Nos (The Nose), 1930.
Ledi Makbet Mtsenskago uezda
(Lady Macbeth of Mzensk;
Katerina Ismailova), 1934.

Silva, Antonio José da, 1705-
1739.
La vidado grande D. Quixote
de la Mancha, 1733.
(Earliest opera in Portu-
guese.)

Škroup, František, 1801-
1862.
Dráteník (The Tinker), 1826.
(The first opera in
Czech.)

Smetana, Bedřich, 1824-1884.
Prodaná nevěsta (The Bar-
tered Bride), 1866.
Dalibor, 1868.
Dvě vdovy (Two Widows), 1874.
Hubička (The Kiss), 1876.
Tajemství (The Secret), 1878.
Libuše, 1881.

Smyth, Ethel, *Dame*, 1858-
1944.
Der Wald, 1902. (First
opera by a woman to be
staged at the Metro-
politan, 1903.)
The Wreckers (Das Strand-
recht), 1906.
The Boatswain's Mate, 1916.

Somers, Harry T., 1925- .
Louis Riel, 1967.

Spohr, Louis, 1784-1859.
Faust, 1816.
Zemire und Azor, 1819.
Jessonda, 1823.

Spontini, Gasparo, 1774-1851.
Milton, 1804.
La vestale, 1807.
Fernand Cortez, 1809.
Olimpie, 1819.
Agnes von Hohenstaufen,
1829.

Staden, Sigmund Theophilus,
1607-1655.
Seelewig, 1644. (Earliest
extant German opera.)

Stanford, Charles Villiers,
1852-1924.
Shamus O'Brien, 1896.

Stefani, Jan, 1746–1829.
Cud, 1794.

Steffani, Agostino, 1654–
1728.
Alarico il Baltha, 1687.
Henrico Leone, 1689.
Rivali concordi, 1692.
Tassilone, 1709.

Storace, Stephen, 1763–1796.
The Siege of Belgrade,
1791.

Stradella, Allesandro, 1644–
1682.
La forza dell' amor paterno,
1678.

Straus, Oskar, 1870–1954.
Ein Walzertraum, 1907.
Der tapfere Soldat (The
Chocolate Soldier), 1908.

Strauss, Johann, Jr., 1825–
1899.
Die Fledermaus (The Bat),
1874.
Der lustige Krieg, 1881.
Eine Nacht in Venedig,
1884.
Der Zigeunerbaron (The
Gypsy Baron), 1885.

Strauss, Richard, 1864–1949.
Feuersnot, 1901.
Salome, 1905.
Elektra, 1909.
Der Rosenkavalier, 1911.
Ariadne auf Naxos, 1912.
Die Frau ohne Schatten,
1919.
Intermezzo, 1924.
Die ägyptische Helena, 1928.
Arabella, 1933.
Die schweigsame Frau, 1935.
Daphne, 1938.

Capriccio, 1942.
Die Liebe der Danae, 1952.

Stravinskiĭ, Igor' Federo-
vich, 1882–1971.
Le rossignol, 1914.
Histoire du soldat, 1918.
Mavra, 1922.
Oedipus rex, 1927.
Perséphone, 1934.
The Rake's Progress, 1951.

Suchoň, Eugen, 1908– .
Krútňava (The Whirlpool),
1949.

Sullivan, Arthur Seymour,
Sir, 1842–1900.
Cox and Box, 1867.
Trial by Jury, 1875.
The Sorcerer, 1877.
H.M.S. Pinafore, 1878.
The Pirates of Penzance,
1879.
Patience, 1881.
Iolanthe, 1882.
Princess Ida, 1884.
The Mikado, 1885.
Ruddigore, 1887.
The Yeomen of the Guard,
1888.
The Gondoliers, 1889.

Suppé, Franz von, 1819–1895.
Dichter und Bauer (Poet
and Peasant), 1846.
Die schöne Galatea, 1865.
Die leichte Kavallerie
(The Light Cavalry), 1866.
Fatinitza, 1876.
Boccaccio, 1879.
Donna Juanita, 1880.

Szeligowski, Tadeusz, 1896–
1963.
Bunt Zaków, 1951.

Szymanowski, Karol, 1882–
    1937.
  Król Roger, 1926.

Talma, Louise, 1906–   .
  The Alcestiade, 1962.
    (First opera by an
    American woman to be
    staged in Europe.)

Taylor, Deems, 1885–1966.
  The King's Henchman, 1927.
  Peter Ibbetson, 1931.

Tchaikovsky, Peter. See:
  Chaĭkovskiĭ, Petr

Telemann, Georg Philipp,
    1681–1767.
  Sokrates, 1721.
  Pimpinone, 1725.

Terradellas, Domingo Miguel
    Bernabé, 1713–1751.
  Mitridate, 1746.
  Sesostri, 1751.

Terrasse, Claude, 1867–1923.
  Le sire de Vergy, 1903.
  Monsieur de la Palisse,
    1904.

Thomas, Ambroise, 1811–1896.
  Le songe d'une nuit d'été,
    1850.
  Mignon, 1866.
  Hamlet, 1868.

Thomson, Virgil, 1896–   .
  Four Saints in Three Acts,
    1928.
  The Mother of Us All, 1947.

Thrane, Waldemar, 1790–1828.
  Fjeldeventyret, 1824. (The
    first opera in Norwegian.)

Tippett, Michael, *Sir*,
    1905– .
  The Midsummer Marriage,
    1955.
  King Priam, 1962.
  The Knot Garden, 1970.
  The Ice-break, 1977.

Traetta, Tommasso, 1727–
    1779.
  Farnace, 1751.
  Ifigenia in Tauride, 1763.

Umlauf, Ignaz, 1746–1796.
  Die Bergknappen, 1778.

Valverde, Joaquin, 1846–
    1910.
  La gran via [with Chueca],
    1886.

Varney, Louis, 1844–1908.
  Les mousquetaires au cou-
    vent, 1880.

Vaughan Williams, Ralph,
    1872–1958.
  Hugh the Drover, 1924.
  Sir John in Love, 1929.
  The Poisoned Kiss, 1936.
  Riders to the Sea, 1937.
  The Pilgrim's Progress,
    1951.

Verdi, Giuseppe, 1813–1901.
  Oberto, 1839.
  Nabucodonosor (Nabucco),
    1842.
  I lombardi alla prima
    crociata (Jérusalem),
    1843.
  Ernani, 1844.
  I due Foscari, 1844.
  Macbeth, 1847.
  I masnadieri, 1847.
  La battaglia di Legnano,
    1849.

Luisa Miller, 1849.
Stiffelio (Aroldo), 1850.
Rigoletto, 1851.
Il trovatore, 1853.
La traviata, 1853.
Les vêpres siciliennes (I
  vespri siciliani), 1855.
Simon Boccanegra, 1857.
Un ballo in maschera, 1859.
La forza del destino, 1862.
Don Carlos, 1867.
Aida, 1871.
Otello, 1887.
Falstaff, 1893.

Verstovskiĭ, Alexei Nikolae-
  vich, 1799-1862.
Askoldova mogila (Askold's
  Tomb), 1835.

Vinci, Leonardo, ca. 1690-
  1730.
Li zite'n galera, 1722.
Didone abbandonata, 1726.

Vivaldi, Antonio, 1678-1741.
La Griselda, 1735.

Wagner, Richard, 1813-1883.
Cola Rienzi (Rienzi), 1842.
Der fliegende Holländer (The
  Flying Dutchman), 1843.
Tannhäuser, 1845.
Lohengrin, 1850.
Tristan und Isolde, 1865.
Die Meistersinger von Nürn-
  berg, 1868.
Das Rheingold, 1869.
Die Walküre, 1870.
Siegfried, 1876.
Götterdämmerung, 1876.
Parsifal, 1882.
Die Feen, 1888. (Composed
  1833.)

Wallace, William Vincent,
  1812-1865.
Maritana, 1845.
Lurline, 1848.

Walton, William, *Sir*, 1902- .
Troilus and Cressida, 1954.
The Bear, 1967.

Ward, Robert, 1917- .
The Crucible, 1961.
The Lady from Colorado,
  1964.

Weber, Carl Maria von, 1786-
  1826.
Abu Hassan, 1811.
Preciosa, 1821.
Der Freischütz, 1821.
Euryanthe, 1823.
Oberon, 1826.

Weigl, Joseph, 1766-1846.
Die Schweitzerfamilie,
  1809. (First opera to be
  sung in Czech.)

Weill, Kurt, 1900-1950.
Die Dreigroschenoper (The
  Three-penny Opera),
  1928.
Aufstieg und Fall der Stadt
  Mahagonny, 1930.
Down in the Valley, 1948.

Weinberger, Jaromir, 1896-
  1967.
Švanda dudák (Schwanda the
  Bagpiper), 1927.

Willan, Healey, 1880-1968.
Transit through Fire,
  1942.
Deirdre, 1946.

Williamson, Malcolm, 1931- .
Our Man in Havana, 1963.
Violins of St. Jacques,
  1966.
Lucky Peter's Journey,
  1969.

Winter, Peter, 1754–1825.
  Der Bettelstudent, 1785.
  Das unterbrochene Opferfest,
  1796.

Wolf, Hugo, 1860–1903.
  Der Corregidor, 1896.

Wolf-Ferrari, Ermanno, 1876–
  1948.
  Die neugierigen Frauen
  (Le donne curiose), 1903.
  Der Schmuck der Madonna
  (Jewels of the Madonna;
  I gioielli della Madonna),
  1911.
  Susannens Geheimnis (The
  Secret of Susanna; Il
  segreto di Susanna),
  1909.

Zandonai, Riccardo, 1883–
  1944.
  Francesca da Rimini, 1914.
  Giulietta e Romeo, 1922.
  I cavalieri di Ekebù,
  1925.

Zemlinsky, Alexander von,
  1871–1942.
  Der Kreidekreis, 1933.

Ziani, Pietro Andrea, ca.
  1620–1684.
  L'innocenza risorta, 1683.

Zingarelli, Nicola Antonio,
  1752–1837.
  Berenice, 1811.
  Giulietta e Romeo, 1796.

Zorin, Dementy Alekseievich.
  Pererozhdenye, 1777.
    (Earliest completely pre-
    served opera by a Russian.
    No data available on the
    composer.)

Zumaya, Manuel de, 1679–
  1756.
  La Partenope, 1711. (First
  Mexican opera, and the
  earliest known full
  opera staged in North
  America.)

Anonymous
  La chercheuse d'esprit,
  1741.
  The Devil to Pay, 1731.
  The Disappointment, 1767.

Title Index

Ariadne auf Naxos (R. Strauss)
Ariane (Cambert)
Ariane et Barbe-bleue (Dukas)
Arianna (Monteverdi)
Ariodant (Méhul)
Ariodante (Handel)
Aristippe (Kreutzer)
Arlecchino (Busoni)
Armida (Haydn)
Armida (Rossini)
Armide (Gluck)
Armide (Lully)
Aroldo (Verdi)
Artaserse (Hasse)
Artaserse (Jommelli)
Artaxerxes (Arne)
Askoldova mogila (Vertovsky)
Askold's Tomb (Vertovsky)
L'assassinio nella catedrale
  (Pizzetti)
Astarto (G. Bononcini)
Astianatte (G. Bononcini)
Astianax (Kreutzer)
Gli astrologi immaginari
  (Paisiello)
At the Boar's Head (Holst)
At the Old Bleaching Ground
  (Kovařovic)
Atlántida (Falla)
Atlántida (Horký)
Atys (Lully)
Aufstieg und Fall der Stadt
  Mahagonny (Weill)
Der Augenarzt (Gyrowetz)
Aurora (Panizza)
Azara (Paine)
Azémia (Dalyrac)
Azora (Hadley)

Babes in Toyland (Herbert)
The Ballad of Baby Doe
  (Moore)
Un ballo in maschera (Verdi)
Bánk-bán (Erkel)
Banuta (Kalniņš)
Barbe-bleu (Offenbach)
The Barber of Seville (Ros-
  sini)

Der Barbier von Bagdad (Cor-
  nelius)
Il barbiere di Siviglia
  (Paisiello)
Il barbiere di Siviglia
  (Rossini)
The Bartered Bride (Smetana)
La basoche (Messager)
The bassarids (Henze)
Bastien und Bastienne
  (Mozart)
The Bat (J. Strauss)
Báthory Mária (Erkel)
La battaglia di Legnano
  (Verdi)
The Bear (Walton)
Beatrice di Tenda (Bellini)
Béatrice et Bénédict (Ber-
  lioz)
Beatrix Cenci (Ginastera)
The Beggar's Opera (Pepusch)
The Beginning of a Romance
  (Janáček)
Die beiden Schützen (Lort-
  zing)
Béla futása (Ruzitska)
Belfagor (Respighi)
La bella addormentata nel
  bosco (Respighi)
La belle Arsène (Monsigny)
La belle Hélène (Offenbach)
Bellérophon (Lully)
Benvenuto Cellini (Berlioz)
Berenice, regina d'Armenia
  (Zingarelli)
Die Bergknappen (Umlauff)
Den bergtagna (Hallström)
The Betrothal (Prokof'ev)
Der Bettelstudent (Millöcker)
Der Bettelstudent (Winter)
Billy Budd (Britten)
Blaise le savetier (Phili-
  dor)
Bluebeard's Castle (Bartók)
The Boatswain's Mate (Smyth)
Boccaccio (Suppé)
Bodas de sangre (Castro)
La bohème (Leoncavallo)

La bohème (Puccini)
The Bohemian Girl (Balfe)
Bomarzo (Ginastera)
Boris Godunov (Musorgskiĭ)
Borislav (Atanasov)
Boulevard solitude (Henze)
Die Brautwahl (Busoni)
De bruid der zee (Blockx)
Bunt Żaków (Szeligowski)
La buona figliuola (Piccinni)
Il burbero di buon cuore
    (Martin y Soler)

La cadi dupé (Monsigny)
Cadmus et Hermione (Lully)
Calandro (Ristori)
Le calife de Bagdad
    (Boieldieu)
La Calisto (Cavalli)
La cambiale di matrimonio
    (Rossini)
Camilla (Paër)
La campagna sommersa (Res-
    pighi)
Il campanello di notte
    (Donizetti)
Candide (Bernstein)
Le cantatrici villane
    (Fioravanti)
The Canterbury Pilgrims (De
    Koven)
Caponsacchi (Hageman)
Il cappello di paglia di
    Firenze (Rota)
Capriccio (R. Strauss)
La capricciosa corretta (Mar-
    tin y Soler)
Le caprice amoureux (Duni)
The Captain's Daughter (Cui)
The Captive in the Caucasus
    (Cui)
I Capuletti e i Montecchi
    (Bellini)
Carattaco (J.C. Bach)
Le caravane du Caire
    (Grétry)
Cardillac (Hindemith)
Carmen (Bizet)
Carmina burana (Orff)

Castaway (Berkeley)
Castor et Pollux (Rameau)
Catalina de Guisa (Paniagua)
La catena d'Adone (Mazzochi)
Caterina di Guise (Coccia)
Cavalieri di Ekebù (Zan-
    donai)
Cavalleria rusticana (Mas-
    cagni)
La caverne (Lesueur)
La cecchina (Piccinni)
Celos aun del aire matan
    (Hidalgo)
Los celos hacen estrellas
    (Hidalgo)
Cendrillon (Isouard)
Cendrillon (Massenet)
La cenerentola (Rossini)
Cephal i Prokris (Araia)
Céphale et Procris (E. La-
    guerre)
Čert a Kača (Dvořák)
Cesare amante (Cesti)
Le chalet (Adam)
Charodyĭka (Chaĭkovskiĭ)
La chatte anglaise (Henze)
Che originali! (Mayr)
La chercheuse d'esprit
    (anonymous)
Chi soffre, speri (Mazzochi
    and Marazzoli)
Chilpéric (Hervé)
The Chocolate Soldier
    (O. Straus)
Christmas Eve (Lysenko)
The Christmas Tree (Rebikov)
Christoph Columbus (Milhaud)
Ciboulette (Hahn)
Der Cid (Cornelius)
La cigale et la fourmi
    (Audran)
Circe (Egk)
La clemenza di Scipione
    (J.C. Bach)
La clemenza di Tito (Mozart)
Cleopatra's Night (Hadley)
Les cloches de Corneville
    (Planquette)
La clochette (Duni)

La clochette (Hérold)
Clotilda (Coccia)
Cola Rienzi (Wagner)
Colas Breugnon (Kabalevskiĭ)
Colegialas y soldados (Hernando)
La colombe (Gounod)
Il combattimento di Tancredi e Clorinda (Monteverdi)
Comedy on a Bridge (Martinů)
La comica del cielo (Abbatini)
Le Comte d'Ory (Rossini)
Comus (Arne)
La confusione nata dalla somiglianza (Portugal)
The Consul (Menotti)
Les contes d'Hoffman (Offenbach)
Le coq d'or (Rimskiĭ-Korsakov)
Der corregidor (Wolf)
Una cosa rara (Martin y Soler)
Così fan tutte (Mozart)
The Cossack Poet (Cavos)
Costanza e fortezza (Fux)
The Countess Maritza (Kálmán)
Cox and Box (Sullivan)
The Cradle Will Rock (Blitzstein)
A Cremonai hegedűs (Hubay)
Crispo (G. Bononcini)
Cristoforo Colombo (Carnicer)
Il crociato in Egitto (Meyerbeer)
Croesus (Keiser)
The Crucible (Ward)
Die csárdásfürstin (Kálmán)
Cud (Stefani)
The Cunning Little Vixen (Janáček)
Cupid and Death (Gibbons)
Curlew River (Britten)
Cyrano (Damrosch)
Czaar und Zimmermann (Lortzing)
Czinka panna (Kodály)

Dafne (Caccini)
La Dafne (Gagliano)

La Dafne (Peri)
Dafne (Schütz)
Tō dakhtilidi tis manas (Kalomiris)
Dal male il bene (Marazzoli and Abbatini)
Dalibor (Smetana)
La dama soldato (Naumann)
La dame blanche (Boieldieu)
La damnation de Faust (Berlioz)
Les danaides (Salieri)
Dantons Tod (Einem)
Daphne (R. Strauss)
Dardanus (Rameau)
David (Milhaud)
Death in Venice (Britten)
Debora e Jaéle (Pizzetti)
The Decision (Musgrave)
Deirdre (Willan)
Dekabristi (Shaporin)
La délire (Berton)
Demetrio (Pérez)
Demofoonte (Jommelli)
Demon (Rubinstein)
Démophoön (Cherubini)
Deseret (Kastle)
Le déserteur (Monsigny)
Destiny (Janáček)
Les deux avares (Grétry)
Les deux aveugles de Tolède (Méhul)
Les deux chasseurs et la laitière (Duni)
Les deux journées (Cherubini)
Deux mots (Dalayrac)
Les deux nuits (Boieldieu)
Les deux petits savoyards (Dalayrac)
The Devil and Daniel Webster (Moore)
The Devil and Kate (Dvořák)
The Devil to Pay (anonymous)
The Devils of Loudun (Penderecki)
Le devin du village (Rousseau)
Diably z Loudun (Penderecki)

Les dialogues des carmélites
(Poulenc)
La diavolessa (Galuppi)
Dichter und Bauer (Suppé)
Dido and Aeneas (Purcell)
Didon (Piccinni)
Didone (Cavalli)
Didone abbandonata (Vinci)
A Dinner Engagement (Berkeley)
Dinorah (Meyerbeer)
The Disappointment (anonymous)
Il dissoluto punito (Mozart)
Djamileh (Bizet)
Doctor und Apotheker
(Dittersdorf)
The Dogheads (Kovařovic)
Doktor Faust (Busoni)
Die Dollarprinzessin (Fall)
La Dolores (Bréton)
Dom Sébastien (Donizetti)
Le domino noir (Auber)
Don Carlos (Verdi)
Don Giovanni (Mozart)
Don Giovanni Tenorio (Gaz-
zaniga)
Don Pasquale (Donizetti)
Don Quichotte (Massenet)
Don Rodrigo (Ginastera)
Das Donauweibchen (Kauer)
La donna del lago (Rossini)
Donna Diana (Rezniček)
Donna Juanita (Suppé)
La donna serpente (Casella)
Le donne cambiate (Portugal)
Le donne curiose (Usiglio)
Der Dorfjahrmarkt (Benda)
La Dori (Cesti)
Down by the Greenwood Side
(Birtwistle)
Down in the Valley (Weill)
Les dragons de Villars
(Maillart)
Dráteník (Škroup)
Dream on the Volga (Arenskiĭ)
Die Dreigroschenoper (Weill)
Drottningen av Golconda (Ber-
wald)
Dubrovskiĭ (Napravnik)

Il duca d'Alba (Donizetti)
I due Foscari (Verdi)
The Duenna (Linley)
The Duenna (Profof'ev)
Duke Bluebeard's Castle
(Bartók)
Dvě vdovy (Smetana)

L'éclair (Halévy)
Edgar (Puccini)
Edmea (Catalani)
Einstein (Dessau)
Elda (Catalani)
Elegie für junge Liebende
(Henze)
Elektra (R. Strauss)
Les éléments (Destouches)
Elena e Malvina (Carnicer)
Eliogabalo (Boretti)
Élisa (Cherubini)
Elisa e Claudio (Mercadante)
L'elisir d'amore (Donizetti)
The Emperor Jones (Gruen-
berg)
L'enfant et les sortilèges
(Ravel)
Die Entführung aus dem
Serail (Mozart)
L'Eraclea (Scarlatti)
Ercole amante (Cavalli)
Ercole in Tebe (Melani)
Erismena (Cavalli)
Erminia sul Giordano (M.
Rossi)
Ernani (Verdi)
Ero s onaga svijeta (Goto-
vac)
Erwartung (Schoenberg)
O escravo (Gomes)
Estrella de Soria (Berwald)
L'étoile (Chabrier)
L'étoile du nord (Meyerbeer)
L'étranger (d'Indy)
Eufemio di Messina (Carnicer)
Eugene Onegin (Chaĭkovskiĭ)
Euphrosine (Méhul)
L'Euridice (Caccini)
L'Euridice (Peri)

Europa riconosciuta (Salieri)
L'Europe galante (Campra)
Euryanthe (Weber)
Eva (J. Foerster)
Eva (Lehár)
Der Evangelimann (Kienzl)
Evangelina (Berutti)
Evgeniĭ Onegin (Chaĭkovskiĭ)

The Fair of Sorochinsk
  (Musorgskiĭ)
The Fairy Queen (Purcell)
Falstaff (Verdi)
The Family of Taras (Kabalev-
  skiĭ)
La fanciulla del west (Puccini)
Faniska (Cherubini)
Farnace (Traetta)
Fate (Janáček)
Fate of a Man (Dzerzhinskiĭ)
Faust (Gounod)
Faust (Spohr)
Le faux lord (Piccinni)
La favola d'Orfeo (Monteverdi)
La favorite (Donizetti)
La fede tradita e vendicata
  (Gasparini)
Fedora (Giordano)
La fée Urgèle (Duni)
Die Feen (Wagner)
Fernand Cortez (Spontini)
Fernando nel Messico (Portu-
  gal)
Fervaal (d'Indy)
Festes de Thalie (Mouret)
Les festes vénitiennes
  (Campra)
Fetonte (Jommelli)
Feuersnot (R. Strauss)
La fiamma (Respighi)
La fiancée (Auber)
Il fidanzato del mare (Paniz-
  za)
Fidelio (Beethoven)
Fierrabras (Schubert)
Figlia di Jorio (Pizzetti)
La fille de Madame Angot
  (Lecocq)

La fille du régiment
  (Donizetti)
La fille mal gardée (Duni)
Il filosofo di Campagnia
  (Galuppi)
La finta giardiniera (Mozart)
La finta pazza (Sacrati)
Le finte contesse (Paisiello)
Fiskerne (Hartmann)
Fjeldeventyret (Thrane)
The Flaming Angel (Prokof'ev)
Flauto solo (d'Albert)
Die Fledermaus (J. Strauss)
Fleur-de-thé (Lecocq)
Der fliegende Holländer
  (Wagner)
The Flying Dutchman (Wagner)
Une folie (Méhul)
Fortunio (Messager)
La forza del destino (Verdi)
La forza dell' amor paterno
  (Stradella)
La forza dell' amore e dell'
  odio (Araia)
Four Saints in Three Acts
  (Thomson)
Fra diavolo (Auber)
Fra due litiganti (Sarti)
Fra gamle dage (Haarklou)
Francesca da Rimini (Rach-
  maninoff)
Francesca da Rimini (Zan-
  donai)
Frasquita (Lehár)
Lo frate 'nnamorato (Pergo-
  lesi)
Die Frau ohne Schatten
  (R. Strauss)
Frederica (Lehár)
Der Freischütz (Weber)
From the House of the Dead
  (Janáček)

Galatée (Massé)
The Gambler (Prokof'ev)
La gazza ladra (Rossini)
The Geisha (Jones)
Gergana (Atanasov)
Gianni Schicchi (Puccini)

Giannina e Bernadone (Cimarosa)
Giants in the Earth (Moore)
Il giasone (Cavalli)
La Gierusalemme liberata (Pallavicino)
La gioconda (Ponchielli)
I gioielli della madonna (Wolf-Ferrari)
Giroflé-girofla (Lecocq)
Giuditta (Lehár)
Giulietta e Romeo (Zandonai)
Giulietta e Romeo (Zingarelli)
Giulio Cesare in Egitto (Handel)
Giulio Sabino (Sarti)
Il giuramento (Mercadante)
Il Giustino (Legrenzi)
Gloria (Cilea)
Die glückliche Hand (Schoenberg)
Götterdämmerung (Wagner)
The Golden Cockerel (Rimskii-Korsakov)
Der goldene Bock (Křenek)
The Gondoliers (Sullivan)
Gonzague (Ibert)
The Good Soldier Schweik (Kurka)
Gorenjski Slavček (A. Foerster)
I goti (Gobatti)
Goyescas (Granados)
Gräfin Mariza (Kálmán)
Der Graf von Luxembourg (Lehár)
La gran via (Chueca and Valverde)
La grand-duchesse de Gérolstein (Offenbach)
Gražina (Karnavičius)
Greek Passion (Martinů)
Grieschesche Passion (Martinů)
Griffelkin (Foss)
Griselda (Paër)
Griselda (Scarlatti)
La Griselda (Vivaldi)

Die grossmüthige Tomyris (Keiser)
La grotta di Trofonio (Salieri)
O guaraní (Gomes)
Il guarany (Gomes)
Guillaume Tell (Rossini)
Gulistan (Dalayrac)
Gunlöd (Cornelius)
Gustave III (Auber)
Gwendoline (Chabrier)
The Gypsy Baron (J. Strauss)
Gypsy Love (Lehár)

H.M.S. Pinafore (Sullivan)
Habanera (Laparra)
Halka (Moniuszko)
Hamlet (Thomas)
Hans Heiling (Marschner)
Hänsel und Gretel (Humperdinck)
Die Harmonie der Welt (Hindemith)
Háry János (Kodály)
The Haunted Manor (Moniuszko)
Haydée (Auber)
Heksen (Enna)
Héléna (Méhul)
Helena rapita da Paride (Freschi)
Help! Help! The Globolinks! (Menotti)
Henrico Leone (Steffani)
Herbergprinses (Blockx)
Herculanum (David)
L'hermitage fleuri (Albéniz)
Hérodiade (Massenet)
L'heure espagnole (Ravel)
Hin und zurück (Hindemith)
Hippolyte et Arcie (Rameau)
Histoire du soldat (Stravinskiĭ)
The House of the Dead (Janáček)
Hubička (Smetana)
Hugh the Drover (Vaughan Williams)
Les huguenots (Meyerbeer)

Hulda (Franck)
Hunyady László (Erkel)
Hus med dubbel ingang (Rosen-
  berg)
Husitská nevešta (Šebor)

Ĩamshchiki na podstave (Fomin)
The Ice-break (Tippett)
L'Idalma (Pasquini)
L'Idaspe fedele (Mancini)
Idomeneo (Mozart)
L'Ifigenia (Jommelli)
Ifigenia in Tauride (Majo)
Ifigenia in Tauride (Traetta)
Igrok (Prokof'ev)
Ildegonda (Morales)
Ilya Bogatir (Cavos)
L'incognita perseguitata
  (Anfossi)
L'incoronazione di Poppea
  (Monteverdi)
Les indes galantes (Rameau)
Gl'inganni felici (Pollarolo)
L'inganno felice (Rossini)
L'innocenza risorta (Ziani)
Intermezzo (R. Strauss)
The Invisible City of Kitezh
  (Rimskiĭ-Korsakov)
The Invisible Prince (Cavos)
Iolanthe (Sullivan)
Ione (Abbatini)
Iphigénie en Aulide (Gluck)
Iphigénie en Tauride (Gluck)
Iphigénie en Tauride (Pic-
  cinni)
L'irato (Méhul)
Iris (Mascagni)
Irische Legende (Egk)
Isis (Lully)
The Island God (Menotti)
L'isle des foux (Duni)
Ismalia (Carnicer)
L'isola d'amore (Sacchini)
Issé (Destouches)
L'italiana in Algeri (Rossini)
L'italiana in Londra (Cima-
  rosa)
Ĩudith' (Serov)

Ivan' Susannin' (Cavos)

Jadwiga (Kurpinski)
Jakobín (Dvořák)
Jean de Nivelle (Delibes)
Jean de Paris (Boieldieu)
Jeanne d'Arc au boucher
  (Honegger)
Její pastorkýna (Janáček)
Jenufa (Janáček)
Jérusalem (Verdi)
Jessika (J. Foerster)
Jessonda (Spohr)
The Jewels of the Madonna
  (Wolf-Ferrari)
Jocelyn (Godard)
Joconde (Isouard)
La jolie fille de Perth
  (Bizet)
Le jongleur de Notre Dame
  (Massenet)
Jonny spielt auf (Křenek)
Joseph (Méhul)
Le joueur de viole (Laparra)
Judith (Serov)
Jugar con fuego (Barbieri)
Le jugement de Midas
  (Grétry)
La juive (Halévy)
Julietta (Martinů)
The Jumping Frog of Cala-
  veras County (Foss)

Kammenyĭ gost' (Dargomyzhskiĭ)
Kapitanskaĩa dochka (Cui)
Karl V (Křenek)
Kat'a Kabanová (Janáček)
Katerina Ismailova (Shos-
  takovich)
Kavkazskiĭ plennik (Cui)
Kazak' stikhotvorets'
  (Cavos)
A Kékszakállú herceg vára
  (Bartók)
Két pisztoly (Erkel)
Khovanshchina (Musorgskiĭ)

King Priam (Tippett)
The King's Henchman (Taylor)
The Kiss (Smetana)
Kitezh (Rimskiĭ-Korsakov)
Die Kluge (Orff)
Kniâz' Igor' (Borodin)
Kniâz' Nevidimka (Cavos)
The Knot Garden (Tippett)
Koanga (Delius)
König Hirsch (Henze)
Kola Briûn'on (Kabalevskiĭ)
Die Königin von Saba (Gold-
    mark)
Königskinder (Humperdinck)
Kosara (Atanasov)
Der Kreidekreis (Zemlinsky)
Król Lokietek (Elsner)
Król Roger (Szymanowski)
Krútňava (Suchoň)

The Lady from Colorado (Ward)
Lady Macbeth Mtsenkago uezda
    (Shostakovich)
Lady Macbeth of Mzensk (Shos-
    takovich)
Ein ländisches Verlobungs-
    fest in Schweden (Berwald)
Lakmé (Delibes)
Lalla-Roukh (David)
Das Land des Lächelns (Lehár)
Der lange Weihnachtsmahl
    (Hindemith)
Lanzelot (Dessau)
The Last Savage (Menotti)
Lazaro (Gaito)
Ledi Makbet Mtsenskago uezda
    (Shostakovich)
La leggenda di Sakuntala
    (Alfano)
Die leichte Kavallerie
    (Suppé)
Leonida in Tega (Draghi)
Leonora (Fry)
Leszek bialy (Elsner)
La liberazione di Ruggiero
    (F. Caccini)
Libuše (Smetana)

Die Liebe der Danae (R.
    Strauss)
A Life for the Czar (Glinka)
The Light Cavalry (Suppé)
Linda di Chamounix (Doni-
    zetti)
Lišky příhodi Bystroušky
    (Janáček)
Liubov k trem apelsinam
    (Proko'fev)
Ljubav i Zloba (Lisinski)
Lodoïska (Cherubini)
Lodoïska (Kreutzer)
Lohengrin (Wagner)
I lombardi (Verdi)
Loreley (Catalani)
Louis Riel (Somers)
Louise (Charpentier)
The Love for Three Oranges
    (Prokof'ev)
Love in a Village (Arne)
Loves of Ergasto (Greber)
Lucia di Lammermoor (Doni-
    zetti)
Lucile (Grétry)
Lucky Peter's Journey
    (Williamson)
Lucrezia (Respighi)
Lucrezia Borgia (Donizetti)
Luisa Miller (Verdi)
Lulu (Berg)
Lurline (Wallace)
Lustige Krieg (J. Strauss)
Die lustige Witwe (Lehár)
Die lustigen Weiber von
    Windsor (Nicolai)
Lycksalighetens ö (Rosen-
    berg)

M. Attilio Regulo (Scar-
    latti)
Ma tante Aurore (Boieldieu)
Macbeth (Verdi)
Le maçon (Auber)
Madama Butterfly (Puccini)
Madame Chrysanthème (Mes-
    sager)

Madeleine (Herbert)
The Magic Flute (Mozart)
The Magic Opal (Albéniz)
Mahagonny (Weill)
The Maid of Artois (Balfe)
The Maid of Orleans (Chaĭkov-
skiĭ)
The Maid of Pskov (Rimskiĭ-
Korsakov)
Maĭskaia noch' (Rimskiĭ-
Korsakov)
Maison à vendre (Dalayrac)
Le maître de chapelle (Paër)
Maître Pathelin (Bazin)
The Makropoulos Affair
(Janáček)
Les mamelles de Tirésias
(Poulenc)
Mam'zelle Nitouche (Hervé)
The Man without a Country
(Damrosch)
Manon (Massenet)
Manon Lescaut (Puccini)
Maometto (Rossini)
Le marchand de Venise (Hahn)
Marco Attilio Regulo (Scar-
latti)
Le maréchal ferrant (Philidor)
María del Carmen (Granados)
Maria di Rohan (Donizetti)
Maria Egiziaca (Respighi)
Maria Golovin (Menotti)
Maria Padilla (Donizetti)
Maria Stuarda (Donizetti)
Maria Tudor (Gomes)
Marie (Hérold)
Marina (Arrieta)
Marionetter (Rosenberg)
Maritana (Wallace)
Il marito giogatore (Orlan-
dini)
Mârouf (Rabaud)
The Marriage of Figaro
(Mozart)
Martha (Flotow)
Les martyrs (Donizetti)
Mary, Queen of Scots (Mus-
grave)
Masaniello (Carafa)

Le maschere (Mascagni)
La mascotte (Audran)
Maskarade (Nielsen)
I masnadieri (Verdi)
Massimo Puppieno (Palla-
vicino)
Massimo Puppicno (Scarlatti)
Mat' (Khrennikov)
Mathis der Maler (Hindemith)
Il matrimonio segreto (Cima-
rosa)
El matrero (Boero)
Mavra (Stravinskiĭ)
May Night (Rimskiĭ-Korsakov)
Mazepa (Chaĭkovskiĭ)
Medea (Benda)
Medea (Pacini)
Medea in Corinto (Mayr)
Le médecin malgré lui
(Gounod)
Médée (Cherubini)
Medio evo latino (Panizza)
The Medium (Menotti)
Mefistofele (Boito)
Die Meistersinger (Wagner)
Memet (Sammartini)
Merry Mount (Hanson)
The Merry Wives of Windsor
(Nicolai)
The Midsummer Marriage
(Tippett)
A Midsummer Night's Dream
(Britten)
Mignon (Thomas)
The Mikado (Sullivan)
Milton (Spontini)
Mireille (Gounod)
The Miserly Night (Rach-
maninoff)
Miss Hélyett (Audran)
Il mistero di Venezia (Mali-
piero)
Mitridate (Terradellas)
Mitridate eupatore (Scar-
latti)
Moïse (Rossini)
Les moissonneurs (Duni)

La molinara (Paisiello)
Molodoya gvardia (Meytus)
Mona (Parker)
Mona Lisa (Schillings)
Der Mond (Orff)
Il mondo alla roversa (Galuppi)
Il mondo della luna (Galuppi)
Il mondo della luna (Haydn)
Monsieur Beaucaire (Messager)
Monsieur de la palisse
  (Terrasse)
Montano et Stéphanie (Berton)
La morte d'Orfeo (Landi)
Mosè in Egitto (Rossini)
Moses und Aron (Schoenberg)
Mother (Khrennikov)
The Mother of Us All (Thomson)
Les mousquetaires au convent
  (Varney)
Mr. Brouček's Excursions
  (Janáček)
La muette de Portici (Auber)
El músico y el poeta (Car-
  nicer)
Die Mutter (Haba)

Na starém bělidle (Kovařovic)
Naboth's Vineyard (Goehr)
Nabucco (Verdi)
Nabucodonosor (Verdi)
Ein Nacht in Venedig (J.
  Strauss)
Das Nachtlager von Granada
  (K. Kreutzer)
Nanon (Genée)
Natalka Poltavka (Lysenko)
Natoma (Herbert)
La navarraise (Massenet)
La nave (Montemezzi)
Nędza uszczęśliwiona (Kamién-
  ski)
Neues vom Tage (Hindemith)
Das Neusonntagskind (Müller)
Ni amor se libra de amor
  (Hidalgo)
Nikita Vershinin (Kabelevskiĭ)
Nina (Dalayrac)
Nina (Paisiello)
Nina et Lindor (Duni)

Ninette à la cour (Duni)
No for an Answer (Blitz-
  stein)
O noapte furtunoasă (Con-
  stantinescu)
Les noces de Jeannette
  (Massé)
Norma (Bellini)
I normanni a Parigi (Merca-
  dante)
The Nose (Shostakovich)
La notte di un nevrastenico
  (Rota)
Le nozze di Figaro (Mozart)

Oberon (Weber)
Oberto (Verdi)
Obruchenie v monastyre
  (Prokof'ev)
Oedipe (Enesco)
Oedipe à Colone (Sacchini)
Oedipus der Tyrann (Orff)
Oedipus rex (Stravinskiĭ)
The Old Maid and the Thief
  (Menotti)
Olimpiade (Arne)
L'Olimpiade (Caldara)
Olimpiade (Jommelli)
L'Olimpiade (Leo)
Olimpiade (Mysliveczek)
Olimpie (Spontini)
Ollantay (Gaito)
L'ombra di Don Giovanni
  (Alfano)
Omphale (Destouches)
Oprichnik (Chaĭkovskiĭ)
L'orfana di Lloret (Carietta)
L'Orfeide (Malipiero)
L'Orfeo (Monteverdi)
L'Orfeo (L. Rossi)
Orfeo ed Euridice (Fux)
Orfeo ed Euridice (Gluck)
Orione (J.C. Bach)
Orlando (Handel)
Orleanskaîa deva (Chaĭkov-
  skiĭ)
L'Ormindo (Cavalli)
Orontea (Cesti)

Orphée aux enfers (Offenbach)
Orpheus og Euridice (Naumann)
Ossian (Lesueur)
Osud (Janáček)
Otello (Rossini)
Otello (Verdi)
Our Man in Havana (Williamson)
Owen Wingrave (Britten)

The Padlock (Dibdin)
Padmavati (Roussel)
Paganini (Lehár)
I pagliacci (Leoncavallo)
Il palazzo d'Atlante incantato
   (L. Rossi)
Palestrina (Pfitzner)
Pampa (Berutti)
Pan y toros (Barbieri)
Panfilo and Lauretta (Chávez)
Panurge dans l'isle des lan-
   ternes (Grétry)
Le pardon de Ploërmel
   (Meyerbeer)
Paride e Elena (Gluck)
Parsifal (Wagner)
La part du diable (Auber)
Partenope (Zumaya)
Il pastor fido (Handel)
Patience (Sullivan)
La patienza di Socrate
   (Draghi)
Paul et Virginie (R. Kreutzer)
Paul et Virginie (Le Sueur)
Paul et Virginie (Massé)
Le pauvre matelot (Milhaud)
The Pearl of Iran (Bantock)
Les pêcheurs (Gossec)
Les pêcheurs de perles (Bizet)
Peer Gynt (Egk)
Le peintre amoureux de son
   modèle (Duni)
Pelléas et Mélisande (Debussy)
Pénélope (Fauré)
Pepita Jiménez (Albéniz)
Pererozhdenye (Zorin)
The Perfect Fool (Holst)
La périchole (Offenbach)

La perle du Brésil (David)
Persée (Lully)
Perséphone (Stravinskiǐ)
Peter Grimes (Britten)
Peter Ibbetson (Taylor)
Le petit duc (Lecocq)
Le petit Faust (Hervé)
Petru rares (Caudella)
Phaéton (Lully)
Philémon et Baucis (Gounod)
Il piccolo Marat (Mascagni)
Pickwick (Coates)
La pietra del paragone
   (Rossini)
Pikovaía dama (Chaǐkovskiǐ)
The Pilgrim's Progress
   (Vaughan Williams)
Pimmalione (Cherubini)
Pimpinone (Telemann)
The Pipe of Desire (Converse)
Pique dame (Chaǐkovskiǐ)
Il pirata (Bellini)
The Pirates of Penzance
   (Sullivan)
I Pirenei (Pedrell)
Los Pirineos (Pedrell)
Pirro (Paisiello)
Pirro e Demetrio (Scarlatti)
Il più fedele frà i vassalli
   (Gasparini)
Počátek románu (Janáček)
Poet and Peasant (Suppé)
Pohjalaisa (Madetoja)
Pohjan neito (Merikanto)
The Poisoned Kiss (Vaughan
   Williams)
Polifemo (G. Bononcini)
Poliuto (Donizetti)
Polly (Pepusch and Arnold)
Il pomo d'oro (Cesti)
Pomone (Cambert)
Porgy and Bess (Gershwin)
Porin (Lisinski)
Le postillon de Longjumeau
   (Adam)
La poupée (Audran)
Povest' o nastoíâschchem
   cheloveke (Prokof'ev)

Le pré aux clercs (Hérold)
La preciosa (Weber)
Le premier jour de bonheur
(Auber)
Il prigioniero (Dallapiccola)
Prima Donna (Benjamin)
Prince Igor (Borodin)
Princess Ida (Sullivan)
Der Prinz von Homburg (Henze)
Prodaná nevěsta (Smetana)
Le prophète (Meyerbeer)
Proserpina y el entranjero
(Castro)
Proserpine (Lully)
Ho prōtomastoras (Kalomiris)
Der Prozess (Einem)
Pskovitîânka (Rimskiĭ-Kor-
sakov)
Psohlavci (Kovařovic)
Psyche (Locke)
Psyche (Lully)
Les p'tites Michu (Messager)
Punch and Judy (Birtwistle)
Puntila (Dessau)
I puritani di Scozia (Bellini)
Pygmalion (Benda)

The Queen of Spades (Chaĭkovskiĭ)
The Quiet Don (Dzerzhinskiĭ)

Radamisto (Handel)
The Rake's Progress (Stravin-
skiĭ)
The Rape of Lucretia (Britten)
Il re pastore (Mozart)
Il re Teodoro in Venezia
(Paisiello)
Rebecca (Josephs)
Le rencontre imprévue (Gluck)
Regina (Blitzstein)
La reine de Chypre (Halévy)
La reine topaze (Massé)
Les rendez-vous bourgeois
(Isouard)
Resa till Amerika (Rosenberg)

El retablo de Maese Pedro
(Falla)
Der Revisor (Egk)
Das Rheingold (Wagner)
Ricciardo e Zoraide (Rossini)
Richard Coeur de Lion
(Grétry)
Riders to the Sea (Vaughan
Williams)
Rienzi (Wagner)
Rigoletto (Verdi)
Les rigueurs du cloître
(Berton)
Rinaldo (Handel)
Der Ring des Nibelungen
(Wagner)
Rip van Winkle (Bristow)
Rip van Winkle (Planquette)
Risdivîâna nich (Lysenko)
Risurrezione (Alfano)
Rita (Donizetti)
Il ritorno d'Ulisse (Monte-
verdi)
Rivali concordi (Steffani)
Robert le diable (Meyerbeer)
Roberto d'Evereux (Donizetti)
Robin Hood (De Koven)
Robin Hood (Shield)
Rodelinda (Graun)
Rogneda (Serov)
Le roi David (Honegger)
Le roi d'Ys (Lalo)
Le roi d'Yvetot (Adam)
Le roi et le fermier (Mon-
signy)
Le roi l'a dit (Delibes)
Le roi malgré lui (Chabrier)
Roland (Lully)
Roméo et Juliette (Gounod)
Romeo und Julie (Benda)
Romeo y Julieta (Morales)
La rondine (Puccini)
Rose et Colas (Monsigny)
Rose of Castille (Balfe)
Der Rosenkavalier (R. Strauss)
Les rosières (Hérold)
Le rossignol (Stravinskiĭ)

Ruddigore (Sullivan)
Rusalka (Dargomyzhskiĭ)
Rusalka (Dvořák)
Ruslan i Lĭudmila (Glinka)
Ruth (Berkeley)
Ruy Blas (Marchetti)

Il S. Alessio (Landi)
Les sabots (Duni)
Sadko (Rimskiĭ-Korsakov)
Saffo (Pacini)
The Saint of Bleeker Street
  (Menotti)
Salammbô (Reyer)
Salome (R. Strauss)
Salvator Rosa (Gomes)
Samson et Dalila (Saint-Saëns)
San Antonio de la Florida
  (Albéniz)
La sangre de las guitarras
  (Gaito)
Sant Alessio (Landi)
Saracen (Cui)
Saraĉsin (Cui)
Šárka (Janáček)
Sarrona (Howland)
Saul og David (Nielsen)
Savitri (Holst)
La scala di seta (Rossini)
The Scarlet Letter (Damrosch)
Der Schatzgräber (Shreker)
Lo schiavo (Gomes)
Der Schmuck der Madonna
  (Wolf-Ferrari)
Die schöne Galatea (Suppé)
Schwanda the Bagpiper
  (Weinberger)
Die schweigsame Frau (R.
  Strauss)
Die Schweizerfamilie (Weigl)
Die Schwestern von Prag (Mül-
  ler)
Scipione Africano (Cavalli)
La scola de maritati (Martin
  y Soler)
The Secret (Smetana)
The Secret of Susanna (Wolf-
  Ferrari)

Seelewig (Staden)
Il segreto di Susanna (Wolf-
  Ferrari)
Šelma sedlák (Dvořák)
Sem'ĭa Tarasa (Kabalevskiĭ)
Semiramide (Rossini)
Semiramide riconosciuta
  (Porpora)
Semyon Kotko (Prokof'ev)
Serse (Handel)
La serva padrona (Paisiello)
La serva padrona (Pergolesi)
Sesostrate (Hasse)
Sesostri (Terradellas)
Shadowplay (Goehr)
The Shamrock (Shield)
Shamus O'Brien (Stanford)
Shanewis (Cadman)
Showboat (Kern)
Siberia (Giordano)
La siège de Corinthe (Rossini)
The Siege of Belgrade
  (Storace)
The Siege of Rhodes (Locke)
The Siege of Rochelle
  (Balfe)
Siegfried (Wagner)
Il signor Bruschino (Rossini)
Sigurd (Reyer)
Simon Boccanegra (Verdi)
Sir John in Love (Vaughan
  Williams)
Le sire de Vergy (Terrasse)
Siroe (Hasse)
Skazanie o nevidimom gradie
  Kitezhie (Rimskiĭ-Korsakov)
Skazka o ĉsare Saltane
  (Rimskiĭ-Korsakov)
Skupoĭ ryĉsar' (Rachmaninoff)
The Sly Little Fox (Janáček)
Snegurochka (Rimskiĭ-Korsa-
  kov)
The Snow Maiden (Rimskiĭ-
  Korsakov)
Socrate (Satie)
Socrate immaginario (Pais-
  iello)
Sokrates (Telemann)

Le soldat magicien (Philidor)
Solimano (Pérez)
Le solitaire (Carafa)
Le songe d'une nuit e'été
  (Thomas)
La sonnambula (Bellini)
The Sorcerer (Sullivan)
Le sorcier (Philidor)
Sorochinskaiâ iârmaka
  (Musorgskiĭ)
La sortija (Albéniz)
Lo spazzacamino principe
  (Portugal)
Lo speziale (Haydn)
Stiffelio (Verdi)
Stoertebecker (Keiser)
The Stone Guest (Dargomyzh-
  skiĭ)
A Stormy Night (Constantines-
  cu)
The Story of a Real Man
  (Prokof'ev)
Das Strandrecht (Smyth)
Straszny dwór (Moniuszko)
Der Sturm (Martin)
Sud'ba cheloveka (Dzerzhin-
  skiĭ)
Suor Angelica (Puccini)
Susannah (Floyd)
Susannens Geheimnis (Wolf-
  Ferrari)
Švanda dudák (Weinberger)
Székely fonó (Kodály)
Szép Ilonka (Mosonyi)

Il tabarro (Puccini)
Le tableau parlant (Grétry)
Tajemství (Smetana)
The Tales of Hoffmann
  (Offenbach)
Tamerlano (Handel)
The Taming of the Shrew
  (Giannini)
Tammany (Hewitt)
Tancrède (Campra)
Tancredi (Rossini)
Tannhäuser (Wagner)

Der tapfere Soldat
  (O. Straus)
Tarare (Salieri)
Taras Bul'ba (Lysenko)
Tarass Bulba (Berutti)
Tassilone (Steffani)
Taverner (Davies)
The Telephone (Menotti)
Il templario (Nicolai)
The Temple of Minerva
  (Hopkinson)
Der Templer und die Judin
  (Marschner)
The Tender Land (Copland)
Der Teufel ist los (Hiller)
Die Teufel von Loudon
  (Penderecki)
Die Teufelsmühle am Wiener-
  berg (Müller)
Thaïs (Massenet)
Thémire (Duni)
Thésée (Lully)
Thétis et Pélée (Colasse)
Thomas and Sally (Arne)
The Three-penny Opera
  (Weill)
Thyl Uylenspiegel (Blockx)
Tiefland (d'Albert)
Tigrane (Scarlatti)
Tikhiĭ Don (Dzerzhinskiĭ)
La Tilda (Cilea)
Till Eulenspiegel (Reznicek)
Tinker (Škroup)
Tobias and the Angel (Bliss)
Toinon et Toinette (Gossec)
Tom Jones (Philidor)
La Tosca (Puccini)
Die tote Stadt (Korngold)
Die toten Augen (d'Albert)
Totila (Legrenzi)
Toussaint (Blake)
Tragödie in Arezzo (Hageman)
Transatlantic (Antheil)
Transit through Fire (Willan)
La traviata (Verdi)
Treemonisha (Joplin)
Le trésor supposé (Méhul)

Trial by Jury (Sullivan)
Il trionfo di Camilla (M.
  Bononcini)
Tristan und Isolde (Wagner)
Il trittico (Puccini)
Troilus and Cressida (Walton)
Der Trompeter von Säckingen
  (Nessler)
Trouble in Tahiti (Bernstein)
Il trovatore (Verdi)
Les troyens à Carthage
  (Berlioz)
The Tsar's Bride (Rimskiĭ-
  Korsakov)
T͡sarskaĭa nevesta (Rimskiĭ-
  Korsakov)
Tsefal i Prokris (Araia)
Tsveta (Atanasov)
Turandot (Busoni)
Turandot (Puccini)
Il turco in Italia (Rossini)
The Turn of the Screw
  (Britten)
Two Widows (Smetana)

Ulisse (Dallapiccola)
L'ultimo giorno di Pompei
  (Pacini)
L'ultimo selvaggio (Menotti)
Undine (Hoffmann)
Undine (Lortzing)
Das unterbrochene Opferfest
  (Winter)
Uthal (Méhul)

V buri͡u (Khrennikov)
Le valet de chambre (Carafa)
Der Vampyr (Marschner)
Vanessa (Barber)
Věc Makropulos (Janáček)
Vendetta (Berutti)
Venus and Adonis (Blow)
Les vêpres siciliennes (Verdi)
Das Verhör des Lukulus
  (Dessau)
Verlobung in San Domingo (Egk)
Véronique (Messager)

Die Verschworenen (Schubert)
Die Verurteilung des
  Lukulus (Dessau)
Veselohra na mostě (Martinů)
I vespri siciliani (Verdi)
La vestale (Spontini)
I viaggiatori felici (An-
  fossi)
La vida breve (Falla)
La vida do grande don
  Quixote (Silva)
La vie brève (Falla)
La vie parisienne (Offenbach)
Vil'i͡am Ratklif (Cui)
A Village Romeo and Juliet
  (Delius)
Le villi (Puccini)
Le vin herbé (Martin)
The Violins of St. Jacques
  (Williamson)
La virtù al cimento (Paër)
Le virtuose ridicole
  (Galuppi)
I virtuosi ambulanti (Fiora-
  vanti)
La visita meravigliosa
  (Rota)
The Visitors (Chávez)
La viviandière (Godard)
Voina i mir (Prokof'ev)
Les voitures versées
  (Boieldieu)
La voix humaine (Poulenc)
Volo di notte (Dallapiccola)
Von Heute auf Morgen
  (Schoenberg)
Vrazh'i͡a sila (Serov)
Výlety páně Broučkovy
  (Janáček)

Der Waffenschmied (Lortzing)
Der Wald (Smyth)
Die Walküre (Wagner)
La Wally (Catalani)
Ein Walzertraum (O. Straus)
The Wandering Scholar
  (Holst)

War and Peace (Prokof'ev)
The Waterman (Dibdin)
Die werwandtelten Weiber
   (Hiller)
Der widerspänstigen Zähmung
   (Goetz)
Der Wildschütz (Lortzing)
William Ratcliff (Cui)
William Tell (Rossini)
Wings of the Dove (Moore)
Wozzeck (Berg)
The Wreckers (Smyth)

Xerse (Cavalli)
Xerxes (Handel)
Ta xotika nera (Kalomiris)

Yelka (Rebikov)
The Yeomen of the Guard
   (Sullivan)
Yupanki (Berutti)

Z mrtvého domu (Janáček)
Zabobon (Kurpiński)
Zamek na Czorsztynie (Kur-
   piński)
Zampa (Hérold)
La zapatera prodigiosa (Castro)
Zaporozhets a Dunayem (Gulak-
   Artemovskiĭ)
Zapustyalata vodenitsa
   (Atanasov)
Die Zauberflöte (Mozart)
Die Zaubergeige (Egk)
Zaza (Leoncavallo)
Zelmira (Rossini)
Zémire et Azor (Grétry)
Zemire und Azor (Spohr)
Zenobia di Palmira (Anfossi)
Zhizn' za tsaria (Glinka)
Der Zigeunerbaron (J. Strauss)
Zigeunerliebe (Lehár)
La zingara (Rinaldo di Capua)
I zingari in fiera (Paisiello)
Die Zirkusprinzessin (Kálmán)
Li zite 'n galera (Vinci)
Zenobia, regina di Palmireni
   (Albinoni)

Zolotoy petushok (Rimskiĭ-
   Korsakov)
Zoška (Kamieński)
Zum Grossadmiral (Lortzing)

AUTHOR-TITLE INDEX

Entries are given here for all authors, including joint authors, and for editors; and for all book titles, including variants and including English translated versions of non-English originals. There are certain exclusions: names of translators; titles of articles, dissertations, and parts of books; translated titles of English originals. Series titles are indexed selectively.

Citations are by item number, or to the comments following a given item (indicated by "n" following the number), or in some cases to the comments preceding an item (indicated by "p" after the number).

The filing mode is word by word (New York before Newman). Numerals in any language--such as numbers for centuries--are filed before letters, not as though they were spelled out. Initial articles in all languages are included in the title but are ignored in filing; thus *Die deutsche romantische Oper* comes before *Das deutsche Singspiel*.... The following list of definite and indefinite articles in various languages may be helpful:

```
Danish--den, det, de, en, et
Dutch--de, het, 't, een, eene, 'n
English, the, a, an
French--le, la, l', les, un, une
German--der, die, das, ein, eine
Hungarian--a, az, egy
Italian--il, la, lo, i, gli, le, l', gl', un, uno, una, un'
Portuguese--o, a, os, as, um, uma
Romanian--un, una, o
Spanish--el, la, lo, los, las, un, una
Swedish--den, det, de, en, ett
```

There are no definite or indefinite articles in the other languages found in this volume.

In German words only, letters bearing the umlaut are treated as though followed by e: ä is filed like *ae*, ö like *oe*, and ü like *ue*. The umlaut is ignored in languages other than German, and all other letter modifications in all languages are ignored in filing order.

Most Spanish and Portuguese compound surnames are filed under the penultimate element: Sopeña Ibáñez, Frederico. But some appear under the final element: Vasconcellos, Joaquím Antonio dá Fonseca. Library of Congress practice has been followed in these and other languages to establish the authoritative form of the personal names.

Surname entries are grouped, ahead of titles that make use of the name: Wagner, Richard precedes *The Wagner Companion*. Hyphenated compounds are treated like two words, except in German, where they are treated like a single word in filing. Names beginning with the prefix Mc are arranged as if written Mac: McDonald before Marcello. Titles or names made up of initials (including acronyms) are filed as though they were ordinary words. The Library of Congress transliteration is used for Cyrillic.

150 anos de música no Brasil, 1800-1950 (Corrêa de Azevedo), 574p

150 Jahre Theater an der Wien (Bauer), 565

200 Jahre Münchener Theaterchronik, 1750-1950 (Wagner), 615n

300 Jahre Oper in Hamburg, 1687-1978, 615n

300 Jahre Wiener Operntheater (Pirchan), 554

400 años de música caraqueña (Calcaño), 697

5000 Nights at the Opera (Bing), 153

A travers chants, études musicales... (Berlioz), 266

Abascal Brunet, Manuel. *Apuntes para la historia del teatro en Chile*, 581

Abbate, Carolyn. "The Parisian 'Vénus' and the Paris Tannhäuser," 533

Abbiati, Franco. *Giuseppe Verdi*, 448

Abert, Anna Amalie. *Anthology of Music*, 30; *Claudio Monteverdi und das musikalische Drama*, 329; *Claudio Monteverdis Bedeutung für die Enstehung des musikalischen Dramas*, 328; "German Opera," 15; "Italian Opera," 15; "Die Oper zwischen Barock und Romantik," 704; "The Operas of Mozart," 15; "Promotion and Patronage," 15; *Richard Strauss--die Opern*, 414

Abitare la battaglia (Baldini), 449

Abraham, Gerald. "The Early Development of Opera in Poland," 648n; *Handel, a Symposium*, 288; *A Hundred Years of Music*, 531n; "Music in the Soviet Union," 15; *On Russian Music*, 263n; "Opera in Other Countries," 15; "Opera in Spain," 15; "Pskovityanka: the Original Version of Rimsky-Korsakov's First Opera," 381p; "Satire and Symbolism in The Golden Cockerel," 381p; *Slavonic and Romantic Music*, 662n; *Studies in Russian Music*, 263n

Abravanel, Claude. *Claude Debussy: a Bibliography*, 248

Angelis, Marcello de. *La musica del Granduca*, 631n
Angermüller, Rudolph. "Wer war der Librettist von *La finta giardiniera?*" 341
Annales de la musique et des musiciens en Russie au XVIIIe siècle (Mooser), 664
The Annals of Covent Garden Theatre from 1732 to 1897 (Wyndham), 677n
Annals of Music in America (Lahee), 681p
Annals of Opera (Loewenberg), 28
Annuaire du spectacle, 607n
Anthology of Music (Fellerer; Abert; Wolff), 30
Anthony, James. *French Baroque Music from Beaujoyeulx to Rameau*, 592p
Antonio Carlos Gomes (Vetro), 274n
Apel, Willi. *Harvard Dictionary of Music*, 1; *Historical Anthology of Music*, 32
Apkalns, Longīns. *Lettische Musik*, 669n
Appel, David H. *Prokofiev by Prokofiev*, 365
Apuntes para la historia del teatro en Chile (Abascal Brunet), 581
Archibald, Bruce. "Tonality in *Otello*," 476
Architetture per lo spettacolo (Aloi), 60
Ariadne auf Naxos by Hugo von Hofmannsthal and Richard Strauss (Forsyth), 419
The Ariadne auf Naxos of Hugo von Hofmannsthal and Richard Strauss (Daviau; Buelow), 417
Arizaga, Rodolfo. *Enciclopedia de la música argentina*, 545p
Arkhymovych, Lidiīa Borysivna. *Shīaky rozvytku ukraïns'koï radīans'koï opery*, 671n; *Ukraïns'ka klasychna opera*, 671n
Armstrong, W.G. *A Record of the Opera in Philadelphia*, 692
Arnese, R. *Cronache del Teatro di San Carlo (1737-1960)*, 638n
Arnold, Dennis. *The Monteverdi Companion*, 332
L'arpa festante (Bolongaro-Crevenna), 615n
Arruga, Lorenzo. *La Scala*, 634n
L'art du ballet de cour en France, 1581-1643 (McGowan), 592
The Art of Singing (Henderson), 178
El arte lírico en el Teatro Colón (Guardia; Herrera), 545n
Arts Council of Great Britain. *A Report on Opera and Ballet in the United Kingdom, 1966-69*, 680n
Arundell, Dennis. *The Critic at the Opera*, 175; *The Story of Sadler's Wells, 1683-1964*, 677n
Asaf'ev, Boris Vladimirovich. *Izbrannye trudy*, 263n; *M.I. Glinka*, 263n; *Russkaīa muzyka ot nachala XIX stoletiīa*, 664n
Ash, Lee. *Subject Collections*, 84
Ashbrook, William. *Donizetti and His Operas*, 250; *The Operas of Puccini* 375

Bauer, Oswald Georg. *Richard Wagner; die Bühnenwerke von der Uraufführung bis Heute*, 504

Baur-Heinhold, Margarete. *Baroque Theatre*, 58

Baxter, W.H. "Agostino Steffani: a Study of the Man and His Work," 404

Becker, Heinz. *Quellentexte zur Konzeption der europäischer Oper im 17. Jahrhundert*, 24; "Zur Situation der Opernforschung," 704n

Beckett, Lucy. Richard Wagner: *Parsifal*, 520

The Beggar's Opera; Its Predecessors and Successors (Kidson), 358

Beijer, Agne. *Drottningholms Slottsteater...*, 660n

Belorusskiĭ Gosudarstvennyĭ Ordena Lenina Bol'shoĭ Teatr Opery i Baleta (Smol'skiĭ), 668n

Belorusskiĭ muzykal'nyĭ teatr (Smol'skiĭ), 668n

Belza, Igor' Fedorovich. *Cheshskaiả opernaiả klassika*, 586n

Benjamin Britten: His Life and Operas (White), 226

Benjamin Britten: "Peter Grimes" (Brett), 231

Benton, Rita. *Directory of Music Research Libraries*, 82; "Libraries--Europe," 90

Bergfeld, Joachim. *Das braune Buch* (Wagner), 489n; *The Diary of Richard Wagner, 1865-1882; the Brown Book*, 489n

Berkenstock, James T. *Joseph Haydn in Literature: A Bibliography*, 295

Berlioz, Hector. *A travers chants, études, musicales*, 266; *Gluck and His Operas*, 266; *The Memoirs of Hector Berlioz*, 208; *New Edition of the Complete Works*, 214; *New Letters of Berlioz 1830-1868*, 209

Berlioz and His Century (Barzun), 210

Berlioz and the Romantic Century (Barzun), 210

Berlioz Society Bulletin, 215n

Bernandt, Grigoriĭ Borisovich. *Slovar' oper*, 666

Bibliography of Black Music (DeLerma), 99

A Bibliography of the Musical and Literary Works of Hector Berlioz (Hopkinson), 207

A Bibliography of the Printed Works of C.W. von Gluck, 1717-1787 (Hopkinson), 267

A Bibliography of the Works of Giacomo Puccini (Hopkinson), 374

A Bibliography of the Works of Giuseppe Verdi, 1813-1901 (Hopkinson), 461

Bibliothèque musicale du Théâtre de l'Opéra (Lajarte), 599n

Bignami, Luigi. *Cronologia di tutti gli spettacoli rappresentati nel Gran Teatro Communale di Bologna*, 630n

Biks, Rozaliả Aleksandrovna. *Bŭlgarski operen teatŭr*, 579p.

Bing, Rudolf, *Sir. 5000 Nights at the Opera*, 152; *A Knight at the Opera*, 153

Bio-base, 95n

Breuer, J. *Institutionen des Musiklebens in Europa*, 62n
Briede-Bulavinova, Vija. *Latviešu opera; lidz 1940 g.*, 669n;
     Opernoe tvorchestvo latyshskikh kompozitorov, 669n
A Brief Outline of Czechoslovak Opera (Eckstein), 584
Bringing Opera to Life (Goldovsky), 149
British Broadcasting Corporation. *Choral and Opera Catalogue*,
     43
British Federation of Music Festivals. *Yearbook*, 680n
British Library. *The Catalogue of Printed Music in the British*
     Library to 1980, 47
British Music Yearbook, 680n
Brocca, Ambrogio. *Il Teatro Carlo Felice; cronistoria dal*
     7 aprile 1828 al 27 febbraio 1898, 632n
Brockpähler, Renate. *Handbuch zur Geschichte der Barockoper*
     in Deutschland, 609
Brockway, Wallace. *The World of Opera*, 14
Brod, Max. *Leoš Janáček*, 305n
Brody, Elaine. "The King's Henchman: Fifty Years Later,"
     439; *The Music Guide to Austria and Germany*, 67; *The Music*
     Guide to Belgium, Luxembourg, Holland and Switzerland, 68;
     The Music Guide to Great Britain, 69; *The Music Guide to*
     Italy, 70; *Music in Opera: a Historical Anthology*, 31
Brook, Claire. *The Music Guide to Austria and Germany*, 67;
     The Music Guide to Belgium, Luxembourg, Holland and Swit-
     zerland, 68; *The Music Guide to Great Britain*, 69; *The*
     Music Guide to Italy, 70
Brook, Donald. *Singers of Today*, 110
Brosche, Günter. *Richard Strauss: Autographen in München und*
     Wien, 410
Brown, A. Peter. *Joseph Haydn in Literature: a Bibliography*,
     295
Brown, David. *Mikhail Glinka: a Biographical and Critical*
     Study, 244; *Tchaikovsky: a Biographical and Critical Study*,
     244
Brown, Howard Mayer. *Peri, Jacobo. Euridice: an Opera in*
     One Act, Five Scenes, 361; *Italian Opera, 1640-1770*, 32b
Brown, James Duff. *Biographical Dictionary of Musicians*,
     107n
Brown, Malcolm Hamrick. *Musorgsky: in Memoriam, 1881-1981*,
     347
Brown, Matthew. "Motivic and Tonal Interaction in Verdi's Un
     Ballo in maschera," 469n
Brown, Maurice J.E. "Schubert's Two Major Operas--a Considera-
     tion of the Possibility of Actual Stage Production," 398n
Bruce, George. *Festival in the North*, 680n
Brunel, Pierre. *Vincenzo Bellini*, 194
Brunner, Herbert. *Altes Residenztheater in Munich*, 616
Bruyas, Florian. *Histoire de l'operette en France, 1855-1965*,
     598

Christout, Marie-Françoise. *Le ballet de cour de Louis XIV 1643-1672*, 593
Chronik des weimarischen Hoftheaters, 1817-1907 (Bartels), 618n
Chronologisch-thematisches Verzeichnis samtlicher Werke von Jean-Baptiste Lully (Schneider), 317
A Chronology of Music in the Florentine Theater, 1590-1750 (Weaver; Weaver), 631
Churgin, Bathia. *Thematic Catalogue of the Works of Giovanni Battista Sammartini...*, 388
Churión, Juan José. *El teatro en Caracas*, 697n
Chusid, Martin. "Casts for Verdi Premieres...," 447n; *A Catalog of Verdi's Operas*, 460; "Drama and the Key of F Major in 'La Traviata,'" 479; *Verdi Companion*, 444
Cien años de teatro musical en España, 1875-1975 (Fernández-Cid), 658
Cinquenta años de ópera en México (Diaz), 643n
Citron, M.J. "Schubert's Seven Complete Operas: a Musico-Dramatic Study," 398
La ciudad y su música (Calcaño), 697n
Clapham, John. *Dvořák*, 256
Claro Valdés, Samuel. *Historia de la música en Chile*, 580n
Claude Debussy: a Bibliography (Abravanel), 248
Claudio Monteverdi, lettere, dediche, e prefazioni (De Paoli), 331n
Claudio Monteverdi und das musikalische Drama (Abert), 329
Claudio Monteverdis Bedeutung für die Enstehung des musikalischen Dramas (Abert), 328
Clément, Félix. *Dictionnaire des opéras*, 33; *Dictionnaire lyrique*, 33
Clercx, Suzanne. *Grétry, 1741-1813*, 278
Clinckscale, Martha Novak. "Pier Francesco Cavalli's *Xerse*," 238
The Collected Correspondence and London Notebooks of Joseph Haydn (Landon), 296n
The Collected Correspondence and Papers of Christoph Willibald Gluck (Mueller von Asow), 269
Collins, Michael. "The Literary Background of Bellini's *I Capuleti ed i Montechi*," 197
The Complete Book of Light Opera (Lubbock), 137
The Complete Operas of Verdi (Osborne), 463
Conati, Marcello. *Carteggio Verdi-Boito*, 459
A Concise Biographical Dictionary of Singers (Kutsch; Riemens), 108
The Concise Oxford Dictionary of Opera (Rosenthal; Warrack), 5
Cone, John Frederick. *Oscar Hammerstein's Manhattan Opera Company*, 690

East Central and Southeast Europe (Horecky), 89
Eaton, Quaintance. *The Boston Opera Company*, 683; *Opera Caravan*, 686; *Opera Production, a Handbook*, 148
Eckhoff, Annemarie. *Oper, Operette, Singspiel*, 42
Eckstein, Pavel. *A Brief Outline of Czechoslovak Opera*, 584; *The Czechoslovak Contemporary Opera...*, 585
Einstein, Alfred. *Mozart, His Character, His Work*, 333
Eisenberg, Anna. "Jacques Offenbach: Hoffmanns Erzählungen," 353
Eisenschmidt, Joachim. *Die szenische Darstellung der Opera Händels auf der Londener Bühne seiner Zeit*, 292
Ellis, W.A. *Richard Wagner's Prose Works*, 489n
En passant par Paris; opéras (Liebermann), 161
Enciclopédia da música brasileira (Marcondes), 574p
Enciclopedia de la música argentina, 545p
Enciclopedia dello spettacolo, 8
Encyclopedia of Music in Canada, 107
Encyclopedia of Opera (Orrey), 10
Encyclopedia of the Opera (Ewen), 9
"English National Opera Guides," 188
English Theater Music in the Eighteenth Century (Fiske), 679
Ente Autonomo del Teatro di San Carlo. *Cento anni di vita del Teatro di San Carlo, 1848-1948* (638n)
Entsiklopediia na bŭlgarskata muzikalna kultura, 579n
Die Enstehung des Ring (Westernhagen), 526
Ernst Kreneks Opern... (Rogge), 311
Erwin, Charlotte Elizabeth. "Richard Strauss's 'Ariadne auf Naxos' ...," 419n
Essays in Musicology in Honor of Dragan Plamenac, 245n
Essays on Opera (Wellesz), 184
Essays on Opera and English Music: in Honor of Sir Jack Westrup, 648n
The Essence of Opera (Weisstein), 26
Estonia (1906-1966), 668n
Eugène Scribe and French Opera of the Nineteenth Century (Pendle), 190
Euridice (Peri), 361
Evans, Peter. *The Music of Benjamin Britten*, 227
Ewans, Michael. *Janáček's Tragic Operas*, 305
Ewen, David. *The Book of European Light Opera*, 137n; *Encyclopedia of the Opera*, 9; *New Encyclopedia of the Opera*, 9

Famous Singers of Today and Yesterday (Lahee), 119
Les fantômes de l'opéra (Leibowitz), 172
Faris, Alexander. *Jacques Offenbach*, 352
Favre, Georges. *Boieldieu: sa vie, son oeuvre*, 221; *Histoire musicale de la Principauté de Monaco du XVIe au XXe siècle*, 644n

Historia de la música española e hispanoamericana (Subirá),
    656
Historia de la música teatral en España (Subirá), 656n
Historia de la zarzuela (Cotarelo y Mori), 656n
La Historia del Teatro Colón, 1908-1968 (Caamaño), 545
Historia del teatro en Buenos Aires (Bosch), 547n
Historia del teatro en La Habana (Tolón; Gonzáles), 583n
Historia y anecdotario del Teatro Real (Subirá), 659n
Historical Anthology of Music (Davison; Apel), 32
Historijski razvoj muzičke kulture u Jugoslaviji (Andreis),
    699n
A History of English Opera (White), 674
A History of Musical Style (Crocker), 15p
A History of Opera in the American West (Davis), 682
A History of Russian Music (Leonard), 663
A History of Sadler's Wells Opera (Jarman), 677n
A History of Western Music (Grout; Palisca), 15p
Hitchcock, H. Wiley. *Music in the United States: an Historical
    Introduction*, 681p
Hixon, Donald L. *Women in Music: a Bibliography*, 98
Hodgson, Julian. *Music Titles in Translation*, 52
Hofmannsthals Weg zur Oper Die Frau ohne Schatten (Knaus),
    423
Hogarth, George. *Memoirs of the Musical Drama*, 179; *Memoirs
    of the Opera...*, 179
Holland, Dieter. *Giacomo Puccini. La bohème*, 375n; *Richard
    Wagner: Die Meistersinger von Nürnberg*, 517; *W.A. Mozart.
    Die Zauberflöte*, 344n
Hollander, Hans. *Leoš Janáček: His Life and Work*, 303
Holmes, William C. "Giacinto Andrea Cicognin's and Antonio
    Cesti's *Orontea* (1649)," 242; "Orontea: a Study of Change
    and Development...," 241
Holoman, D. Kern. "The Present State of Berlioz Research,"
    206
Honolka, Kurt. *Grosse Reader's Digest Opernführer*, 143n;
    Die grossen Primadonnen, 115
Hoorickx, P. Reinhard van. "Les opéras de Schubert," 396
Hopkinson, Cecil. *A Bibliography of the Musical and Literary
    Works of Hector Berlioz*, 207; *A Bibliography of the Printed
    Works of C.W. von Gluck, 1714-1787*, 267; *A Bibliography
    of the Works of Giacomo Puccini*, 374; *A Bibliography of
    the Works of Giuseppe Verdi, 1813-1901*, 461
Horányi, Mátyás. *The Magnificence of Eszterháza*, 619n
Horecky, Paul. *East Central and Southeast Europe*, 89
Horn, David. *The Literature of American Music in Books and
    Folk Music Collections*, 681p
Horsbrugh, Ian. *Leoš Janáček; the Field that Prospered*, 302

National Theaters in Larger German and Austrian Cities (Dace), 569
National Union Catalog: Pre-1956 Imprints, 44
Nederlands componisten van heden en verleden (Monnikendam), 645
Nederlands theater- en televisie jaarboek, 645n
Nederlandsche zangeressen (Bottenheim), 645n
Nejedlý, Zdeněk. *Dějiny opery Národního Divadla*, 589n
Nelson, Molly Sue. "Operas Composed in America in the Nineteenth Century," 682n
Němeček, Jan. *Opera Národního Divadla v období Karla Kovařovice 1900-1920*, 587
Nestyev, Israel V. *Prokofiev*, 364
Neue Zeitschrift für Musik, 618n
Neues historisch-biographisches Lexikon der Tonkünstler (Gerber), 107n
Neuhaus, Max. "Antonio Draghi," 253
Neuls-Bates, Carol. "Verdi's Les vêpres siciliennes (1855) and Simon Boccanegra (1857)," 482
The New Encyclopedia of Music and Musicians (Pratt), 4
New Encyclopedia of the Opera (Ewen), 9
The New Grove Dictionary of Music and Musicians, 3
The New Kobbé's Complete Opera Book (Kobbé), 136
New Letters of Berlioz 1830-1868 (Berlioz), 209
New Looks at Italian Opera (Austin), 620
New Oxford History of Music, 15
New York (City). Public Library. The Research Libraries. *Second Edition of the Dictionary Catalogue of the Music Collection*, 46
The New York City Opera: an American Adventure (Sokol), 689
Newman, Ernest. *Gluck and the Opera: a Study in Musical History*, 264; *Life of Richard Wagner*, 493; *More Stories of Famous Operas*, 140; *Seventeen Famous Operas*, 140; *Stories of Famous Operas*, 140; *Stories of Great Operas*, 140; *The Wagner Operas*, 509
Newman, Joyce. *Jean-Baptiste de Lully and His Tragédies Lyriques*, 315
Niccolò Jommelli: the Last Years (McClymonds), 309
Nicolaisen, Jay. *Italian Opera in Transition, 1871-1893*, 629
Nitulescu, Petre. *Muzica românească de azi*, 653n
Nomus katalog, 590
Norris, Christopher. *Shostakovich, the Man and His Music*, 399
Northouse, Cameron. *Twentieth-century Opera in England and the United States*, 680
Noske, Frits. *The Signifier and the Signified: Studies in the Operas of Mozart and Verdi*, 336

Povoledo, Elena. *Li due Orfei, da Poliziano a Monteverdi*,
625; *Music and Theater from Poliziano to Monteverdi*, 625
Powers, Harold S. *Studies in Music History; Essays for
Oliver Strunk*, 527n
Pozzi, Emilio. *I teatri di Milano*, 634
Pratt, Waldo Selden. *The New Encyclopedia of Music and
Musicians*, 4
Prawy, Marcel. *The Vienna Opera*, 564; *Die Wiener Oper*, 564
Prentice-Hall History of Western Music, 16p
Prestige, Colin. "D'Oyly Carte and the Pirates," 434
Prieberg, Fred K. *Musik und Musikpolitik in Schweden*, 660
Prieto, Juan Sixto. "El Perú en las música escénica," 647n
Prod'homme, Jacques-Gabriel. *Gounod; sa vie et ses oeuvres*,
276p; *L'Opéra (1669-1925)*, 599n
Prokof'ev, Sergeĭ Sergeevich. *Avtobiografiiâ*, 365; *Prokofiev
by Prokofiev*, 365
Prokofiev (Nestyev), 364
Prokofiev by Prokofiev (Appel; Daniels), 365
Prosnak, Jan. *Kultura muzyczna Warszawy, XVIII w.*, 650n
Prunières, Henry. *Cavalli et l'opéra vénitien au XVIIe
siècle* 237; *L'opéra italien en France avant Lulli*, 596
Przewodnik operowy (Kański), 648n
Puccini, Giacomo. *Letters of Giacomo Puccini*, 373; *Puccini,
276 lettere inedite*, 371
Puccini (Greenfield), 370
Puccini, 276 lettere inedite (Puccini), 371
Puccini: a Critical Biography (Carner), 369
Puccini com' era, 372

Quaderni (Istituto di Studi Verdiani, Parma), 446
*Quellentexte zur Konzeption der Europäischer Oper im 17. Jahr-
hundert* (Becker), 24
*The Quiet Showman: Sir David Webster and the Royal Opera
House* (Haltrecht), 168

*La R. Accademia degli Immobili ed il suo teatro "La Pergola,"
1649-1925* (Morini), 631n
Radice, Mark A. "The Anatomy of a Libretto; the Music In-
herent in Buchner's Woyzeck," 205
Radiciotti, Giuseppe. *Giovanni Battisti Pergolesi*, 359
Rank, Mathias. "Leitmotive der Dresdner Opern Geschichte,"
614n
Rasponi, Lanfranco. *The Last Prima Donnas*, 125
Il Real Teatro Carolino e l'ottocento musicale palermitano
(Tiby), 639n
O Real Theatro de S. Carlos de Lisboa (Fonseca Benevides),
652n

SUBJECT INDEX